THE JESUS GENE

Ray Hudson

There is no doubt that the research that you have completed is unparalleled in the history of Freemasonry. You have truly brought to light many important facts and issues.

Dr. N Paul Branden
Freemason USA

The authors' theory draws on cutting edge genetic research, recent archaeological advances in the Holy Land, and on a vast wealth of Masonic knowledge. Indeed, it is probably true to say that without this encyclopaedic familiarity with the traditions of the Brotherhood the correspondences and connections revealed in these pages would never have fully come to light.

Dr. Keith Laidler
Author of **The Head of God** and **Female Caligular**

Also by Patrick Byrne - Templar Gold

THE JESUS GENE

A MESSIANIC BLOODLINE, THE JEWS AND FREEMASONRY

PATRICK BYRNE MA
ENRIQUE BOZZO
RAY HUDSON

CARDON BOOKS

Published by Cardon Books.

For enquiries or orders:
cardonbooks@btinternet.com

ISBN: 0-9552680-01

Printed in the United Kingdom by:

Lightning Source UK Ltd
Milton Keynes

CONTENTS

TABLE OF ILLUSTRATIONS

PREFACE

This book reflects continuing research after the publication of Templar Gold[1], which was written by one of the authors, Patrick Byrne. Although Templar Gold went a long way into new theories for the origins of Freemasonry, some questions remained unanswered. Two other researchers, Ray Hudson and Enrique Bozzo, joined Patrick Byrne in this investigation.

As the enquiries developed, one particular line became so powerful as to bring the whole endeavour into question. This line of enquiry was the significant Judaic content in both the symbolism and ritual of Freemasonry - this in spite of the fact that the Masonic authorities vigorously insist that it is neither a religion, nor a substitute for any religion; furthermore that it is non-denominational. We must at this point explain that the Judaic symbolism within Freemasonry is there for all to see. What we were finding, as we delved deeper into Judaic symbolism and practice, was the relationship between Judaism and Freemasonry was much stronger than had previously been perceived. As our researches continued, it became clear that Freemasonry was, in fact, a Judaic institution and had, most probably, been created by Jews themselves. Various researchers have hinted at this possibility – and we quote several of them at the end of chapter 1 – but none have explored this concept to a definitive conclusion, and published their findings in book form.

In making these comments, we know that Freemasonry is a "system of morality, veiled in allegory and illustrated by symbols". So it was not only essential to be sure that our findings were correct, but to be confident that our interpretation of any allegory was reasonable and realistic. What then were the possible consequences of pursuing a line of argument that was pointing towards Freemasonry as an organisation that had most likely been created by Jews? For at least two hundred years it has been perceived wisdom that Freemasonry was, originally, a Christian creation, and no one seemed concerned by that observation. Why should the revelation that it was actually a group of Jews who started Freemasonry make any difference to anyone, apart from those with anti-Semitic views? On the one hand, Christianity developed from a sect of Judaism: indeed, Christianity is sometimes referred to as Judeo-Christianity. Freemasonry, on the other hand, is an institution, which encourages and inspires self-discipline and a deeper appreciation of the spiritual value of life: it should have nothing to fear from the truth.

We neither had nor have any problem with this new reality, or with Judaism as a faith or a culture: for that matter, none of us had or have any problem with Freemasonry as a social belief system. This investigation started out as a search for the truth and ended as just that. As questions arose, we have strived to answer them using research rather than offering our own views. It soon became clear that our research was bringing the non-denominational argument seriously into question. We were faced with a choice:

1. Continue with the research and risk the wrath of the Masonic authorities, a serious problem for two of us, who hold senior rank in the institution.
2. Turn our backs on the third of the grand principles on which the order is founded, namely "truth".

Indeed, so important is "truth", to Freemasonry, that the following quotation was by Zerubbabel, after whom the occupier of the senior chair in a Royal Arch Chapter is named. Indeed, the incident referred to is also enacted in one of the Allied Masonic Degrees. Zerubbabel was the Israelite prince who led his people back to the "promised land" when their captivity in Babylon ended.

> The first wrote, Wine is the strongest,
> The second wrote, The King is the strongest,
> The third wrote, Women are strongest but above all TRUTH beareth away the victory.
>
> *From the Canon of the Septuagint*

After much soul-searching, we decided to continue – supporting this decision with the Order of the Garter motto, "Shame to him who thinks ill of it", and our findings are laid out for the reader in the pages that follow.

The first chapter explains how the overwhelming Judaic content of Freemasonry brought the notion that the order is non-denominational seriously into question. The second chapter, corroborates the first, from an examination of many of the earliest written records of Masonic ritual. The third chapter shows how, when viewed from a Judaic perspective, the underlying meaning of the ritual can take on a wholly different interpretation. The three ceremonies which a candidate undergoes to become a Freemason can now be seen as an allegory of the process of proselytism. We do not suggest that the ceremonies of making a Mason are, even remotely, acts of proselytism, simply that they bear a strong metaphorical likeness to it.

This is such a profound observation that it demanded an explanation. If, as our researches were showing, Freemasonry is a Judaic vehicle, then who on earth began it, when and why? The central part of the book is accordingly concerned with an investigation of the recorded history of the Jews, from the Jerusalem Temple period until the eighteenth century. This study identified one period when a probable forerunner to Freemasonry provided an obvious device to overcome the problems that Jews then faced. It was a period when Jews were banned from England and some other European countries. During this period, many Jews openly converted to Christianity but secretly continued to practice their faith. To find out about the latest dictates of rabbinical law, and other Jewish news, they needed a secure and secret method of identifying other crypto-Jews who brought that news to them: for being uncovered meant likely death.

During the research into the development of the Jewish race, a Messianic bloodline emerged that also demanded further examination. Templar Gold has already identified that the Ark of the Covenant is probably in the hands of the Freemasons and this Messianic bloodline is clearly linked to the family who – during the Temple period – were guardians of the Ark. Here, then, is a bloodline that links Freemasons, Jews, the Jerusalem Temple and the Ark of the Covenant, arguably the greatest treasure on earth. The final part of this book concludes with an examination of whether this Messianic bloodline is connected with the one identified in the fictional Da Vinci Code[7], or any of the many non fiction books on the Rennes-le Château mystery. The final chapter ends with a most surprising conclusion.

PART 1

FREEMASONRY

CHAPTER 1

MODERN FREEMASONRY

Templar Gold[1], by co-author Patrick Byrne asserted that the Knights of St. John of Jerusalem, who are better known as the Knights Hospitaller, created Freemasonry. While the evidence supporting this conclusion remains persuasive his research into this subject has continued. Patrick has been assisted during this four-year period of research by two fellow researchers. One, Ray Hudson, is a senior member of over twenty Masonic Orders and has occupied the chair of most of them. The other, Enrique Bozzo, is a resident of Uruguay; his Spanish mother tongue and excellent English proved very helpful as the enquiry proceeded.

Byrne speculated that it was the Ark of the Covenant, God's seat on earth during the Jerusalem Temple period, that linked the Knights Hospitaller to the Freemasons. He further ventured to suggest that all the signs are that the Ark still exists and is guarded by the Freemasons.

An underlying weakness in Byrne's theory - that at first the Knights Templar and after they were disbanded the Knights Hospitaller guarded the Ark - is the Jewish nature of Freemasonry. The Judaic content of Freemasonry is plain to see. Indeed, anti-Semitic groups have long suggested that there is a grand Jewish-Masonic conspiracy to take over the world. The idea that Freemasons could, with the help of Jews or anyone else, rule the world will bring a wry smile to the face of any practicing Mason. Conspiracies apart, the Judaic nature of Freemasonry must be examined and explained. If Byrne[1] is correct and the Masons are the guardians of the Ark of the Covenant, then it is very likely that some Jews, particularly the sons of Aaron who were charged by God to look after the Ark – and "Ark" in Hebrew is "Aron" - will be close by.

> In the tabernacle of the congregation without the vail, which is before the testimony, Aaron and his sons shall order it from evening to morning before the Lord: it shall be a statute for

> ever unto their generations on the behalf of the children of Israel.
>
> *Exodus 27:21*

Possessing the Ark would indeed tie the Jews and Freemasonry together, and yet it all appears too naïve, too easy. If, as Templar Gold suggests it was the Knights Templar and later the Knights Hospitaller who were guardians of the Ark for around 1,000 years, then where do the Jews come into the modern equation? To throw some light on this conundrum, we will need to examine at least two subjects in more depth: Freemasonry and Judaism.

Turning first to Freemasonry, this brotherhood is usually put forward as originally a Christian organisation, which later became non-denominational. Such an arrangement makes a Judaic involvement harder to explain and so we will begin our search there, within the esoteric world of Freemasonry. It is almost a given to say that Freemasonry has a Judaic foundation, for the ritual is configured around the construction of King Solomon's Temple in Jerusalem. The question that we must address is – whether there is more Judaism in Freemasonry than simply borrowing the Temple as a location for the Masonic initiation ceremonies?

We will begin by looking at some of the typical questions posed to English Freemasons. We will also provide the answers given on the web site of the United Grand Lodge of England (hereafter UGLE), and contained in two well-distributed pamphlets.

Q. What is Freemasonry?

A. Freemasonry is one of the world's oldest secular fraternal societies … Freemasonry is a society of men concerned with moral and spiritual values. Its members are taught its precepts by a series of ritual dramas, which follow ancient forms, and use stonemasons customs and tools as allegorical guides.

Q. Is Freemasonry a religion?

A. Freemasonry is not a religion. It has no theology and does not teach any route to salvation. A belief in God, however, is an essential requirement for membership and Freemasonry encourages its members to be active in their own religions as well as in society at large. Although every lodge meeting is opened and closed with a prayer and its ceremonies reflect the essential truths and moral teachings common to many of the world's great religions, no discussion of religion is permitted in lodge meetings.

Q. Aren't you a religion or a rival to religion?

A. Emphatically not. Freemasonry requires a belief in God and its principles are common to many of the world's great religions. Freemasonry does not try to replace religion or substitute for it. Every candidate is exhorted to practise his religion and to regard its holy book as the unerring standard of truth. Freemasonry does not instruct its members in what their religious beliefs should be, nor does it offer sacraments. Freemasonry deals in relations between men; religion deals in a man's relationship with his God.

By its own admission, the Holy Royal Arch, a Masonic order that was until very recently part of Craft Freemasonry, deals almost exclusively with man's relationship with his God. To be more correct, it deals with his association with YHWH or Jehovah the Jewish God; therefore, this Order at least "instructs its members in what their religious beliefs should be" but with particular regard to Judaism.

Before we look closer at the validity of these replies, based as they are on ancient and modern rituals, let us look first at what is "carved in stone". What is carved or moulded into the building that houses the Headquarters of Craft Freemasonry for England and Wales, including the Degree known as Holy Royal Arch. This Headquarters building is large and impressive and enjoys an enviable situation in Great Queen Street, London. Thousands pass by it every day, possibly not even giving it a second glance. Its doors are open and visitors, Masonic and non-Masonic, welcomed. For those interested, guided tours are regularly available. Within this building are many Masonic temples, or lodge meeting rooms, of varying sizes. There are a museum, library, shop and many administrative offices. As one might expect, the building contains everything necessary for the effective running of this large fraternal organisation, its visitors, and the membership who use its facilities.

On the front, high above the main entrance, "carved in stone", is the distinctive UGLE seal. This seal or coat-of-arms contains much heraldic information that reflects particular aspects of its history and change, and is its frontispiece to the world. In modern language, it is its logo. A seal, or heraldic device of this type, gives important information about the individual or organisation it represents. In this respect the UGLE seal is no different; it carries the history, aims and objects of the organisation it represents. The seal is impressed on all its official documentation, membership certificates, and embossed in gold on the front of the Masonic Book of Constitutions. The many thousands of members hold it in highest respect. Indeed, positioning the Seal on the front of the building bears witness to this fact. The prominent position and design carries its message to the world. But what is that message? What is it saying?

FIGURE 1 – THE SEAL OF UNITED GRAND LODGE OF ENGLAND

Let us examine what Harry Carr[2], an eminent Masonic scholar, had to say on this subject;

> The Arms of the United Grand Lodge of England were a combination of the Arms of the Antients (*sic*) and Moderns,

> preserving the best features of each, and the Hebrew inscription was corrected.
>
> *Harry Carr*
> *The Freemason at Work*

We might ponder what exactly was the correction Harry Carr referred to. It appears to suggest the original Hebrew of the Ancients was faulty. Here is a good place briefly to explain the "Ancients" and "Moderns". Again we quote from The Freemason at Work:

> After 1751, the Ancients' and Moderns' Grand Lodges existed side by side, not always without display of intense rivalry. In the late 1700s, however, there were many prominent Masons who held high rank in both bodies and in the early 1800s efforts were being made, behind the scenes, to effect a union. Eventually, and with the help of three Royal Brothers, all sons of George III, the negotiations proved successful and the Union took place in December 1813 ... In 1919, the shield was enhanced by a wide border bearing eight lions, suggesting the Arms of England and marking the long association of King Edward VII and many other members of the Royal Family with the Craft.
>
> *Harry Carr*
> *The Freemason at Work*

Laurence Dermott, the first Grand Secretary of the Grand Lodge of the Ancients was sufficiently impressed by the designs and models of Rabbi Jacob Jehudah Leon (1603-1675), that he adopted one of his designs for the Ancient's Seal. This Seal was incorporated into the new coat of arms when the Ancients and Moderns merged in 1813. Rabbi Leon was also known as Leon Templo and was a Jewish heraldic expert: Laurence Dermott was a noted linguist who regularly gave lectures in Hebrew. In his second edition of "Ahiman Rezon" – the Book of Constitutions of the Ancients - he called Leon Templo "the famous and learned Hebrewist Architect and Brother".

If we cxamine the UGLE seal, what does it tell us? Looking first at the shield on which the bearings or coat of arms are placed. The shield is called the escutcheon or field and can take other forms such as a lozenge or circle. The three castles on the left half of the shield symbolise grandeur, solidity and unity. The square and compasses that split the castles are the main symbols of the order. On the right of the shield are a lion, ox, man and an eagle. These are according to Harry Carr meant to represent, respectively, strength, assiduity, humanity and speed. They are also the four faces of the cherubim that guarded the Ark of the Covenant.

> As for the likeness of their faces, they four had the face of a man, and the face of a lion, on the right side: and they four had the face of an ox on the left side; they four also had the face of an eagle.
>
> *Ezekiel 1:10*

Freemasonry, like many other such fraternal organisations, is one of progression. Each level or degree contains descriptive and dramatic displays, which highlight the particular lessons to be drawn from it. Various symbols, such as the operative tools - that is to say the real working tools used by the ancient builders - are used to explain moral values to which the Candidate should aspire. Craft Freemasonry comprises the first three Degrees and these ceremonies take place in a lodge. The culmination of the Craft Degrees is the Holy Royal Arch, and this ceremony occurs in a Chapter. Until 2004, according to its own statutes, UGLE recognised only these three Craft degrees plus the Holy Royal Arch. In 2004 UGLE recognised the Royal Arch as a stand-alone fourth degree. A meeting of the Royal Arch is called a Chapter meeting and takes place in a Chapter temple. A Chapter represents the Grand Sanhedrin or ancient Jewish ruling Council. Five banners, with images, adorn the eastern wall, of which four are said - in the ritual - to represent each of the four divisions of the army of Israel. These four banners hold an image of a lion, ox, man and eagle, the same four symbols that appear in the UGLE seal, emphasising the position of the Royal Arch within Freemasonry. We will return to the banners later.

Having given this brief description of the structure of English Freemasonry let us return to the seal of UGLE. We will now examine the symbol above the shield, the Ark of the Covenant, which rests under the protective cover of the two cherubim's wings. The Ark of the Covenant is the most powerful symbol of the Jewish faith since it is the symbol of the unique rapport between the Children of Israel and YHWH. God's "chosen people", the Jews, take this Covenant so seriously that they literally carve it on their own bodies with the ritual of circumcision. It is therefore surprising that any other organisation - especially one which declares that it is not a religion - should make such prominent use of it. The Ark, after all, is where the Hebrew God, YHWH, sat when visiting his people. The Ark was so sacred to the Jews that usually only the high priest could enter into its presence and then after many washings or purifications. On the UGLE seal, above the Ark of the Covenant are some Hebrew characters, which should be written and read from right to left.

קרשל יהזה

The obvious question is why should the UGLE seal contain Hebrew characters? Does this seal represent an alliance between the Hebrews and UGLE? This Hebrew text translates, according to UGLE and many eminent Masonic scholars such as the Harry Carr, as "*Kodesh la-Adonai*" meaning "*Holiness to the Lord"*, and most Freemasons accept this translation without question. It is understandable that Harry Carr should choose not to give the literal translation for it is written of him:

> My eminent friend and brother, Harry Carr, the secretary of Quatuor Coronati Lodge No. 2076 (English Constitution), who is not only a prominent British Mason, but also a prominent Jew - and proud of it.
>
> *The Royal Arch Mason*
> *Spring 1972*

What is hardly surprising, though, is not that a learned Jew should avoid using the correct translation, which is "Sacred YHWH", because Jews prefer not to write down the tetragrammaton - YHWH - in case it is subsequently amended or deleted. It is, though, curious that Freemasonry - a nonreligious organisation - should feel the need to respect this Jewish tradition to the point of mistranslating the wording on their Seal.

The fact is that the popular English language Christian Bible, the King James version, generally uses "Lord God" or "Jehovah" as the transliteration of "YHWH". The second transliteration, "Jehovah", is attributed to a mistake by a Bible translator. This arose because - as discussed above - it is Jewish practice to substitute "Adonai" or "Lord" for YHWH, and the Masorites - self-appointed guardians of Jewish tradition from the reign of Tiberius who were engaged in copying Hebrew texts - inserted the vowels of "Adonai" under "YHWH" to remind the reader to pronounce "Adonai" in place of YHWH. In the sixteenth century, a German scribe engaged in transliterating the Bible into Latin for the Pope wrote YHWH as it appeared in his texts, that is to say, with the consonants of YHVH and the vowels of Adonai, and came up with the word JeHoVaH. This name has stuck ever since.

Manly Hall[2] followed the party line when writing about the headdress of the ancient Jewish Priests:

> Over the plain white cap of the ordinary priests the High Priests wore an overcloth of blue and a band of gold. On the front of the golden band were inscribed the Hebrew words "Holiness to the Lord".
>
> *Manly Hall*
> *Masonic, Hermetic, Qabbalistic & Rosicrucian Symbolical Philosophy*

There is a common misunderstanding that Jews are prohibited from writing the name of God because they must not take the name of God in vain. In fact that requirement refers to not taking oaths on God's name lightly. What Judaism does forbid is the erasing or defacing of God's name, and this directive comes from the Bible:

> And ye shall overthrow their altars, and break their pillars, and burn their groves with fire; and ye shall hew down the graven

> images of their gods, and destroy the names of them out of that place.
>
> Ye shall not do so unto the LORD your God.
>
> *Deuteronomy 12:3 and 4*

Rather than risk the accidental defacing of God's name, Jews normally do not write it down in the first place. There is another instruction for Jews not to pronounce God's name and this refers only to the Tetragrammaton, YHWH, or in Hebrew, יהוה. To overcome this restriction, they have substitute names. Three: El, Elohim and YHWH are - more precisely - alternative names; Shaddai, Elyon, Adonai and others are considered in rabbinical literature to be attributes rather than names. Then there are seventy-two names derived in a Kabbalastic exercise from Exodux chapter 14, verses 19 to 21. Freemasonry follows this tradition by referring to God by a number of sobriquets. "Great Architect of the Universe" is one and "Grand Geometrician of the Universe" is another, to name but two. This strict adherence to religious Law is appreciated and respected, but should be unnecessary outside the Jewish faith. This begs another question. Why would a self-professed non-denominational and non-religious organisation, with a known Christian ancestry feel the need to be understanding of and obedient to Jewish religious Law? UGLE does not show a similar respect to either of the other Abrahamic religions, Islam and Christianity.

On entering the UGLE's headquarters building there are many Jewish and non-Jewish references in symbolic or artistic form. Various virtues and moral attitudes are pictorially displayed, with commemorations to the dead of two world wars. The temples, or lodge rooms, that occupy the building – and there are in total twenty-three temples including those for the Royal Arch - are furnished with various artefacts that assist in the ceremonies. Every door has fingerplates and on each one is emblazoned the Magen David (Shield of David) or six-pointed Jewish Star.

At the entrance to the Great temple there are two enormous bronze doors with depictions of the building of King Solomon's

Temple and other incidents portraying Jewish life and legend. Above the doors is a curious symbol which looks like a slightly inverted "S"; at first glance it appears to symbolise very little. But if it is turned at an angle of 120 degrees clockwise, it becomes a Jewish character Yod " י " the first letter of the Sacred Name of YHWH. Remember that Hebrew is written right to left.

יהוה

This forms part of the architrave above the doors and is supported by the two Masonic Pillars. As if supporting Judaic Law, part of the Masonic Ritual goes as follows:

Q. Brother Smith in this position what have you discovered?
A. The Sacred Symbol.
Q. Where is it situated?
A. In the centre of the building.
Q. To whom does it allude?
A. To God, the Grand Geometrician of the Universe.

Freemasonic ritual is by its own admission "illustrated by symbols and veiled in allegory." Could this "sacred symbol" and its strategic placing - symbolically in the centre of a Masonic lodge - allude to the central placing of the Hebrew "Yod" above the centre of the Grand temple doors within United Grand Lodge? As if to confirm the fact, the symbol also appears on the ceiling of the Great temple. If so, then the God referred to is YHWH. There is yet another relief on the bronze doors which merits our attention. This relief depicts the Ark being wheeled away with a model of the Temple on top of the Ark. This curious metaphor seems to be making two points:

1. The Ark is with the Temple of Solomon.
2. The Temple of Solomon is also mobile.

Considerable weight is added here to Byrne's[1] suggestion that the Freemasons are guardians of the Ark of the Covenant if this interpretation is correct. Freemasonry does call its lodges "temples of Solomon"; it has symbolic columns, the Star of David, the name of YHWH, and in older times, the menorah, or seven-branched candlestick included among the lodge furniture.

There is another interpretation which leads to much the same conclusion. Godfrey Higgins[3], in discussing the Mercavah or chariot described by Ezekiel that carried God, refers to the four animals of the cardinal points, and their connexion in the text with the wheel. Higgins maintains that the word "Caaba" was derived from the last part of the word "Mercavah" or "Mercaba" - from the noun Recab as the temple of the cabalistic cycle or circle of the sun or the heavens.

> For this reason it had a circle of 360 stones around it, and the black stone in the inside of the circle is still adored as the emblem of the sun as the generative principle ... A Temple was the circle or wheel of the heavens... The Caaba, with its 360 pillars around it, was the Temple of Mohamed (like the Temple of Solomon) or circle or wheel of Mohamed ... To have called it the Temple of Mercaba would have been a tautology. All the oldest Temples of Zoroaster and the Indians were caves, acknowledged to be in imitation of the vault or circle or wheel of heaven. From all these considerations I am induced to believe that the word Mercavah is formed of M, (meaning chief or arch), cb, cav or cavah (meaning the chief or head of a circular vault of M). The idea of wheel applied to the revolving planetary bodies is peculiarly appropriate. The Cavah is the origin of our word cave.
>
> *Godfrey Higgins*
> *Anacalypsis*

It must be said with justification that the ultimate aim of Freemasonry is to build oneself as the temple, housing the "Ark" represented by the heart, as the supreme receptacle for God. In so doing, Freemasonry differs little from the three Abrahamic religions of Judaism, Islam and Christianity. For Freemasonry, though, God is clearly identified as YHWH. The other Masonic orders, although not formally recognised by UGLE, exemplify this point in the following attitude:

> We may hereafter be found worthy to receive the approving mark of the Great Overseer of the Universe, as fitted to form part of that spiritual edifice, that temple not made with hands, eternal in the heavens.
>
> *Mark degree ritual*

Although these other orders are not formally recognised by UGLE, the craft ritual makes the claim "Freemasonry is a progressive science". We can thus assume that any "progression" is a few steps beyond the craft. Within its ritual, Freemasonry also claims to be a "system of morality, veiled in allegory, and illustrated by symbols". What Freemasonry does not say - and the point we are making - is that the symbolic illustrations are almost universally Judaic. Freemasonry also claims for itself a "Universal Brotherhood"; however, the preponderance of Judaic form and principle casts doubt on the Universality. In making this last point, we are not closing our eyes to the Judaic ambition to be the universal religion.

We will close this examination of UGLE's headquarters building with an observation. Consider two hermits, a Christian and a Jew, who spent all their lives in the wilderness contemplating their faiths. If these two hermits visited London and wandered into the UGLE building, the Jew would be the first to pray.

We now turn to the Masonic apron, or one particular aspect of it. There is a different apron for each degree and all have a triangular flap at the top. In the first degree, that of "entered-apprentice", the flap is raised so that it is pointing upwards. In the second-degree, that of "fellow-craft", the flap is lowered so that it is pointing downwards. Originally, Freemasonry consisted of only two degrees and so the symbolism was intended only for those two degrees. Symbolism is always open to many interpretations, but this feature of the aprons fits securely within the theme of this book.

If you place these triangles, one pointing upwards and the other downwards on top of each other, you will get the Magen David or "Seal of Solomon" as it is better known. The Shield of

David originated in Prague in 1648 CE. It comprises the first and last letters of David's name, "D", and reflects a pre 400 BCE Jewish language - identical with the Punic letters – where the letter D was a triangle, similar to the Greek letter delta. Thus, two superimposed triangles form the Shield of David.

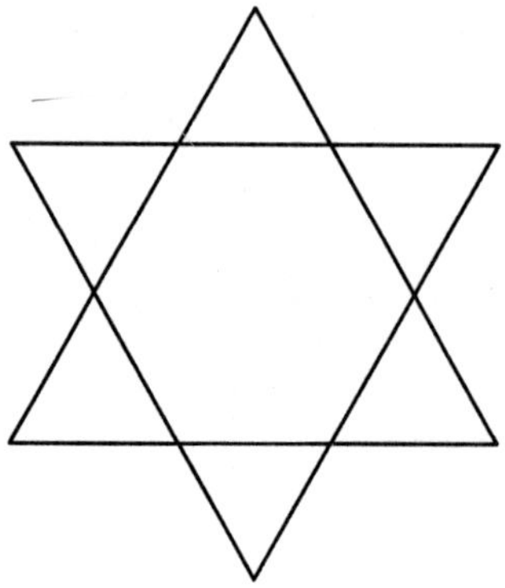

FIGURE 2 – THE STAR OF DAVID FROM TWO MASONIC APRON FLAPS

Similarly the master Masons' apron and a master's collar can be overlaid on the Hebrew Tree of Life as depicted in the Kabbalah. Introducing the Tree of Life uncovers another example of Judaic influence on craft Freemasonry. The two second-row circles, marked 3 and 2, which support the top corners of the Collar are called *Chocmah* and *Binah* respectively. There is an ancient Masonic password that Stevenson[4] uncovered in an early Masonic ritual, The Sloane Manuscript. That word is "mahabyn," and strangely we can identify that word within the two words *Chocmah, Binah.* Furthermore, there is another current Masonic password also plainly visible within the names of these two circles.

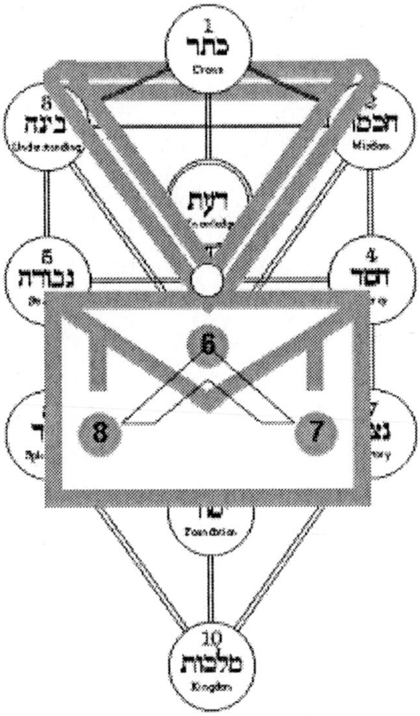

FIGURE 3 – THE HEBREW TREE OF LIFE WITH MASONIC APRONS OVERLAIN

To have one such word drawn from the Hebrew Tree of Life might be coincidence, to have two looks intended.

In making these observations, the reader is asked to understand that Masonic passwords suffer from regional variations. Over time, they become slightly changed not only for different regions but even from lodge to lodge. Bearing in mind that the old Masonic rituals were rarely written down but passed on by oral tradition, one cannot be surprised at these differences. The old Hebrew culture was passed down by word of mouth in much the same way. It is, however, stretching credibility to deny a connection between the ancient passwords and the Hebrew Tree of Life.

A further intriguing Masonic feature, emanating from UGLE, is the dating system. The ritual states "Freemasons, like the

Jews, measure time from the creation of the world". For Freemasons, 4,000 years are added to the Gregorian calendar, while the Jews add 3,750. The words, "like the Jews", confirm the creation is that depicted in Genesis of the Old Testament. For Freemasons these time measures are referred to as *Anno Lucis*, meaning the "Year of Light", and the year 2004 CE is thus changed to AL 6004. All UGLE authenticating documents and certificates of membership are dated this way. Now this could be regarded as just a romantic link with the ancient world, but taken with the other similar links with Judaism a different picture and possibility emerge.

It is notable that UGLE takes no positive stance on the origins of Freemasonry. It is assisted in this by the absence in the public domain of definitive evidence, due in part to the paucity of written ritual in the formative years. Despite many research papers by eminent scholars, UGLE contends that its proven provenance is from 1717 CE. It is understandable that if UGLE decided to endorse one of the many theories that proliferate about the origin, then it might upset those holding different views. This may be an acceptable explanation for fence-sitting, but why use the Jewish dating system? Why not use the Gregorian system? The term *Anno Lucis* refers to a Jewish time measurement – albeit with slightly different numbers - it is not Muslim, Christian or any other, it is clearly Jewish. If, as is claimed, UGLE wish to emphasise its fence-sitting status, why not date everything from 1717, or even 1813 when the Union took place? The term *Anno Domini* is no more and no less categorical than the use of *Anno Lucis*. Both terms underpin a religious viewpoint, and yet religion is a subject that UGLE studiously avoids to the point of banning religious discussion in Masonic lodges. From a commonsense perspective, the term *Anno Domini* is used throughout the world, commercially and privately, without any religious inference or preference given or received. It is therefore intriguing that UGLE should adopt the same time measuring system of the Jews. *Anno Domini*, the Year of the Lord, is a Christian reference, just as *Anno Lucis* is a Jewish one. *Anno Domini* relates to the arrival of a Messiah whom Jews do not recognise as such and so baulk at its use, apart from employing it in commercial transactions. Jewish resistance to

Christian symbolism extends to the modification of mathematical symbols. The plus sign (+) is a cross and a cross is a Christian symbol, and so Jews use an inverted T (⊥). The undeniable observance by UGLE of Judaic tradition invites the question of whether the banning of other Masonic Orders, including the Christian Orders such as Knights Templar and Rose Croix, from UGLE's building has anything to do with them being seen as profane or unclean.

The Great temple at the headquarters of UGLE acts as a model for the Masonic temples scattered around the cities, towns and villages of England. The furniture, ornaments and fittings of a Masonic lodge room symbolise and represent some aspect of King Solomon's Temple. The lodge flooring, of black-and-white chequered carpet or tiles, represents the surface of the original Temple. This flooring is referred to as the "mosaic pavement" and the provenance for this term is somewhat vague. Reference to a "pavement" in the Temple complex appears in II Kings and St John's gospel.

> And king Ahaz cut off the borders of the bases, and removed the laver from off them; and took down the sea from off the brasen oxen that were under it, and put it upon a pavement of stones.
>
> *II Kings 16:17*

> When Pilate, therefore, heard that saying, he brought Jesus forth, and sat down in the judgement-seat in a place that is called the pavement, but in Hebrew, Gabbatha.
>
> *St. John 19: 13*

The Aramaic word "gabbatha" actually translates to "raised ground", which, was presumably covered with a pavement. Mackey[5] has this to say on the use of the word "pavement".

> The word here translated as "pavement" is in the original *Lithostroton,* the very word used by Pliny to denote a Mosaic Pavement. The Greek word, as well as its Latin equivalent, is

> used to denote a pavement formed of ornamental stones of various colours, precisely what is meant by a Mosaic Pavement.
>
> *Albert Mackey*
> *Encyclopaedia of Freemasonry*

We will now turn to another facet of Freemasonry. It is generally accepted that charity is the foundation stone that underpins Masonry. The generous sums of money raised for Masonic and non-Masonic charities worldwide is a source of pride and encouragement for Freemasons. Interestingly, this concept is also rooted in Judaism. Charity is as much a foundation stone of Judaism as it is of Freemasonry. Charity is one of the Hebrew *Mitzvot* or laws. Jewish workers in the many cities where they have settled, continue to give some of their income to a central charitable fund. Some of these funds go to a society to pay for the burial of the poor. Every Jew who is able contributes to this society, so we can clearly see how charity is also at the heart of Judaism. Clearly, many organisations are involved in charitable works but few also share Judaic philosophical precepts.

The attitude of Freemasons towards charity is demonstrated in their observable actions, but the link between charity and Solomon's Temple goes deeper. We have earlier discussed the Jerusalem Temple high priesthood in this investigation and the name of the high priest during King David's and King Solomon's reigns was Zadok; and Zadok is from the same root – "sedec" - as "Tzedakah". We can now quote an extract from Louis Jacobs[6]:

> Charity: Alms-giving and care for the poor; Heb. *Tzedakah.* This word in the Bible denotes 'righteousness' in general but in post-biblical Judaism it is used to denote charity, as if to suggest, according to many exponents of the idea, that there should be no condescension in alms-giving. The poor are not to be patronised but given the assistance they need because they have a just claim on the wealthy.
>
> *Louis Jacobs*
> *The Oxford Concise Companion to the Jewish Religion*

When the early Masonic ritual promoted the excellent qualities of charity, it said "the sick and needy have a 'just claim' on your kind office". Once again we see a commonality of Masonic and Judaic terminology; or must we assume that this identical use of the term "just claim" is yet another coincidence?

Having explained some of the openly visible Judaic connections with Freemasonry, let us turn our attentions to the ceremonies. We will keep in mind that in studying Masonic rituals for research purposes, we must be careful not to reveal anything that might spoil a ceremony for an aspiring Freemason. The first-degree, or that of an Entered Apprentice, is one of introduction and preparation. It is an illustration of and encouragement of the basic moral principles that should guide all Freemasons. Undertakings are given to obey the laws of the country and uphold high moral standards. Loyalty to the monarchy and/or the civil authorities is demanded, and a firm belief in God must be confirmed. Promises are made that Freemasonry will not have a higher priority than important family and business commitments. Serious warnings are given not to use Freemasonry for any financial gain or self-promotion. Finally the qualities of charity are demonstrated in a dramatic form. The conclusion involves some of the working tools of an operative mason or building worker. The actual usage of each tool is described, plus a symbolic use whereby each tool represents a moral virtue. In this way a pictorial image is set alongside the various moral virtues in the mind of every new Freemason.

An important element in earlier ceremonies, although less practised today, was the "rough-ashlar". The rough-ashlar is a cubic stone with edges about 150mm in length, and, as its name suggests, uneven and irregular surfaces. It symbolises the candidate's mind as being rough and unfinished as it has yet to receive the complete Masonic knowledge. Lodges now display this stone in a prominent place, usually the pedestal of the Junior Warden, but little more reference is made to it. What is significant is that many lodges obtain a stone hewn from the same quarries as the stones used for the original Temple of King Solomon. When this is so, a small brass plate is usually proudly affixed to the stone confirming this fact. If Freemasonry developed from the operative guilds of the Middle Ages, as some Masonic scholars claim, then why this boast. Why the need to link Freemasonry directly to the building that symbolises Judaism more than any other? Indeed, the Temple exemplifies Judaism more than anything else apart from the Ark of the Covenant, which it once held.

While we do not wish in any way to diminish King Solomon's Temple, there are plenty of extant majestic buildings that bear tribute to the masons who built them. Indeed, as if to highlight the intruder nature of the Temple, the earliest surviving Masonic manuscripts have the Tower of Babel [see appendix C] as the symbolic birthplace of masonry. York Minster and Canterbury Cathedral are but two majestic examples that stand today although built long before 1717. St. Paul's Cathedral was designed by Christopher Wren, whose life from 1632 to 1723 spanned the creation of the first Grand Lodge, and who is thought by many to have been a Freemason. Any of these buildings would serve as symbols of the creative power of the working mason demonstrating attributes that could be moralised and symbolised, and there are many similar examples. The choice of King Solomon's Temple, of which not a standing stone remains, to display the masons' art, seems at best curious. It is paradoxical that UGLE is unable or unwilling to claim any definitive provenance before 1717, while using Masonic ritual that refers to Moses as "Our great and illustrious founder". As if to confirm the conclusions that are beginning to stare us in the face, the Bible states that the only "founding" done by Moses was that of the Hebrew Nation. This inference is underlined by the Holy Royal Arch ritual, which describes the first Masonic Grand Lodge – the Holy Lodge – as having been established:

> At the foot of Mount Horeb, in the wilderness of Sinai. By Moses, Aholiab and Bezaleel.

Mount Horeb is Mount Sinai and this "Grand Lodge" was the Tabernacle. The Tabernacle was the temporary goat-hair tent that - according to the Bible - housed the Ark of the Covenant. It was a structure of immense significance to Christian and Jew alike, facilitating as it did direct contact with God. However, it contained not a single example of the stonemason's art. No building blocks, no statues, no carvings, nothing at all created by hitting metal against stone. The statement that the Tabernacle was the first Freemasons' Grand Lodge strongly implies that Freemasonry has little to do with the art and science of operative stonemasonry.

The preparation of a candidate for Freemasonry is also of interest to our Judaic connections. We will only discuss what is relevant to our enquiries, thereby preserving the element of surprise to future candidates. Much of this preparation is similar to other popular organisational entry rituals. Each facet of the preparation has relevance to a moral question, which is dramatised and explained during the ceremony. We can illustrate this with what is probably the biggest misconception prevalent among non-Masons - the "rolled up trouser leg". Like much Masonic ceremonial, this has become an object of fun with the public. In reality an innocent yet serious connotation underpins it. When the candidate kneels to take his obligation – or oath to abide by the regulations of Freemasonry - there should be nothing between him and the earth on which he kneels. This is to give greater solemnity to the important commitment he is making and permanently imprint the occasion on the candidate's mind.

Similarly all money and metal objects such as rings and watches are removed from candidates. Here the object is to ensure that he has nothing of value when he enters the lodge for the first time. Every candidate is thus admitted "poor and penniless", to give him a greater appreciation of the need for charity. It is also worth noting from the perspective of this book that the workers engaged in building King Solomon's Temple were not allowed to use any tools made of iron within the Temple precincts:

> And the house, when it was in building, was built of stone made ready before it was brought thither: so that there was neither hammer nor axe nor any tool of iron heard in the house, while it was in building.
>
> *1 Kings 6:7*

There is another practice that bears on this investigation: it is having one foot made bare or "slipshod". This is a Judaic custom dating from ancient times. The removal of a shoe was a sign of an agreement and is explained in the Bible:

> Now this was the manner in former time in Israel concerning redeeming and concerning changing, for to confirm all things; a man plucked off his shoe, and gave it to his neighbour; and this was a testimony in Israel.
>
> Therefore the kinsmen said unto Boaz, Buy it for thee. So he drew off his shoe.
>
> *Ruth 4:7 and 8*

Shoes, and feet for that matter, have a great significance to Jewry, even down to the order they tie their shoelaces. This importance comes from disciplines laid down in the Kabbalah. For example, when entering the home of a friend, a Jew should enter with the left foot going first. In Masonic ritual, when escorted around the lodge room floor during the ceremonies, the candidate is instructed to "step off with the left foot." It is easy to see where this tradition comes from.

There have over the years been many exposés, or books containing the Masonic ritual in written form. A popular and often referred to disclosure is Jachin and Boaz, the author of which is unknown. In this exposure the Master Masons' word is said to be "Macbenach". The pronunciation of this word after years of slight changes resulting from oral transfers has varied it in many areas of modern Freemasonry to "Machbenah". The constant connections we have made between Freemasonry and Judaism could finally be settled by this single revelation. We have demonstrated that throughout Masonic ritual there are constant references to the Patriarchs. We have also touched on the connection between Judaism, Christianity, and Islam as the Abrahamic religions. Can it once again be simply coincidence that the name of the cave where Abraham is buried is "Machpelah"? The syllabic and phonetic similarities are remarkable for a word that has for hundreds of years been verbally transferred from man to man. We are not putting this example forward as definitive proof of the link between Freemasonry and Judaism, rather yet another instance that is particularly compelling.

When a Masonic temple or lodge room is in use, outside the door is an "outer-guard" as he is now known, or more traditionally the "tyler". He guards the temple from intrusion and prepares prospective candidates for the ceremonial. Another of the tyler's jobs is to ensure the temple is properly laid out for whatever ceremony is to be conducted. At the "festive board" or dinner after the ceremony, there are various toasts to the Queen and Masonic dignitaries. The final toast is given by the tyler and it is to "all poor and distressed Freemasons". We quote it in its entirety to further illustrate the point, although we recognise that the odd word may vary from lodge to lodge.

> To all poor and distressed Freemasons, where're dispersed over the face of earth and water, wishing them a speedy relief from all their sufferings and a safe return to their native land should they so desire.

We will now quote, in its entirety, a Hebrew prayer, which is said in every Synagogue throughout the world, every Monday and Thursday, prior to the Scroll of the Law being returned to the Ark.

> As for our Brethren, the whole house of Israel, who are in distress or captivity, on sea or land, may the All-Present have compassion on them, and lead them from trouble to deliverance, from darkness to light, from oppression to freedom, now, speedily and very soon; and let us say Amen.

Normally we would attach little importance to what may be regarded as a simple coincidence. However, in the light of all the other evidence, it is now difficult not to draw the obvious conclusion. Another duty of the tyler is "to keep out all intruders and cowans to Freemasonry", and it is the word "cowan" which catches our attention. Traditionally, according to Masonic legend, it means someone aspiring to be a Mason, speculative or operative, who does not posses the correct and necessary qualifications for either. He is a person to whom we do not trust our secrets, or our lives. This definition has found its way into the dictionary:

> Cowan
> \Cow'an\ (kou'an), n. [Cf. OF. couillon a coward, a cullion.] One who works as a mason without having served a regular apprenticeship. [Scot.]
>
> *Webster's Revised Unabridged Dictionary 1998*

The word "cowan" is claimed to have appeared first in Scottish Freemasonry in connection with the Knights Templar. It is suggested that an old Gallic word "couenne", which translates as "bumpkin" or "idiot", is the root. Another explanation for the origin of "cowan" arises when it is used as a name, a name that will pervade this enquiry, "Cohen". Cowan, just like "Cohn", "Koln" and "Cohan" is simply an alternative phonetic transliteration from the Hebrew and all refer to the Cohanim, the sons of Aaron, the family of the Temple priesthood. It is difficult to discern any reason why Freemasons should wish to keep the Cohanim out of their lodges unless the suspicion that the Masons have the Ark is correct and they fear that the Cohanim would claim it back from them. This is, though, a somewhat simplistic attempt to make the evidence fit the theory.

We will continue with the long list of commonalities between Freemasonry and Judaism, turning next to headwear. There is a feature of all three Craft degrees and the Royal Arch when a candidate first enters and a prayer is invoked on the proceedings. The candidate kneels, and if he is Jewish, he stands and his head is covered, in respect for the Jewish custom for males to cover their heads at prayer. However, there are no such formal "written" arrangements for any other religious persuasion or cultural custom, only for being Jewish. By way of reinforcing this arrangement, in earlier times it was normal for all of the lodge members to wear hats. This practice gradually declined until only the Worshipful Master wore a hat and now that tradition too has gone.

We have analysed part of the ceremonial and symbolism of Craft Freemasonry at length and we now turn to the "completion of the craft three degrees", the Holy Royal Arch. These words identify the earlier three degrees as a preparation for this, the ultimate objective. The earlier degrees have, as we have indicated, introduced a candidate slowly to Judaic symbolism and culture. As we move into the Royal Arch, matters Judaic become more overt. This ceremony will likely take place in a lodge room, although special Chapter rooms do exist. The room is accordingly laid out to represent the ancient Sanhedrin, the Jewish ruling Council held in Jerusalem. The three equal masters or principals, are called Zerubbabel, who is referred to as a "prince of the people"; Haggai, referred to as "the prophet" and Joshua, referred to as "the son of Josedech the High Priest". It can also be noted that these three principals represent a trinity of prophet, priest and king, and this trinity is usually associated with the Christian Holy Trinity. It is worth noting that Jews believe that a prophet, priest or king – or a combination of these – will be their Messiah. The three principals are dressed in garments of the period in colours traditionally associated with kingly, priestly or prophetical roles. In some old Chapters, and still to this day in Scotland, the principals wore hats like those worn by the leaders of the ancient Sanhedrin.

FIGURE 4 – SENIOR COMPANIONS OF THE HOLY ROYAL ARCH

The Holy Royal Arch degree re-enacts events that took place some 70 years after the Children of Israel were captured by Nebuchadrezzar and taken into Babylonian captivity. It details their return to Jerusalem to rebuild the Temple a task led by Zerubbabel the purported royal heir to the throne of Israel.

Three stonemasons leave Babylon and go to Jerusalem to help in the building work. They are employed on preparing the foundations of the new Temple on the site where the Temple of Solomon formerly stood. While digging, they make a major discovery and rush back to the Sanhedrin to report it. What they have discovered are the supposed lost secrets of a Master Mason, lost with the murder of Hiram Abif in the Craft third degree ceremony. In modern times they discover the "Sacred Word" of God, although in early ritual it was the Ark of the Covenant.

Having made this great discovery, they are promoted to membership in the Sanhedrin, that is to say, the Chapter. There then follow three long-established lectures, one given by each of the three Principles namely:

Joshua delivers the Historical Lecture
Haggai the Symbolical Lecture
Zerubbabel the Mystical Lecture.

The Historical lecture, as its name implies, is a history of the first three Masonic Grand Lodges and these are specified as the tabernacle, Solomon's Temple and the second or Zerubbabel's Temple. From within the very ritual of Freemasonry comes the most unequivocal evidence that Freemasonry has its origins in the Temple complexes of the early Hebrews.

The Symbolical Lecture provides an explanation of the imagery and ornaments within a Royal Arch Chapter. Finally, the Mystical lecture delivers a powerful message detailing the rewards for loyalty and punishments or non-allegiance to YHWH. This lecture relates sections of the Old Testament and contains powerful words of penalty for failure to abide by the Laws of the Almighty. It would be easy to believe one had suddenly relocated to a Pentecostal Tabernacle in the Bible Belt of the American South. Gone are the soft words of traditional Christian teachings of, "love thy neighbour" and "turn the other cheek" and in come more vivid wording:

> It intimates by the very act, that the stiff-necked and disobedient shall be cut off from the land of the living by the judgement of God, even as the head is severed from the body by the sword of human justice.

In the Mystical lecture, all the signs are demonstrated and explained. They are either signs of punishment for failing to observe God's word or methods of showing humility and submission to YHWH. There follows a detailed explanation of the importance and power of the name YHWH and its significance. This section concludes with instructions on how to communicate this Name without breaking the Judaic observance of not uttering it. The power, content and objective of this degree is best summed up in the closing paragraph of this Mystical Lecture:

> This Supreme Degree inspires its members with the most exalted ideas of God, and leads to the exercise of the purest and most devout piety; a reverence for the incomprehensible Jehovah, the eternal Ruler of the Universe, the elemental life and primordial source of all its principles, the very spring and fount of all its virtues.
>
> *Mystical Lecture of Holy royal Arch degree*

This paragraph from Masonic ritual needs no further explanation. As we mentioned earlier, UGLE recognises only the three degrees of Craft Masonry plus the Holy Royal Arch, nothing else. Although UGLE does not recognise any other Masonic order, most of the senior Freemasons who manage UGLE are involved in managing the other Masonic Orders, such as Mark Master Masons and the Red Cross of Constantine. In making this statement we are simply reiterating UGLE's stance. However, when a companion is elevated to the second Principal's chair, he is instructed thus:

> It instructs you that the harmony and union of the Chapter should be your constant aim - to which end you are studiously

> to avoid all occasions of giving offence or of entertaining any subject which might create discord or division in the Chapter - and by all means in your power to establish permanent union and good understanding in the different orders of Freemasonry.
>
> *Address to Haggai's robes*

It is well known that friction existed between the original Ancient Grand Lodge and the Modern Grand Lodge. This resulted in the compromise arrangement whereby the Royal Arch was included within Freemasonry but not as an independent degree. As explained above, the Royal Arch has only recently been recognised as a fourth degree. The above ritual suggests that the Ancients – who wanted the Royal Arch included – managed to get at least one reference into the ritual about the other "side" orders of Masonry.

The other Masonic Orders – just referred to - fall into different categories such as Chivalric or the Knightly Orders, like the Knights Templar, Knights of Malta, St. John the Hospitaller and the Red Cross of Constantine. There are other orders that continue the Solomonic legend. There are also the so-called Christian Orders and it is one of these that we will examine, the one usually regarded as the most Christian of all the orders. We refer to the "Rose Croix of Heredom of the Ancient and Accepted Rite for England and Wales", usually shortened to "Rose Croix".

The qualifications for joining this Order are to have taken the three Craft degrees and to declare a belief in the Christian trinity. Although the ceremony of "perfecting" a candidate is a metaphor of the Easter events, throughout the ritual there is little mention of Jesus Christ, no mention of the Holy Ghost or the Virgin Birth. In fact, none of the usual New Testament stories associated with Christianity are mentioned, even the Easter story is allegorical. However, part of this dramatic ceremonial involves an ornately decorated altar covered by a white altar cloth. On the front of this white altar cloth is emblazoned a red and gold cross, made up from five squares thus:

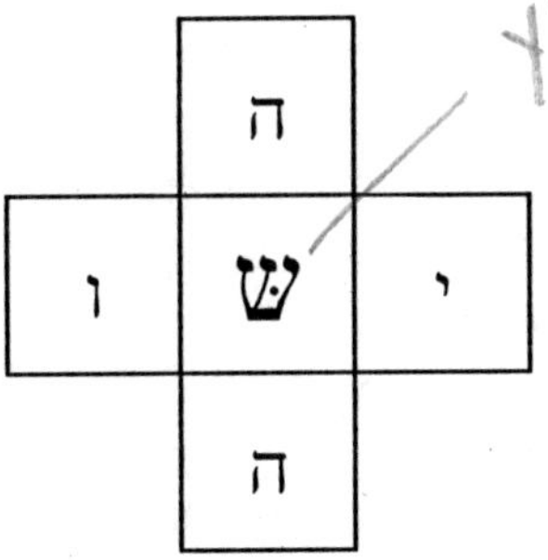

FIGURE 5 – FEATURE ON ROSE CROIX ALTAR CLOTH

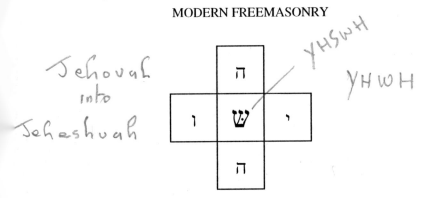

In the outside squares are the Hebrew characters YHWH, and in the centre is the Hebrew shin, which converts YHWH to YHSWH; and this, the ritual slightly infers, changes Jehovah into Jeheshuah, the Hebrew name of Jesus.

> The letter Shin in the centre refers to our Saviour, through whom Jehovah is revealed as Jeheshuah of the New Law.
>
> *From the Rose Croix ceremony of enthronement of a Sovereign*

In fact the addition of Shin (ש)t o Yod-He-Vah-He (י ה ו ה) does not result in Jeheshuah, which, in Hebrew, is written (from right to left) as Yod-He-Vau-Shin-Vau-Ayin (י ה ו ש ו צ). The reference to "Shin", as the Saviour, actually draws on a Kaballistic reference to it as evidenced by Manly Hall[3]:

FIGURE 6 - THE HEBREW TRIAD

> The Kabbalists used the letter Shin, to represent the trinity of the first three *Sephiroth*. The central circle slightly above the

> other two is the first *Sephira-Kether*, the White Head, the Crown. The other two circles represent *Chochmah*, the Father, and *Binah*, the Mother. From the union of the Divine Father and the Divine Mother are produced the worlds and the generations of living things. And again, from the Hebrew names attached to these two circles the astute Master Mason will notice one of his important words. The three flame-like points of the letter Shin have long been used to conceal this Creative triad of the Kabbalists.
>
> *Manly Hall*
> *Masonic,Hermetic, Qabbalistic and Rosicrucian Symbolical Philosophy.*

Christians usually consider the Trinity to be theirs, but here is evidence to suggest that a branch of Judaism is also comfortable with the concept. Here we find evidence that within the Kabbalah is a precursor of the Christian Trinity. With the five squared altar cross containing the Hebrew characters YHSWH, it is almost as if Judaic Freemasonry has been brought full circle to encompass Christianity. The five squared altar cross might be seen as a metaphor placing Christianity back within the religion from which it sprang some 2,000 years ago.

Most Christians readily accept Christ as of one-substance-with God, but Jews do not. This degree, Rose Croix, ostensibly the most Christian Masonic order, can be seen to remind its membership of the origins of Christianity from within Judaism. The ritual further explains how the rose is an emblem of God as mentioned in the Bible:

> I am the rose of Sharon, and the lily of the valley.
>
> *Song of Solomon 2:1*

Like many other Masonic Rituals, this degree is a journey during which questions are put to the candidate:

Q. Whither go thou?
A. To Jerusalem.

The candidate is then read a quotation from the Bible including:

> Behold, we go up to Jerusalem; and the Son of man shall be betrayed unto the chief priests and unto the scribes, and they shall condemn him to death.
>
> *Matthew 20:18*

It is curious that a Christian order should quote a piece of scripture containing the words "Son of man" in reference to Christ, instead of "Son of God". The "Catholic Encyclopaedia" has this to say on the subject:

> The employment of the expression in the Gospels is very remarkable. It is used to designate Jesus Christ no fewer than eighty-one times -- thirty times in St. Matthew, fourteen times in St. Mark, twenty-five times in St. Luke, and twelve times in St. John. Contrary to what obtains in the Septuagint, it appears everywhere with the article, as *ho huios tou anthropou*. Greek scholars are agreed that the correct translation of this is "the son of man", not "the son of *the* man". The possible ambiguity may be one of the reasons why it is seldom or never found in the early Greek Fathers as a title for Christ. But the most remarkable thing connected with "the Son of Man" is that it is found only in the mouth of Christ. It is never employed by the disciples or Evangelists, nor by the early Christian writers. It is found once only in Acts, where St. Stephen exclaims: "Behold, I see the heavens opened, and the Son of Man standing on the right hand of God". The whole incident proves that it was a well-known expression of Christ's. Though the saying was so frequently employed by Christ, the disciples preferred some more honorific title and we do not find it at all in St. Paul nor in the other Epistles.
>
> *Catholic Encyclopaedia*
> *www.newadvent.org*

Clearly Catholic theologians are comfortable with the use of "Son of man" but even they are surprised at its use in the New Testament. The use by a Christian Masonic order must therefore be questioned. It is as if the Masonic ritual is drawing attention to Jesus, not as the Son of God but rather as the Son of man, and that is without doubt how Judaism views Jesus Christ.

One of the authors is a member of over twenty different Masonic Orders and can attest that they all follow similar paths with respect to Judaism. Some Masonic orders are a little more overt, some milder and some subtler. However, they all adopt a similar Biblical theme almost entirely based around the Old Testament.

This chapter has demonstrated that Freemasonry is inextricably linked to Judaism. To close the chapter we will quote from some other creditable sources who have presented a similar theme over the centuries.

> Masonry is a Jewish institution, whose history, degrees, charges, passwords and explanations are Jewish from beginning to end, with the exception of only one degree and a few words in the obligation.
>
> *Rabbi Isaac M. Wise*
> *The Israelite of America*

> The Grand Lodge Masonry of the present day is wholly Jewish.
>
> *Richard Carlile*
> *Manual of Freemasonry*

> It is certain that there were Jews around the cradle of Freemasonry; certain rites prove that they were cabbalistic Jews.
>
> *Bernard Lazare*
> *L'antisemitisme*

Our rite is Jewish from beginning to end; the public should conclude from this that we have actual connections with Jewry.

Brother Rudolph Klein
Latomia

The Coat of Arms used by the Grand Lodge of England is entirely composed of Jewish symbols.

Transactions of the Jewish Historical Society; Vol. 2

The Freemasons erect a building in which the God of Israel will live forever.

Freemasons' Guide

The most important work of the Freemason must be to glorify the Jewish race, which has preserved unchanged the divine standard of wisdom. You must rely upon the Jewish race to dissolve all frontiers.

Le Symbolisme

Each Lodge is and must be a symbol of the Jewish Temple; each Master in the Chair, a representative of the Jewish king; and every Mason a personification of the Jewish workman.

An Encyclopædia of Freemasonry

The true reason why members of the Masonic Craft address each other as Brother so and so ... is purely because of Hebraic Influence.

Bernard Shillman
Hebraic Influences on Masonic Symbolism

Bro. Benas expressed the view that the Israelitish tradition is of the very tissue of Masonic substance, and the spirit of that tradition is its vitalising element.

The Freemason

This chapter now leaves us in no doubt the influence of Judaism over Freemasonry goes far beyond the simple borrowing of the

Temple at Jerusalem for initiation ceremonial. There is something about the relationship between the Jews and Freemasonry that has so far not been generally aired in public. To suggest a role for Jewry in early Freemasonry is not new[5] but more recent research of the various theories of the origins of Freemasonry has not given much credibility to the works of Mackay[5] and his contemporaries.

To pursue the origins of Freemasonry we will need to examine the earliest examples of its ceremonies. We will scrutinize the early written manuscripts of Masonic ritual to see whether they cast light on the Judaic nature of Freemasonry.

CHAPTER 2

EARLY FREEMASONRY

In chapter 1, we established that the Judaic content of Freemasonry goes far beyond the borrowing of the Temple at Jerusalem for Masonic ceremonies. What we must now do is to examine the rituals and "ancient charges" where copies are available.

There is an immediate problem with this approach. Most of the existing early rituals originated in England, and although books began to be published towards the end of the fifteenth century, they were expensive. Apart from the clergy, Jews and some rich people, reading was not a generally available skill. The earliest copies of masonic material are therefore most likely the creation of members of the clergy, either as a scribe paid for by the artisans or as an interested spectator. We know from Dr. Bing Johnson[8] that the first guild of masons was inaugurated in London in 1356. Twelve working masons approached the Mayor of London and his Aldermen at Guildhall and had a code of rules drawn up. The document still survives and makes the point that they needed a guild because they considered that masons were not governed as other trades were. Their first rule stated:

> Every man of the trade may work at any work touching the masons trade if he be perfectly skilled and knowing in the same.

A blindingly simple approach to the complex area of training and apprenticeships if ever there was one. It also brings into immediate focus the lack of any need for passwords, secret signs and handshakes. This rule was uncomplicated, if someone could do the job, no one could stop him from doing it. Some twenty years later, the London Masons Company became the first trade guild for working masons in England.

There are several alternative suggestions for the origins of Freemasonry - as distinct from organisations of working masons -

the website of UGLE has a couple of comments that merit examination:

> Freemasonry is one of the world's oldest secular fraternal societies.
>
> *www.grandlodge-england.org*

This generally unquestioned comment is not helped by UGLE's insistence that they began in 1717. There are many fraternal societies of far greater age and so it must be the use of the adjective "secular" that distinguishes Freemasonry from other, much older fraternal societies. In discussing "what Freemasonry is", UGLE continues:

> The origins of Freemasonry are the subject of great debate. That there is a connection with the operative stonemasons who built the great medieval cathedrals and castles is generally accepted by Masonic historians – but whether that connection was direct or indirect is the subject of speculation.
>
> *www.grandlodge-england.org*

If Freemasonry finds its origins in the "guilds of masonry", then we are looking at a start date of around 1356, for as we have just seen that was when the first English "masons' guild" was formed. The linking of Freemasonry to the old masons' guild does, though, create a problem. What was it, or is it, about Freemasonry that makes it so different from the original masons' guild as to require distinguishing secret passwords and signs. Indeed, we have questioned the livery companies of London that still exist today and none appears ever to have had distinguishing passwords or signs. There was clearly no need for passwords to protect the original masons as their first rule clarifies:

> Every man of the trade may work at any work touching the masons trade if he be perfectly skilled and knowing in the same.

If someone claimed to be a mason it was only necessary to put a chisel and maul in his hands and seek a demonstration of his abilities. So, what is it about Freemasonry that requires signs and passwords? Passwords that are so secret, that to betray them to a non-member was punishable by death, and a fairly gruesome death at that. Working masons were certainly not paid any more, or less, than other tradesmen and working masons had no special rights that other tradesmen lacked. There is a persistent Masonic tradition that Middle Ages stonemasons had a unique right to travel both within countries and between them. In reality there is no evidence to support this suggestion apart from the Statute of Cambridge (Parliament met there on that occasion) of 1388, which forbade servants to move out of their "hundred" without legal authority. A hundred was an area of land in England supposed to have contained one hundred families. In England the concept of serfdom was breaking down. The outbreak of the Black Death in the fourteenth century resulted in far fewer workers being available for hire and so strenuous, but futile, attempts were made to freeze wages at pre-Black Death levels. The Peasants Revolt of 1381 records how Watt Tyler met with the king in London, after travelling up from Maidstone. His resulting death was not because of his "unauthorised" travelling, rather for his unacceptable demands. Apparently, as with many matters Masonic, the accepted wisdom is flawed.

Forming part of the Masonic legendary "unique right to travel" is another "remodelled" fable and this is that the "Poor Laws" put pressure on local communities to turn away visitors. The argument is that visitors who might be work-shy would become a financial burden on the community, who were then obliged to support them. This suspicion against travelling people prompted masons to create Freemasonry as a means of identifying each other and so protecting themselves. In fact, there were several "Poor Law" Acts in England.

1. In 1349, as just mentioned, because of the labour shortages brought on by the Black Death, the "Ordinance of Labourers", banned the giving of relief to able-bodied beggars, this was to compel people to work for their living.

2. In 1388 the "Statute of Cambridge" restricted the movements of servants and beggars and made the county "hundreds" responsible for their own "impotent poor".
3. In 1494 the "Vagabonds and Beggars Act" subjected "vagabonds, idle and suspected persons" to three days in the stocks on bread and water. Beggars who were too infirm to work were allowed to stay in their "hundred" and could beg.
4. In 1547 the "Statute of Legal Settlement" allowed sturdy beggars to be branded or enslaved. The impotent poor received relief and had cottages erected for their use.
5. In 1576 an act for "Setting of the Poor on Work, and for the Avoiding of Idleness" insisted that every town set up stocks of materials to allow the poor to work. A "House of Correction" was established for those who refused to work.
6. In 1597 an act for the "Relief of the Poor" passed parochial responsibility for the poor and suppression of begging to churchwardens or overseers (from two to four, depending on the size of the parish).
7. In 1601 providing work and the use of county "Houses of Correction" for vagrants as well as the setting to work and apprenticeships for children was added to the duties of the churchwarden and overseers.
8. In 1662 the "Settlement Act" decreed that newcomers to a parish could be removed upon the orders of two Justices of the Peace. A complaint had first to be made against them within 40 days of arrival, provided they had not rented a house worth at least £10 a year.
9. In 1697 an act "For Supplying some Defects in the Laws for the Relief of the Poor" made newcomers with certificates liable for removal only when they sought benefits; and those in receipt of relief were required to wear identifying badges. Fines were levied on those who refused to take pauper apprentices.
10. In 1723 the "Workhouse Test Act" allowed workhouses to be set up by a parish, or in combination with neighbouring parishes. Relief was offered only to those willing to enter the workhouse.

11. In 1782 "Gilbert's Act" allowed parishes to set up a common workhouse controlled by a board of guardians appointed by Justices of the Peace. The poor who were able to work were dealt with by providing them with work and supplementing wages.

It is clear from this summary of Poor Law Acts that there was little to deter a healthy and willing workman from travelling into any village. The fear for any village or hamlet was of persistent beggars, who had no intention of working for their keep, from imposing themselves on to the village overheads. In making this statement, it would be wrong to imply that England had been overtaken by an epidemic of idleness. It was simply that after the Black Death, the population increased rapidly and ahead of the economy and so there was not enough work to go around. It is unlikely that skilled masons would have been caught up in this "poverty trap". If they were travelling at all then they would have been heading for a large building project where their skills would be gainfully employed.

Returning to the guild movement, guilds were popular as the distinguishing bodies for the different trades, not least because they had the right to nominate two representatives to sit on their town council. There is, though, only a record of one masons' company outside London, and that was in Newcastle-upon-Tyne, it was formed in 1581. The advantage for any artisan of holding guild membership was that after serving an apprenticeship for (usually) seven years the craftsman would gain his "freedom". The medieval term "freeman" meant that they were not the property of a feudal lord, and enjoyed the right to earn money and own land. People who lived in towns were usually protected by the charter of their town – from which came the term "freedom of the City". A free-mason was thus one who was not attached to, or the property of, a feudal lord. A free-mason was therefore likely to have been a town or city dweller.

During its 200 or so years of existence, the London Guild of Masons experienced something of a roller coaster existence. As the Tudors settled the country, large-scale palace building work was available in plenty. When Henry VIII's marriage plans led to the break from the papacy, the reformation that followed resulted in mass looting and destruction of the monasteries, which, in turn deterred anyone from building church buildings. The guild of London Masons declined as the wealth shifted from royalty, nobility and the Church to the merchants, gentry and the universities. The old system whereby the king or a bishop would take a direct interest in his new building project shifted to merchants. The merchants would agree a drawing or plan and demand a fixed price from a builder, just like any other commodity they bought. By the mid-seventeenth century the Guild of London Masons was almost finished; at the end of that century their building was taken over by Freemasons (forerunners of UGLE) who sold it on around the middle of the eighteenth century.

We will now turn to the early Freemasonic and operative Masonic documentation. In all, there are some 130 documents of various types and all but a few dating from around 1800. It is generally accepted that the earliest record is the Regius or Halliwell Manuscript, which has been dated by the British Museum to around 1400. Euclid is mentioned, as are the seven liberal arts and sciences. Importantly, there are no secret words, symbols or signs in this document. Instead, there are three elements. The manuscript, which is in rhyming verse, begins with a Christian prayer. It contains a schedule of "rules for good and moral behaviour" that every mason should follow, and a brief history of the origins of masonry in Babylon. These, then, are the three elements:

1. An opening prayer.
2. A legendary history of masonry from its pre-biblical origins to its establishment in England.
3. A code of regulations for member masons, covering both craft practices and morals, prefigure a ceremonial approach to the institution that would eventually appear.

Clearly, each meeting would begin with a prayer. If a man or woman was to be admitted as an apprentice or operative mason, then an embryo "ceremony" would follow and this probably comprised a "reading" of the history of masonry. It is here that one of those opportunities existed for Masonic ritual to be "amended" or "fashioned" to suit any particular cause. In the early days of working masonry few ordinary people could read or write and so the guild would need to call on the services of someone who could. That would inevitably have meant a member of the clergy. In medieval England, few people other than the clergy could read. This was not accidental; it was the means by which the Church kept control over knowledge, over "the word". Therefore, if a piece of masonic history was to be read out at a ceremony of making an apprentice or a mason then the shortlist of possible readers was small. The choice would usually have been limited to a minor member of the clergy, and this would not have been difficult to arrange because the financial arrangements connected with the construction of church buildings were usually overseen by the clergy. We will discuss in later chapters how Jewry taught their children to read and write as a matter of course, and this raises the question of why Jews did not become involved in this matter. The answer is simple. In 1290 all Jews were expelled from England and it was not until 1656 that Oliver Cromwell reversed this decision. For some 366 years it was illegal for a Jew to live in England on pain of death.

We have examined the earliest surviving masonic document and noted that apart from the three elements of prayer, Masonic history and regulations, there is nothing to link it with modern Freemasonry. We are seeking to establish how, and when, the Judaic content – identified in chapter 1 - got into the ritual. We can readily imagine how the three elements of the early manuscript came together. It is reasonable to assume the Charges might be imposed on each new candidate by requiring them to swear an oath of obedience to them. We need look no further than the fourteenth point in the Regius Manuscript to find out that their use of oaths was little different to those used in everyday life today. We have included a small sample to provide a flavour, and, as we read the charges below we can picture the young man, probably kneeling with a hand or two on the Bible slowly repeating the charges as they are read to him. The left column approximates the original format and the right-hand column a more recent interpretation:

Xiijus punctus.	**Fourteenth point.**
The fowrtethe poynt ys ful good lawe To hym that wold ben under awe;	The fourteenth point is a full good law To him that would be under awe;
A good trwe othe he most ther swere To hys mayster and hys felows that ben there;	A good true oath he must there swear To his master and his fellows that be there;
He most be stedefast and trwe also To alle thys ordynance, whersever he go,	He must be steadfast and also true. To all this ordinance, wheresoever he go,

After the Regius Manuscript, the next is known as the Cooke Manuscript, and dates from around 1500. The Cooke MS is depicted in Appendix C where examples of the roots of some modern ritual can be seen. This manuscript, like the Regius MS mentions Babylon, Euclid and the seven liberal arts and sciences, but also brings in Enoch and the briefest mention of the Temple at Jerusalem.

> What time that the children of Israel dwelt in Egypt they learned the craft of masonry. And afterward, [when] they were driven out of Egypt, they came into the land of behest, and is now called Jerusalem, and it was occupied and charges there held. And the making of Solomon's Temple that King David began. (King David loved well masons, and he gave them right nigh as they be now.) And at the making of the Temple in Solomon's time as it is said in the Bible, in the 3rd book *of Regum in tercio Regum capitolo quinto*, that Solomon had 4 score thousand masons at his work. And the king's son, of Tyre, was his master Mason. And [in] other chronicles it is said, and in old books of masonry, that Solomon confirmed the charges that David, his father, had given to masons. And Solomon himself taught them there manners [with] but little difference from the manners that now are used. And from thence this worthy science was brought into France and into many other regions.
>
> *The Cooke manuscript*

Introducing king Solomon's Temple is the first tentative indication of Jewish hands on the ritual. If this observation is correct, then we need to explain how this could have happened when Jews were banned from living in England. Within the Cooke Manuscript are several passages in Latin, including the one just above, and this suggests that a member of the clergy was the scribe. Once again, in this manuscript there are no secret words or signs. An earlier United Grand Lodge of England Librarian, John Hamill[9], had this to say on the subject of passwords:

> When the authentic school [in the 18th Century] came to examine the English records they could find no evidence at all of the existence of operative lodges. In medieval times the operatives' lodge had simple been a hut or lean-to on the site in which they stored their tools and took their refreshment and ease. By the 1600s the guild system, with the exception of the London Livery companies, was virtually moribund. Nor was there any evidence of an English Mason word or of the English operatives having had secret modes of recognition.... Accepted masonry simply seems to have appeared in England as a new organisation **without any prior connections with the operative craft.**
>
> *John Hamill*
> *The Craft; A History of English Freemasonry*

John Hamill's final paragraph is telling. He concluded that Freemasonry had no connection with operative masonry at all and simply appeared as a "new organisation". This innocuous comment is laden with potential answers to some of the questions we have raised. If Hamill is correct, and no Masonic historian has challenged his analysis, then the date when Freemasonry "appeared" coincides with the slightly earlier return of the Jews to legal residence in England. We will return to this theme later.

Although the lack of documents means that we cannot be totally sure, it does appear that in those early days there was only one ceremony and that would have been to admit a newly qualified mason. It must be acknowledged that in the thirteenth century an apprentice was effectively the property of the craftsman to whom he was bonded. This made it unlikely that an apprentice could have sworn an oath to anyone other than his master. The law of England changed for apprentices in the sixteenth century when apprenticeships became voluntary. As might be expected, the old manuscripts show that during the sixteenth century the single ceremony of admission of a mason changed to two ceremonies, one for the craftsman and one for the apprentice. The Harleian Manuscript c. 1650, which is in effect a copy of the Old Charges from about 1550, gave the first hint of two degrees.

The Edinburgh Register House Manuscript dated c. 1696 is to be found in the Public Records Office of Edinburgh. This manuscript describes the actual ceremonies for the two degrees. It should be noted that this manuscript is only thirty or so years after the Jews had been readmitted to England. This was the first time a concise document was assembled detailing how the Masonic ceremonies should be conducted in enough detail to let anyone perform them. This is the defining moment - for this investigation – when a totally new form of masonry, Freemasonry, entered onto the public scene. This is the moment, which John Hamill described as when:

> Accepted masonry simply seems to have appeared in England as a new organisation.

If, as we suspect, Freemasonry was an earlier Jewish creation, then the act of publication of this, and other manuscripts suggests two things. Firstly, that gentiles were being admitted into the new society, for there is no earlier sign of a Jew betraying – by publishing - the earlier organisation. Secondly, the ceremonial was being developed into something quite different from the old operative masonic ceremonies. The Edinburgh Manuscript begins with a series of questions and answers:

Q. Are you a mason?
A. Yes.
Q. How shall I know it?
A. You shall know it in time and place convenient. Remark the first answer is only to be made when there is company present

> who are not masons. But if there be no such company by, you should answer by signs, tokens and other points of my entry.

Here then, for the first time are specific signs and signals to display that the individual is indeed a mason. This begs the serious question of why? Why would masons need a password that identified them as either:

1. An apprentice mason?
2. A journeyman mason?

Even today, when building site workers serve apprenticeships, it is almost unheard-of for an employer to ask to see any academic proof of, say, a bricklayer's credentials. The first test that any potential new bricklayer is given is a look at his hands and his tools of the trade. Both need to look suitably worn down by the rigours of handling bricks and mortar day in and day out. The next test is to give the bricklayer a place in line, some bricks and some mortar. The foreman will pass by after an hour or so and will know immediately if the bricklayer is a time-served tradesman or not. No protests of knowing a password will save the bogus bricklayer from being sent packing if his technique and speed are not what a time-served bricklayer ought to achieve. There is also no short cut to developing the techniques and skills necessary to lay bricks neatly and at speed. This observation is to some extent repeated in Masonic ceremonies. At each degree ceremony the candidate is asked to prove that he has the correct words and signs of the degree he claims to hold as a proof that he is worthy to advance to the next degree.

When the London Guild of Masons was inaugurated, they saw no need to give their new journeymen-masons a password or signs to identify them as warranted, so why would this requirement be added some three hundred years later? It is worth repeating also that no other guild provides it craftsmen with passwords or signs or tokens of membership. This observation is not limited to England. Gould[10] examined the stonemasons' guild of Germany during the middle-ages and his conclusions support our findings:

> There is not the slightest proof or indication of a word, and the existence of a sign is very doubtful.
>
> *Robert Gould*
> *History of Freemasonry, Its Antiquities, Symbols, Constitutions, Customs*

The Edinburgh MS continues:

Q. What makes a true and perfect lodge?
A. Seven masters, five entered apprentices, A days journey from a boroughs-town without bark of dog or crow of cock.
Q. Does no less make a true and perfect lodge?
A. Yes, five masons and three entered apprentices

The reference to a lodge being a day's journey from town is, to say the least suspicious. Plainly an air of overwhelming secrecy has being introduced. This raises the question of what on earth could a group of operative masons be getting up to that required them to travel – presumably on foot - a whole day's distance from their town?

The reference to the numerals seven, five and three is another suggestion of Hebrew influences on the Masonic ritual. These three numbers add up to fifteen. All Hebrew characters represent a number as well as the letter and thus the number fifteen, when written as *Yod-Heh* (because *Yod* = 10 and *Heh* = 5), just happens to be one of God's Hebrew names. Therefore, fifteen, or *Yod-Heh* is usually written as *Tet-Vav*, which is 9 + 6 = 15. As we mentioned in chapter 1, Jews do not write God's name to avoid the possibility of it later being altered or defaced. Freemasons too take an oath not to write, carve, mark or engrave the Masonic passwords. Now this is usually interpreted as a security measure to prevent those secrets becoming known. Some passwords for orders other than craft are, though, names or attributes of God, and so the directive not to write them down might be construed as an instruction to observe Judaic practice. Returning to the Edinburgh MS, it continues:

Q. How stands your lodge?

A. East and west as the Temple of Jerusalem.
Q. Where was the first lodge?
A. In the porch of Solomon's Temple.

We can see in the Edinburgh MS a stronger move towards a relationship with king Solomon's Temple, in parallel with the gradual introduction of Judaic influences on the ritual.

Q. Which is the key to your lodge?
A. A well hung tongue.
Q. Where lies the tongue?
A. In the bone box.

The "bone box" is an old term for the head, or sometimes the mouth as enclosed behind teeth. This plainly implied that the secrets of masonry are held in the mason's head and can only be communicated verbally. This was a curious suggestion for a trade that relied almost entirely on manual dexterity. The "ceremony" then appears to move into a second part or degree.

Q. Are you a fellow craft?
A. Yes.
Q. How many points of the fellowship are there?
A. Five. [The ritual then describes what Freemasons know as the five points of fellowship. The "words" of the first and second degrees of Freemasonry are also here mentioned, exactly as they are today.]

The modern ceremony has changed somewhat and the five points of fellowship no longer belong to the degree of a Fellowcraft. The manner in which the five points of fellowship are given is the first clear indication that the Judaic influences are sophisticated. The mystical form of Judaism called the Kabbalah, that should not be given to Jews under the age of forty, was transferred from one person to another by oral tradition and the secrets were given "mouth to ear" and this is exactly how the five-points-of-fellowship works.

The numeral five was important for early Jews as the number of books in the Torah and the hour of the day when they took their lunch break. It has a similar origin in the skies, being the number of planets visible to the naked eye. Further, the planet Venus is the next planet after Earth in closeness to the sun. Being closer to the sun the gravitational pull from the sun is stronger and so Venus must travel faster than the earth in order not to be pulled into the sun. The orbit of Venus is also shorter than that of the Earth because it is nearer to the sun and so it takes fewer days to travel around the sun. At various points in time, the Earth, Venus and the Sun are in conjunction; that is to say "in line". If Venus is between the earth and the Sun this is called an "inferior conjunction" and if Venus is the far side of the Sun then it is a superior conjunction". If we start with the planets in either conjunction, it takes eight years before the planets are similarly aligned again. During those eight years, Venus will have completed ten orbits and the Earth eight. Also during that time, there will have been five superior and five inferior conjunctions. If the positions of the inferior or superior conjunctions are plotted, they mark out five equal divisions of a circle which when joined describe a pentagram or five pointed star. A pentagram is carved in stone outside each of the three entrances to the UGLE headquarters.

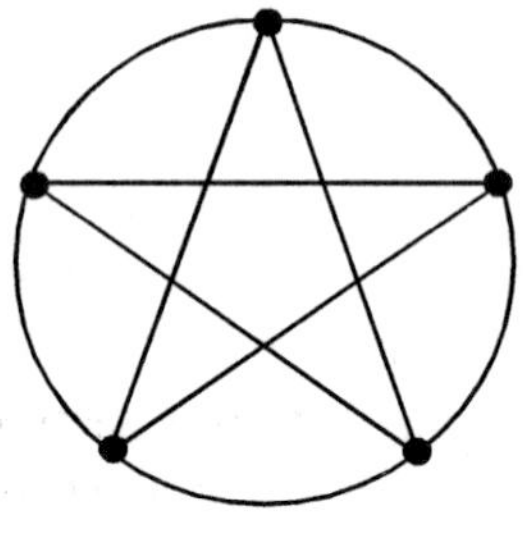

Returning to the Edinburgh Register House MS, there follows a description of how the "Mason Word" should be given. The "fearful" nature of the threats is in stark contrast to the form of words used by the masons who founded the London Masons Guild:

> Every man of the trade may work at any work touching the masons trade if he be perfectly skilled and knowing in the same.

It is worthy of repetition that there is nothing in these words to suggest for one moment that these masons considered anything in their particular vocation to be in any sense secret. Indeed they appeared to welcome anyone as a member if he could perform the skilled work that a mason was required to carry out. This, perhaps surprising, observation is reinforced by the comment we made earlier in this chapter that none of the other London Livery or Guild Companies ever had passwords or secret signs to distinguish their membership. The Masonic order known as "The Operatives" has only "keywords" that are various names of God, or His attributes.

Two of the authors have between them over fifty years Masonic experience including membership in nearly every order as well as mastership, or its equivalent, in most orders. Thus, we are able to say with considerable authority that nowhere in Freemasonry is there any secret that refers to how to carry out the trade of masonry. There is not even the simplest explanation of how best to hold a hammer and chisel; there are equally no directions on the best way to split a rock or the best mix of mortar or even the most effective types of sand, lime and cement to use. In short there is not a single word on how to perform the job of a mason. There is a lot about personal moral values, but the majority of Freemasonic ritual is about philosophy. Philosophy is variously defined as "the search for truth", or "understanding the universe and human existence by means of reflection, reason and argument". Once again we must mention that philosophical societies are almost as legion as the stars in the sky but none except Freemasonry imposes physical penalties for revealing any passwords. Such penalties were exacted in ancient Greek organisations such as the Pythagoreans, but those were times when arithmetic and algebra were deemed to be magic. Philosophy also includes any belief system and therefore encompasses religion, but this topic is banned from discussion in a Masonic lodge room. The only secrets, secrets that a mason must keep under threat of the most awful punishments, are the secret words and signs. This raises the question of why a secret word or a secret sign should be so important and there is only one answer. The secret words and signs are to protect the holder from being identified to anyone other than a fellow member. Let us look at "The Forme Of Giveing The Mason Word" included in the Edinburgh MS:

> Imprimis (Latin for "first or foremost") you are to take the person to take the word upon his knees and after a great many ceremonies to frighten him you make him take up the Bible and laying his right hand on it you are to conjure him to secrecy. By threatening him that if he shall break his oath the sun in the firmament will be a witness against him and all the company then present, which will be an occasion of his damnation and that likewise the masons will be sure to murder him.
>
> *Edinburgh manuscript*

There follows a section that is the earliest form of not "writing, inditing, carving, marking, engraving or otherwise delineating" the words on anything and these words are largely still included in the modern ritual. When the new mason had completed his sworn oath never to reveal the "mason word", he would be taken out by the "youngest member":

> Where, after he is sufficiently frightened with 1,000 ridiculous postures and grimaces, he is to learn from the said mason the manner of making his due guard which is the sign and the postures and words of his entry which are as follows. First when he enters again into the company he must make a ridiculous bow, then the sign and say "God bless the honourable company". Then putting off his hat after a very foolish manner only to be demonstrated then (as the rest of the signs are likewise) he says the words of his entry which are as follows.
>
> Here come I the youngest and last entered apprentice. As I am sworn by God and St. John by the square and compasses, and common judge to attend my masters service at

> the honourable lodge, from Monday in the morning till Saturday at night and to keep the Keys thereof, under no less pain than having my tongue cut out under my chin and of being buried, within the flood mark where no man shall know, then he makes the sign again with drawing his hand under his chin alongst his throat which denotes that it be cut in case he breaks his word. Then all the masons present whisper amongst themselves the word beginning with the youngest till it come to the master mason who gives the word to the entered apprentice.
>
> *Edinburgh manuscript*

In the Edinburgh Manuscript, we find the first reference to a "square", albeit here appended to the "compasses". We will return to the "square", later. Not until a Mason achieves the "Chair of King Solomon" will ritual approaching that described in the first paragraph above be seen by him. When the Edinburgh MS was in use, there were two degrees "apprentice" and "fellow", and there were two passwords that are still in use today. The ceremony of "fellow" was almost the same as for the apprentice but with a different "word" given on the five points of fellowship.

The question that must now be posed is "How reliable are these manuscripts given that they were written in violation of the severe oaths taken by a mason"? The ceremony as described in the Edinburgh MS is replicated in the Chetwode Crawley MS, which is dated about 1700 and the Kevan Manuscript of around 1714. Overwhelming proof of authenticity came from a lodge minute book for a lodge formed in Scotland in 1710. The lodge secretary wrote the ceremony on the first ten pages of the book and the last twenty-nine words ran on to the first page of lodge minutes, page eleven. Rather than waste paper, the secretary did not start on a fresh page but continued immediately underneath the ritual. At some point in time during the following sixty-one years, somebody decided the ritual should not be so openly displayed and ripped out the first ten pages. However, the final twenty-nine words agree exactly with the end of the Edinburgh Register House Manuscript, and the Chetwode and Kevin Manuscripts.

The Sloane Manuscript, which also dates to around 1700 and now housed in the British Museum, introduces various new signs and grips. Some of these signs and grips are still in use today and others are noticeably curious. Take, for example, the method of identifying another mason at work:

> Another sign is placing their right heel to the inside of their left in the form of a square so walk a few steps backward and forward and at every third step make a little stand placing the feet square as afores. This done, any if masons perceive it they will presently come to you if you come where any masons tools lie in the form of a square. It is a sign to discover him.
>
> *The Sloane Manuscript*

right heel

This section is unequivocally saying that not all masons were Freemasons and to discover the Freemasons from within the ranks of masons, certain elaborate rituals were to be carried out. Explaining these curious "identification" rituals continued a little later in the same text:

> To discourse [speak to] a mason in France, Spain or Turkey (say they) the sign is to kneel down on his left knee and hold his right hand to the sun and the outlandish [foreign] brother will presently take him up but believe me if they go on their knees on that acc[ount] they may remain there; or any persons observe their signs as long as the Jews will remain on their belief to receive their wished for Messiah from the east.
>
> *The Sloane Manuscript*

This latter paragraph tells us several things. Firstly that this form of Freemasonry was not a trade protection organisation for English masons but was international. Thc reference to Jews and their long awaited Messiah is, by any reckoning a most peculiar comment to include in a piece of English guild ceremonial. This is especially true so soon after Jews had been permitted to live in England and bearing in mind that they had been banned for several hundred years. The Sloane MS included the mason words as "Maha Byn" with "Maha" spoken by one mason into another's ear, and the reply "Byn" given by the second Mason.

The Sloane Manuscript is interesting for another reason. It is there that we see a further reference to a "square", this time as a means of identification.

> Another sign is placing their right heel to the inside of their left in the form of a square.

The word, "square", has become so central to Freemasonry that it is now commonplace to refer to a Freemason by the epithet of being "on the square". We spent chapter 1 describing the inordinate Judaic influence on Masonic symbolism and already in this chapter we have identified Jewish influences on the Masonic ritual. The use of the word "square" in such a central role within Freemasonry begs the question of what have squares got to do with Judaism? The answer is surprisingly obvious once it has been pointed out. When the Israelites returned from captivity in Babylon, towards the end of the 6th century BCE, they found that the Aramaic alphabet had largely displaced their ancient Hebrew one. Over the next four centuries they developed and introduced a new alphabet, which gradually replaced the Aramaic alphabet. This "new" Hebrew alphabet is called "**Square** Hebrew". Square Hebrew became firmly established by the first century BCE and further developed into the modern Hebrew alphabet that is used today. It is immediately clear that any reference to the word "square" to a Jew would immediately hit a nerve in the way that the same word will cause a Freemason to "prick up his ears". Indeed, it is clear that the term, "on the square", can equally apply to "square Hebrew", and so it is equally as significant to Jews as it is to Freemasons.

It is, though, the reference to steps - with the feet peculiarly placed – that provides the strongest link between Jews and Freemasonry:

> Another sign is placing their right heel to the inside of their left in the form of a square so walk a few steps backward and

> forward and at every third step make a little stand placing the feet square as afores.

Placing one's feet in the position described above, and the modern ritual invites a Mason to "take a short pace with the left foot and bring the right heel into its hollow", creates a shape that any Jew, brought up on the language of the Torah, Hebrew, would instantly recognise. Standing in this position, a Freemason's, feet describe three possible square Hebrew characters:

ז - Zayin
ד - Dalet
ך - Khaf

The early - Sloane Manuscript – version of the unusual Freemasons' gait required the mason to stop at every third step and bring the feet into the form of a square as described above. Emphasis is placed on each "third" step. Modern Masonic ritual requires an initiate to:

> Step off with your left foot bring the right heel into its hollow.
> Take another, a little longer, heel-to-heel as before.
> Take another, longer still, heel-to-heel as before.

We can now see that the three increases, in size, of the steps, replicates the increasing size of the three square-Hebrew characters, zayin, dalet and khaf. What is most remarkable is that these same three square-Hebrew characters, Z, D and K, make up the vowel-free word "ZDK", which can clearly be seen as "Zadok" without the vowels. Because ancient Hebrew did not have vowels, ZDK can – from a Hebrew perspective - be viewed as the name of the high priest who officiated over King Solomon's Temple. Why the secret steps described above should find their way into Masonic ritual is – for the moment – unknown because it is clear that their purpose was to allow one Jew to recognise another without a word being spoken.

We must introduce a note of caution at this point. The observation that a candidate's steps symbolize the three Hebrew characters Z, D and K is there for all to see. These letters do transliterate to "Zadok", and this is the way Solomon's high priest's name is spelt throughout the Bible. However, the Hebrew language is somewhat more complex. In reality, the correct first letter of Zadok is "tsadi", which has no English equivalent. Equally the last letter (on the far left) is ק (Qof) and the full Hebrew spelling of "Zadok" is צ ד ו ק, or written in English, from left to right, Tz-Z-D-Q. The final Hebrew letter "Qof" is regularly transliterated as "K" as seen in such words as Kaballah, which is also spelt as Cabbala or Qaballah.

We can, though, be fairly sure that this explanation – that is to say of Hebrew characters - of the initiate's steps towards the pedestal have been correctly interpreted because in the second-degree ceremony, that of a Fellowcraft, the candidate takes an entirely different set of steps. In the Fellowcraft's ceremony the candidate's footsteps trace out the Hebrew character "Yod", the first letter of the name of God, YHWH. To complete the association with the Hebrew alphabet, in the third degree ceremony the candidate traces out the Hebrew character "lamed". "Lamed" has the value – thirty – and this number was important to Freemasonry at the time the third degree ceremony was introduced; as explained in Templar Gold[1]. Indeed, the evidence is now overwhelming that Freemasonry was some sort of secret Jewish organisation, although for what purpose we do not, as yet, know. One fact which we can bear in mind is that between the years 1290 and 1656, it was illegal for Jews to reside in England and so, if any Jews were residing there, they would have needed to observe a special secrecy as discovery probably meant death.

The next manuscript we will examine is the Dumfries Manuscript. This dates from around 1710 and introduced the "cabletow", which remains as a symbolic item in modern ritual. The use then was "to hang me by, if I should betray my trust." Further penalties included "my heart taken out alive, my head cut off, my body buried within ye sea mark." This manuscript is large, running to twenty-eight sides of paper of about the size of a shorthand book, 11cm x 20cm. It begins with a distinctly Christian prayer in which mention is made of "the wisdom of the glorious Jesus", as well as "three persons in one Godhead".

The seven liberal sciences are treated at length in this work and as with the number five, mentioned above, the number seven also holds a special place in early Judaism. Before the invention of the telescope only five planets, plus the sun and the moon, were visible to the human eye - and clearly moving differently to the stars in the night sky. The earliest Biblical reference to seven comes with the seven commandments that God gave to Noah, for him to keep when He saved Noah from the flood. These Noahic laws form the basis of the later Ten Commandments. As mentioned before, seven symbolises "completeness". Other uses of the number seven include the number of deadly sins, the number of days in a week and the number of arms on the menorah, the candlestick placed in the Temple at Jerusalem.

In the Dumfries Manuscript, the seven liberal arts and sciences are followed by the story of Noah – also supporting the number seven - and the beginnings of geometry and various trades such as iron-working. The history section then Abraham and David, who:

> Began ye Temple of Jerusalem which is called ye temple of Diana and David loved masons well and cherished them by giving them good wages. And he gave them their charge on this manner that they should truly [know] the ten words which was written by the finger of God in characters of stone.
>
> *Dumphries No. 4 Manuscript*

Hiram, a man from Tyre, is introduced to bring his "exquisit knouledge" to bear on the Temple. Hiram is closely followed in the story by a "courious masson Minus Greenatis", who, after building king Solomon's Temple, went to France and taught Charles Martle's subjects. Minus Greenatis is most likely Naymus Grecus (a curious figure also mentioned in the Grand Lodge MS) and Charles Martle is undoubtedly Charles Martel. The legend continues with masonry reaching England in the time of St. Albans. The manuscript continues with a comprehensive schedule of "rules for good and moral behaviour" and ends with catechism of questions and answers to test the new masons' knowledge. An early question points to the involvement of the knights Hospitaller:

Q. What lodge were you entered in?
A. In ye true lodge of St. John

Most of the manuscripts make reference to St. John or the "true lodge of St. John" and this is strong support for the speculation of Byrne[1]. His premise was that, because the Masonic ritual can be decoded to identify a mountain in the south of France, then it probably follows that the mountain had something to do with the French order of Knights Templar. Byrne further surmised that this "secret" was carried to the present time within the ranks of the Knights Hospitaller who were earlier known as the Knights of St. John.

The next manuscript – known as the Trinity College, Dublin MS - is a short one, contained on only one side of roughly A4 paper and is dated 1711. It is in the form of a catechism and begins with the Jesuit sign of the cross standing on an extended letter "H":

This sign would later be modified by removing the upper arm of the cross to create the Royal Arch symbol of the triple tau.

The catechetical exchange between the master of the lodge and the candidate is much the same as earlier manuscripts until it gets to the master-word. In the manuscript two are given, "backbone" and "matchpin". These are sufficiently close to the modern words as to confirm that whoever wrote this document had indeed heard the correct version but forgotten or misheard. The first and second-degree words in this manuscript are correct.

The next manuscript that we will examine is A Mason's Examination dated 1723; it is an exposé that was reproduced in *The Flying Post* of April of that year. The author of *The Flying*

Post wrote a lengthy eulogy to Freemasonry to accompany the exposé, in which he pointed out that:

> The Worshipful Society are no Innovators in religious Affairs, no perjured Plotters or Conspirators against the established Government; that they in no way interfere or clash with any other Society or Corporation, however dignified or distinguished; for all which excellent Qualifications, a reasonable Person would be willing to pay their Persons, their lodges, their Constitutions, all due respect and Honour.

We can reasonably assume from this disclosure, that its purpose was to set right some information - that the author of the exposé believed to be wrong – that was already circulating. This disclosure makes no attempt to suggest that the "Worshipful Society" had anything to do with operative masonry. Indeed, this manuscript continues much on the lines of the ones described above until the catechism begins:

Q. Are you a Free-mason?
A. Yes, indeed, that I am.
Q. How shall I know it?
A. By signs and Tokens רסמ, from my Entrance into the Kitchen, and thence to the Hall.

The reference to kitchen and hall was the old method of identifying whether a brother was an apprentice or fellowcraft. Similar metaphors are still in use in orders such as Mark Master Masons. It is, though, the introduction of Hebrew characters that is arguably the strangest aspect of this particular manuscript.

According to Knoop[11] the characters in the manuscript are incorrect; the second character, *samech*, ought to be *shin* and should thus read רשמ. This Hebrew word is RôSHeM (*Resh, Shin, Mem*) meaning a symbol or token. We are advised that this word actually means "to record". Either way, it appears that whoever wrote this exposé was not a Hebrew scholar and so was most unlikely to have inserted the Hebrew text. Whether this surmise is also correct or not, we are still left with the obvious question of why would a Hebrew word be included in the Masonic ritual? Freemasonry was then the preserve of English gentlemen.

This correction by Knoop[11] allows another interpretation. Perhaps the use of the Hebrew character *samech* was a deliberate attempt to cover up the genuine character *shin.* There is a good reason for this deception because *shin* is the first letter of the Hebrew word *Shaddai*, one of the Hebrew words for God. Its visual appearance can be represented by forming two "V" signs with the first two forefingers of each hand, palms facing away from the body, and touching the two index finger together to make a "W" sign. If this sign is placed on the forehead and raised slowly up and down, it displays the way in which – according to some Masonic orders - Aaron blessed the Children of Israel. Clearly this particular use of a Masonic sign cannot be authoritative, but it demonstrates the importance of the Hebrew character *shin* within Freemasonry.

The next strange aspect of this manuscript comes a few lines later:

Q. What lodge are you of?
A. I am of the lodge of St. Stephen's.

We have discussed earlier how most manuscripts refer to the lodge of St. John, thereby providing a possible link back to the knights of St. John. The use of St. Stephen appears to be unique to this manuscript and this calls for an explanation. Stephen was one of the seven first Christian deacons in Jerusalem as well as the first Christian martyr. He was a member of a minority group within the Christian community who complained about the quality of care given to elderly widows. Because of their complaint seven deacons were chosen to perform this task. Stephen's evangelical talents led to a number of Jewish converts including many Temple priests and this brought a violent reaction. Stephen was taken before the Sanhedrin and charged with "speaking against this holy place"; his defence was uncompromising:

> Ye stiffnecked and uncircumcised in heart and ears, ye do always resist the Holy Ghost: as your fathers did, so do ye.
>
> Which of the prophets have not your fathers persecuted? and they have slain them which shewed before of the coming of the Just One; of whom ye have been now the betrayers and murderers.
>
> *Acts 7:51 and 52*

We mentioned in chapter 1, how Masonic "stiff-necked and disobedient shall be cut off from the land of the living", and here we find Stephen using similar words. For his audacity, Stephen was taken out of Jerusalem and stoned to death. It may have been St. Stephen's high regard for widows which endeared him to Freemasons because they consider themselves to be "sons of the widow". This belief results from Hiram Abif, a legendary Masonic character who was purportedly the architect for the building of the first Temple at Jerusalem and was a "widow's son". What may also have attracted the ritual compilers was Stephen's closing remarks to the Sanhedrin.

> But he, being full of the Holy Ghost, looked up steadfastly into heaven, and saw the glory of God, and Jesus standing on the right hand of God
>
> *Acts 7:55*

Apart from the use of Hebrew text and St. Stephen, this manuscript follows the pattern of Freemasonry of the time fairly closely. The various passwords are correct, as are the punishments.

The next manuscript we will consider is The Grand Mystery of Freemasons Discovered, which is dated to 1724. This includes the reference to St. John with correct words and signs. This manuscript also includes the first reference to a meridian. Interestingly, Byrne[1] linked the inaccurate positioning of the Paris meridian in relation to a temple shaped mountain in the South of France. This was identified by decoding the Masonic ritual.

Q. How is the meridian found out?

A. When the sun leaves the South and breaks in at the West-end of the Lodge.

This document also introduces the "arch", as in the Holy Royal Arch Masonic degree, into the ritual. Byrne also pointed out that the discovery of the error in the positioning of the Paris meridian coincided in time with the introduction of the Holy Royal arch degree into Freemasonry:

Q. Whence is an arch derived?
A. From architecture.

The five points of fellowship are incorporated with the five architectural orders. The last paragraph of this exposé includes a reference to king Henry VI's Act of Parliament making it a felony for masons to confederate themselves into chapters or assemblies. In reality this Parliamentary Act, instituted by Henry, was simply part of a legislative series designed to break the power of guilds to increase rates of pay. They were:

1423 Reinstitution of penalties for excessive wages.
1424 Prohibition of annual gatherings.
1427 Power given to justices of the peace to determine wages.
1429 Revoked the 1406 ruling on the taking of apprentices.
1436/7 Another attempt to control wage inflation.
1444/5 Curtailed the wages of a "frank mason".

The use of the term "frank mason" suggests that the legislators considered masonry to be a French institution. Henry VII continued with the legislation:

1495 Regulating of the wages of "free mason, master carpenter, and rough mason".

So did Henry VIII:

1514 Constrained the wages of a "free mason".

None of this legislation had any purpose other than to keep down wage inflation of all craftsmen including masons.

The manuscript The Whole Institution of Masonry dated 1724 is a short version of another similarly named document dated 1725. This one also originates from "Holy St. John", and contains Christian expressions.

Q. How many Lights in a Lodge?
A. Twelve.
Q. What are they?
A. Father, Son, Holy Ghost, Sun, Moon, Master Mason, Square, Rule, Plum Line [sic], Line, Mell [mall] and Chizzel [sic].

The Mason-words are correct as well as the method of receiving them. What is interesting is that this manuscript is some two years after Dr Anderson had published his Book of Constitutions, which had the approval of the Grand Master, the Duke of Montagu, as well as the Grand Lodge. The first code, or regulation was:

> Concerning God and Religion
> A Mason is oblig'd, by this Tenure, to obey the moral Law; and if he rightly understands the Art, he will never be a stupid atheist, nor an irreligious libertine. But though in ancient Times Masons were charg'd in every Country to be of the Religion of that Country or Nation, whatever it was, yet 'tis now thought more expedient only to oblige them to that Religion in which all Men agree …
>
> *Dr Anderson*
> *Book of Constitutions*

This was a clear direction to de-Christianise Freemasonry but this aim would not be fully achieved until nearly a century later. The use of "to oblige them to that religion in which all men agree" is by any measure a phrase laden with possibilities. We have already identified the overwhelming Judaic content of Freemasonry and now an injunction to drop the religion of the land. It is difficult not to conclude that Dr. Anderson was knowingly or otherwise suggesting that Judaism is "the religion on which all men can agree".

The first Grand Lodge, the Moderns, dropped the opening Christian prayer but retained many other references including the one to St. John. The later competing Grand Lodge, the Ancients, kept the prayer until the amalgamation of the two Grand Lodges in 1813. The second code gives the further lie to this being in any sense an organisation of operative masons:

> Of the Civil Magistrate Supreme and Subordinate
> A Mason is a peaceable Subject to the Civil Powers ... nor to behave himself undutifully to **inferior Magistrates** ...
>
> *Dr Anderson*
> *Book of Constitutions*

This then is an organisation of men who are socially superior to Magistrates. The fourth regulation is equally telling:

> Of Masters, Wardens, Fellows, and Apprentices
> Only Candidates may know, that no Master should take an Apprentice, unless he has sufficient Employment for him, and unless he be a perfect Youth, having no Maim or Defect in his Body, that may render him uncapable to learning the Art, of serving his Master's Lord...
>
> *Dr Anderson*
> *Book of Constitutions*

At first sight, it could be argued that it is perfectly normal for a physical trade such as masonry to exclude those who have physical defects. However, a little later in this particular regulation we find:

> [No Brother can be] Grand-Master unless he has been a Fellow-Craft before his Election, who is also to be nobly born, or a Gentleman of the best Fashion, or some eminent Scholar, or some curious Architect, or other Artist, descended of honest Parents, and who is of singular great Merit in the Opinion of the Lodges.
>
> *Dr Anderson*

Book of Constitutions

Further proof, if proof were needed, that this is not an organisation of working masons. This brings us back to the issue of "why exclude those with physical defects"? One obvious observation – in the light of the lodge room representing king Solomon's Temple - is that no unclean (sick or disabled) person was allowed into the original Temple at Jerusalem.

> And he set the porters at the gates of the house of the Lord, that none which was unclean in any thing should enter in.
>
> *2 Chronicles 23:19*

We find yet another curious comment in the sixth regulation:

> Of Behaviour in the Lodge while constituted.
> ... to pay due Reverence to your Master, Wardens, and Fellows, and put them to worship.
>
> *Dr Anderson*
> *Book of Constitutions*

"Put them to worship" seems a strange regulation for an organisation that goes to considerable lengths to insist that it is not a religion.

The next exposition we will consider is The Graham Manuscript dated to 1726. This version also quotes its beginnings from "the Holy Saint John". It is quite clearly a Freemasonic document for it contains the words and signs of the apprentice and fellowcraft degrees. It also holds the first evidence of what is now the third degree ceremony including the five points of fellowship, which were transferred to the new third or "Masters'" degree from the fellowcraft degree. Within the text are references to Jesus and to the Trinity, but in addition is the first reference to the manner in which a Freemason enters on to his Masonic career, that is to say "slipshod".

Q. What poster (posture) did you pass your oath in?
A. I was neither sitting standing going running riding hinging (hanging) nor flying naked nor clothed shod nor barefoot…

"Nor … shod nor barefoot", this phrase requires an interpretation. The words are used in a slightly more understandable form in a later manuscript, Masonry Dissected, which was published by Samual Pritchard and is accurately dated to 1724. This disclosure was translated into French and published in France and is generally recognised as the primary source for several later exposés.

Q. Who brought you to the Lodge?
A. An enter'd Prentice
Q. How did he bring you?
A. Neither naked nor clothed, barefoot nor shod…

A full explanation of this curious conduct is given in a later version of the Masonic ritual, Avery Allyn's, A Ritual of Freemasonry[12], which is dated around 1830. This two-hundred and fifty page book contains most of the ritual in use today, albeit now arranged into different degrees and orders.

Q. Why was you neither barefoot nor shod?
A. It was an ancient Israelitish custom adopted among Masons; and we read in the book of Ruth concerning their mode and manner of redeeming, and changing 'for to confirm all things, a man plucked off his shoe and gave it to his neighbour, and this was testimony in Israel'. This then, therefore, we do in confirmation of a token, and as a pledge of our fidelity; thereby signifying that we renounce our own will in all things, and become obedient to the laws of our ancient institutions.

We discussed in chapter 1 how, by handing over a shoe, new masons would have renounced their beliefs in favour of "the laws of our ancient institutions". Which "ancient institutions" is this referring to? By inference, none other than those of "Israel", for this is where the custom held sway according to the Bible and this portion of the ritual. It is as if new Masons are becoming converts to Judaism - what a remarkable possibility. This can only be coincidence, and so we must look further.

There was not another Masonic disclosure until 1760 and this purported to be the ritual of the Ancients lodges. It is called Three Distinct Knocks. Some two years later a similar exposure gave details of the ritual for Moderns lodges. It is called Hiram or the Grand Master Key to the Door of both Ancient and Modern Freemasonry.

Three Distinct Knocks has this to say about the removal of shoes:

Q. Why were both your shoes taken off your feet?
A. Because the place I stood on, when I was made a mason, was holy ground.

In fact, it is not until a Mason joins the Holy Royal Arch and gains a senior rank that he will experience both-shoes removal as a reality. The conclusion is now unavoidable; the removal of the shoe(s) makes the subsequent oath a testimony or covenant; it was made to God and it was made in a place that was deemed to be holy. A Freemasons' lodge represents king Solomon's Temple and that – apart from occasional desecration by the Babylonians and the Romans - was the Jewish Temple to YHWH. Perhaps this is not coincidence after all.

The ancient manuscripts of early Masonic ritual are telling us that a clear and deliberate process of increasing the Judaic content went on over many years. It also appears that the aim was to transfer a new Mason's allegiance to YHWH. This possibility is far too controversial to be left unchecked. This chapter has thrown up a number of issues that will bear on the solution. We will summarise them for future reference:

1. The earliest manuscript, circa 1400, contained no Jewish references and no secrets.
2. The next manuscript, circa 1500, includes a reference to King Solomon's Temple and yet Jews were banned from England at this time.

3. Freemasonry "appeared" on the scene around 1700, which is only 50 years after Jews were permitted to live in England.
4. The Sloane Manuscript introduced a reference to "square", which is also the name of the Hebrew alphabet.
5. The position into which a Freemason arranges his feet corresponds to the name of the high priest, Zadok, who officiated at King Solomon's Temple.
6. The new Freemasonry was overwhelmingly secretive.
7. Masonic meetings were held "a whole day's distance from their town".
8. Jewish Kaballah practices appear in early Masonic ceremonial.
9. Not all operative masons were Freemasons.
10. Freemasonry was international from the beginning.

Within this list of issues that we have uncovered lies the germ of an answer to the question of how did Freemasonry begin. We will continue to explore these themes in the next chapter.

CHAPTER 3

PROSELYTISM?

The last chapter ended with the surprising observation that the oath which a Masonic initiate takes on the Bible amounts to a testimony made to God. Further, in earlier times the new Mason would make this oath, to "renounce his own will in all things, and become obedient to the laws of the ancient institutions of Freemasonry", on ground believed to be Holy. Those "ancient institutions" could only have referred to Israel.

So, what of the other oaths that a Freemason takes? If we turn back to the exposure just mentioned, Masonry Dissected, there was only one obligation or oath to cover the three degrees of apprentice, fellow and master. The obligation required an initiate to swear – in the presence of Almighty God - that he will always conceal and never reveal any of the secrets that are about to be communicated. He further promised never to write the secrets anywhere in any way. Finally, he accepts that the punishment for breaking this oath is a somewhat slow and painful death. These requirements have changed little in today's Freemasonry.

So, what are these secrets that are about to be imparted to him. In a few words, not much. Indeed, not a great deal more than was available to the mason joining a guild several hundreds of years earlier, and who was not threatened with dire consequences if he betrayed them. In fact, the only "new" information that a Freemason receives are the signs and words by which one Brother identifies another.

We have just cautiously hinted that to become a Freemason is akin to converting to Judaism and this demands further examination. To begin with, a Jew has to abide by the 613 commandments or *Mitzvot* or *Mizva* given in the Torah. The first ten, deal with respect for God and a Freemason would automatically have no problems with these.

Mitzvot 11 to16 - deal with the Torah and as most of Freemasonic ceremonial is taken from Biblical stories this too would present no problem. If a Freemason perseveres and joins other orders or degrees that are available, each order generally – but not exclusively - deals with a new Biblical character such as Noah or Melchezedek. Similarly to the Craft ritual, the other orders provide a historical narration of the life of a newly introduced Biblical character, stressing their dedication to God and the rewards that flow from such dedication. Thus, by following his Freemasonry through the various degrees, a Mason will learn "by heart" each new Biblical story, and repeat it during the actual ceremony. He will thus be "teaching" the Biblical stories to other new masons present at the ceremonials. Without realising it, he is actively conforming to Mitzvot number 12:

To learn Torah and to teach it

Mitzvot 17 - requires ones children to be circumcised and this must be a deliberate act.

Mitzvot 18 - requires the wearing of *tzitzit* or tassels from the corners of ones clothing, exactly as many Masonic aprons have.

Mitzvot 19 to 20 - require the wearing of a *tefillin* or pouch containing passages from the Torah on the head and arms.

Mitzvot 21 - requires one to fix a *mezuzah* or long pouch also containing passages from the Torah to ones gate-post.

Mitzvot 22 to 25 - require formal prayers to be said during the day and Grace to be said after meals also not to make stone altars. Masons always return thanks to God after a Masonic meal. There is also a piece of ritual, delivered to a Freemason at his initiation, which unambiguously supports these Mtzvot:

> By imploring his [God's] aid in all your lawful undertakings, and by looking up to Him in every emergency for comfort and support.

Mitzvot 26 to 39 - are about brotherhood and as such are very close to a Freemason's heart.

Mitzvot 40 to 52 – charity, concern and care for the poor, another subject close to the heart of a "good" Mason. We have already mentioned in chapter 1 the "tyler's" toast, "to all poor and distressed Freemasons". Later in this book we will show how the Hebrew suffix for the high priest, the word "*tzedech*" or "*zedek*", also meaning "charity" overlaps with Freemasonry.

Mitzvot 53 to 58 - concern treatment of gentiles and apart from the injunction not to marry a gentile would cause no problems for a Mason.

Mitzvot 59 to 81 - are rules on marriage some; such as 67 – "Not to exclude a descendant of Esau from the community of Israel for three generations", are probably observed today more in the breach.

Mitzvot 82 to 106 - detail forbidden sexual relations most of which are contained in English Law. During his third degree ceremony, a new Mason promises:

> I will maintain a Master Mason's honour and carefully preserve it as my own ... and most strictly respect the chastity of those nearest and dearest to him, in the persons of his wife, his sister, and his child.

Mitzvot 107 to 142 – lists the Jewish festivals and feast days.

Mitzvot 143 to 169 - describes dietary rules, which today are followed only by Orthodox Jews. There rules include the instruction not to mix dairy products with meat and this clearly reflects the ancient days when these foods were all that was available on the mountaintops of the southern Levant.

Mitzvot 170 to 613 – are rules of business and rules that mostly apply to days long gone and are scarcely if at all relevant to today.

Clearly, apart from strict Orthodox Jews, a "conscientious" Freemason would probably meet nearly as high a proportion of the 613 Mitzvot as many, perhaps most, Jews. It is plain the 613 Mitzvot do not present an insurmountable barrier between Freemason and Jew. We can accordingly continue with this comparison of the process of conversion to Judaism with Masonic initiation. Before a potential convert to Judaism - a proselyte - can be admitted, he must be brought before *Beit Din*, a rabbinical court, which will decide if he is ready to become a Jew - just as every potential Freemason is interviewed by a lodge committee and questioned on his beliefs before the lodge members have an opportunity to vote on his application.

If the proselyte is successful at the *Beit Din,* he advances to circumcision and if he is already circumcised then a pinprick of blood is drawn for symbolic purposes. This appears at first sight to be an overwhelming barrier to the idea that becoming a Freemason amounts to conversion to Judaism, or is it? Consider the initiate standing at the door of the lodge where a dagger is placed at his breast to prevent him rushing forward:

Q. Do you feel anything
A. Yes

During earlier Freemasonry the wording was slightly different. Three Distinct Knocks had this to say:

Q. Why had you a Sword, Spear or some other war-like Instrument, presented to your naked left breast?
A. Because the Left-breast is nearest to the Heart, that it might be the more a Prick to my Conscience as it prick'd my flesh at the time.

The wording for the other major exposure Jachin and Boaz was identical, suggesting a common source document for both. Finally the latest exposure during this period, Shibboleth, which Jackson[13] felt was a record of a "genuine Modern[s] procedure" - despite several errors - had this to say:

Q. What was your manner of entering?
A. With three distinct steps, and a sharp instrument presented to my left breast.

It is not clear whether actual blood – albeit a pinprick – was drawn in the early days but it copies this action. There is a common assumption that circumcision is a condition to becoming a Jew, but this is not the case. As with so many matters, the question of circumcision is a cause for disputation within Judaism as the following extracts show:

> The issue between the Zealot and Liberal parties regarding the circumcision of proselytes remained an open one in tannaitic times. Rabbi Joshua asserting that the bath, or baptismal rite, rendered a person a full proselyte without circumcision, as Israel, when receiving the Law, required no initiation other than the purificative bath. While Rabbi Eliezer makes circumcision a condition for the admission of a proselyte, and declares the baptismal rite to be of no consequence. A similar controversy between the Shammaites and the Hillelites is given regarding a proselyte born circumcised. The former demanding the spilling of a drop of blood of the covenant; the latter declaring it to be unnecessary.
>
> The abolition of circumcision in the case of proselytes, on the ground of its being a measure of extreme cruelty when performed upon adults, was proposed by Isaac M. Wise at the rabbinical conference in Philadelphia in 1869. It was finally agreed to by the Reform rabbis of America at the New York conference in 1892.
>
> *JewishEncyclopedia.com*

It is apparent that even circumcision cannot be held up as an argument that the Masonic ceremonial is not a ceremony of conversion.

The next ritual for the proselyte is immersion in the *mikvah*, which is a ritual bath for spiritual purification. In Freemasonry the candidate in his final craft degree goes through a process of spiritual rebirth – not, as is sometimes mistakenly claimed, a resurrection. The Masonic character, Hiram Abif, who is being impersonated, never does recover. He dies and stays dead. In early French ceremonies a brother other than the candidate would lie down to symbolise the dead Hiram Abif and he would move just before the candidate lay down, confirming the symbolic nature of rebirth or spiritual purification.

Of the various Masonic allegories, which we are suggesting are metaphors for the process of conversion to Judaism, it is this last ceremony, of spiritual rebirth equating to a ritual bath that is arguably the most contentious and so deserves a more comprehensive explanation. In using a *mikvah,* the proselyte is immersed completely in water to wash away past sins. In the Masonic ceremony, the candidate is lowered into a grave – quite literally a recess in the floor in some lodge rooms. He is then raised from a "**figurative** death to be reunited with the companions of his former toils". There can be no doubt that this ceremony represents a spiritual rebirth and that would necessitate the leaving behind of past sins, for one cannot be born again with any sin other than "original sin". In fact, the concept of rebirth is a requirement for Bible-based Christians as well as Jews:

> Jesus answered and said unto him, Verily, verily, I say unto thee, except a man be born again, he cannot see the kingdom of God.
>
> *St. John 3:3*

Perhaps the following extract from the internet Jewish Encyclopedia makes the issue indubitably clear:

> The proselyte is regarded as a newborn child; hence his former family connections are considered as ended.
>
> *JewishEncyclopedia.com*

Almost the final act for a Jewish convert is to take a Jewish name and be introduced into the Jewish community. A Freemason adds the title "brother" to his name and it is not unusual for a new Mason to be similarly formally introduced to the members of his lodge.

During the Jerusalem Temple period, a converted Jew took a sacrifice or offering to the Temple. When the Temple was destroyed, this ceremony disappeared. Some Orthodox rabbis propose this moment as an opportunity to engage in an act of charity as a symbolic offering. Charity is central to Freemasonry, and, during his initiation, a candidate is strongly reminded of his commitment to charity.

Notwithstanding the fascinating case we have put forward above, we can safely say that the procedure of becoming a Freemason is **not** an act of proselytism – indeed, it would be offensive to suggest that Jews were deliberately ensnaring gentiles into Judaism in this way. All the available evidence on Judaism is that this would be the last thing that Jewry would wish to happen. Indeed, the opinion of Jews towards gentiles cannot be better demonstrated than by their directive not to drink wine made from grapes grown by gentiles. The wilful act of conversion to Judaism is neither quick nor easy to achieve. We include below a few extracts from the Jewish Encyclopedia, which graphically demonstrate the antipathy of Jews towards proselytes:

> In modern times conversions to Judaism are not very numerous. Marriage is, in contravention of the rabbinical caution, in most instances the motive, and proselytes of the feminine sex predominate. Instruction in the Jewish religion precedes the ceremony, which, after circumcision and baptism, consists in a public confession of faith, in the main amounting to a repudiation of certain Christian dogmas, and concluding with the reciting of the Shema (confession of the Jewish faith).
>
> Certain restrictions regulating the status of women proselytes are found in the *Mishnah.* Girls born before the conversion of their mothers were not regarded as entitled to the benefit of the provisions concerning a slanderous report as

> to virginity set forth in Deuteronomy, and if found untrue to their marriage vows, their punishment was strangulation. Proselytes could contract marriages with men who were barred from marrying Jewish women. While a proselyte woman was deemed liable to the ordeal of jealousy the provisions of the Law regarding the collection of damages in the case of injury to pregnant women were construed as not applicable to her.
>
> In these passages the strict interpretation of the Pentateuchal texts, as restricted to Israel, prevails, and in a similar spirit, in the order of precedence only the manumitted slave is assigned inferior rank to the proselyte, the bastard and the natin (low "caste" Temple servant tribe) taking precedence over him.
>
> *JewishEncyclopedia.com*

It is, though, plain that the Masonic ceremonies of initiating, passing and raising a new Mason amount to a passable allegorical representation of proselytisation. How then, could such an august body as the Freemasons, who number many intellectuals in their membership, allow their organisation to mimic – albeit in an allegorical manner – the act of conversion to Judaism? We have identified that Freemasonry contains a large amount of Judaism, and in order to understand how the apparent allegorical proselytisation was allowed into the ceremonial we must try and identify who actually did it, who put the Judaism into Freemasonry? It seems unlikely that the brethren who brought Freemasonry into the light of day thought of such a notion and if they did, how on earth did they gather enough like-thinking people to achieve this end? The Judaic content is undeniable and its "mock proselytism" nature suggest that Jews must have been responsible either for the words and rubric of Masonic ceremonial or in guiding (perhaps misguiding would be a better description) the hands of those who did compile the ritual. There appears to be no other logical explanation for the nature of the ritual. It is going to be hard enough to find an explanation as to why those early Jews created - or guided the creation of - Masonic ritual that so obviously replicates in allegorical form the act of proselytisation.

Perhaps it was all a harmless joke that simply got too big, a "thumbing of Jewish noses" at the establishment that had until so recently banned them from living in England. Maybe they never intended or expected Freemasonry to "take-off" and become so huge. One thing is for sure: fairly quickly the early Jews must have lost control and with it the capability of influencing Masonic ritual to the extent that they could undo the proselytising nature of the ceremonies.

Let us now continue with our analysis of the extant manuscripts. There is at least one piece of ritual that suggests a foreign origin for Freemasonry. In A Mason's Confession, 1727, only four years after introducing the "slipshod" ritual, the first Judaic rite, we find the following exchange:

Q. What's a mason's livery?
A. A yellow cap and blue breeches.

These garments are explained as the compasses: the yellow jacket is the hinged arms of the brass compasses and the blue breeches are the steel points. We saw how the word, "square", came to be associated with Freemasonry and now we can add the compasses. These two navigational instruments, when overlain, create the emblem of Freemasonry. This emblem, visible at the head of nearly every Masonic document and Masonic web page, holds within it the Seal of Solomon or Magen David, the symbol of Judaism.

FIGURE 7 – SQUARE AND COMPASSES WITH SEAL OF SOLOMON

The next manuscript we examined was published in 1730. It was Masonry Dissected and in it the words have changed slightly:

Q. Have you seen your master today?
A. Yes.

Q. How was he clothed?
A. In a Yellow Jacket and Blue Pair of Breeches.

So, what does this curious line of enquiry mean? Perhaps the answer lies in the inclination of those people who at various periods in history have encouraged anti-Semitism: to make Jewry wear easily identifiable clothing. The oldest known reference to the ordering of distinctive clothing by the Jews was in 807 CE. It was Abbassid caliph Haroun al-Raschid who ordered all Jews to wear a yellow belt and a tall, cone-like hat. Not exactly what the ritual compasses signify, but the colour yellow has been introduced as a special distinguishing mark of a Jew. During the Spanish inquisition, when the "heretics" were given the result of the trial at the *auto-da-Fés*, before usually being burned alive, the accused were dressed in black with a yellow scarf with a red cross on it. Alternatively they wore the *Sanbenito,* which was a yellow slipover with two diagonal red crosses. In 1215, CE, the Church of Rome joined in this particular form of persecution:

> In some provinces a difference in dress distinguishes the Jews or Saracens from the Christians, but in certain others such a confusion has grown up that they cannot be distinguished by any difference. Thus it happens at times that through error Christians have relations with the women of Jews or Saracens, and Jews and Saracens with Christian women. Therefore, that they may not, under pretext of error of this sort, excuse themselves in the future for the excesses of such prohibited intercourse, we decree that such Jews and Saracens of both sexes in every Christian province and at all times shall be marked off in the eyes of the public from other peoples through the character of their dress. Particularly, since it may

> be read in the writings of Moses [Numbers 15:37-41], that this very law has been enjoined upon them.
>
> *Canon 68*
> *Fourth Lateran Council*

So, what does the Biblical text of Moses tell us about any dress code for Jews:

> And the LORD spake unto Moses, saying,
>
> Speak unto the children of Israel, and bid them that they make them fringes in the borders of their garments throughout their generations, and that they put upon the fringe of the borders a ribband of blue.
>
> *Numbers 15:37 and 38*

The above depiction is clearly not the yellow that would have supported the premise we are exploring but the description provides us with unexpected support for our general thesis, for the Biblical description is of none other than a Masonic apron:

FIGURE 8 - MASONIC PROVINCIAL RANK APRON

The use of "yellow" as the distinguishing colour to identify Hebrews did not occur until 1269. It was Louis IX who ordered that "both men and women were to wear badges on the outer garment, both front and back, round pieces of yellow felt or linen, a palm long and four fingers wide". Although the evidence here is not decisive, it does strongly hint that the reference to "yellow jacket" for the compasses was an allegory for Jewry. The Biblical description above, from Numbers 15:38 for the Jewish dress code, looks remarkably like a Masonic apron and adds force to our argument.

How, then, might the Jews have achieved this remarkable early control of the Masonic ritual? We have identified earlier that Jews were permitted back into England in 1656 and that by 1730 only 74 years later, Judaic influences were appearing in the Masonic ritual. We have John Shaftesley[14] to thank for a most comprehensive paper that allows us to examine just how popular Freemasonry was with male Jews. Shaftesley makes an early reference to the Book of Constitutions drawn up for the Ancients lodges by their secretary Laurence Dermott and entitled *Ahiman Rezon*. The meaning of the title has not been translated or deciphered to this day, although Dermott did include the subtitle A Help to a Brother in later editions. *Ahiman Rezon*, referring to lodge meeting prayers, includes these words:

> A Prayer used at Opening the Lodge, or making a Brother; used by Jewish Freemasons.

Ahiman Rezon also mentions "likewise the Prayers used in Jewish and Christian Lodges". *Ahiman Rezon* was compiled in 1764 and so here is compelling evidence that Jewish lodges existed by this date; only forty-seven years after Freemasonry entered the public arena.

Shaftesley[14] quotes a Lodge No. 84, based at Daniel's Coffee-House in Lombard Street, as including the Jews Solomon Mendez, Abrahm Ximenex, Jacob Alvarez, Abraham de Medina, Benjamin Adolphus and Isaac Baruch among its membership. He also makes an interesting point that supports much of what has been posed above:

> Katz [Professor Jacob Katz – Rector of the Hebrew University of Jerusalem] suggests that Christians generally did not know

> of the Talmudic and medieval Judaic references to obedience to the Commandments of Noah as constituting grounds for tolerance of righteous Gentiles …
>
> *John Shaftesley*
> *Jews in English Regular Freemasonry from 1717 to 1860*

Shaftesley also quotes Herbert Lowe, a non-Mason and Lecturer in Rabbinic Hebrew at the University of Oxford:

> He [Lowe] praised Freemasonry and the 'amazing affinity' between it and Judaism on moral principles; 'in three important principles [they] resemble one another: in theory, in practice, and in ceremonial'.
>
> It is your great achievement that you have made it possible at your gatherings for all who believe in God to worship Him together without in any way abating each man the fidelity due to his particular creed.
>
> *John Shaftesley*
> *Jews in English Regular Freemasonry from 1717 to 1860*

The observation that Freemasonry mirrors the process of religious conversion is not confined to the authors. Shaftesley mentions the beliefs of many rabbis that Freemasonry is another road to conversion – not of Christians to Judaism, though, but of Jews to Christianity!

Shaftesley lists the names of some 930 Jews whom he considers to have been Freemasons between 1717 and 1860. From this list is it possible to identify at least one hundred Jews who were Freemasons during the formative years for the ritual of between 1717 and 1730. In those early days, the catechetical part of the ceremony was carried out with the brethren seated around a table. The meetings were held in Public Houses and so it is not an unreasonable assumption to put the membership – at meetings – at not more that say twenty. It is important to say "at meetings", because then as today, it will have been those who attended meetings who were the activists.

In his paper, Some Sephardic Jews in Freemasonry, delivered at his installation as Master of the Montefiore Lodge of Installed Masters, Leon Zeldis had this to say on early English Jewish Masons:

> It is not surprising, then, that the first known Jewish Mason, dating from 1716 (one year *before* the creation of the first Grand Lodge) was an English Sephardi: Francis Francia, also known as the "Jacobite Jew". He was tried and later exonerated from an accusation of high treason. In an English newspaper of 1877, recounting this incident, Francia is called a Mason.
>
> In 1732, another Jew, Edward Rose, was initiated in a Lodge presided over by Daniel Delvalle, 'eminent Jew snuff merchant' as characterized in a report in the *Daily Post* of 22 September 1732. Without doubt, Delvalle must have preceded Rose by several years, to have reached the high position of Master of the Lodge. Furthermore, Bro. Mathias Levy, in an article entitled 'Jews as Freemasons' published in *The Jewish Chronicle* in 1898, claims that the initiation took place 'in the presence of Jews and non-Jews.' These other Jews present must have been Masons themselves, initiated at an earlier date.
>
> *Leon Zeldis*
> *Some Sephardic Jews in Freemasonry*

The exposure Masonry Dissected 1730 records the names of 67 lodges of which 13 were outside London and one was in Spain. This leaves 53 lodges in London and at roughly 20 active members per lodge (enough to sit around a table) there were around 1060 active Freemasons in London of who some 100 were Jews. At ten per cent, the number of Jews in English Freemasonry is clearly well above the proportionate number of male Jews in the male population. The mathematics used in this calculation are approximate and so no great stress should be put on the result, other than to suggest that in the formative years of Freemasonry in England Jewry was strongly represented. The assumption, implied in the analysis so far, suggests that one or more of these Jews was involved in developing the Masonic ritual. This is certainly not an excessive claim because, as we said in chapter 1, Rabbi Jacob Judah Leon Templo designed the original coat of arms of the Ancients Grand Lodge, a design that is now incorporated into the coat of arms of the United Grand Lodge of England.

It may be hard to imagine that in the mere fifty years from 1656, when Jews were readmitted to England, until 1717 when Freemasonry became public, male Jewry could become so well established in what would become a worldwide institution. That is, until we examine their success in another area. In the traditional Jewish – and Knights Templar when they existed - business arena of banking, the inroads made by the Jews in an equally short time displays their capacity for control. An archivist of the Bank of England, J. A. Giuseppi, F.S.A., published a paper in *Transactions XIX* listing the names of the Proprietors of the Bank of England. These data were summarised by Sir John Clapham[15] with the conclusion that no less that a ninth of the 107 Proprietors of Bank of England stock in 1701 were Sephardic Jews. This number is clearly out of all proportion to their representation in England at that time.

In 1809 the two Grand Lodges, the Ancients and the Moderns, appointed commissioners to negotiate a merger. The negotiations were completed and on 27 December 1813 – Saint John the Evangelist's day - the United Grand Lodge of England was inaugurated. Interestingly, the Duke of Sussex is reported[14] to have been "a friend of the Jews and in favour of their political emancipation". It is also on record[14] that he was the first Royal patron of the Nevei Zedek, a Jewish Hospital. Shaftesley[14] also reports how Hyppolito Joseph da Costa escaped from the Portuguese Inquisition and fled to London where he became a Provincial Grand Master and a friend of the Duke of Sussex. From this we can readily acknowledge that by 1813 Jewry had a place at the high table of Freemasonry. That some Jewish organisation existed prior to 1717 cannot be proved but we do know that before that date middle-class gentlemen were being made Masons. In a Masonic paper, J. Ward stated that:

In 1721 the Grand Charter of the Grand Lodge of England, John, Duke of Montagu, instructed Dr. Anderson and several other prominent Masons to revise the Ancient Charter so as to make them more suited to the period, these were issued in 1723. The most striking change was with regard to religion, for instead of demanding that a Mason should be a "true son of the Holy Church," it ran as follows: "But though in ancient times, Masons were charged in every country to be of the religion of that country or nation, whatever it was, yet it is now thought more expedient only to oblige them to that religion in which all men agree; leaving their own particular opinions to themselves." To alter Freemasonry from a Christian to a vaguely Deistic basis was a complete revolution.

In 1816, the last traces of Christianity were removed from the Constitutions, the Duke of Sussex being Grand Master at the time; of the Duke, the Jewish Daily Post, 6th May, 1935, states "The Duke of Sussex was an open friend of the Jewish community ... he opened his doors to Jews with great affability."

J. S. M. Ward
Freemasonry, its Aims and Ideals

The most often quoted "first recorded Freemason on English soil" is Elias Ashmole, who founded the Ashmolean Museum in Oxford. His diary contains an account of how he was made a Free Mason in a lodge held at his father-in-law's house in Warrington in 1646. In fact there is an earlier record. In 1641, Robert Moray – who was then the quartermaster-general of the Scots Covenanters - was admitted into the lodge of Edinburgh. The minutes of the meeting survive to this day:

At Neucastell the 20th day off May 1641 the quilk day one serton nomber off Mester and others being lafule conveined, doeth admit Mr the Right Honerabell Mr Robert Moray, General quarter Mr to the Armie of Scotlan, and the sam bing

> aproven be the hed Mester off Mesons of the Log of Edenbroth guherto they heaue set to ther handes or markes.
>
> *The minutes were signed by A. Hamilton, Johne Mylln, James Hamilton and the candidate Robert Moray.*

We have spent much time examining the Judaic content of Freemasonry and the evident influence of Jews before its entry onto the public stage in 1717. There are, though, indications that another group of people were, at around 1830, involved in modifying the early Freemasonic ritual. The first clue that may identify this second group occurs with the office of "Deacon", which first makes a formal appearance in Three Distinct Knocks, in 1760. Deacons must have been in place earlier because no mention is made of their being in any way innovative.

> The earliest record of a Deacon is Industry Lodge No.48 in 1734, it had two such officers – Senior Deacon or Steward, and Junior Deacon or Steward. In 1743 another Lodge recorded "a Masters Deacon" and "a Wardens Deacon", but they were not generally known until 1809 when the Lodge of Promulgation resolved that "Deacons were useful and necessary Officers".
>
> *Aspects of the Craft (Masonic Paper)*
> *Ray Hudson*

What is significant is that the first Masonic Deacons carried black wands or rods. This knowledge comes from Jachin and Boaz:

> The Senior and Junior Deacons have each a black Rod, with the **Compass** hanging around their necks …
>
> *Jachin and Boaz*

The reference to "compass" may simply be an error, but the next description, for the Pass-Master [sic] says:

> The Pass-Master has the **compasses** and Sun, with a line of Cords about his neck.
>
> *Jachin and Boaz*

The difference between "compass" – an instrument for locating magnetic north, and "compasses" – an instrument with two hinged legs for drawing circles, is clearly significant. It was an error of 3° between magnetic north and true north, which Byrne[1] suggests created the need for a third degree in Freemasonry. It is, though, the black rods that are another a give-away. That inheritor of mediaeval British pageantry, the "Gentleman Usher of the Black Rod" is more usually known simply as "Black Rod". His important role in the ceremony of the State Opening of Parliament is to summon MPs to the House of Lords to hear the Queen's Speech. When he reaches the chamber of the House of Commons, the door is slammed in his face. He then knocks three times – a Masonic knock if ever there was one - on the door with his black rod and the doors of parliament are opened to him.

> The earliest reference to the Black Rod dates from 1361 when the knights, moving in procession from one point to another as part of the frequent festivals at Windsor Castle, were led by an usher who carried a Black Rod.
>
> *From an Article by Tom Barton*
> *President Alberta Royal Canadian Legion*

The Black Rod, then, is clearly a staff associated with knighthood rather than anything to do with operative masons. There are a few other supporting aspects of Masonic ritual to support the premise that Freemasonry developed out of the Knights Hospitaller. Firstly, there is the matter of the age at which a man may become a Mason. This is usually twenty-one although exceptions may be made in such cases as University students who are members of a University lodge, when the age may be reduced to eighteen. In the exposure Shibboleth, 1765, the minimum age was even higher at twenty-five. This hardly mirrors anything to do with operative masonry where an apprentice would, even now, be admitted at sixteen and much younger in earlier times. Secondly, there is the question of Masons carrying swords. Today it is usually only the Tyler, outer guard - or perhaps "sentry" is a better description - who carries a sword to protect the lodge. There is, however, reference in Jachin and Boaz, 1762, to suggest that many, if not all, Freemasons carried swords in the lodge:

> The Chamber is also guarded within and without, by some of the Brethren, who have drawn Swords in their Hands.
>
> *Jachin and Boaz*

The Chamber referred to here, is the "Chamber of reflection", a darkened room which no longer forms part of the Craft ceremony. It has been moved to the Order of the "Ancient and Accepted Rite", which is colloquially known as the "Rose Croix" and originated in France. A further sign of the sword carrying tendencies of Freemasons is given later in the same ceremony, when the blindfold is removed:

> They then take the Handkerchief from his eyes, and whilst they are so doing, the Brethren form a Circle round him with their Swords drawn in their hands, the Points of which are presented to his breast.
>
> *Jachin and Boaz*

Jackson[13] expresses concern about this manoeuvre, known as the "circle of swords" and attributes its origin to the French, based on two factors:

1. The author of Jachin and Boaz draw somewhat on an earlier exposure, The Master Key, which plagiarised a French exposure, the *L'Ordre des Francs-Maçons* which in turn drew from earlier French exposures *Catéchisme des Francs-Maçons* and *Le Secret des Francs-Maçons*.
2. The "operative background in England makes it unlikely that it started in England".

Jackson[13] does concede that the "circle of swords" was in operation in Ancients lodges although the wearing of swords was banned in Moderns lodges until 1780. At first sight this appears a minor matter but in reality it is intriguing. During the early period of Freemasonry it was customary for a gentleman to carry a sword as a normal part of his dress. Not until around 1750 was the sword replaced by a cane, although in rougher areas of towns the cane might well house a sword inside it. The intriguing aspect of Masonry and swords then, was that it was the "Moderns" Grand Lodge members who were in the main gentlemen and therefore expected to carry swords. The "Ancients" Grand Lodge members were considered to be from a lower social class, and would not have usually carried a sword. Indeed, this class difference is attributed by some as the reason for the hostility between the two Grand Lodges. So why would the gentlemen – the Moderns – leave their swords outside the lodge while the Ancients – who perhaps would not normally have carried a sword – take one in to the lodge room? Little happens in Freemasonry that does not have some reason behind it and this example seems to be saying that the swords define the Grand Lodges. The Moderns appear to be laying down their swords at the door of the lodge to distance themselves from the Ancients.

What began as an investigation to try and identify how the Judaic content entered Freemasonry has ended up identifying two separate and distinct sources for the ritual:

1. A Judaic source.
2. A knightly group. This may simply be the propensity of Jews during the Middle Ages to consider themselves knights, or it may signify the involvement of a group of knights and their early use of the title Knights of St. John connects us with the Knights Hospitaller.

This assertion is strengthened by the obvious polarisation of the Judaic influences within the Moderns lodges and the Hospitaller influence within the Ancients' lodges. It is now apt to summarise the evidence in support of this claim.

<u>Evidence for the Moderns being the Judaic source.</u>

1. The Moderns dropped the opening Christian prayer from an early date and led the way for de-Christianising the order.

2. The exposé Three distinct Knocks – which is accepted as a Moderns exposure has each of the words that "belong to the gripes [grips]" written in Hebrew.
3. Swords were banned in Moderns lodges until 1780.
4. The exposure Masonry Dissected, 1730, may be taken as a Moderns exposure because the author of Three distinct Knocks admits to drawing on it. The date was also long before the Ancients came into the public glare. Masonry Dissected mentioned the "yellow jacket and blue breeches" pointing to a Jewish master.

Evidence for the Ancients being a knightly source.

5. The Ancients kept the opening Christian prayer until the Grand Union on 27 December, 1813.
6. Swords were extensively used in Ancients ritual.
7. The master was usually installed on St. John's day, 27th December.
8. The "Deacons" with their black-rods were introduced in Ancients lodges.
9. St Stephen was mentioned in Jachin and Boaz and he was the first Christian martyr, just as the Templars and Hospitallers considered their Knights who fell in defence of the Holy Christian Church to also have been martyrs.
10. In Jachin and Boaz the "new" Deacon wore a compass around his neck, not compasses. This points to Templar Gold's thesis about the error in positioning the meridian in France.

In all, ten clear differences between the Ancients and the Moderns Grand Lodges that point to their being different organisations. How the second "knightly group" became involved can only be a matter of further speculation. Byrne[1] suggested that around 1740 the Knights Hospitaller discovered that the location of Pech Cardou was not exactly on the Paris meridian. He further speculated that Pech Cardou, a mountain in the south of France, had for centuries sheltered the Ark of the Covenant. This helped to explain why the Hospitallers decided that they needed to record the location of the mountain in new Masonic ritual by creating an extra Freemasonic degree. This would clearly explain the involvement of knightly symbolism but it does not explain why it was necessary to separate the initial Grand Lodge into two entirely different Grand Lodges, the Ancients and the Moderns. Perhaps when the Knights Hospitallers approached the English rulers of Freemasonry with their request for an additional Masonic degree, the idea was met with less than enthusiasm.

Whether the Knights Hospitaller or some other "knightly" order was also involved in the creation of Freemasonry is to a large extent a red-herring. It is clear from the early manuscripts and other records discussed above that the Judaic ritual was in place long before the "Ancients" entered the Masonic arena in 1751. Indeed, we are now looking towards a date of around 1641 as the earliest public signs of Freemasonry, as the minutes of Robert Moray's admittance into the lodge of Edinburgh corroborate. We will accordingly set aside the question of two influences on Freemasonry and concentrate of the earliest forms of ritual, that containing the Judaic content.

What we also need to address is what it was about the new Freemasonry that attracted so many initiates? We know that early Freemasons met in public houses and that the meetings were considered effectively to be fashionable drinking and dining clubs. We can gain an idea of this from an explanation to clarify yet another Masonic myth.

There is a Masonic lecture that is regularly given to brethren, which says that in early times the tracing board was drawn on the floor by the Tyler, and at the end of the ceremony the candidate was given a mop and bucket and told to wash it off. In reality, because meetings took place in rooms in public houses, it was the lodge layout – somewhat different to modern lodge layouts – that was marked on the floor with chalk. On completion this was indeed cleaned up by the candidate or the Tyler. The occurrence of Masons seeking a mop and bucket after their meeting became a source of merriment for the non-Masons present in the drinking establishment. For this reason, tapes were usually pinned to the floor to mark out the lodge area and then taken up on completion.

The exposure made during the 1760s, Three Distinct Knocks makes mention of the ceremony continuing "after the brethren had partaken of a toast to the candidate". In those days the second half of the ceremony took place with the members seated around a large table on which was wine and beer. Indeed, there is a tale of one lodge where the members partook of the toasts with such enthusiasm that they were incapable of completing the ceremony. This humorous vignette might explain how, in such a relaxed and alcohol affected atmosphere, it would be possible to introduce or revise ritual in such a way people were unaware of any sub-context. Masonic meetings today are more abstemious affairs.

If, as we have suggested, the early Jewish influences on the Masonic ritual were overtaken by events and the organisation grew rapidly beyond their control, a question remains. This question is: what is it that makes Freemasonry so popular with men? There can be little doubt that then, as today, gaining the "handshakes, words and signs" empowered the new Freemason and set him apart as a member of an exclusive club. Knowledge, and handshakes, signs and passwords are all instruments of power, just like keys. If one holds the key, or word, one can enter; if not one cannot. Most men have an innate drive to rise in the social order, and the ability to rise is attributable in part to an individual's power. For a few, power is a birthright, but for the vast majority power must be acquired. Freemasonry offers early access to the five types of power, which most social psychologists recognise:

Coercive power - is the ability to punish others. Employers have coercive power because they can sack an employee. Even a new Freemason has the power to "blackball" or exclude someone he dislikes, from joining his lodge.

Reward power – employers also have this power because they can give an employee a pay increase. As "Master" of his lodge, a Mason is in total control and appoints most of his officers; Freemasonry is not a democracy. Normally, though, a Freemason would not have full "reward power" until he has reached some seniority; then he can recommend other Masons for promotion.

Legitimate power – is the power granted to an individual by some authority, such as that of a headmaster. For a Freemason, legitimate power links closely with "reward" power above, for he has the authority of his Provincial and Grand Lodge underpinning his position. At the opening of every lodge the Warrant or Charter from the Grand Lodge is displayed.

Expert power – is the power that a doctor has over his or her patients. It is about the acquisition of knowledge and clearly the Freemason with his passwords and signs has some distinct knowledge that sets him apart.

Referent power – is about being admired or respected. For most of the period since 1717 Freemasons have been looked up to because of the aura of exclusivity that surrounded them. In consequence recruitment of new Masons was relatively easy. In recent years, as respect for established societal "order" has been eroded, a concerted attempt to darken the name of Freemasonry has diminished much of the "referent power" it enjoyed. In consequence Freemasonry membership is falling around the world.

In addition to the five types of power, which make Freemasonry attractive to many men, it also has the ability to meet social needs. Abraham Maslow[16] defined, in 1954, a hierarchy of human needs that is still widely recognised today. Maslow's research was in the general area of motivation – what motivates us to do things, to work harder etc. He identified two groups, "deficiency needs" and "growth needs". What Maslow concluded was that for the deficiency needs the lowest need must be met before the next could be addressed and so on up the scale. The first four levels are:

1. Physiological needs such as hunger, thirst and bodily comfort.
2. Safety and security and freedom from danger.
3. Belonging and love, the need to affiliate with others and to be accepted.

4. The need for self-esteem, to achieve, to be competent and to gain the approval and recognition of others.

These four deficiency needs – according to Maslow – have to be met before the "growth" needs can be addressed. They are if you prefer basic human needs that must be met before an individual can move on towards the highest goal of self-actualisation. It is immediately obvious that Freemasonry can offer any man satisfaction at levels three and four of his deficiency needs. In fact, what Maslow is suggesting is that membership of Freemasonry, or some such similar organisation, is only slightly less important than such issues as eating and being safe. Clearly this is an oversimplification because many men find complete satisfaction for these deficiency needs within marriage or a long-term relationship. Maslow does, however, explain the attraction for men that Freemasonry holds. Maslow went on to complete his list of human drives with four growth needs:

5. Cognitive or mental activity, to know, to understand and to explore.
6. The aesthetic search for symmetry, order and beauty.
7. Self-actualisation or to find self-fulfilment and to realise one's full potential.
8. Maslow later added self-transcendence, which is helping others to find self-fulfilment.

Others have varied Maslow's proposition but they usually distil down to three levels of human needs. Material, social and spiritual and Freemasonry addresses the latter two to an advanced level, particularly if a member wishes to pursue the philosophical side of the institution.

Recognising the various forms of "power", which Freemasonry holds, it is important how that power is exercised – both individually and organisationally. In this area, it might be argued that Freemasonry, as an organisation, has not recently displayed the finely honed survival strategies, which MacDonald[17] maintains have been exhibited over centuries by international Jewry. This further suggests that if the Jews ever did control

Freemasonry they have relaxed their grip of late. This bald statement requires an explanation and it also lies within the framework of psychology.

It is a fact that peoples beliefs and behaviours generally agree. For example, a person who strongly believes that it is wrong to drop litter is unlikely to do so. If that person should accidentally allow some litter to fall out of her moving car, she will usually decide that the area was full of litter anyway, and so her piece of litter didn't make any difference. This is the first step down the road to changing her strongly held belief about not dropping litter. When someone's beliefs get out of sync with their behaviour it might be reasonable to assume that the person will change the way they act. We have, though, a curious attribute called "cognitive dissonance", which dislikes discord in our personal belief systems and so more usually we will change our beliefs to fit our behaviour. As seen in the hypothetical example just given of the lady who hated litter louts, when faced with accidentally committing the "crime" of creating litter, decided that in her case it didn't count because the area was already littered.

In the last twenty or so years, Freemasonry has modified its ritual in response to external criticism, and we see in these actions grounds for believing that the hands on the "tiller" are less than infallible. An example of Freemasonry being modified for the wrong reasons can be seen when it was decided some time ago to alter the ceremonial ritual and to remove the physical punishments from the obligation. This change was to deflect the demands of some Methodist critics who found the ritual offensive. In fact, the critics did not reduce in number and most individual Masons resented their ceremonial being modified. It would have been more effective to find ways of stopping the critics from being critical; that way their behaviour change would have influenced their beliefs, positively towards Freemasonry. This simple comment conceals a complex subject close to the hearts of the advertising profession. Advertisers can create demand for a product, or create a demand and then devise a product to meet that new demand; such is their power. How you stop your critics is less important than stopping them because once they are stopped, cognitive dissonance will attack the disharmony caused by them disliking

Freemasonry and yet doing nothing about it. The anticipated outcome should be that they would adopt a more tolerant view of Freemasonry.

The reaction to criticism by the most senior Freemasons of complying with the demands of an external religious body in the expectation the criticism would go away was less than successful. Perversely, it only encouraged others to join in the general criticism. The senior Freemasons appear to have overlooked the fundamental requirement to successful behavioural change and that is trust or respect. As mentioned above, Freemasonry already has the five power factors at its disposal and so power is not an issue to be considered. The factor where Freemasonry is weak is "believability" – put simply, it is not trusted, and it is not trusted because it has secrets. The harsh reality is that if we don't trust someone and we don't think that they are believable then they are unlikely to influence us. Initially Freemasonry went to considerable lengths to display its charitable generosity but this did little to alleviate the criticism or change the widely held views on its trustworthiness. Generosity and trustworthiness are on different personality scales and so influencing one is unlikely to affect the other. Far better has been the more recent approach of opening the doors of Freemasonry to non-Masons to look around their lodge buildings. It doesn't really matter how unfair the basis of the poor reputation for trustworthiness towards Freemasons is, what is important is to show there is nothing to hide.

As we saw in the previous chapter, before the Masonic gatherings were held in London hostelries, the early ritual states that they took place "a whole day's distance from their town", where there was no chance of being overheard. This is suggesting that the secrets a Freemason held were such as to endanger his life if they were revealed to a non-Mason. This is extraordinary. We have already explained how there is nothing in the Masonic secret words and signs worth the proverbial jot or tittle, simply some words, gestures and names that Masons must keep secret. We have also made it clear that no other guilds or similar organisations have or had such secretive passwords and signs. There is only one rational explanation and that is that the old passwords were just that. They were a means of identifying individuals who for some reason in days gone by were at risk of their lives and whose identity had to be kept secret. When we identify who those people were and if we can tie them to Judaism, then we will most likely have identified the originators of Freemasonry.

This need for secrecy is central to our investigation. Clearly what has been suggested above is our interpretation of the available evidence. There will doubtless be those who will dismiss it out of hand. However, if this is to be done, then an alternative explanation for the Judaic content of Freemasonry and its apparent similarity to a process of proselytism must be postulated.

So, after a careful examination of the available early Masonic manuscripts, we are left with a number of issues. To the eight listed at the end of the last chapter, we can now add five more:

1. The ancient Masonic ritual introduced the navigational instrument, the compasses.
2. When combined with the "square", which was introduced in the previous chapter, we get the Masonic emblem, the square overlain by the compasses. These two instruments mark out an approximate Magen David, the symbol of Judaism.
3. Why does the Masonic ceremonial of making a Mason mimic proselytisation?
4. How can we explain the large number of Jews involved with early Freemasonry.
5. Why were early meetings held "a days journey from the village"?

We now have in total thirteen issues that clearly bear on the answer to the question of how and when was Freemasonry created. We know who created Freemasonry or at least we can say with confidence that Jews were present at its creation and exerted an enormous influence on the development of the ceremonials. Masonic myths and legends abound to suggest that early Jews, from the Essenes to Roman slaves, created Freemasonry but none are given any credibility by Masonic researchers. There is no alternative but to examine in detail the history of the Jewish people to uncover where, when, why and how they managed to bring Freemasonry into being.

PART 2

THE JEWS

CHAPTER 4

EARLY ISRAEL

In Part 1, we identified the remarkable quantity of Judaic symbolism contained within Freemasonry and concluded that it cannot be accidental. It is clear that some Jews were heavily involved in the creation of Freemasonry, going so far as the create entry ceremonials as an allegorical representation of the process of conversion to Judaism. Let us begin by defining Jewishness. Whatever happened before the exile of the Children of Israel in Babylon, on their return the prophet Ezra had this to say to them:

> And Shechaniah the son of Jehiel, one of the sons of Elam, answered and said unto Ezra, We have trespassed against our God, and have taken strange wives of the people of the land: yet now there is hope in Israel concerning this thing. Now therefore let us make a covenant with our God to put away all the wives, and such as are born of them, according to the counsel of my lord, and of those that tremble at the commandment of our God; and let it be done according to the law.
>
> Arise; for this matter belongeth unto thee: we also will be with thee: be of good courage, and do it. Then arose Ezra, and made the chief priests, the Levites, and all Israel, to swear that they should do according to this word. And they swear.
>
> *Ezra 10:2 - 5*

From that time, a Jewish birthright is passed only down the female line; it mattered not until recently whether the father was a Jew or a gentile. Anyone not a birthright Jew could of course become one by converting to Judaism.

Turning now to early Hebrew history, this arguably began with the Habiru people. The word "Hebrew" is generally mooted as deriving from Habiru, who - it is suggested - left Egypt to find a new life under the leadership of Moses. Or did they? This explanation has become accepted wisdom but questions abound. Küng[18] points out that "*habiru*" of the Mesopotamian cuneiform texts do not so much stand for a particular people as a lower social stratum. Kathleen Kenyon[19] has this to say of them:

> Unlike the Hurri, the Habiru, in the opinion of most scholars, cannot be recognised as an ethnic group, since no characteristic names can be associated with them. Nor can they be recognised as following some definite occupation, for sometimes they are apparently professional soldiers, sometimes they are labourers, and sometimes slaves. The only common characteristic is that they are foreigners, and the best explanation would appear to be that they were bands of adventurers and soldiers of fortune.
>
> *Kathleen Kenyon*
> *Archaeology in the Holy Land*

Indeed, the story of Moses' life and his leadership of the Exodus raises more questions than it provides answers. That not a single piece of archaeological evidence has turned up, outside of Egypt, to support the story of the Exodus is but one aspect that calls the tale into question. The birth of Moses when, to escape from the pharaoh's instruction to kill all male newborn Hebrews, his mother floated him off in a reed basket down the river Nile has an earlier echo. So, but to a lesser extent, does his discovery and resulting upbringing by the pharaoh's daughter. Around 1,000 years previously, Sargon of Akkad (2334 – 2279), a Mesopotamian ruler, who conquered Syria, Anatolia and western Iran, had an almost identical early childhood. His mother, a priestess, set him adrift as a baby on the Euphrates where a gardener found him and raised him up in humble surroundings. Sargon then rose socially, by merit, to the post of cupbearer to the ruler of the city of Kish, before becoming ruler.

If we examine the Biblical version of events for the Exodus, we can immediately identify another weakness in the Moses story, it is the case for Aaron as the brother of Moses. Moses was, as the reader will recall, set adrift in a wicker basket as a baby. He was discovered by the pharaoh's daughter and brought up in the pharaoh's household. According to the Bible, Moses spent sixty years in the Sinai desert after running away from Egypt when he killed a slave-master who was beating an Israeli slave. When God instructed Moses to return to Egypt to "free his people" Aaron was miraculously available to act as Moses' spokesperson. Moses was eighty years old at the time and Aaron was three years older.

> And Moses was fourscore years old, and Aaron fourscore and three years old, when they spake unto Pharaoh.
>
> *Exodus 7:7*

The only way this particular story can hold up is with the hand of God supporting it. There was without doubt a Moses, or a Moses-like character, because someone brought the monotheism of Akhenaten out of Egypt to the central highlands of the southern Levant. That the Bible should have both Moses and the patriarch, Joseph, both having close links to Egyptian pharaohs is far too coincidental for us to dismiss it. We will return to Moses, Aaron and his descendants later, but first we need a better understanding of how Judaea survived and became Israel.

Moses is not the only Biblical character to find an earlier resonance. Stories written some 4,000 years ago on clay tablets in the Sumerian language survive today, and they concern a king of Uruk in Babylonia called Gilgamesh, who lived around 2,700 BCE. The most complete surviving version derives from twelve stone tablets, written in the Akkadian cuneiform language and were found in the Nineveh library of Ashurbanipal, who was king of Assyria from 669 to 633 BCE. One of the stories about Gilgamesh concerns his discussions with Utnapishtim, who told him about the great flood. One of the gods had let Utnapishtim know of the impending flood and advised him to build a great boat and to bring all living things into the boat. The flood duly came and lasted seven days, and the earth became an ocean. Eventually Utnapishtim's boat came to rest on the top of Mount Nimush. The story continues almost word for word from the later story of Noah's flood. On the seventh day Utnapishtim released a dove and a raven from the boat until the waters receded. On being saved, Utnapishtim offered an animal sacrifice to his gods.

It is immediately apparent that the Bible as a tool to describe early Hebrew history is proving to be less than reliable, and so we will need to examine other historical sources. A cursory examination of Palestine and Israel reveals at once how it became such a crucial influence on later western lifestyles. It sits not just on the edge of the fertile-crescent, but bordering the narrow strip of land that joins the two main halves of the crescent together.

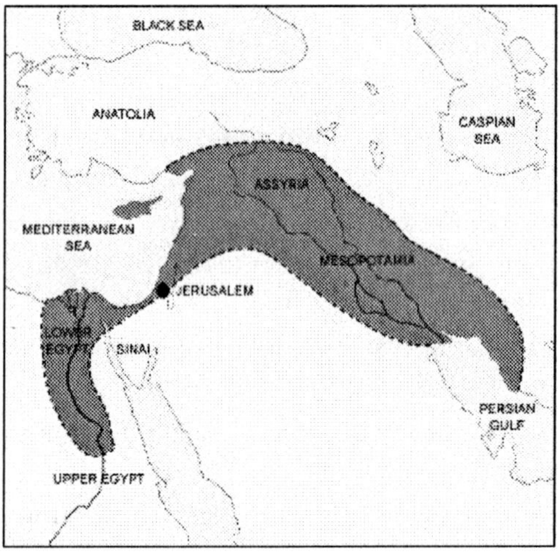

FIGURE 9 – THE FERTILE-CRESCENT

The American Orientalist James Henry Breasted (1865–1935) coined the term "fertile-crescent".

Before continuing, we must mention that the recent conflicts over the land of the southern Levant, known variously as Canaan, Israel and Palestine has made the latter two terms value-laden for the protagonists. This book takes no side in that dispute nor offers any opinion. It is, however, unavoidable as the story unfolds, to make reference to the exact location under discussion, because, as the reader will discover, location and topography are critical to the development of the region. In using the terms, "Palestine" and "Israel", the purpose is simply to identify the area with the title it held during the period under discussion.

The reality is that for the critical thousand years of the Jerusalem Temple period the Levant was a buffer state between Egypt and either Assyria or Babylonia (Mesopotamia). That Israel survived at all as a nation is not just a function of location, but also of geography, or more specifically the topography of the region. The area that was Judaea is very hilly, almost mountainous land that for most of its time was good for nothing more than nomadic sheep and goat herding. Not until the inhabitants discovered around the ninth century BCE that olives and grapes would grow there did the country hold out any hope that it could support an advanced civilisation.

Figure 5 shows a simplified topographical map of the southern Levant using only three shades to denote differing contour levels to stress the physical nature of the region:

White is the lowest and denotes plains
Mid-grey denotes hilly areas
Dark-grey denotes the highest areas above 1,000 metres

The presence on the map of some towns and boundaries lines does not mean that they existed concurrently. What the map demonstrates is that the country of Judaea comprised the Neghev Desert plus the highlands of the southern Levant as far north as Bethel. Provided the occupants of this land posed no threat to their powerful neighbours, they were most likely to have been left alone.

Immediately we can see that the southern Levant is split north-south by two mountain ranges. If someone starts from Ashdod and travels eastwards, he initially crosses the 30 kilometre wide coastal plain before rising slowly into the Central mountain range. Only 50 kilometres from the sea the mountains drop rapidly into the Jordan valley and at the Dead Sea arrive at the lowest place on earth. The Jordan valley is about 30 kilometres wide and then the land climbs steeply up and over the eastern mountain range.

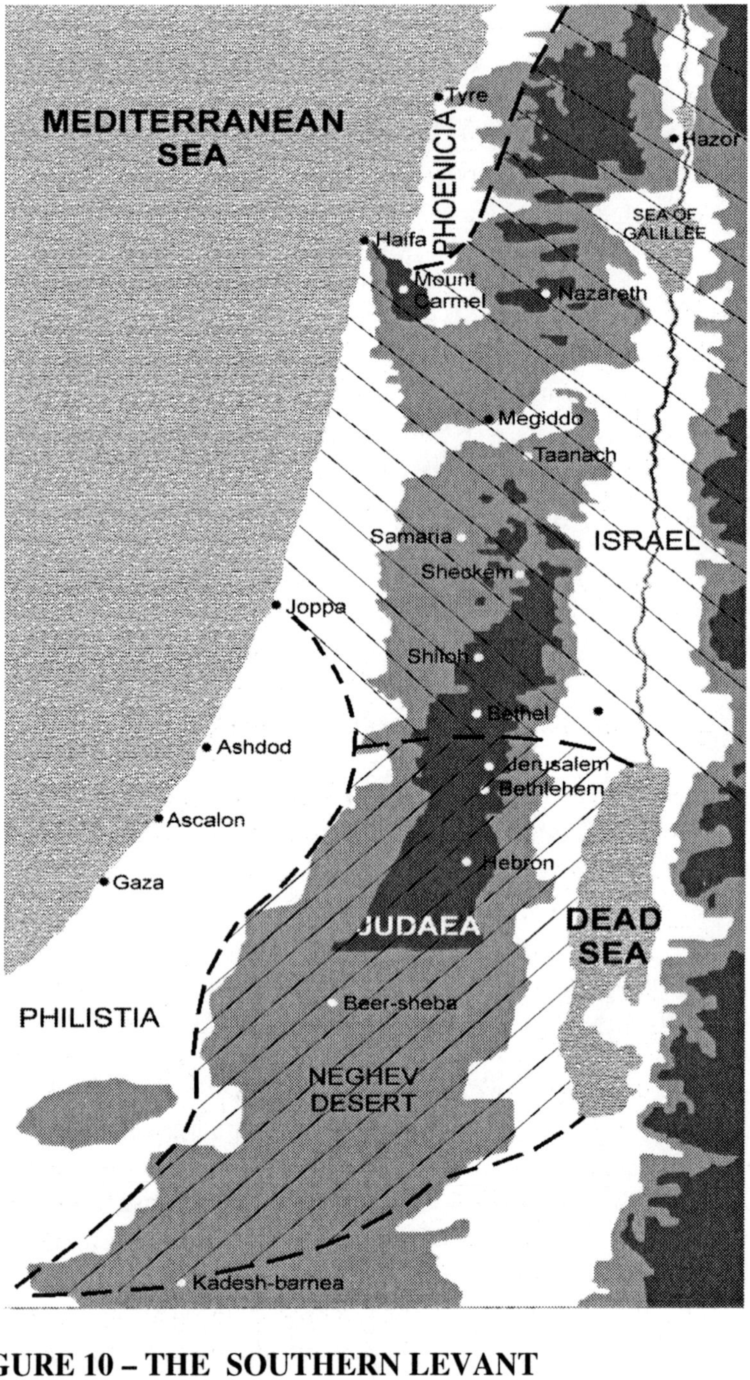

FIGURE 10 – THE SOUTHERN LEVANT

We have already mentioned how the Levant was the corridor between two regional superpowers and two major trade routes went either side of the mountainous country of Judaea. To the west, the "Way-of-the-Sea" trade route, known to the Romans as *Via Maris* began in the Nile delta and went along the coast via Gaza, Ascalon and Ashdod to Joppa. Just north of Joppa, the Way-of-the-Sea turned eastwards through the Meggido valley and then north up the Jordan valley as far as Hazo where once again it branched off to the east towards Damascus. From Damascus this trade route joined the other major route in the region and headed east towards Assyria and Mesopotamia.

The second major trade route was known as the "Kings Highway" and also started in the Nile delta at Heliopolis, just north of Cairo. The King's Highway made first for Clysma (modern Suez) and then struck off across the Sinai Desert to Elath (modern Aqaba). It was here, on one of the major trade routes in the region, when camel trains stretched for miles, that we have to believe that Moses and the whole Israelite race were lost for 40 years. The King's Highway then travelled north, keeping close to the eastern foothills of the Eastern range of mountains and sometimes crossing plateaux formed by its flattened peaks. The route also avoids the Arabian Desert, immediately to the east. Following this line north, the "King's Highway" went through Petra, Kerak and on to Philadelphia (modern Amman). From there, the route continued through Gerasa (modern Jerashal) and then to Damascus where it joined the Way-of-the-Sea trade route. Sandwiched between these two superpower arteries were Israel and Judaea.

Having earlier cast doubt on the reliability of the Bible as a source of historical data, we can only turn to archaeologists for answers. Curiously, the conclusions that academics from this discipline are reaching are markedly different from accepted knowledge as described in the Bible. The modern-day archaeologist is able to call on a vast range of scientific support to help him unravel the secrets of his excavations. To carbon 14 dating techniques we can add neutron activation tests that "fingerprint" the sources of clay used in pot making. Gas chromatography allows archaeologists to examine the chemical content of minute residues. Electron microscopes make tiny surface variations visible to identify the individual potter. DNA analysis has facilitated previously undreamed of avenues of research. These scientific tools now allow archaeologists to assess the materials they recover from excavations far more precisely. In addition to these superior analytical tools, there is modern equipment that makes potential excavation-sites easier to select. Aerial photography identifies interesting ground formations. Ground penetrating radar, and electrical-resistivity surveying then identify whether there are likely to be any manmade structures underground. After all this technology has isolated a promising site, the earth is carefully dug and the samples tested until every piece of knowledge is extracted. If necessary, other academic disciplines will join in to support the archaeologist: anthropology, botany, climatology, ecology, hydrology, morphology plus the paleao branches of each. It was with the help of aerial photography, backed up by non-invasive subsoil investigative techniques, that every potential site of ancient civilisation in the southern Levant has been identified and excavated. It is probably true to say that we now know more about the ancestry of this region than any other in the world.

So what does all of this knowledge tell us? For a start we can reappraise the Biblical patriarchal period. We now know that the central highlands area, from Hebron to the Megiddo valley and what would later become Judaea (see figure 5), had regular cycles of settlement and abandonment.

<u>Phase 1</u> (around 1,300 years)
Between 3,500 BCE and 2,200 BCE the first settlements arrived on the central highlands, creating some 200 sites. Each settlement site was roughly oval in shape and housed an extended family of roughly eighty souls. There was a series of rooms strung around the perimeter forming an outside wall enclosing a courtyard where the animals would shelter at night.

Phase 2 (around 200 years)
From 2,200 BCE to 2,000 BCE there was a crisis coinciding roughly with the end of the wet neolithic pluvial period after which the climate turned much drier. During phase 2, the settlements were abandoned although there is evidence that nomadic sheep and goat herders continuously occupied the highlands.

Phase 3 (around 450 years)
From 2,000 BCE to 1,550 BCE the central hills were again settled with some 220 sites and a total highland population of perhaps 40,000. During this settlement period larger settlements – towns might be a more suitable term – and even fortified regional centres begin to develop. Hebron, Jerusalem, Bethel, Shiloh and Sheckem were later to expand into major fortified regional centres. Cities is the term usually used to describe these centres but the populations were much smaller than modern cities.

Phase 4 (around 400 years)
Then between 1,550 BCE and 1,150 BCE the cycle of abandonment repeated itself. It seems likely that on this occasion the depopulation was due to the Egyptian pharaoh, Amenhotep II, who took 89,600 slaves from the southern Levant as punishment for their support of a Hittite uprising. Only 25 settlements have been found that were active during this period, although, as earlier the land had nomadic sheep and goat herders throughout this phase.

Phase 5 (around 250 years)
Finally, from 1,150 BCE to 900 BCE the resettlement began yet again, this time creating around 250 sites, and a population of roughly 45,000. It was the north central highlands – between Taanach and Bethel in the area that became Israel - that were settled first and the most densely. The ratio of settlements in the northern central highlands (Israel) to those in the south - from Jerusalem to the southern tip of the highlands (Judaea) - was 5:1.

Phase 6 (around 314 years)
Between 900 BCE and 586 BCE the number of sites increased to 500, with a population of some 160,000. This expansion, way above what the highlands had previously supported, was doubtless due to the discovery that olives (for their oil) and grapes would grow there. We will contend that there was a further reason, which we will discuss later. Both olive oil and grapes were at the top end of value for agricultural produce and so promoted trade with the more fertile lowlands as well as the adjacent superpowers of Assyria, Babylonia and Egypt. Canaanite storage jars with residues of olive oil and grapes have been found in Egypt.

It is relevant to mention that during all of these periods of expansion and abandonment, there was nothing special or different about the central highlands of the southern Levant. Exactly the same housing, cooking utensils and other implements of everyday life are to be found in the surrounding hills whether the residents were Ammonites, Moabites or Philistines. To be accurate there was one difference, the Canaanites occupying the central highlands did not eat or keep pigs. This is a significant difference and one for which there is no known explanation. The matter has turned into an issue of religion for both Jews and Muslims on the basis the pig is a cloven-hoofed animal that does not chew the cud and is therefore odd. Perhaps the answer lies in the thinness of the topsoil on the central highlands that would have made the disposal of human excrement difficult. If this were to be the case then it is easy to see why pigs would be less than welcome given their inclination to eat anything just below the surface of the ground. It would also go some way to explain the later Judaic obsession with cleanliness, but this is speculation because pigs are also difficult to herd.

To gain a better understanding of the central highlands and why events turned out the way they did, we need to understand that this land was marginal. "Marginal" land is that which cannot produce a surplus. In modern times we would define "marginal land" as that which would earn enough to cover wage and interest costs but not leave any profit. Such land now has only a tiny rental value because there is no profit available to an investor from its current use. However, in ancient times such concepts as "profit" were irrelevant to the important matter of survival.

In those days, as today, it was possible to eke out a living on land that would not grow the staple foods such as wheat. If sheep or goats were moved whenever the grass was cropped too short to sustain them, the land would support human life. Such a nomadic existence does, however, require vast areas of land to support only a few people, but life is sustainable. The sheep and goat herders would annually take their flocks down the mountainsides to graze the adjacent lowland arable farms immediately after the lowland farmers have harvested their crops. The farmers welcomed the animals that cropped the stubble and fertilised the ground with their droppings ready for the next sowing. There would be an exchange or barter of goods, a few animals for the farmers' stew-pots in return for grain to see the nomads through the winter months. This was important to the nomads who needed grain to balance the fat-rich diet of meat and milk, but less so to the agricultural farmer who can easily keep a cow for the family milk needs. When the farmer was ready to re-sow his land and all barter business completed, the nomads would move back onto the hills where new growth of the grass awaited the remorseless mastication of the herbivores.

If, over many years, the symbiotic cycle of highland grazing and lowland field cropping continued successfully, then inevitably as family groups expanded, some family members could remain in the highlands. There they would guard the land that had proved itself of value. The growth in numbers in the family unit provided the sort of redundancy that can be put to use grow supplementary crops to improve the family lifestyle. The big problem, with settling on marginal land, is that the settlers are more than usually dependent on the weather. For settlers on marginal land to survive there must be a surplus of grain during the good years to feed them during the unavoidable poor years. In the southern Levant the poor years averaged one in three. If the drought years began to bunch up then the lowland surplus grain would have become unavailable. This is because the lowland farmers would have kept the reduced surplus for their own use rather than bartering it. At that point, the marginal land – in this instance the central highlands – became unviable and abandonment was inevitable. Dever[20] postulates that the resettlement cycle – phase 5 above - might have come about because the Egyptian control of Canaan had weakened by the twelfth century BCE. In consequence, the lowland farmers did not have to produce a surplus to their harvest for the Egyptian tribute. With no - or reduced – surplus, there was nothing to barter with the nomads and this would have forced the nomadic herders to begin to cultivate the highland pastures.

We mentioned above how, during the period 1,150 BCE to 900 BCE, the resettlement of the central highlands of the southern Levant was slow and continuous, a conclusion that all archaeologists agree on. It is also a pattern of settlement that is mutually exclusive with the Biblical version of Moses leading the Israelites out of Egypt. The archaeological evidence, and the conclusions of the academics who have studied that evidence is uncompromising.

The Exodus from Egypt did not happen.

This is a profound statement and demands further explanation. It is not surprising to find that expert opinion over what did occur varies, not to any great extent, but differences there are. There is a consensus that the resettlement, which began around 1,150 BCE, was gentle and continued over a long period. The possibility of an influx of fewer families who procreated as an explanation of the increases in population numbers is also ruled out. Professor Dever[20] sets out the position concisely, and with sympathy to his Judaic beliefs:

> The whole "Exodus-Conquest" cycle of stories must now be set aside as largely mythical, but in the proper sense of the term "myth": perhaps "historical fiction," but tales told primarily to validate religious beliefs. In my view these stories are still "true" in that they convey forcefully later Israel's self-awareness as a "liberated people".

William Dever
What Did the Biblical Writers Know and When Did They Know It?

Professor Redford[21] is a little more circumspect:

> It is ironic that the Sojourn and the Exodus themes, native in origin to the folklore memory of the Canaanite enclaves of the southern Levant, should have lived on not in the tradition but among two groups that had no involvement in the historic events at all – the Greeks and the Hebrews. In the case of the latter, the Exodus was part and parcel of an array of "origin" stories to which, lacking the traditions of their own, they appropriated from the earlier culture they were copying.
>
> *Donald Redford*
> *Egypt, Canaan, and Israel in Ancient Times*

Israel Finkelstein and Neil Silberman[22] come to a similar conclusion:

> Putting aside the possibility of divinely inspired miracles, one can hardly accept the idea of a flight of a large group of slaves from Egypt through the heavily guarded border fortifications into the desert and then into Canaan in the time of such a formidable Egyptian presence. Any group escaping Egypt against the will of the pharaoh would have easily been tracked down not only by an Egyptian army chasing it from the delta but also by the Egyptian soldiers in the forts in northern Sinai and in Canaan.
>
> *Israel Finkelstein and Neil Silberman*
> *The Bible Unearthed*

Another reason for these self-confident assertions is that the growth in the central hill population cannot be put down to the natural increase of population. Archaeologists know from comparison with the recorded growth of other similar communities, that increases from 12,000 people in 1,200 BCE to 55,000 by 1,150 BCE and another 20,000 only 100 years later have no precedent. They are fully satisfied that the growth was due to the continuous influx of migrants over the whole period, this in direct contradiction of the Biblical account of Exodus.

The acceptance of a gentle migration into the central uplands of the southern Levant is almost universal across the academic discipline of archaeology, but who those migrants were is open to speculation. Some academics prefer the idea that the re-population of the hills was simply another cycle of Canaanite occupation, while others prefer to cite the nomadic tribes of central Arabia, who – to be fair – had a history of commandeering adjacent lands. The answer may of course lie in a combination of local people and others migrating to the region for the usual reasons of escaping wars and famine.

In addition to the evidence from archaeologists, Dr. Michael Hammer supports the suggestion of a gentle and continuous migration from the immediately surrounding areas.

> Both Jewish and Middle Eastern non-Jewish populations share a common pool of Y chromosome biallelic haplotypes.
>
> *Proceedings of the National Academy of Sciences*
> *9th May 2000*

What Dr. Hammer's scientific language means is that both Middle Eastern Jews and Arabs share a similar genetic structure confirming that they share a common male ancestor.

Other archaeological evidence supports the examples cited above in suggesting that the Exodus did not occur. One of the curious facts about this region is that the two superpowers to the east and to the west of Judaea and Israel both left extensive contemporary records. These accounts include information sent from Canaan to the superpowers. Conversely, from Judaea and Israel we have the Bible as almost the only written historical record. During the period discussed above, when the uplands were repopulating, Canaan was under the suzerainty or control of Egypt. From Egypt we know there was a presence in the southern Levant, and that the people there were known as Israel. This knowledge comes from the stele of the pharaoh Merneptah, which specifically mentions "Israel".

The stele, or carved slab, contains a eulogy to the pharoah Merneptah who reigned from 1,213 BCE until 1,203 BCE. This stele provides us with the first record of the existence of a state called Israel. It appears that the Egyptians used the same name for a people as for the land they occupied, and this is not dissimilar to our present-day practice. The stele must refer to the lowland areas of Canaan because we now know that the highlands were sparsely populated then. Wherever the people referred to in the stele were located in Canaan, it seems almost self-evident that they were the people who later repopulated the highlands and named the region after themselves. This does support the Canaanites as the original Hebrews. Furthermore, the Egyptians had unfriendly epithets for wandering people and so clearly by the time of this stele Israel was a settled state.

Flinders Petrie discovered the stele in Merneptah's tomb in Thebes by in 1896, and it contains the phrase:

> Israel is laid waste and his seed is not.

As expected, this stele has attracted a vast amount of debate and research, the above words in particular. Michael Hasel[23] argues that, from Israel's perspective, the two important words are "Israel" and "seed". He rejects both the idea that Israel interprets as the northern valley of Jezreal, as well as the idea that the word has the meaning "the wearers of the side lock". Hasel concluded that Israel was a state:

> Israel, identified by the determinative for people, is a socioethnic unity powerful enough to be mentioned along with major city-states that were also neutralised.
>
> *Michael Hasel*
> *Israel in the Merneptah Stele*

In his consideration of the word "seed", Hasel decides that it refers to grain rather than offspring:

> We may perceive Israel within the context and information of the Merneptah stele to be a rural sedentary group of agriculturalists without its own urban city-state support system.
>
> *Michael Hasel*
> *Israel in the Merneptah Stele*

With these conclusions, Hasel is confirming the Biblical picture, portrayed in Judges 6, of Gideon - who lived around the time of the Merneptah Stele - as a farmer living in a small village, exactly as we have described above. Hasel concludes:

> Israel functioned as an agriculturally-based/sedentary socioethnic entity in the late 13th century BCE, one that is significant enough to be included in the military campaign against political powers in Canaan.
>
> While the Merneptah stele does not give any indication of the actual social structure of the people of Israel, it does indicate that Israel was a significant socioethnic entity that needed to be reckoned with.
>
> *Michael Hasel*
> *Israel in the Merneptah Stele*

In addition to the stele, there are copious records of affairs in Canaan in the form of diplomatic letters, lists of conquered cities, scenes engraved on Temple walls, annals of Egyptian kings, literary works and hymns[24]. Egyptian records, as well as those from Assyria and Babylonia regularly include references to astrological events, such as solar eclipses or passing comets. These records allow us - with the aid of modern computer software - to date astrological events to the very day. There are also some 400 Amarna tablets that include letters from the rulers of various towns in Canaan, such as Jerusalem, Shechem and Megiddo. These tablets show that Canaan was a closely supervised province of Egypt, as befits the land through which Egypt's main trade routes ran. Indeed, contrary to the version reported in the Bible, Egyptian troops were stationed in Canaan. Unfortunately for the particular subject under discussion, the Amana letters do not cover the period of the claimed invasion of Canaan by the Israelites led by Joshua. But Biblical dating has the pharaoh for this period as none other than Rameses II, perhaps the strongest of all the pharaohs. There is no reason to consider that Rameses II relaxed Egypt's grip over Canaan and with it his principal trade routes to the north and east.

Indeed, his reaction to the threat from the Hittites, as mentioned below, proves his iron grip over the territory.

There were at least two occasions during the second period 1,550 BCE to 1,150 BCE when external forces intruded dramatically. This was when the population of the hill country of the southern Levant was declining. The first occasion demonstrates clearly the hold that Egypt held over Canaan and it was the battle of Megiddo. Pharaoh Thutmose III became aware that the Hittite King of Kadesh was aligning with various Canaanite town mayors. Thutmose took his army north, in 1482 BCE, and laid siege to Megiddo for seven months before it fell. For the following three years the Egyptians carried out detailed inspections, to collect tribute and to ensure the town and its surroundings were maintaining a pro-Egyptian status. Flushed with his success at Megiddo, in 1,476 BCE, Thutmose again took his army into Phoenicia and suppressed two more towns, Ullaza and Ardata, which had been party to the earlier uprising. He repeated his attacks on Phoenicia in 1,473 and returned to Egypt with the Levantine coast securely under his control.

Around 1,300 BCE the Hittites, from Anatolia (Turkey), targeted Syria and Egypt as the next territories that they intended to bring under their rule. Ramses II was aware of their plans and took his army north and joined battle at Kadesh, which is about 80 kilometres due north of Damascus. A victory stele has Rameses claiming a triumph but an honourable draw seems more likely. Either way, it was enough to halt the advance of the Hittites into Egypt. Only a few years later a dynastic marriage was arranged between the ruling Hittite and Pharaonic houses thus cementing the peace between the two nations. This battle demonstrates the ability of Rameses II to march his army the length of the Levant. To the very doorstep of his opponent and there, if not defeat the Hittites at least to give them such a bloody nose as to convince them that Egypt was a conquest too far. This surely demonstrates most clearly how Rameses II could easily have swatted any threat to the central Canaan highlands from purported runaway slaves from his own backyard.

The collapse of the Hittite empire occurred around 1,190 BCE and seems to have been due to a revolt by one of the northern regions, Phrygia. It seems likely that because of this revolt, there was a large-scale migration from the southern coastal regions of Greece, which led to the capture and settlement of the southern coastal plain of the Levant, Philistia on figure 5. The arrival of the "Sea Peoples" is well recorded and dated in existing Egyptian records and classical Greek literature. Yet, according to the Bible the Philistines were present at the time that Abraham was in Canaan, some seven hundred years earlier:

> And there was a famine in the land, beside the first famine that was in the days of Abraham. And Isaac went unto Abimelech King of the Philistines unto Gerar.
>
> *Genesis 26:1*

There are further references to the Philistines at the time of Abraham in Exodus 13:17 and 23:31. Both of these Biblical records call into question the infallibility of the Bible.

We have already mentioned how climatic changes can tip marginal land into untenable land. We must also concede that the various military actions along the Levantine coast resulted in substantial deathtolls to the farmers living outside of the town defences. This siege strategy of destroying the adjacent food-stocks and those who grew them would continue for nearly three thousand years, and the result was always the same. When the aggressor eventually retired, there was plenty of farmland available for anyone who chose to occupy it. That temptation was also available to the people eking out a living in the Canaanite uplands, and may partially explain the cycles of population drift off the hills.

There is another facet of the Biblical story of the Exodus that calls the whole account into question, and it is the suggestion that the escapees were slaves. For the Children of Israel to have been slaves creates several difficulties. The Bible suggests that these slaves were all in the ownership of the pharaoh and on building work, but the numbers quoted are highly questionable.

> Therefore the King of Egypt rose up against them, and dealt subtly with them, and brought them low with labouring in brick, and made them slaves.
>
> *Judith 5:11*

> And the children of Israel journeyed from Rameses to Succoth, about six hundred thousand on foot that were men, beside children.
>
> *Exodus 12:37*

The Bible is suggesting that more than half a million male Israelite slaves were engaged on a building project or projects. This number is far more than those employed on building the great pyramids at Giza and we now know the pyramid builders were not slaves at all. The Greek travel-writer, Herodotus, visited Egypt around 450 BCE. He was told by his Egyptian guides that it took twenty-years for a workforce of 100,000 slaves to build Cheops' pyramid. Scientists now put the number at fewer and less years, but even these numbers are dwarfed by the half-million quoted in the Bible. There is nothing in Egypt to compare with the great pyramids at Giza, so what were the Children of Israel, all half-million of them, building? There is little doubt that this is a later fabrication and clearly if the numbers (of Israelites) are wrong, then so can be everything else. Indeed, let us consider the impact on Egypt of losing – let us say - half a million workers, at a stroke. The effect would have been financially devastating and the incident would certainly have been recorded.

The fact is that what Egyptian records there are about slaves shows that if they tried to escape – and doubtless some did – they were pursued. Besides, the main routes out of Egypt were lined with forts that guarded the route and the food and water stores. Any escaping slaves would take the main routes north and east because there would be little point in them going south into deepest Africa. In reality, if a slave wished to escape from a sadistic owner, he, or she, needed only to seek refuge in a Temple and offer their services to the god.

> Now there was upon the shore, as still there is now, a Temple of Heracles, in which if any man's slave take refuge and have the sacred marks set upon him, giving himself over to the god, it is not lawful to lay hands upon him; but this custom has continued still unchanged from the beginning down to my own time.
>
> *Heroditus*
> *Histories Volume II*

Even if a slave decided to head for freedom he would have been aware that Egypt had extradition agreements with its neighbours, and these included the mutual return of slaves. The following excerpt is from a treaty between Rameses II and the Hittite King Hattusili III.

> If a man or two men who are unknown flee, and if they escape from the country of Egypt and if they don't want to serve him, then Hattusili, the great king, the King of the country of Hatti, has to deliver them into his brother's hands and he shall not allow them to inhabit the country of Hatti.
>
> *Peace treaty Rameses II and Hattusili III*

To further highlight the point, the following extract[24] is from an exchange of papyrus between chief bowmen (equivalent to modern army majors):

> I say to the Re-Har-akhti: "Keep Pharaoh - life, prosperity, health! our good lord - life, prosperity, health! - in health! Let him celebrate millions of jubilees, while we are in his favour daily!"
>
> Another matter, to wit: I was sent forth from the broad-halls of the palace - life, prosperity, health! - in the third month of the third season, day nine, at the time of evening, following after these two slaves… When my letter reaches you, write to me about all that has happened. Who found their tracks? Which watch found their tracks? What people are after them? Write

> to me about all that has happened to them and how many people you send out after them.
>
> *James Pritchard*
> *Ancient Near Eastern Texts*

It would be wrong simply to pour cold water onto the Biblical records, for one fact comes out of the extant Egyptian records and it is that Canaan was certainly a slave nursery for Egypt. Redford[21] reports many examples of Canaanite mayors filling quotas of slaves for dispatch to Egypt, and the aftermath of the various Egyptian conquests invariably resulted in the deportation of large numbers of slaves. Thutmose III took 7,300 slaves back to Egypt and his son, Amenhotep II, a further 89,600. The mass deportations were usually accompanied by the razing of offending towns and this created a "destruction layer" of burnt timbers and other flammable materials. The "destruction layer" can, in subsequent archaeological excavations, be accurately dated using carbon 14 tests and then linked to other contemporaneous records of the event. Pottery found at or close to the "destruction layer" will also provide clues to the date of the event.

The Exodus, which we have just suggested did not happen, was preceded - according to the Bible - by the sale of Joseph, by his brothers, into slavery in Egypt. The story of how Joseph caught the eye of pharaoh and became the pharaoh's ruler over Egypt, is an example to us all of how anyone can rise to greatness. At the end of the Bible book of Genesis, Joseph buries his father accompanied by pharaoh and is finally given a state funeral himself in Egypt. The problem with this story is that on opening the next Bible book, Exodus, we find all the descendants of Joseph and his family are in bondage to the pharaoh. The implausible explanation is given in Exodus:

> Now there arose up a new king over Egypt, which knew not Joseph.
>
> *Exodus 1:8*

It requires a suspension of disbelief to accept that a "new Pharaoh" might arise who did not know the man who was the nation's second-in-command under the previous Pharaoh. Clearly – from the evidence quoted above - this is all a later fabrication, but, in saying that, one has to ask the questions:

1. Was this a straightforward invention?
2. Did these stories grow from some distant recollection?

If the answer to the first question is "yes", then there is nothing more to be said. However, if the answer to the second question is "yes", then we can seek a reasonable explanation of what those earlier events might have been. It is almost as if the Bible is saying to us that there were two groups of ancestors, one group were slaves and the other was close to the pharaoh.

If the kingdom of Israel was - contrary to the Biblical account - created by Canaanites resettling in the central highlands of the southern Levant, where does that leave us? And if - also contrary to the Biblical account - there was no Exodus and no mass escape from Egyptian bondage, then who introduced the monotheistic worship of YHWH into Israel. We cannot avoid the likelihood that Moses or a Moses-like figure, or figures, did indeed come out of Egypt although we will deal with that suggestion in greater depth later.

We can make this statement with confidence because for the periods of settlement and later abandonment, through to the periods of the kingdoms, the worship of a pantheon of gods, including Baal, was the indigenous religion. The whole region that was Canaan is littered with hilltop altars erected to the fertility god Baal and lowland Temples serving the same purpose. Therefore, at some point in time monotheism must have been introduced to the region and that point appears to be close to the end of the second millennium or the beginning of the first. If it was the beginning of the first millennium then we are looking at a time close to the claimed building of the first Temple, the Temple which Solomon dedicated to the worship of YHWH.

Returning to the location of Judaea and Israel. The huge trade that went on between Egypt and Greece can explain the importance to Egypt - during the period 1,400 BCE to 1,200 BCE - of the "Way-of-the-Sea" trade route through Canaan. Although much trade went by sea there was still a lot carried overland through Anatolia and down the coastal plain of Canaan. Egypt's surplus grain went to Greece and in return they received olive oil. It was the discovery that olive trees could survive on the central highlands that transformed the marginal land into productive land capable of supporting a nation.

We have, so far, questioned the Biblical account of the Exodus based largely on archaeological evidence. Others have put more effort into critical examination of the Biblical texts, or exegesis. It is doubtless true to say that no other book has experienced the same degree of critical analysis as the Bible, particularly the Old Testament texts. It is probably also true to recognise that most other books would crumple under such intense inspection. However, few books apart from the Bible claim inerrancy (literally free from error). Unfortunately Judaeo-Christian belief depends heavily on the Bible as God's-revealed-will and on that basis it is difficult to accept that God could possibly make mistakes. Judaism and Christianity both recognise God as the Supreme Ruler of the Universe and have a duty to obey His commandments as revealed in the Bible.

Judaism has 613 *mitzvot* or commandments, drawn from the first five books of the Bible, the Torah, and which are binding on all Jews. They include:

> To learn the Torah (the Pentateuch or first five books of the Bible) and to teach it.
> Not to add to the commandments of the Torah, whether in the Written Law or in its interpretation received by tradition.
> Not to take away from the commandments of the Torah.

The Torah was purportedly written by Moses, the man whom God chose to lead the Children of Israel out of Egypt, an action that we have just said did not happen. Moses, according to the Bible, was chosen by God, not only to lead his people out of Egypt, but also to be conduit of the Torah, from God to the Jewish People.

Christians also believe in the inerrancy or infallibility of the Bible, and Walter Elwell[23] provides a revealing analysis of the subject. For Protestants, the Bible became an essential weapon to prise infallibility and therefore supreme authority away from the Pope. For them, ultimate authority rests in inspired scripture. The Catholic Church has maintained infallibility for the pope and has reserved inerrancy for the Bible. The observation that parts of the Bible appear to contradict other parts is nothing new: indeed some reformers have devised elegant solutions. One such solution says that "if a passage appears to permit two interpretations, one of which conflicts with another passage and one of which does not, the latter must be adopted". The idea that the Bible is inerrant does in fact come from the Bible itself:

> All scripture is given by inspiration of God, and is profitable for doctrine, for reproof, for correction, for instruction in righteousness:
>
> *2 Timothy 3:16*

The Bible also defines criteria by which one can distinguish God's message from false prophets. In so doing it undeniably stakes out for itself the high ground of absolute truthfulness.

> When a prophet speaketh in the name of the Lord, if the thing follow not, nor come to pass, that is the thing which the Lord hath not spoken, but the prophet hath spoken it presumptuously: thou shalt not be afraid of him.
>
> *Deuteronomy 18:20*

For Christians, the message of inerrancy is reinforced by the words of Jesus Christ:

> Think not that I am come to destroy the law, or the prophets: I am not come to destroy, but to fulfil. For verily I say unto you, Till heaven and earth pass, one jot or one tittle shall in no wise pass from the law, till all be fulfilled.
>
> Whosoever therefore shall break one of these least commandments, and shall teach men so, he shall be called the least in the kingdom of heaven: but whosoever shall do and

> teach them, the same shall be called great in the kingdom of heaven.
>
> *Matthew 5:17:20*

Having expressed – through Moses, the other prophets and disciples – His revealed will, in the form of the books of the Bible, God's veracity is reinforced in both the Old and the New Testaments:

> God is not a man, that he should lie; neither the son of man, that he should repent: hath he said, and shall he not do it? or hath he spoken, and shall he not make it good?
>
> *Numbers 23:19*

> And also the Strength of Israel will not lie nor repent: for he is not a man, that he should repent.
>
> *Samuel 15:29*

> In hope of eternal life, which God, that cannot lie, promised before the world began;
>
> *Titus 1:2*

There are many examples of eminent churchmen commenting on Biblical inerrancy. In the early church Augustine writes, "I have learned to yield this respect and honour only to the canonical books of Scripture: of these alone do I most firmly believe that the authors were completely free from error." The two great Reformers, Luther and Calvin, bear testimony to Biblical infallibility. Luther says, "But everyone, indeed, knows that at times they (the fathers) have erred as men will; therefore I am ready to trust them only when they prove their opinions from Scripture, which has never erred." While Calvin does not use the phrase "without error," there can be little question that he embraced inerrancy. Of the writers of the Gospels he comments, "The Spirit of God . . . appears purposely to have regulated their style in such a manner, that they all wrote one and the same history, with the most perfect agreement, but in different ways."

It is apparent then that the problem of Biblical inerrancy is that once you accept one or even a few errors, then the whole edifice of Judaeo-Christian faith is undermined. This is understandable but not something that should deter the curious from examining what archaeologists and other scientists have to say on the matter. For many it is possible to accept and believe in God and at the same time view the Bible as the work of man and so fallible. With this view very much in mind we may continue the exegesis of the Bible's written word, with particular reference to the period we are examining.

Redford[21] provides analysis that must cause all but the most devout to consider the Bible to be a human creation and so prone to error, just like every other human construct. Professor Redford begins by pointing to the complete absence of mention in the Bible of the great Egyptian empire on its border. The marching Egyptian armies or Hittite armies, no subservient town mayors or governors no ruling Canaanite cities, no mention of the arrival of the Sea Peoples. The great Egyptian kings get only the briefest of mentions, and when they do it is usually wrong: The Egyptian King who was to help Hoshea in his rebellion (2 Kings 17:4) has his name confused with his city "So". The pharaoh Shabtaka (697 – 690 BCE) is listed in the Table of Nations (Genesis 10:7) as a Nubian tribe. All of this supports the claim that the Bible was written some time later, probably in the seventh and sixth centuries BCE. The environment as described in the Bible would certainly have applied more accurately to that period, for by then the Egyptian empire had almost disappeared and the power had moved to Assyria. Even the dates are wrong, and Redford[21] explains how totalling the lengths of the reigns of the kings of Judaea, from Solomon's fourth year - when the Temple was dedicated - to the destruction in 586 BCE gives 430 years. However, adding 430 to 586 gives 1,016 BCE, which is at least 60 years too soon for the first Jerusalem Temple. Professor Redford provides a similar example for the time of Abraham. Redford added the years of the sojourn plus the wanderings in the desert. He concluded that Joshua conquered Canaan just as Thutmose III was completing his successful subjugation of all Canaan. It was only a few years later when Amenhotep II deported vast numbers – 89,600 is the number in Egyptian records – of Canaanites to Egypt.

> The inescapable conclusion is that the Exodus simply did not happen.

The problems that this conclusion raises are immense for Jews everywhere. If there was no Exodus then it follows – because it was an even earlier event - that there probably was no Abraham, although this is not a prerequisite to this thesis. On the other hand, the Biblical period called "Judges" does indeed present a picture wholly compatible with a scattered system of settlements, each one containing an extended family unit.

> In those days there was no King in Israel, but every man did that which was right in his own eyes.
>
> *Judges 17:6*

Although Abraham originated from Ur in Babylon, only the Bible provides any record from his life. This is curious for the man who founded a whole nation, especially when the capability to write was available there and at that time. To demonstrate this capability from the region, Bierbrier[24], reports on a popular story of an Egyptian, Sinuhe, a political refugee from the pharaoh, Senwosret I, who did spend several years in Canaan at around 1,960 BCE. It would be unrealistically speculative to suggest that this person might be the Biblical Abraham. It does, though, confirm that relatively minor characters were recorded for posterity then, and that this was a well-known story, to the Egyptians, as late as 1,080 BCE.

Certainly the region known as Judaea did exist, was populated and eventually became a kingdom, as we will see. There is, though, simply no way the archaeological evidence and Biblical exegesis can be squared for the period covering Abraham down to the first kingdom. There are suggestions in the Bible account that what is written is based on some distant memories from the past, perhaps there were written records - long since lost - that formed the basis of the Biblical account. We have suggested that, if the

Exodus did not occur then some Moses-like figure must have brought Judaism to the region and we will need to consider carefully how this may have happened. Perhaps some of the answers lie in later Biblical writings and so we will examine the next important period in Israeli history. This next period is the transition from a loose-knit community of scattered settlements into a kingdom complete with an administrative structure and centrally managed defences.

CHAPTER 5

TWO KINGDOMS

In the preceding chapter we came to some remarkable conclusions:

1. There was no exodus.
2. Moses, or someone like him introduced monotheism to Israel and Judaea.
3. During the first and second millennia BCE, Judaea and the highlands of Israel were insignificant to the adjoining superpowers. Their location, though, was strategically important.

We also reported how sparsely populated the central highland ridge through Canaan was during the years 1550 BCE to 1150 BCE with around 25 settlements, each housing an extended family of about 80 people. The next 250 years, to 900 BCE, saw the number of settlements increase tenfold to around 250, and two discoveries allowed this expansion. The first was iron for tools to cut large water storage tanks, or cisterns, into the highlands limestone rock. This statement requires some explanation because limestone had previously been cut with bronze tools for many years as the Egyptian pyramids attest. The point made here is that it is more difficult to cut a cistern sized hole into rock using a bronze saw – where sand between the teeth was the cutting medium – than in an open quarry where there is room at each end for men to stand and wield a two-man cross-cut saw. A cistern would have been laboriously cut with a hammer and chisel and bronze was simply too soft for this purpose. The second discovery was how to crush, burn and slake the limestone to make lime-mortar, and use it to line the cisterns and so prevent leakage. The new capacity to store water meant that land, which previously only had access to spring water for part of the year, could now store enough water to support the settlers through the dry spells. The entire area of the highlands had roughly divided into three distinct farming types. Agriculture provided for the inhabitants of the north-eastern end, and the south-eastern end was largely pasture. The western slopes concentrated on more valuable crops of olives and grapes. What had developed was a self-sufficient agrarian economy providing all the essentials for life, plus two potentially cash crops of wine and olive oil. The two "cash crops" could be traded with the lowland peoples and the nearby superpowers of Egypt and Assyria for luxuries. Archaeological evidence tells us that as the region approached the end of the second millennium there were few luxuries suggesting the highland economy was only just self-sufficient with little surplus available for external trade.

It appears from Part 1, that the Temple period in Jerusalem may somehow be at the heart of this enquiry. We need carefully to examine this period of history comparing the archaeological findings against the Biblical version. We will therefore devote this chapter to a brief résumé of the history of the region, as reported in the Bible. In attempting to condense one thousand years of Biblical history into a few pages, we are not intending to produce a textbook for future historical students, but rather to try to gain an understanding of the psyche of the early Jewish people.

The scene was set Biblically for a defensive alliance between the tribes when the Philistines defeated the Israelites in battle and carried off the Ark of the Covenant.

> And the Philistines put themselves in array against Israel: and when they joined battle, Israel was smitten before the Philistines: and they slew of the army in the field about four thousand men.
>
> *1 Samuel 4:2*

According to the Bible the Philistines gave the Ark back because it caused them great illness. Whether this is myth or history is irrelevant to the observation that the Israelites needed to combine as a "kingdom" to fight off aggressors. It is equally true to say that a combined army provided the potential for aggression by the Jews. Samuel – the last of the Judges – was asked by his people to appoint a King to rule over them:

> And [the people] said unto him, Behold [Samuel], thou art old and thy sons walk not in thy ways (Samuel's sons had been made judges but took bribes): now make us a King to judge us like all other nations.
>
> *1 Samuel 8:5*

Although this request was against his own inclination, the Bible tells us that God supported the people and commanded Samuel to make Saul king. Saul was from the tribe of Benjamin and this tribe occupied the northernmost part of Judaea including Jerusalem. Saul displeased God who then sent Samuel to Jesse in Bethlehem, whose son David He had identified as the next King of Israel. Jesse paraded each of his sons in turn before Samuel, and David, the last had to arrive from the hills where he had been tending sheep. It was David who Samuel then anointed.

> Then Samuel took the horn of oil, and anointed him in the midst of his brethren: and the Spirit of the Lord came upon David from that day forward. So Samuel rose up, and went to Ramah.
>
> *1 Samuel 16:13*

What followed was David's defeat of the Philistine giant champion, Goliath, and subsequent falling-out with Saul, causing David to flee into exile. Later, after Saul committed suicide David ascended the throne. This is all well known, but did it all really happen? Until recently archaeologists would have said, "in all probability, yes, these events can be evidenced in archaeological excavations". The archaeological evidence of the destruction of the Philistine town of Tel Qasile, on the outskirts of Tel Aviv, and other excavations containing ash layers were all attributed to David's subjugation of the country[22]. Similar evidential ash layers were also found in the major Canaanite centres of Megiddo, Hazor and Gezer. There was, in addition to the ash layers, a most interesting find of a particular gate construction – essentially an entrance and exit passageway through the city walls with two chambers contained by the gates.

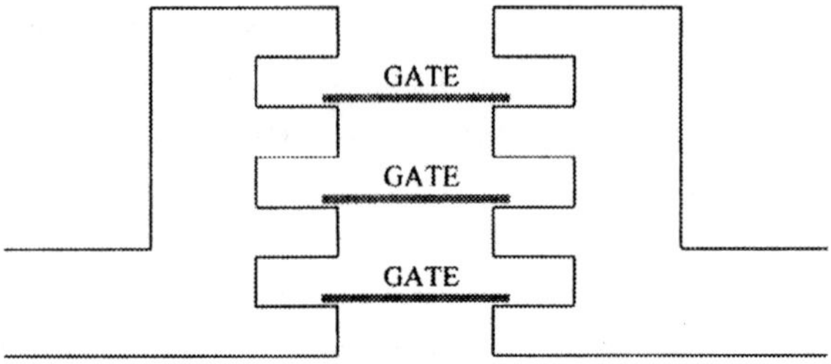

FIGURE 11 – CANAANITE CITY GATE

This arrangement – rather like a prison "airlock" system - would allow visitors to be isolated between the gates, unable to move forward or to retreat until they had been searched for weapons or other unacceptable goods. It also provided added defence during a siege, because even if the attackers broke through the first gate they had two more to break down during which time they could be attacked from immediately above. Megiddo, Hazor and Gezer were three Canaanite cities reported in the Bible as having defensive walls built by King Solomon to enable them to stand as storage cities:

> And this is the reason of the levy which King Solomon raised; for to build the house of the Lord, and his own house, and Millo and the wall of Jerusalem, Hazor, and Megiddo, and Gezer.
>
> *1 Kings 9:15*

The likeness of the construction methods of these city gates, pointed to the centralised administration, including standard designs for defensive structures, usually associated with statehood. The conclusion was unavoidable that David and Solomon were kings over a united Judaea and Israel, just as the Bible claims.

The breakthrough that cast doubts on the dating of the destruction layers and the six-chamber gates came with improved knowledge about the distinctive Philistine pottery found in the relevant ash layers. It became clear that contrary to earlier opinion, Philistine pottery did continue in use well into the first millennium[22]. The crucial evidence, though, came about courtesy of the scientists. In the past few years, carbon 14 dating techniques have advanced to the point where they were usable in this particular investigation. Until recently the margin of probability, or possible error, was measured in centuries and so any results were meaningless. However, recent improvements have dramatically reduced this margin of error. Modern tests on samples of timber from the Megiddo ash layer push the date towards 950 BCE, well after the death of David and before the destruction of Megiddo by the Egyptian pharaoh Shishak in 926 BCE. Furthermore, the six-chamber gates which looked so promisingly Davidic or Solomonic were two layers above the destruction layer and so much later. Whereas a destruction layer in David's time allowed Solomon to have built the gates, for the destruction layer to have been towards the end of Solomon's reign moved the gates into the reigns of his successors. We are probably now looking at the reigns of Jehoshaphat in Judaea and Omri in Israel. Tests on the archaeological remains from several other Canaanite towns[22] support these dates.

Setting aside the absence of the city gates and the destruction layers in Megiddo, Hazor and Gezer leaves us with the archaeological evidence of numbers of settlements and total population. We also have the lack of larger settlements or towns that would suggest some movement towards statehood. It is now apparent that the Biblical "kingdoms", of Saul, David and Solomon could not have been as militarily advanced as the Bible suggests, nor did they have well-developed construction techniques. The reality of the tenth century BCE is that Judaea and Israel - on the central highlands of the southern Levant - were agrarian societies. There is simply no trace of the record keeping on which monarchies float. The records of local assets, who owns what and who pays what taxes, and more to the point what those taxes were spent on, no records whatever. The fact is that only ten per cent of the total population of the highlands lived in Judaea, the vast majority, ninety per cent, lived in the northern region of Israel. With this in mind, it is curious that the Bible has Judaea as the political centre of a united monarchy over both Judaea and Israel. We have already mentioned how, by 900 BCE the total population of the highlands was only some 45,000 and that puts around 4,500 people in Judaea. This is nowhere near enough people to fund a stone-built heavily fortified city - such as Jerusalem - as described during the reign of Solomon, let alone a temple lined with gold. These 4,500 people were pastoralists living at the very margins of life, and dependant on the adjoining lands of the northern highlands for the grain supplement to their meat and milk diets. There is a huge disparity between the account recorded in the Bible and the reality shown by archaeological excavation and analysis.

We have shown that the highlands rural economy was just self-sufficient. It is also a matter of topographical fact that logistically it was easier to trade on the hilltops than to move produce up and down the hillsides to the lowland market. It is necessary to explain that statement. The track along the ridge of the central highlands provided relatively easy access between north and south. Along the line of the ridge but off this track north–south travel was more difficult. This was due to the deep and steep valleys that strike off to east and west, valleys which were cut by rainwater runoff millions of years earlier. It is also appropriate now to make the point that Jerusalem sits directly on this north–south track and effectively acts as a gateway between the two old Biblical countries of Judaea and Israel.

It is perfectly reasonable to acknowledge that the highland communities began to co-operate with each other commercially. One inevitable consequence of such trade is that dealers would have appeared - to manage the trade - and then political leaders would also have emerged. Large assemblies of people always need the forces of law and order to bring stability to their lives and to settle disputes. The forces of law and order are an essential support to the leadership role. The self-sufficient economy, which had developed on the central mountains of the southern Levant, produced three different foodstuffs:

1. Arable grain and vegetables;
2. Pastoral sheep and goat husbandry;
3. Olive oil production and viticulture.

This specialisation, fitting the best crop to each area of land, compelled the three different farming communities to trade with one another. Although the idea may be attractive, even the wine producers could not live on their produce alone. It is not hard to imagine how disputes would have become endemic in the highland society. The olive oil and wine would have demanded the highest prices on the open market but their producers would have incurred heavy transport costs to ship them off the mountainsides. Some years one or other crop or yield would have been greater or smaller than usual. Centralised storage of surpluses was an obvious way forward particularly with grain, and the model was readily available to them in nearby Egypt. It cannot be coincidence that it was just this advice the Bible tells us brought the patriarch, Joseph, to the attention of the pharaoh. This was a region that cried out for a central administrator, a centralised arbitrator and overseer of stored grain and other foodstuffs. It is reasonable to presume that such a central administration came into effect sooner rather than later in the developing highlands.

What may be curious is the Biblical insistence that the highlands were two separate countries, Judaea and Israel, which only combined during the reigns of David and Solomon. These are periods that we can now say could not have sustained a single kingdom of the population-size and power described in the Bible, let alone two. We can, of course, indulge in semantic debate as to whether what existed in the highlands was a state, a kingdom or a simply a community with an elected leader. The fact is that in the highlands the geography dictated that all the people co-operated with each other. They were dependent on each other, not for survival, because they could always trade with the lowlands, but rather they were mutually dependent for the most convenient way of life. The Bible says that after Saul came David and at this point we can be sure that David was indeed the first of a dynasty of kings because there is an extant record. In 1993 a fragment of a black basalt stele was discovered, reused as a building block at Tel Dan (right at the top of figure 5, above Hazor), containing the inscription:

> [I killed Jeho]ram son of [Ahab] King of Israel, and [I] killed [Ahaz]iahu son of [Jehoram kin]g of the House of David. And I set [their towns into ruins and turned] their land into [desolation].
>
> *Israel Finkelstein and Neil Silberman*
> *The Bible Unearthed*

The stele was carved for Hazael, the King of Damascus who lived only 100 years after David, and records a battle that was fought around 835 BCE. So, if David was the first King of a united Judaea and Israel, and there is nothing but good reason to believe that the highlands would have been united because of mutual interdependence and where does that leave us? What aspects of the Biblical account can we accept?

We have reached the point in time – around 930 BCE – when David and Solomon are dead and the Bible tells us that the unified realm split into two, Judaea to the south and Israel to the north. What we now want to draw out is the way that these two nations behaved over the next one thousand years. We wish to show how both nations, perched on the top of an inhospitable mountain range, and with superpower neighbours each side of them could not resist conspiring against their overlord of the time. We also wish to show that when the adjacent superpowers were quiescent then the rulers of Israel and Judaea would turn on each other or on themselves. In short, this was a most turbulent people, and some might conclude that they were almost ungovernable, indeed, were it not for their important strategic location it seems likely that they would have been left alone. As we progress through this period of southern Levantine history, we will test the veracity of Biblical records against the available archaeological evidence.

In order to develop this argument, we will now put Judaea on "hold" for a while, and concentrate on Israel. This is not, in any sense to discount Judaea, or to deny its existence as a separate entity. It does though recognise the reality that, as a separate kingdom, it could only have existed because no one else wanted it. Judaea was bounded to the south by the Negev desert, to the east by the Judean desert, to the north Jerusalem acted as a gatekeeper and to the west the slopes down to Philistia were steep and fairly inaccessible. Why would anyone want Judaea where the living was pastoral and at best marginal? We will, therefore, concentrate our attentions on Israel. The Bible explains how, when Solomon died, his son Rehoboam was unpopular and arrogant and so Israel broke away from the rule of the united monarchy.

> So when all Israel saw that the King hearkened not unto them, the people answered the king, saying, What portion have we in David? neither have we inheritance in the son of Jesse: to your tents, O Israel: now see to thine own house, David. So Israel departed unto their tents.
>
> *1 Kings 12:16*

There followed, for Israel's monarchy, a turbulent forty or so years, but a period during when the population continued to grow and with it the nation's wealth. An Ephraimite, Jeroboam, had led a futile revolt against Solomon and fled to Egypt when it failed. He returned when Rehoboam acceded after his father's death and again led a rebellion, which proved successful. Israel then had a new dynasty at its head and the House of David was left with Judaea. Jeroboam's son Nadab succeeded him in 986 BCE. Nadab ruled for only two years when Baasha, who began the second dynasty, killed him and then reigned for some twenty-four years. His son, Elah, succeeded Baasha and also managed only a couple of years before being murdered while drunk by Zimri. Seven days was all Zimri lasted before committing suicide when under attack from the next dynastic ruler Omri. Unable to take the throne immediately Omri needed four years of war against another claimant to the throne Tibni. Omri's was the fourth dynasty of Israel and would last for the next four generations.

Having described a period in Israel's history when internecine squabbles were the order of the day, we turn to the first major external shock. There can be little doubt that this event helped Israel to expand her borders, and it was the invasion of the southern Levant by the Egyptian pharaoh, Shishak (Egyptian Sheshonq). Shishak, the founder of the 22nd Dynasty, which lasted for some 200 years, was a Libyan from Bubastis in the eastern delta region. In order to stabilise his unruly neighbouring vassals, Shishak launched a campaign against the Levant in 925 BCE. Carvings at the temple at Karnak record that he devastated some 150 villages and towns. Moving from the delta region of Egypt, Shishak cleared Philistia before moving into the hills to take Jerusalem, after which he turned north to clear Israel. The Bible records his attack on Jerusalem:

> And it came to pass in the fifth year of King Rehoboam, that Shishak King of Egypt came up against Jerusalem: And he took away the treasures of the house of the Lord, and the treasures of the king's house; he even took away all: and he took away all the shields of gold which Solomon had made.
>
> *1 Kings 14:25-26*

This is an important Bible entry because it demonstrates synchronicity between the Bible and archaeological findings. It is generally accepted that the first Bible was written sometime around the seventh and sixth centuries BCE and by then Egypt was an ex-superpower and a shadow of its former self. There was simply no way that the first Bible scribes – in the seventh century BCE - could have known about Shishak's invasion unless they had some earlier record to guide them. Unlike our earlier conclusions about the Exodus, it is now clear that records available to the Bible scribes, about Shishak, were accurate. This is one of the early examples of how archaeology can prove the veracity of the Bible from around the end of the tenth century BCE.

After clearing the northern hilltops, Shishak turned his attentions on Megiddo where he razed the city and left a victory stele to record his victory. Apart from his influence on developing the Levant, Shishak has another side to him that may prove relevant to this enquiry. He was very involved with the priesthood particularly that of Amun and this patronage continued under his successors. We can therefore assume that the priests who accompanied Shishak would have become familiar with the remoteness of the highlands of the Levant. We can also speculate that if they or their successors were later part of a move from

Egypt to Canaan they would have been armed with that knowledge.

The overall result of Shishak's invasion was to leave behind a leadership vacuum when he returned to Egypt. It is not felt that Shishak extended his campaign into Judaea, apart from Jerusalem, and why would he? Judaea, as we have described above was an isolated area of sheep and goat herders with a few scattered settlements with eighty or so people in each. The efforts of Shishak would, though, have opened opportunities for some of those goat herders to move onto vacant property in Israel. Equally, the Israeli survivors could have moved into vacant areas of Philistia or north-east of Megiddo.

Despite the setback of Shishak's invasion, Israel recovered and continued to increase its population and wealth. By 750 BCE, archaeologists believe that the population of Israel had grown to around 350,000. It is hardly surprising that, as the wealth of Israel increased so did the curses of their poorer Judaean neighbours rain down on them:

> But Omri wrought evil in the eyes of the Lord, and did worse than all that were before him.
>
> *1 Kings 16:25*

Omri's son Ahab fares even worse in the eyes of the Judaeans as do the following two generations of Israeli kings, until Jehu fulfils their wishes:

> And when he came to Samaria, he slew all that remained unto Ahab in Samaria, till he had destroyed him, according to the saying of the Lord, which he spake to Elijah.
>
> *2 Kings 10:17*

It is immediately clear that even by 850 BCE, the worship of YHWH had not taken hold in Israel to the extent that it is reported as doing in Judaea. This is supported by archaeological evidence of altars dedicated to Baal across the highlands region. Jehu killed the Baal priesthood and their followers but appears to have permitted other cults to continue:

> But Jehu took no heed to walk in the law of the Lord God of Israel with all his heart: for he departed not from the sins of Jeroboam (worship of the golden calf), which made Israel to sin.
>
> *2 Kings 10:31*

It was around twenty years later when, according to the Bible, God's punishment on the Israelites – foretold by the Judaean prophets - was exacted. This was a period when Egypt was weakened and Assyria had not yet achieved dominant superpower status. Ahab, king of Israel, interfered in the succession of the neighbouring kingship of Damascus, and as a reward, the new king, Hazael, swept into Israel from Damascus and defeated the Israeli army. This was a fairly short-lived setback and when Joash ascended to the throne of Israel, one of his early actions was to recover the territory lost to Hazael. After Joash, came his son Jeroboam II (788 – 747 BCE), who enjoyed a peaceful reign of around forty years, still centred on Samaria. The death of Jeroboam was the signal for another period of bloodletting in the royal household. His son, Zechariah reigned for only six months before being murdered by Shallum who succeeded him. Shallum was in turn killed by Menahem before his first year was out and he ruled until 738 BCE at which point the region's new superpower, Assyria, took an interest.

At first, Assyria was content to exact a swingeing levy on Israel. Menahem "went to join his fathers" and his son Pekahiah took over as king, but he was soon murdered by an army officer, Pekah. The Assyrian ruler, Tiglath-pileser, became bored with the tribute from Israel and decided to go one step more and add Israel to his empire. He proceeded to overrun Israel and – as was their custom – deported many Israelites back to the region around Babylon. What was left of Israel was renamed Ephraim and was a dependency of Assyria. Pekah was assassinated for his failure, and his assassin and successor, Hoshea, declared himself a faithful vassal of Assyria. The death of Tiglath-pileser, in 723 BCE, provoked a rebellion in Ephraim, and Hoshea sought the assistance of Egypt to fight off their new suzerain. Tiglath-pileser's son, Shalmaneser V, had by then assumed his fathers' throne and he ferociously put down the revolt. His army laid siege to the capital city of Samaria for three years and meanwhile swept through Ephraim – ignoring Judaea – and carried off anyone they caught alive. Shalmaneser V replaced the deportees with captives from other regions and the Israelites never returned to their native land. The founding tribes of Israel have henceforth been referred to as "the lost ten tribes of Israel". The mixed races, which then populated what had been Israel, became known as Samaritans and the region as Samaria.

Before we turn our attentions to Judaea, to continue with a similar historical analysis to that which we have just completed for Israel, we will examine the archaeological evidence, which supports the Biblical account. We can gain a clear idea of how far Israel had extended its borders by the time of Omri; that is to say, some 50 or so years after Shishak, because there is a stele, dating from the ninth century BCE. This one was found in 1868 during the excavation of Dhiban, east of the Dead Sea in southern Jordan:

> I am Mesha, son of Chemosh[-yatti], the King of Moab, the Dibonite. My father was King over Moab for thirty years, and I became King after my father. And I made this high-place for [my god] Chemosh in Qarcho . . . because he has delivered me from all kings, and because he has made me look down on all my enemies. Omri [was] King of Israel, and he oppressed Moab for many days, for Chemosh was angry with his land. And his son reigned in his place; and he also said, "I will oppress Moab!" In my days he spoke thus. But I looked down on him and on his house, and Israel has been defeated; it has been defeated forever! And Omri took possession of the whole land of Medeba, and he lived there in his days and half the days of his son: forty years.
>
> *From the Mesha or Moabite stele*

This is supporting the Bible text and shows that, by the time of Omri, Israel had extended its borders considerably and ruled over Moab (modern west-central Jordan):

> And Mesha King of Moab was a sheepmaster, and rendered unto the King of Israel an hundred thousand lambs, and an hundred thousand rams, with the wool.
>
> But it came to pass, when Ahab was dead, that the King of Moab rebelled against the King of Israel.
>
> *2 Kings 3:4-5*

The Mesha stele continues:

> But [my god] Chemosh restored it in my days. And I built Baal Meon, and I built a water reservoir in it. And I built Qiryaten. And the men of Gad lived in the land of Atarot from ancient times; and the King of Israel built Atarot for himself, and I fought against the city and captured it. And I killed all the people of the city as a sacrifice for Chemosh and for Moab. And I brought back the fire-hearth of his uncle from there; and I brought it before the face of Chemosh in Qerioit, and I made the men of Sharon live there, as well as the men of Maharit. And Chemosh said to me, "Go, take Nebo from Israel." And I went in the night and fought against it from the daybreak until midday, and I took it and I killed the whole population: seven thousand male subjects and aliens, and female subjects, aliens, and servant girls.
>
> *From the Mesha or Moabite stele*

The discovery of the Mesha stele has confirmed the existence of the Moabites, who were previously only known of from the Bible. Their culture is thought to date from about the late 14th century BCE to 582 BCE, when the Babylonians conquered them. We must, however, be circumspect because we have to rely on the Jewish historian, Josephus, for this further information and he didn't live until the first century of the modern era. Interestingly, the Moabite language used on the stele resembles Biblical Hebrew[22].

The Old Testament (Genesis 19) also tells us that the Moabites were from the same stock as the Israelites. Moab was a son of Lot's firstborn daughter and sired by her father, who was a nephew of Abraham. Chemosh, the god mentioned throughout the stele, was the national god of Moab and is mentioned several times in the Bible. Perhaps the most appropriate quotation is where King Solomon is led astray:

> Then did Solomon build an high place for Chemosh, the abomination of Moab, in the hill that is before Jerusalem, and for Molech, the abomination of the children of Ammon.
>
> *1 Kings 11:7*

The Mesha stele continues with one of the earliest mentions of Yahweh (YHWH) outside of the Bible:

> For I had destroyed them for [the god] Ashtar Chemosh. And from there I took the vessels of Yahweh, and I presented them before the face of [my god] Chemosh. And the King of Israel had built Yahaz, and he stayed there throughout his campaign against me; and Chemosh drove him away before my face. And I took two hundred men of Moab, all its division, and I led it up to Yahaz. And I have taken it in order to add it to Dibon. I have built Qarcho, the wall of the woods and the wall of the citadel; and I have built its gates; and I have built its towers; and I have built the house of the king; and I have made the double reservoir for the spring in the innermost part of the city. Now the innermost part of the city had no cistern, in Qarcho, and I said to all the people, "Each one of you shall make a cistern in his house." And I cut the moat for Qarcho by using Israelite captives. I have built Aroer, and I constructed the military road in Arnon. I have built Beth-Bamot, for it had been destroyed. I have built Bezer, for it lay in ruins. And the men of Dibon stood in battle formation, for all Dibon were in subjection. And I am the King over the hundreds in the towns which I have added to the land. And I have built Beth-Medeba and Beth-Diblaten and Beth-Baal-Meon, and I brought there . . . flocks of the land. And the House of [Da]vid dwelt in Hauranen, . . . Chemosh said to me, "Go down, fight against Hauranen!" I went down . . . and Chemosh restored it in my days . . .
>
> *From the Mesha or Moabite stele*

The mention, close to the end, of the "House of [Da]vid" provides further support for the existence of this dynastic house. However, some caution is necessary because the final lines are damaged and difficult to read. The words used in the above translation are attributed to a French scholar, Andre Lemaire, who was able to identify a previously indistinguishable letter as a "d". The end of the above translation must therefore be treated as controversial. If the translation is confirmed, and advances in science will probably bring this about in due course, then the mention of the "House of David" dwelling in Hauranen is curious. Hauranen was in Moab (modern Jordan), south of the river Arnon, and this implies either that Judaea also had extended its boundaries or there is some blurring of the Biblically separate states of Judaea and Israel.

We have devoted rather a lot of space to the Mesha stele to demonstrate the quality of the archaeological evidence now available to support the conclusions being drawn. There are, in fact, other extant archaeological records that provide support, of sorts, for the Biblical account after Solomon. There is an Assyrian monolith inscription, on which King Shalmaneser III, in 854 BCE, had inscribed the details of his battle against the combined forces of Phoenicia, Israel and Syria:

> He brought along to help him 1,200 chariots, 1,200 cavalrymen, 20,000 foot soldiers of Adadidri of Damascus; 700 chariots, 700 cavalrymen, 10,000 foot soldiers of Irhuleni from Hamath; 2,000 chariots, 10,000 foot soldiers of Ahabbu Sirila.
>
> *From the Monolith Inscription of Shalmaneser III*

Ahabbu of Sirila is assumed to be King Ahab of Israel, and Finkelstein[22] and Dever[20] are content with this interpretation. However, James Jordan[27] argues that the use of Sirila as the country of Ahabbu suggests strongly that it is not Israel; the usual Assyrian reference for Israel is "the land of Omri", and therefore Ahabbu is not King Ahab. James points out that "even if '*sir*' is correct, the name is a poor spelling of Israel; and it is doubly questionable because nowhere else on Assyrian tablets is Israel given this name".

We can, though, set this disputed artefact to one side because there are others, including the absence of evidence where some should be found. Indeed, the University of Calgary and Finkelstein[22] provide summaries:

EVENT	DATE BCE	SOURCE
David conquers Jerusalem	990	No evidence of any change in the settlement systems on the highlands or in the valleys
Solomon builds the temple	960	No sign of grand scale building in Jerusalem, Megiddo, Hazor or Gezer
Omri establishes Samaria	880	Mesha stele from Moab Foundations excavated
Ahab's various exploits	860	Shalmaneser III mentions Ahab at battle of Qarqar Buildings excavated at Samaria, Megiddo and Hazor
Jehoram defeats Moab	848	Mentioned on Tel Dan inscription. Destruction of Jezreel and other destruction layers
Jehu pays tribute to Shalmaneser III	841	Annals: 18th yr. of Shalmaneser III
Joash pays tribute to Adad-nirari III	796	Stele inscription
Jeroboam III defeats Damascus	760	Large scale building at Hazor, Gezer and Megiddo Samaria ostaca and seal found at Megiddo
Menahem pays tribute to Tiglath-pileser III	740	Stele inscription
Ditto	738	Annals: 8th year of Tiglath-pileser III
Ahaz pays tribute to Tiglath-pileser III	734	Summary inscription Tiglath-pileser III
Pekah removed; Hoshea ascends throne in Israel	732	Summary inscription Tiglath-pileser III
Fall of Samaria	722	Babylonian Chronicle: 5th year of Shalmaneser V

Recapture of Samaria and exile of inhabitants	720	Annals: 2nd yr. of Sargon II
Assyrian campaign to Judah	701	Annals: Sennacherib
Manasseh pays tribute and service to Assyria	c. 674	Prism B: Esarhaddon
Ditto	c. 668	Annals Prism C: Ashurbanipal
Battle of Carchemish	605	Babylonian Chronicle: 21st year of Nabopolassar
Capture of Jerusalem	597	Babylonian Chronicle: 7th yr. of Nebuchadrezzar
Release of Jehoiachin	561	Accession yr. of Amel-Marduk

This weight of evidence, supporting and contrary to Biblical records enables us to accept the Bible for the period after Solomon as a reasonable record of events, *parri passu* with other evidence. In other words, after Solomon we can confirm a strong thread of historical accuracy running through the Biblical text to support it as a realistic record for the time. This means that while some parts of the Bible can now be seen to be invention, it is simply as a means of filling the gaps between the known historical facts. Let us, for the sake of discussion, set aside the issue of inerrancy of the Bible. We can then admit the Biblical record in the knowledge that – just like all other historical records – it embodies the belief systems of the scribes who compiled it. The glossing over of events that others see as important should not alter our perspective of them and should not prevent us from drawing conclusions from the Biblical data that are available to us.

In addition to archaeological evidence to support or discredit the Biblical account, there are other analyses going on to examine each and every word in the Bible, and subject it to rigorous scrutiny. It will come as no surprise that the Bible, which has had such a powerful effect on humankind, has been the subject of such extensive analysis. Judeo-Christian theologians and those of other religions have often devoted their lives to interpreting each word and line of the Bible, to meet the needs of an evolving population. As new techniques of literary analysis have developed, so they have been applied to the Bible texts. This process has been made all the more complex because of the several transliterations that have taken place from initially Hebrew into Greek and then Greek into English, or whatever language the reader uses. More recently, the arrival of the computer has allowed what might be termed a "word-crunching" approach to textual analysis to take place. Computers can add the number of times particular words and phrases are used in proximity. They can examine the percentage uses of various words in any given text. The results of this computer analysis can identify different authors, for authors have individual styles which dictate how they string words together.

Yet another approach to exegesis has been to examine the form the writing takes. In an attempt to uncover the oral traditions that underlie much of the Bible texts, analysts have used the supposition that language takes on a particular form suitable to the use to which it is being put. For example, reports of political news items will usually appear differently in "left-wing" newspapers to what is written in "right-wing" newspapers. Therefore, by identifying often, short "core" material that recurs across more than one Biblical entry, this technique – known as redaction – provides, according to its proponents, a window into the use or purpose of any particular text. It is also asserted that the true meaning - when the text first originated - and its subsequent uses until the final version was set down in the original Bible can be uncovered.

The result of all of these textual analytical methods has been to identify the Torah – the first five books of the Bible - not as the work of one man, Moses, but rather of four different authors. These four authors are called:

Deuteronomy	- given the label "D"
Elohist	- given the label "E"
Yahwist	- given the label "J"
Priestly	- given the label "P"

The particular variable that resulted in the labels "J" and "E" is the use of particular variations of the name for God. "J" uses YHWH or Jahweh (Yahweh is the German spelling that we now use) and

"E" uses Elohim. The "P" author adopts a style that emphasises the priesthood, while "D" has an exhortatory style. It is usually agreed that E and J are the oldest sources originating probably in the tenth century BCE, while D and P probably date from around the fifth century BCE. Of the five books that make up the Torah, there is a consensus that the first two and the fourth books, Genesis, Exodus and Numbers, contain sections from E, J and P. The third book Leviticus is entirely P and the fifth book, Deuteronomy, is entirely D.

In terms of literary style, the Yahwist, defines his people by anecdotes and stories, he also nearly always refers to God as YHWH. Only occasionally does the Yahwist refer to God as Elohim; indeed, to the Yahwist, God is very humanlike in speech and actions.

The Elohist, conversely, treats God as a more remote being, he also avoids the use of YHWH until after God has revealed His proper name to Moses.

Ritual directions and laws often interrupt the Priestly code, and there are also extensive genealogical lists found in Genesis as well as Leviticus. The Priestly code, like the Elohist, uses Elohim for God until Moses was given the name YHWH; it also stresses the supernatural power of God.

The Deuteronomist calls for Israel to conform to YHWH's covenant and emphasises that Israel was identified as God's chosen people.

It is generally considered from extensive exegesis that although the Bible was written around the seventh and sixth centuries BCE, the authors did draw on earlier works. The dating of the Elohist and Yahwist to the tenth century BCE supports this conclusion. Even taking into account this analysis of our present-day knowledge of the Biblical texts, and recognising the important data that underpins that knowledge, we do still have a problem. The fact is that based on the available archaeological evidence Jerusalem simply could not have been of the size to warrant a temple of the grandeur described earlier. How could 4,500 people, living at the margins of existence have amassed treasure and gold shields?

We have examined the Biblical account of the history of the Jerusalem temple period. We have checked this both against archaeological findings and exegesis of the Bible records. It only remains to look at general building techniques of the period to ascertain whether they will help us to determine exactly when king Solomon's Temple was built.

Dating from around 880 BCE, the period of king Omri, evidence of massive fortification begins to appear. Hazor, in the far north, had pillared buildings as well as the casemate city walls. The city of Dan, even further north had a huge gate structure, podium and the remains of well-dressed ashlar stones. At Samaria, the capital city of Israel during the time of Omri, a large casemate "box" inside the city that was filled and paved to create a podium on which was built the royal palace. This pattern of construction is very similar to temple mount in Jerusalem. At Jezreel the feature was repeated but included a sloping rampart outside to prevent the walls from collapsing under the weight of the earth fill. It is abundantly clear that by the early ninth century, the Israelites were competent civil engineers and builders. It was, however, at Hazor and Megiddo where evidence of some impressive civil engineering, which would influence future defences of Israelite cities, was first found. This civil engineering comprised a deep shaft within the city walls, with a tunnel leading from the bottom of the shaft to a nearby spring that provided the city's water supply. The access to the spring from outside the city walls had been bricked up and camouflaged to prevent any attackers from finding it. Because of this impressive work, Megiddo – and some subsequent Israeli cities - had access to water within the city walls and could thus withstand a siege for as long as the food supply lasted. These were times when siege engines, such as the ballista and trebuchet had not been invented and so strongly defended high masonry walls were a very effective defence against any aggressor.

Around 150 years later, when Hezekiah became King of Judaea he improved the fortifications of Jerusalem and copied the Megiddo and Hazor system, by constructing the Siloam tunnel, which provides access to the Gihon spring.

> This same Hezekiah also stopped the upper watercourse of Gihon, and brought it straight down to the west side of the city of David. And Hezekiah prospered in all his works.
>
> *2 Chronicles 32:30*

Having earlier followed the fortunes of Israel until its destruction – both from Biblical records and from supporting scientific evidence, we can now turn our attention to Judaea. According to the Bible and as described above, after Solomon the unified highlands region split into two states. The archaeological evidence available to us reinforces this position, and if anything casts some doubt over the existence of a unified monarchy. During phase 3 (in chapter 4) from 2,000 BCE to 1550 BCE, we have evidence of two separate states. The Amarna tablets, or letters, also referred to in chapter 4 mention two kings; Abdi-Heba ruled from Jerusalem, and Labayu from Sheckem. In addition, fragments of pottery have been found with the names of Sheckem and Jerusalem inscribed on them. These curse pots were inscribed by the Egyptians with the names of their enemies and then smashed and buried, thus sending bad luck to them. Judaea was certainly the poor relation when compared with its neighbour Israel. By as late as 850 BCE, when Israel had vastly expanded its borders, there were not many more than twenty small settlements in Judaea. Most of the population were nomadic shepherds, as shown by the many single graves scattered over the hillsides with no nearby settlement. Even olive oil production, a key factor in the growth of Israeli wealth, did not shift from being a family enterprise to a Judaean state industry until the seventh century BCE, two hundred years after Israel had effected this change. Very little evidence, outside the Bible exists to tell us much about the various monarchs of Judaea. One interesting monarch was Athalia. She was the daughter of King Ahab of Israel and his wife Jezebel. When King Ahaziah, who was her son, died, at the hands of the King of Israel, Jehu, she seized the throne and reigned for seven years. As retribution for the death of her son and other relatives by Jehu, she massacred the remaining royal Judah family members:

> And when Athaliah the mother of Ahaziah saw that her son was dead, she arose and destroyed all the seed royal.
>
> *2 Kings 11:1*

One member survived, Joash, who later returned and organised a successful revolution during which Athaliah was killed and he then assumed the throne of Judaea. It is obvious from this episode, that although there were separate states, the royal families were – as royalty have done before and since – quite happy to marry into each others' households. It was during the reign of Joash that the Syrian King, Hazael, swept through Israel. Hazael was, however, content to collect tribute from Jerusalem rather than bother with a long siege and the eventual destruction of Judaea. The Bible book, 2 Kings, chapter 12, describes at length how King Joash tried to get the priests to repair the damaged temple. When King Joash paid off Hazael with the Temple wealth he was murdered by some of his servants.

It was not until Israel had been destroyed by Shalmaneser V and her people deported that Judaea and Jerusalem in particular began to blossom. Setting aside the temple, which we will return to later, the real evidence of major building work in Jerusalem does not surface until the reign of King Hezekiah, who ruled from about 726 BCE until around 697 BCE. Judaea was then under the suzerainty of King Sargon II of Assyria. Hezekiah had approached the Egyptians for support and began planning a rebellion against Sargon. By way of preparation for the rebellion, he strengthened the defences and extended the wall around Jerusalem to encompass the bordering western hill, now known as Golgotha. This increased level of construction was made possible, or perhaps necessitated by a large increase in the size of the population of Jerusalem, estimated at around 25,000 people. It is likely that many of these extra people were refugees from adjacent Israel as a result of Shalmaneser's offensive. Once again, to put this into a U.K. perspective, 25,000 residents would merit the title of "small-town," certainly not the city that the Bible tells of. Archaeological evidence does, though, indicate that this period - until the destruction of Jerusalem by the Babylonians - was one of prosperity.

In Jerusalem, parts of several fine structures dating to around Hezekiah's time have been uncovered, including the Ashlar House. This, as its name suggests, was a public building constructed from large dressed stone blocks or ashlars. Another two storey house complete with limestone toilet seat and an external staircase built from stone, is known as the House of Ahi'el, from a name inscribed on a piece of pottery found there. The advanced civilisation is demonstrated by the finding of some 50 bullae, or soft clay sealing pieces. These bullae ("scarab" was the Egyptian term) were used to seal papyrus documents in the same way that wax was later used. After binding with string the clay seal would be fixed over the knot and stamped with a seal. The bullae and examples of ostraca, or weight stones for weighing out goods, offer the earliest evidence that a mature state had developed able to cope with the levels of bureaucracy necessary to support its administration.

It is obvious from the amount of ash present at the House of Ahi'el site that the house was burned down and the heat has fired the clay sealing pieces preserving them perfectly. Two of many Hebrew names on the bullae belong to Biblical characters. First is Gemaryahu, the son of Shafan, an official at the court of King Jehoiakim, and second is Azaryahu, the son of Hilkiyahu, who belonged to the Cohanim family of high priests. We can, therefore, be sure that the priesthood existed during Hezekiah's reign, and that improves our confidence in the presence of a temple too.

The strengthening of the walls of Jerusalem, by Hezekiah, turned out to be a fortuitous act on his part. The rebellion against the new Assyrian king, Sennacherib, collapsed when Sennacherib marched against the coalition that had united to stand against him. Egypt came to the support of the rebels but was quickly defeated. With his kingdom overrun and devastated, Hezekiah offered tribute to Sennacherib, but the Assyrian spurned the offer and called for Jerusalem to surrender. The Bible tells how the King asked the prophet Isaiah for advice and was told that Jerusalem would not fall. Armed with this advice Hezekiah stood firm and for reasons unknown - although disease among his troops is the best guess - Sennacherib suddenly struck camp and returned home.

King Manasseh succeeded Hezekiah, and he opted for peaceful subservience to Assyria. This peace delivered to Judaea over fifty years of steady growth and prosperity. To the distress of the Temple priesthood, this period of peace and prosperity brought with it a taste for the dress and culture of the foreigners who brought trade to the region. With this fondness for things foreign came a liking for alternatives to YHWH and so a wide range of pagan goods found sanctuary in Judaea, even at the royal court.

> So Manasseh made Judah and the inhabitants of Jerusalem to err, and to do worse than the heathen, whom the Lord had destroyed before the children of Israel.
>
> *2 Chronicles 33:2*

Retribution, as was so often the case in this Biblical hilltop land, was not long in coming. The death of the Assyrian king, Ashurbanipal, in 627 BCE, was the signal for Assyria's power over the region to decline rapidly. On the eastern side of the "fertile-crescent" Babylonia came to the fore and once again absorbed Assyria, a return to the situation that had prevailed during most of the second millennium BCE. Meanwhile to the west, Egypt was also in an expansionist mood. Judaea as ever, sat uncomfortably between these two superpowers.

After Manasseh's death around 640 BCE, the new young king, Josiah, began to restore YHWH to the position of state religion. The various places of worship to pagan gods that had appeared during the reign of Manasseh were destroyed and the countryside cleansed. It was during this period, when the temple at Jerusalem was being renovated that a previously unknown scroll of the Torah was discovered. This scroll is generally thought to be the work of Deuteronomy or "D" as described earlier. King Josiah continued his reforms by invoking an assembly at which the population was required to enter into a covenant with God recognising the new Torah. This marked a return to the ways of David and Solomon when the state, or more precisely the king, physically intervened to support Judaism. The decline of Josiah's suzerain, Assyria, must have made his reforms easier to enact.

The two new regional powers, Babylonia and Egypt eventually squared up to one another in 605 BCE at Carchemish, a city on the upper Euphrates. Although Carchemish sat at the northern end of the Levant and thus closer to Egypt, Egypt had overestimated her own strength and was soundly defeated. It was around this time that the latest Judaean king, Jehoiakim, tried to break free from Babylonia. This action is not as curious as at first sight it appears, given the obvious military prowess of Babylonia.

When the Judaean King Josiah, died his younger son Jehoahaz was the people's choice for king. However, before Egypt's defeat at Carchemish, Judaea was under Egyptian rule and it was the pharaoh Necho who appointed Jehoiakim as king. Jehoiakim was thus an Egyptian protégé and owed his loyalty to Egypt not Babylon. After Carchemish Jehoiakim simply changed his allegiance to the victor, the Babylonian King Nebuchadrezzar, and remained loyal for the next three years. Neither Judaea nor Israel had a good record over which suzerains to support and so after three years of loyal submission, Jehoiakim decided on rebellion. In 598 by way of response, Nebuchadrezzar led a decisive attack against Judaea and during the siege of Jerusalem Jehoiakim was bound in chains and sealed inside an iron cage. The cage was then propped above the roadway and Jehoiakim allowed to starve.

When Jerusalem finally fell to Nebuchadrezzar, Jehoiakim's successor, Jehoiachin, was taken into exile with the country's elite. The next king, Zedekiah, was another son of King Josiah and had the birth-name of Mattaniah. When Nebuchadrezzar defeated the Judaeans he appointed Mattaniah as regent and made him adopt the name Zedekiah. Curiously, Zedekiah soon succumbed to local pressure and began to plan, with the neighbouring states, to overthrow his suzerain. Inevitably, Nebuchadrezzar heard of the plot and in Zedekiah's ninth year of office he besieged Jerusalem once again. It was during this period that the prophet Jeremiah urged submission to the Babylonians and was imprisoned for doing so. After six months Nebuchadrezzar breached the walls of Jerusalem and had Zedekiah's sons killed and the subversive vassal blinded and taken in chains to Babylon, where he died in prison. As further retribution, Jerusalem was sacked and its buildings and defences reduced to rubble. The temple was burned and the people deported to Babylon. Only the poorest were left behind to tend to the land. The Babylonian Exile had begun and Judaea was no longer a kingdom but now simply a province of Babylonia. The utter destruction of Jerusalem at that time is all too evident from the layers of charred remains in the thick layer of rubble from burned buildings dating to that period.

The reign of Nebuchadrezzar was the zenith of power for the Assyrians, and apart from his conquests over his neighbours he embarked on a dramatic building campaign. Nebuchadrezzar's legacy included the "Hanging Gardens of Babylon" and completing the "Tower of Babel". By 552 BCE, the then King of Assyria, Nabonidus, feeling threatened by the Persians to his east, had moved to northern Arabia for security. Using Jewish mercenaries Nabonidus established an Arabian province, leaving his son Bel-shar-usur to look after Babylonia in his absence. By 546 BCE the King of Persia, Cyrus, conquered what is now Turkey and so encircled Assyria on two sides, to the east and to the north. The priesthood of the national god of Babylonia, Marduk, had never liked Nabonidus and offered Cyrus the surrender of Babylon in return for Marduk remaining the national god. A measure of syncretism is clearly visible between Marduk and the Hebrew God YHWH. On the one hand Marduk later became known as Bel or Lord and acquired no less than 50 names of divine attributes. YHWH, on the other hand, has 72 such different names. Marduk originally conquered Tiamut, who represented primeval chaos, to become lord of the gods of heaven and earth. Everything in nature, including man, owed its existence and destiny to Marduk.

Supported by the offer from the priests, Cyrus attacked Babylonia and seized the country without a fight. The Persian King, Cyrus, had now added lands represented by modern-day Turkey, Iraq and Persia (modern Iran) he then turned east and added Afghanistan, Pakistan, Turkmenistan and Uzbekistan. Cyrus was an enlightened ruler and allowed the subjects of his new lands to worship their existing religions. In support of this objective, he released the Jews who had been exiled in Babylonia and permitted them to return to their homeland. The new governor of Judaea, accountable to Cyrus, was Nehemiah.

> These were in the days of Joiakim the son of Jeshua, the son of Jozadak, and in the days of Nehemiah the governor, and of Ezra the priest, the scribe.
>
> *Nehemiah 12:26*

Jerusalem was thus partly repopulated by Jews released from Babylon. Nehemiah's mission was to fire up the people to rebuild the city walls and increase the greatly reduced population. Nehemiah chose not to rebuild the wall on the line of the old city wall but moved it north to clear the city of David, which from that time was left empty and outside the walled city. Nehemiah went back to Babylon after supervising completion of the rebuilding of the walls and houses; but later returned to Jerusalem to oversee the rebirth of Judaic moral values in the community. He remained there until his death in around 413 BCE.

The arrival on the scene of Alexander the Great in 333 BCE had a profound effect on the people of Jerusalem and particularly their priesthood. The decadent enjoyment of human pleasures that had been honed considerably by the Greeks, sat uncomfortably on the shoulders of an ascetic religious community like the Jews.

The next 150 or so years were relatively peaceful - by Jerusalem's standards - but the tensions were building. When Alexander died and his empire was divided between his various army commanders, Judaea, with its surrounding states went to his marshal, Ptolemy I, who controlled Egypt from Alexandria and from his perspective Palestine did not pose any threat. This did not stop Ptolemy and the ex-general Seleucus – who controlled Babylon – from squabbling over the Levant. Meanwhile, in blissful ignorance of the squabbles among their powerful neighbours, the wealthy aristocrats of Jerusalem grew to like their new Greek lifestyle. So much so that they pooled their resources to pay the Seleucid King to replace the high priest Joshua with an even more extreme Hellenizer, Menelaus.

This brought about a civil war turning the rich against the general population who still supported Joshua. The king, Antiochus IV Epiphanes, had to send forces to intervene and stop the bloodshed. This diversion, which brought the need permanently to garrison Jerusalem, seems to have annoyed him. He subsequently imposed restraining orders against Judaism and provided the necessary force to impose them. Antiochus banned Judaism on pain of death and ordered sacrifices to be made to Zeus on an altar within the Jerusalem temple precincts. Such was the explosive temperament at the time that this attempted suppression of Judaism sparked the Maccabean revolt (so named after the four books that describe the events). The Hasmonean, Mattathias, an old priest refused to participate in the pagan rites – and he and his five sons led the revolt. The insurrection soon turned away from the Seleucids and in on itself towards the underlying cause of the unrest, the Hellenizing Jews. To start with, circumcision was imposed on those who considered it no longer to be an essential requirement of the Jewish State. The limited numbers of rich people meant that their support for Hellenism would fail. The opposition by the great mass of the population guaranteed the success of the uprising. It was during the uprising that Judas Maccabeus – the old priest Mattathias' son - performed the act that is celebrated by Jews to this day - the annual festival of *Hanukka* – when he cleansed and rededicated the Temple to YHWH. The Hasmoneans now turned on the Seleucids and expelled them. Jerusalem settled down once more, this time as an independent state ruled by the priestly Hasmonaean dynasty. The last Hasmonean ruler, Antigonus, was executed on the orders of the Roman general, Mark Antony.

The next ruler of Judaea was Herod and he was proclaimed King by the Roman conquerors, but Herod was not of the Davidic line. Indeed, he was an Arab from the Edomite area between the Dead Sea and the Gulf of Aqaba. Herod rose to fame, or perhaps infamy as Christians would assert, as a direct result of the political foresight of his southern Palestinian father, Antipater. Antipater was a man of wealth and became procurator of Judaea in 47 BCE. He was also given Roman citizenship. Antipater appointed Herod - who held Roman citizenship – as governor of Galilee. In 40 BCE the Parthians invaded Palestine and in the ensuing civil war Herod fled to Rome. In Rome he was appointed King of Judaea and with the assistance of a large army he was dispatched back to Judaea to claim his kingdom, which he did in 37 BCE. Herod had been a practising Jew for many years and now took the opportunity to strengthen his position in Judaea by divorcing his first wife. He then married, Mariame, a Hasmonean princess and niece of Antigonus, the last Hasmonean ruler.

The Greek influence on Judaea reaffirmed itself under Herod, who built a hippodrome, theatre and amphitheatre in and near Jerusalem. Arguably, Herod's greatest contribution to Jerusalem was to rebuild the temple. Work on the temple began in 20 BCE and lasted until 26 CE, some 46 years. The platform, on which the temple sits - Temple Mount - was doubled in area and the temple itself enlarged and faced with white stone. Whatever divisions and tensions still existed in Judaea, they appear to have been assuaged by the role of Jerusalem as the centre of the Jewish religion. The temple itself became an object of compulsory pilgrimage, and by allowing an autonomous Jewish Sanhedrin – the Jewish Court of Elders – Herod turned Jerusalem into a great centre of the Hellenistic world.

When Herod died in 4 BCE there followed a period with three of Herod's sons ruling a divided kingdom. Archelaus governed the South, Philip the North and Herod Antipas a bit of the central region and the East. It was Antipas who placated his wife Herodias by imprisoning John the Baptist. He further succumbed to her wiles when she arranged for her daughter, Salome, to request John's head as a reward for dancing on his birthday. When Jesus was subsequently arrested, Pontius Pilate, the Roman procurator, sent him to Antipas, but Antipas was unwilling to get involved and so returned him to Pilate. The reign of one brother, Archelaus, was short-lived and after complaints to Rome he was deposed and replaced by a Roman administrator. The fifth administrator, Pontius Pilate, held office from 26 CE until 36 CE, and during his term of office ordered the crucifixion of Jesus Christ. Archelaus' full brother Antipas ruled until 39 CE and his half brother Philip ruled until 34 CE. Herod's grandson, Herod Agrippa I, resurrected the dynasty in 41 CE but his rule was also short-lived and in 44 CE the procurators again took over the administration of Judaea.

The Jews had for centuries fought each other when no external power was available, and now it was the turn of Rome. In 66 CE they once again rebelled against their rulers and once again the result was disastrous. Roman forces under Titus besieged the city and in 70 CE the Roman forces reduced Jerusalem to ashes. The Temple was given special attention and every stone block cast over the side of the platform of Temple Mount. When, some 500 years later the Muslims captured the Holy City not a single building block was left on temple mount. Some 65 years after the 66 CE revolt, the partially repopulated city of Jerusalem again rebelled against Rome and this time the emperor, Hadrian, led what was to be his last military campaign to put down this rebellion. Hadrian ordered that a new Roman city, *Aelia Capitolina*, be built over the ruins of Jerusalem and the layout of this town is what is visible today in the Old City of Jerusalem. The years 66 - 131 CE had seen the final rebellions against Rome, which resulted in the virtual annihilation of Jerusalem. Nothing remains of the temple apart from the structure, Temple Mount, on which it stood. A portion of the western-wall of Temple Mount is now called the "wailing wall" and provides a focus of Jewish hope for a new temple.

It is easy to imagine how any religious group might yearn for a return to the straightforward and ordered regime that operated in and around King Solomon's temple. It was a model that for some 900 years survived great traumas. Sometimes these traumas were caused by superior external forces, but more often from internecine disagreements. On several occasions the temple itself was demolished or at least seriously damaged as a lesson and example to the population. Sometimes large sections of the community were taken off to new lands. The beginning of the end, for the Temple, however, was largely self-inflicted when priestly appointments became commodities that could be openly bought and sold. Tradition has it that there were 18 high priests who served in Solomon's Temple (960-586 BCE) and 60 in the Second Temple, including the Herodian temple (516 BCE-CE 70). Since

Titus ordered the complete dismantling of the Jerusalem temple there has not been a single practising Jewish high priest.

This chapter has yielded little in our search for the time when Freemasonry was created. One thing that we can say with certainty is that it was not during the Jerusalem Temple period. There is absolutely no sign of any group showing the slightest inclination to build an organisation, open to all men, and with fraternal objectives. All the evidence about this period of history for the hilltop region of the southern Levant is of a disharmonious society ready to cross the street for a fight with anyone. It was a society, which was often riven with factions, fighting each other over land that for the most part was nearly worthless. We can only speculate on what created this turbulent nation, perhaps the constant heat, living on marginal land off a high protein diet contributed? Was it the isolation of living on top of a mountain range that made the occupants believe that they were immortal? Perhaps the three disparate foodstuffs, which necessitated constant trading between the various growers and sheep and goat herders produced a society in which disputes became a way-of-life. Or was it simply that living between two superpowers provided opportunities for playing politics that was irresistible to the local rulers? We will never know. What we do know, though, is that we must look to later periods for the originators of Freemasonry.

One fact that has emerged from our examination of this period of Jewish history is that the Jerusalem Temple period provides a poor model as the foundation on which to build a world wide organisation dedicated to "brotherly love and fraternity".

CHAPTER 6

A TEMPLE

In chapters 4 and 5 we examined the early history of Judaea and Israel to gain some understanding of the physical and political pressures that brought about the Biblical communities of Judaea and Israel. It is, however, the Jerusalem Temple that provides the obvious link with Freemasonry, so we will now examine the Temple and the family who ran it. From the time of Moses, until King Solomon, the Bible has Aaron, his sons and male descendants, guarding the Ark of the Covenant in a temporary structure, the Tabernacle. There they performed their priestly duties to the satisfaction of most of the Israelites during their sojourn in the Sinai desert. Aaron and his sons did, though, have to fight off at least one challenge to their right to this work.

> And they gathered themselves together against Moses and against Aaron, and said unto them, Ye take too much upon you, seeing all the congregation are holy, every one of them, and the Lord is among them: wherefore then lift ye up yourselves above the congregation of the Lord?
>
> And the earth opened her mouth, and swallowed them up, and their houses, and all the men that appertained unto Korah, and all their goods.
>
> They, and all that appertained to them, went down alive into the pit, and the earth closed upon them: and they perished from among the congregation.
>
> *Numbers 16:3, 32 and 33*

We will probably never find evidence of the Tabernacle, made as it was for the most part of perishable woven goats hair and wood. We will therefore concentrate our enquiries on the stone structure, the Temple at Jerusalem, and the first question we need to address, is exactly when was the first Temple built there.

An immediate problem flows from our assertion in chapter 4 that the Exodus did not occur. This is that if there was no Exodus then what about the tabernacle and the Ark of the Covenant? Both the tabernacle and Ark were fabricated while the children of Israel were at Mount Sinai, in other words during the Exodus. The available evidence does not preclude the existence of either but a different explanation of how they originated is required. We know there was a Temple at Jerusalem because existing non-Biblical records tell of it, mostly those of Josephus. In addition, the platform or casemate - on which the Jerusalem Temple stood – still stands today. We are therefore looking for a different series of events that led to the building of the Temple at Jerusalem. The difficulty is that the Temple for which the records exist was the one built by King Herod. However, we also understand from the writings of Josephus that Herod built his Temple on the site of the earlier Temple. The Temple that preceded Herod's was also a rebuilt Temple, this time by Zerubbabel after the return of the "children of Israel" from their captivity in Babylon. The period of the second Temple from 516 BCE to 68 CE is less contentious. Archaeologists and biblical researchers alike generally accept that the Bible scribes began their work around the seventh and sixth centuries BCE. These scribes were therefore writing contemporaneous records of events. The discovery of the Dead Sea Scrolls went a long way to reinforce the authenticity of the Bible as a historical record, proving as they did to be some of the oldest extant examples of Biblical text.

Before we pick through the evidence for a Temple at Jerusalem, let us first show that there was a settlement there at the time. In fact, there are Egyptian cuneiform engravings dated to 2,000 BCE, mentioning Urshaleim. It is believed that Urshaleim evolved out of "Ur Salem" meaning the "Temple of Salem", a Canaanite god. We well know how "new" religions have an inclination for building their places of worship on the sites of earlier cultic sites and so a Temple to YHWH in Jerusalem would have provided an early example of this unwritten convention.

There is also one archaeological find that provides us with some support for the existence of a Temple at Jerusalem as early as 800 BCE. Called the "House of Yahweh Ostracon", it is a pottery fragment containing a written receipt for a donation of silver shekels to Solomon's Temple. The fragment does not directly mention Jerusalem, simply "According to your order, Ashyahu the king, to give by the hand of [Z]ekaryahu silver of Tarshish for the house of YHWH - 3 shekels". The existence of other altars and temples is known and so this particular item cannot be considered conclusive evidence. Subsequent to this date, we can show that circa 260 BCE, the Egyptian King Ptolemy II ordered the Hebrew Torah to be translated into the Greek language. Copies survive to this day of the resulting work, named the *Septuagint* (meaning seventy) after the seventy-two Jewish scribes who were bilingual in Greek and Hebrew – symbolically six from each of the twelve tribes - who worked on it. The symbolical use of seventy-two scribes, six from each of the twelve tribes, is unlikely to win over any sceptics, especially as ten of the twelve tribes had been "lost" for hundreds of years before the purported activity took place.

The *Septuagint* contains detailed accounts of the second Temple and so Ptolemy and other Greeks who read it must have been aware of the Temple's existence. It is inconceivable that a reference would have been made if no Temple had existed. This observation ignores the mention in III Macabees that Ptolemy actually visited the Temple at Jerusalem. Josephus recorded the account of this visit in his work *Antiquities* and he in turn referred to an earlier work known as the Letter of Aristeas. Aristeas was a member of the court of Ptolemy and had sent this correspondence to his brother Philocrates. The letter describes how he went to Jerusalem to ask the Temple high priest, Eleazer, to organise a translation of the Torah into the Greek language. Ptolemy harboured an ambition to collect in his library a copy of every book in the world. Aristeas mentions that when Ptolemy was in a good mood over this action, Aristeas asked him if he would release 100,000 Hebrew slaves, and the King agreed. Aristeas also wrote that Ptolemy sent lavish gifts to the Temple at Jerusalem. We must mention here that scholars contest the validity of the Aristeas letter and some suggest that it may be a later attempt to justify the existence of a Greek version of the Torah. Clearly the 100,000 quoted as the number of Hebrew slaves seems unrealistically high.

There appears to be no suggestion, however, that the general import of the "letter" is not substantially correct.

The Hebrew scriptures, the TaNaKh, are made up from the Torah, the five books of Moses; the Nevi'im and the Kethuvim. These three also make up the Christian Old Testament. Other Jewish ancient writings, some of which are now included in the Bible, include[28]:

1. I Esdras – the book of Ezra
2. II Esdras – the book of Nehemiah
3. III Esdras – the 1 Esdras of the Septuagint
4. IV Esdras – an apocalyptic work from around 100 CE
5. I Maccabees – written around 100 BCE
6. II Macabees – completed around 120 BCE
7. Tobit – written in Aramaic and could have been written as early as 300 BCE
8. Judith – difficult to date, may be as early as 330 BCE, or as late as 160 BCE
9. Susanna – thought to be quite late, perhaps 100 BCE
10. III Macabees – curious title, for the Macabees are not mentioned and the story is about Ptolemy IV and his visit to the Temple at Jerusalem
11. Letter of Aristeas – dealt with above
12. Greek book of Esther – contains a further 107 verses to the original Hebrew version
13. I Enoch – one of the oldest texts
14. The astronomical book of Enoch – four copies were found among the Dead Sea Scrolls
15. The book of Watchers – also found among the Dead Sea Scrolls and dating from around 200 BCE
16. Aramaic Levi – a reconstruction from fragments dating from around 200 BCE
17. Book of Jubilees – dating from around 125 BCE
18. Testaments of the twelve Patriarchs – purported to be the last will and testaments of Jacob's twelve sons
19. Apocalypses – dating from around 150 BCE
20. Apocalypse of weeks – oldest of the Apocalypse books dating from around 170 BCE

21. Book of Dreams – dating from around 150 BCE
22. Sibylline Oracles – dating from around 150 BCE
23. Testament of Moses – it is though that the most recent entries, concerning King Herod, were added to an older work from perhaps 100 BCE
24. Wisdom of Ben Sura – dating from around 200 BCE
25. Epistle of Enoch – fragments also found among the Dead Sea Scrolls
26. Baruch – dating from around 150 BCE
27. Wisdom of Solomon – dating from around 50 BCE
28. Psalms of Solomon – dating from around the time of Christ
29. Prayer of Manasseh – date unknown
30. Prayer of Azariah – date unknown
31. Letter of Jeremiah - date unknown
32. Bel and the Dragon – date unknown
33. Philo – Jewish chronicler from the first century CE
34. Josephus - Jewish chronicler from the first century CE
35. Elephantine Papyri – oldest Jewish texts outside the Hebrew Bible dating from around 450 BCE
36. Dead Sea Scrolls – over two hundred manuscripts dating from around 200 to 100 BCE

This important store of evidence provides reassurance that the Temple did indeed exist during the "second Temple period". That is to say from soon after the return of the Jewish people from their captivity in Babylon until the destruction of Herod's Temple, by the Romans, in 68 CE.

We can also be confident the Jews did return from their Babylonish captivity because the "Cyrus cylinder", found in Babylon in 1879 CE, confirms the biblical account. These ancient cylinders had reverse image text engraved on them similar to an old newspaper press, albeit on a much smaller scale. When rolled over a portion of flattened clay they reproduced the text on the clay. The rebuilding of Jerusalem is not specifically mentioned, but the cylinder does record the exiles returning home. It also tells of land distribution by local rulers and that local banking and tax systems were established.

We can also take some reassurance that a Temple existed at Jerusalem before the exile, otherwise the return from Babylon and the Temple rebuilding story makes little sense. The Biblical report of rebuilding the Temple is reinforced because, as discussed in the previous chapter, there appears to be little doubt that there was a Temple at the earlier time of Hezekiah. The question still remains - exactly when was the first Temple at Jerusalem built?

The biblical writers attribute the first Temple to Solomon, and this may hold an important clue. David appears to have been the first King – albeit over an immature kingdom – of a monarchy ruling over both Judaea and Israel. It was God, according to the Bible, Who chose David to be King. David is such a significant character in the history of Judaism that his importance almost cannot be overstated. He was the first King to be chosen by God and so to rule by divine right. David was and still is such an important figure in the formation of Judaism that it is most curious that he did not build the first Temple. For some reason, the biblical writers were unable to take this step and attributed the decision to God.

> And, behold, I propose to build an house unto the name of the Lord my God, as the Lord spake unto David my father, saying, Thy son, whom I will set upon thy throne in thy room, he shall build an house unto my name.
>
> *1 Kings 5:5*

In view of his importance, the case for David building the first Temple is overwhelming. We can, therefore, safely premise that the reason why he is not accorded that honour is because he really did not build it. The only reasonable conclusion is that the Bible writers reported the truth - as they knew it - and this observation adds credibility to the Bible. However, we have said earlier that the Exodus did not occur, and in so doing we appear to cast doubt on the veracity of the Bible, or do we?

In chapter 5, we discussed how scholars have identified four original sources, Deuteronomy (D), Elohist (E), Yahwist (J) and Priestly (P) as the primary source data from which the first biblical scribes worked. There is also consensus that the first Bible scribes worked during the seventh and sixth centuries BCE, while E and J can be traced back to the tenth century BCE . Setting aside the question of Exodus for a moment, the real issues become:

1. Were the first biblical scribes truthful?
2. Were E and J truthful?

When considering the question of when the first Temple was built at Jerusalem, we can discount any untruthfulness by the Elohist, Yahwist and Priestly sources. For any of them to say that there would be a Temple, to YHWH, in Jerusalem before it was actually built would have required divine foresight. Perhaps, then, the biblical scribes, knowing that a temple existed in their time, pushed its construction date back to the reign of Solomon. But, if David was the first King appointed by God, why on earth exclude him from the honour of building God's first Temple? There is only one realistic explanation and that is that the earlier records – those of E and J - from which those scribes were working said that David did not build it. It most likely follows that the records of E and J said that it was David's son, Solomon, who built the Temple. We cannot argue that the scribes were unwilling to alter the records of E and J to show King David as the first Temple builder and then argue that they did so to make Solomon the Temple builder. Solomon was known to those same scribes to have led a dissolute life. The same scribes report how he took some seven-hundred wives and three-hundred concubines. Indeed, the scribes later blame Solomon for much of Israel's misfortunes.

> Wherefore the Lord said unto Solomon, Forasmuch as this is done of thee, and thou hast not kept my covenant and my statutes, which I have commanded thee, I will surely rend the kingdom from thee, and will give it to thy servant.
>
> *1 Kings 11:8*

In the face of God's clear displeasure with Solomon, surely he was not the best person to build God's first Temple on earth. The Temple scribes were doubtless members of the priesthood and would have had a serious interest in not making King Solomon the builder of God's first Temple. If we set aside our knowledge – provided by the archaeologists - that Judaea simply could not have had the funds to build the Temple at that time, we can recognise that the biblical account has a "truthful ring" to it. The Biblical authors were writing some three to four hundred years after the event. They could easily have amended their records to make the better man, King David, the builder of the Temple. Why, unless the notes from which they worked bound them to it, did they record Solomon as the builder of the first Temple on Earth to YHWH.

We must now address the matter of the authenticity of the Bible, in particular about our assertion that the Exodus could not have happened. We need here to distinguish between writing a deliberate lie or falsehood in the Bible and inventing a history where none existed. In the former case, we have the obvious fact that the biblical scribes were unwilling to do so in the case of making King David the builder of the first Temple. In the latter we must recognise that lying is most vigorously condemned in Judaism:

> Thou shalt not raise a false report: put not thine hand with the wicked to be an unrighteous witness.
>
> *Exodus 23:1*

That the biblical scribes felt an irresistible need to compose an account of the origins of mankind and the Jewish people is, at the very least, understandable. Their religion, Judaism, unequivocally defines the Jews as God's chosen people, a race who would inherit not just the hilltop land of the Levant but eventually the earth.

> Remember Abraham, Isaac, and Israel, thy servants, to whom thou swarest by thine own self, and saidst unto them, I will multiply your seed as the stars of heaven, and all this land that I have spoken of will I give unto your seed, and they shall inherit it for ever.
>
> *Exodus 32:13*

> His soul shall dwell at ease; and his seed shall inherit the earth.
>
> *Psalms 25:13*

It is plain that the Bible authors considered the Jews would inherit the earth - they after all recorded God's words - and therefore that birthright was important. It is unimportant here, whether we mean E and J, together with the later P and D, or the scribes who actually compiled the Bible that we use today. Obviously a record of the ethnicity of the Jewish people had to be laid down in writing.

However, with a lawyer's eye for detail, we could argue that it might be acceptable to "create" a history for ones people where none existed. For example, there is a story told of a rabbi, *Rav Yehoshua ben Chanina*, who was asked by the Elders of Athens to make a false statement. After some thought the rabbi said "a mule can give birth". The Elders commented "everyone knows that a mule cannot bear offspring, therefore that is not a lie". *Rav Yehoshua's* response to them was, "that is precisely what makes it a lie"!

If the biblical writers only had records going back to the turn of the first millennium BCE, they were faced with a problem. Clearly they would wish to provide the origins of their ethnicity because for Jews ethnicity is more important than for most other races. If, as Judaism states, the Jews are God's chosen people, it would have been self-evident that some earlier history was essential. It was needed to identify exactly who qualified as a "chosen person", precisely who was a Jew? Faced with this problem the biblical scribes "created" a Jewish history. Not from thin air but building on the myths and legends that follow all races and cultures as they settle from a nomadic to a static existence. They may well have considered that what they wrote about the Exodus - even back to the creation story with Adam and Eve - was not a lie. What they recorded was simply their best effort to explain the origins of mankind in general and the Jewish race in particular. The creation story, down to the time of King David would only be a lie if the scribes who wrote it knew it to be a lie, and there is no reason to suppose that this was the case. Professor Dever[20] put it succinctly when he said:

> If we look at the biblical texts describing the origins of Israel, we see at once that the traditional account contained in Genesis through Joshua simply cannot be reconciled with the picture derived above from archaeological investigation. The whole "Exodus-Conquest" cycle of stories must now be set aside as largely mythical, but in the proper sense of the term "myth": perhaps "historical fiction," but tales told primarily to validate religious beliefs.
>
> *William G. Dever*
> *What Did the Biblical Writers Know and When Did They Know It*

It seems clear that the early Bible can now be seen as an attempt to achieve a goal and to provide a history based on the myths and legends of the time. The Bible book of Judges describes a "nation" of self-governing households, which is exactly what the archaeological evidence says was there at the time. The early biblical account was clearly not just "conjured out of thin air".

By the same reasoning, where the biblical scribes had some firmer evidence to work with, they did just that. Palaeography and archaeology are both pointing towards the period of David and Solomon as the earliest time from when the records of E and J began. Thus, from around 950 BCE, until around 550 BCE, the scribes were able to rely on written data plus a fairly reliable oral tradition. An examination of the Bible against other existing archaeological records shows no signs of deliberate falsehood. The Bible may – just like the alternative records – put things in a different light or place more or less weight on actual events, but that is no different to any chronicler. From around 550 BCE, the consensus is that the Bible was being written contemporaneously with events.

Based on these conclusions, we are still left with two conflicting pieces of data:

1. There was a Temple at Jerusalem, which the Bible declares was built by King Solomon.

2. At the time of King Solomon, the argument for a combined monarchy is weak and Judaea was too poor to have financed the building of such a Temple.

We will consider item (1) first. If, as has been argued above the biblical scribes appear to have been truthful when earlier data, such as that of E, J, P and D were available to them; can we find any support for their version of events? We mentioned in chapter 5 how the invasion by the Egyptian pharaoh, Shishak, provided synchronism with events that the biblical scribes could not have known. They compiled the Bible some three to four hundred years after Shishak and could only have used the information if it was in the records of the Elohist or Yahwist. The fact is that Shishak's invasion came only a few years after the death of Solomon, relatively concurrent. So, if the biblical scribes were aware of Shishak's invasion, which we know to be accurate from other independent sources, then it improves the credibility of the Bible account of Solomon building the Temple at Jerusalem. To doubt the Bible on this issue requires an explanation as to why the ancient records recorded Shishak's invasion and then "invented" a Temple. Such an approach required that the biblical scribes deliberately created a false record and there is no obvious example of them doing that apart from for the period <u>before</u> around 950 BCE, as fully discussed above. It is one thing to generate a manuscript based on mythology but another knowingly to create a lie. Furthermore, because records existed in E and J of Shishak's invasion, the Biblical scribes would have no way of knowing that an account did not exist somewhere of exactly when the first Temple was built. A record that might later surface to prove the untruthfulness of their documentation of God's revealed word. It is equally unclear why they would create a record saying that Solomon, of all kings, built it. Why not name any of the later kings – if it wasn't Solomon why not use the King who really did build it?

Dever[20] provides more support for the veracity of the Biblical account for that period by way of Solomon's list of "administrative districts":

> And Solomon had twelve officers over all Israel, which provided victuals for the King and his household: each man his month in a year made provision.
>
> *1 Kings 4:7*

Professor Dever points out that the locations of traditional twelve tribes have largely been identified from archaeological artefacts, adding support for the quality of the ancient data.

Turning to the subject of our direct interest, the Temple at Jerusalem, William Dever is more insistent about the accuracy of the Bible. He points out that we now have archaeological evidence of contemporary Temples that replicate the Biblical description of the one at Jerusalem in every respect.

> The "Phoenician" derivation in Kings and Chronicles thus turns out to be quite correct; there was no native tradition of monumental architecture in Israel's earliest phases of urbanisation in Iron IIA [around 950 – 850 BCE], so models had to be borrowed from neighbouring peoples in the centuries-old Canaanite tradition.
>
> *William G. Dever*
> *What Did the Biblical Writers Know and When Did They Know It*

Dever also points out that the general construction technique for the Temple was used only during the 10th – 9th centuries BCE. This practice involved dressing the blocks of masonry at the quarry so they could then be assembled on-site. The Bible makes much of this method as the means by which the Temple construction site was a peaceful place:

> And the house, when it was in building, was built of stone made ready before it was brought thither: so that there was neither hammer nor axe nor any tool of iron heard in the house, while it was in building.
>
> *1 Kings 6:7*

It is now believed that these construction methods were brought to Canaan by the "Sea Peoples" who arrived in Canaan some one-hundred and fifty years before Solomon. Even the biblical description of cedar lining to the Temple has now been observed in buildings uncovered at Ebla and Hazor.

Finally, two bronze pillars, just like those placed at the entrance to King Solomon's Temple have also been found at other contemporary Temples in the region. The rest of the decoration, down to the cherubim is normal for the period. It is simply not possible that the biblical scribes could have known this, some three to four hundred years after the event, unless they had records or other data from E, J, P and D to inform them. Even if there were extant temples of similar design in the sixth century BCE, the Biblical scribes could not have known when they were built unless records existed.

This analysis forces us to look again at second of the conflicting pieces of data from above:

2. At the time of King Solomon, the argument for a combined monarchy is weak and Judaea was too poor to have financed the building of such a Temple.

Again, there are two possible explanations for the seeming contradiction and they are potentially interdependant.

1. King Solomon really was the ruler over the combined kingdom of Israel and Judaea and used the wealth of Israel to build the Temple at Jerusalem.
2. Some person or persons brought the wealth to Solomon that enabled him to build the Temple.

If we consider the first option, that King Solomon was the ruler over the combined kingdoms of Judaea and Israel. This would make the biblical record correct, and so we need to find an explanation as to how it happened contrary to the archaeological evidence. In this instance, the Bible is not helpful. The first King in the highland region of the Levant was Saul, who was from the tribe of Benjamin, and they had settled in the northern lands of Israel. Saul was predictably chosen because of his military prowess, but during a later war the Philistines killed his three sons in battle and Saul - mortally wounded - fell on his own sword. Around this time David - who had been an aide of Saul's but fell out with him and was forced to flee - was appointed King over Judaea. The Bible then reasonably states that Saul's young son, Ishbosheth, reigned in Israel under the guidance of General Abner. There followed a few skirmishes, then a major battle when David's men defeated the might of Israel. We are asked to accept that David defeated a nation with five times as many people as his kingdom, Judaea. The people of Israel then asked David to be their King as well as his being King of Judaea.

Now it is always dangerous to attempt to try and place oneself metaphorically into the ancient past, but to accept the biblical account of events does require a measure of suspension of disbelief. To transpose these events to modern times it would be rather like the USA going to Mexico and asking the Mexican President to also rule over the USA. Such a move is inconceivable especially for the reason that they could not find a suitable President from within their own ranks. This is not to deny that David ruled over a united Judaea and Israel. We simply point out that it would have needed something more than the fact that David was already a King and so "will do for us too". What is equally remarkable about this biblical account is that if, for the sake of debate, we accept that the biblical scribes invented the whole story, why on earth not make Saul the ruler over a united monarchy. There is no apparent reason to invent any of the above if you simply make the first king, Saul, a ruler over a combined Judaea and Israel. The biblical scribes had the option if they were in a creative mood, but chose to avoid it. Much more likely, surely, is that the scribes were diligently following what E, J, P and later D had recorded.

We will now turn to the second possibility, that person or persons unknown brought sufficient wealth to David or his son Solomon to somehow facilitate his rule over neighbouring Israel. If this wealth also came with a condition, that "a Temple to YHWH must be built at Jerusalem", then the plausibility of the biblical account improves.

So, whom might these "person or persons unknown" who brought wealth to David or Solomon be? The answer may well lie in an alternative possibility for the Exodus. We have already discussed the evidence of the archaeologists, which make clear why the Exodus could not have taken place. Even without this newfound knowledge, the Biblical account is incredible. The idea that 500,000 Israelite males – and that would add up to around 2 million souls when their wives and children are added – left Egypt is implausible. The total population of Egypt then was around 6 million and to have nearly half suddenly decamp would have brought economic chaos on an unprecedented scale. Despite this observation, Egyptian records - and they were extensive - make no mention of departing Israelites or of any other group of people. Then there is the curious fact that the Levites, the priestly family charged with looking after the tabernacle and then the Temple, were not given any land.

> The priests the Levites, and all the tribe of Levi, shall have no part nor inheritance with Israel: they shall eat the offerings of the Lord made by fire, and his inheritance.
>
> *Deuteronomy 18:1*

At first glance this appears a reasonable statement, but not when read with the earlier assertion that some 2 million Israelites left Egypt. There were twelve tribes who got the land plus the Levites and so statistically there should have been one thirteenth of this number who were Levites, or around 150,000 people. There is no way that one Temple, burning animal offerings from dawn until dusk, could feed 150,000 people; let alone house them. Much more likely, surely, is that a group of priests arrived in Jerusalem and somehow managed to persuade the king, David or Solomon, to let them build a Temple to their God. As latecomers they would not be able to take any land because all the workable land was already occupied. Anyway, if the proposition we are now exploring is correct then the arriving priests had no need for land, they had gold.

The next obvious question is "can we identify a group of people who meet the hypothesis we have just floated"? In fact there is, and they were the tomb builders of the pharaohs, whose daily lives are discussed in detail by Morris Bierbrier[24]. There was a village, just across the river from Karnak and Luxor, called *Deir el-Medina* that housed the workers who built the pharaohs' tombs in the nearby Valley-of-the-Kings. For the ancient Egyptians, death was a continuation of life, a concept that fits comfortably with Christianity even if Judaism is somewhat more ambivalent on the issue. The Internet online encyclopaedia of Judaism, at www.jewfaq.org describes "Olam Ha-Ba" - the afterlife - thus:

> Traditional Judaism firmly believes that death is not the end of human existence. However, because Judaism is primarily focused on life here and now rather than on the afterlife, Judaism does not have much dogma about the afterlife, and leaves a great deal of room for personal opinion. It is possible for an Orthodox Jew to believe that the souls of the righteous dead go to a place similar to the Christian heaven, or that they are reincarnated through many lifetimes, or that they simply wait until the coming of the messiah, when they will be resurrected. Likewise, Orthodox Jews can believe that the souls of the wicked are tormented by demons of their own creation, or that wicked souls are simply destroyed at death, ceasing to exist.
>
> *Internet online encyclopaedia of Judaism*

Although there is every reason to believe that earlier pharaohs had groups of workers to build their tombs, including pyramids, we have little detailed knowledge of their day-to-day lives, apart from possible locations of their villages. We are luckier with the inhabitants of *Deir el-Medina* since finding several undesecrated tombs of senior workmen containing many records of daily life in the village. The period for which we have this data is from around 1317 BCE, until around 1069 BCE, when Libyan raids and the Egyptian civil wars encouraged tomb robbing. The village probably existed earlier, from the reign of Thutmose I (circa 1500 BCE) continuously until the reign of Akhenaten (1352 – 1336 BCE). Akhenaten moved the whole construction unit to Akhetaten (El-Amarna) until his death when Tutankhamum moved them back to Thebes (Luxor). There are signs that the village was regularly expanded and rebuilt, probably during periods of relative inactivity on the mainstay of the village, tomb building. Bierbrier makes an interesting comment, in connection with Flinders Petrie's discovery of a workers complex that bears on the question of the Exodus:

> It cannot be emphasised too strongly that these men were not slaves but only temporary conscripts. Apart from domestic servants, slavery did not exist on a large-scale in Egypt: corvée labour [unpaid instead of taxation] made it unnecessary. Even the Hebrews in the Bible, who lived in Egypt over a thousand years after the pyramid age, were not slaves in the modern sense of the word.
>
> *Morris Bierbrier*
> *The Tomb Builders of the Pharaohs*

We know from these records uncovered at *Deir el-Medina*, that during the reign of Rameses II, some 48 men were working on his tomb and that this reduced to 32 when he died. During the short reign of Rameses IV the numbers of hands increased to 120, but on his death this number was halved. This suggests that when wives and children were added, the population of *Deir el-Medina* was around one hundred. While building a tomb the workers were split into two gangs, one for each side of the tomb and each gang had its own supervisor. New recruits usually came from the village, which clearly demonstrates that these were not corvée workers but full-time tomb-builders.

The workforce included stonemasons who carved the tomb and inscribed the messages found on many walls, carpenters, sculptors through to decorators who painted them and other illustrations to decorate the Temple and provide messages for the afterlife of the occupant. These skilled artisans would usually pass their skills on to their sons who would in time take over their duties. There were scribes who kept accounts and recorded every detail of work in the tombs and of village life and disputes. The senior workers even acted up as priests whenever the need arose. Although most of the furniture found in the tombs was made in the royal workshops, which were not located in the village, it was not unusual for the villages to become involved in this sort of work.

The occupants of *Deir el-Medina* can be seen to be self-sufficient, except in food production. The senior overseer would liaise directly with the pharaoh or his vizier, and was clearly a senior member of the royal establishment. All materials were called up and paid for from the treasury and accounted for in the permanent records. The village was served by men and women seconded from the central administration, and most likely corvée workers and slaves. These servants would cut wood, carry water, fish for food, keep the gardens tended and do the washing and other menial tasks. Life in the village appears to have been pretty good by the standards of the time and with all the usual squabbles that village life entails. So well organised was this workforce that they initiated the first ever recorded strike by a workforce. During the reign of Rameses III, around 1158 BCE, when food supplies had failed to arrive for twenty days the scribe Amennakhte was forced to go to the mortuary Temple of Horembeb to obtain rations for the workforce. But when the intermittent delays reached six months, the workers staged a sit-down strike in front of the Temples of Thutmose III and Rameses II. Although this strike brought the necessary response in the form of food rations, the lesson was not lost and strikes became an occasional feature of the life of the workers from the village.

Apart from the regular illnesses from their particular curse - scorpion bites - the villagers had time to indulge in some reading. The literary history of the village runs to over 1,500 published examples, of which the most numerous were "wisdom literature". This particular genre of creative writing offered moral precepts and advice from scribes, officials and pharaohs. Among the examples of popular stories, is one about an Egyptian political refugee called Sinuhe, who was an official of the pharaoh's harem, and whom we touched on in chapter 4. Sinuhe was visiting Libya when he heard of his pharaoh's assassination and decided to flee rather than return home. He appears to have got lost and ended up in Palestine where he wandered for several years until he was invited to settle in southern Syria. There he married the chieftain's eldest daughter and became a veritable patriarch in his own right. In time Sinuhe entertained emissaries from Egypt and eventually the pharaoh Sesostris I invited him to return to Egypt, which he did. In his native land, Sinuhe remarried and lived out his life comfortably in the Egyptian establishment. What makes this individual interesting, and the point we made in chapter 4, is that Sesostris I, was a 12th Dynasty pharaoh who lived around 1950 BCE, which is roughly the time when the Bible has Abraham in the same place. In other words, we have in Sinuhe a prototype for Abraham, and one who was in the right place at the right time, even down to his return to Egypt (the Bible has Abraham visiting Egypt).

Turning now to the religions of *Deir el-Medina*, there were several large Temples and the cliff face was dotted with chapels. The pharaohs of the eighteenth dynasty, who founded the village, were followers of Amun. This successful period, and in particular the Theban victory over the Hyksos ensured that Amun's stature and the wealth of Amun's Temples grew. The Egyptians favoured creating triads of gods to make "families" and Amun was no exception. The sky goddess and great divine mother, Mut (meaning mother), who may have originated either in the Nile delta or in Middle Egypt, became the "wife" of Amun. These two gods, together with the youthful god Khons, who was said to be Mut's son, formed the triad. Over the years, great wealth was lavished on the Temples of Amun to the point where they were able to absorb those of the god Re and transmogrify into Amen-Re. Amen-Re was the supreme god of Egypt at that time and his main Temple was in Karnak, just across the river Nile from the village. The village of *Deir el-Medina* had its own Temple to Amun and the stele found there are dedicated to Amun and Amen-Re.

Yet another, so far unmentioned coincidence of religious practices occurred at Karnak where a Temple oracle would converse with Amun and pass on the god's selection of those whom he wished to act as priests in his Temple. The Bible describes how Moses followed this process quite closely, when God chose Moses' brother Aaron to be the first of a hereditary line of priests. The Egyptian gods were also called on to make decisions, such as who was the rightful owner in property disputes. Some form of lot drawing or dice throwing must have been used to resolve such disputes. The Jewish high priest, using the Urim and the Thummin, apparently followed this practice. These two sacred lots, whose precise function is not known, were kept in the Ephod, a breast piece or pouch, which was part of the ceremonial dress of the high priest and worn outside the robe. The Ephod was probably held in place by a girdle and shoulder pieces.

The final years of *Deir el-Medina*, during which village life gradually disintegrated, is recorded in the personal letters of one of two scribes – Dhutmose and his son Butehamum. It is Dhutmose's letters that were found during the archaeological excavation of the village. The letters tell how the Theban area had become unsafe and so the workers moved for safety to the mortuary Temple of Rameses III at nearby Medinet Habu. Remarkably, work on the tomb, for Rameses XI was successfully completed, in spite of difficulties in supplies, including food. There were also shortages of labour due to conscription for the wars – both civil and against Libya - and by workers absconding to avoid conscription. At the very end, much of the work of the remaining supervisors and whatever workers they could muster, was repairing tombs that had been looted, and reburying the bodies that had occupied them. Other recovered letters show that Dhutmose died in around 1071 BCE, leaving his son more or less in charge of the workforce. There are signs that people visited the village during the period when the workers based themselves at Rameses Temple but soon it was completely abandoned. The discovery of *Deir el-Medina* can probably be attributed to two of Napoleon's engineers, Prosper Jolois and René Devilliers in 1799. It is known that at least two earlier European travellers passed through the valley without noticing the village. Statuettes and other relics from the village began to trickle onto the open market from around 1777 because of many private "digs". By 1820 excavations were initiated by various governments, French, British and Prussian to name a few.

At *Deir el-Medina* then, were a group of workers who had all the skills necessary to replicate anything that Moses and the Children of Israel did during the Exodus. They could readily have made an Ark of the Covenant, a tabernacle and provided the priests to administer them. This was a group of some of the best-educated people in Egypt at that time. Before they deserted the village for good, they knew where every pharaoh in the Valley of the Kings was buried and exactly what wealth was buried with them. Faced, as they were, with leaving the area and beginning a new life elsewhere, the temptation to make their next sojourn more comfortable was enormous. The sheer magnitude of the riches readily available to them placed an intolerable level of inducement before them. It has to be said, though, that prior to the abandonment, there is little evidence of tomb robbing by the villagers. Records do exist of the trials of various workmen and foremen for theft from the tombs under construction, but that proves nothing other than occasionally men succumb to temptation. During the last months, when tomb robbing had become endemic there is, however, evidence of involvement by the community. Around 1110 BCE, six workers and two deputies were arrested for robbing the tomb of Queen Isis, and valuables recovered from their houses. It is probable the workmen were executed. One thing is certain and that is that during the last days of *Deir el-Medina* several of the tombs of the pharaohs buried in the Valleyy of the Kings were desecrated and the contents looted. Our knowledge of the value of the ornaments that were buried with Tutankhamun provides a tantalising sample of the potential treasure in the other tombs.

Here then was a skilled community with nothing to deter them from leaving Egypt. This was a community with all the necessary skills and potential wealth to give them great bargaining leverage. They could certainly have negotiated with King David or Solomon to build a lavish Temple in the remote town of Jerusalem.

If, as we are speculating, they did remove some of the tomb treasures, then undoubtedly the refugees from *Deir el-Medina* did not make their way directly to Jerusalem from Egypt. If they had indeed indulged in some tomb robbing they would have wanted to find suitable places to bury their ill-gotten gains, it was after all evidence against them if they were later apprehended. It is surely likely that they would have selected a remote oasis - why not in the Sinai region - where they could devise a new way of life, one that would keep them all together. They had after all lived as a community for centuries. They would want a location where few would link them back to Egypt and a small hilltop town called

Jerusalem would have been appealing. They needed new identities and so new occupations were required. Doubtless they had cast envious eyes at the Egyptian priesthood over the years and this was a career for which they already had all the necessary skills. As they sojourned at an oasis in the desert, they would doubtless have sent out small parties of men to explore the surrounding lands for a suitable final resting-place for them all. Compared to their years of digging tombs into desert cliff-sides and the ever-present scorpions, Jerusalem would have looked like heaven.

To begin their new life as priests they needed a new religion, nothing that would link them with Egypt. They needed a local ruler who would welcome gold in exchange for allowing them to settle in his lands and they needed somewhere that did not have too strong an affinity to any existing religion. Jerusalem met all of these needs. If this community, of perhaps one hundred souls, does make up the biblical Exodus, then it is easy to see why they chose not to include an afterlife in their new religion. They had after all seen first-hand that nothing happens to the dead when left alone for hundreds of years. The similarity between early Jahwehism and Atenism is too close simply to be disregarded as coincidence. Over three centuries before, pharaoh Akhenaten had decreed that Aten was to be the only god and closed the other Temples, including those to the death-god Osiris. This knowledge would probably have appealed to a group of "escaping" tomb builders. This must, surely, have raised Aten to a high position on their list of preferred religions.

We have suggested above that a group of skilled refugees from Egypt, led by a man whom we can call Moses, arrived at Jerusalem. We have further suggested that they sought from King David or Solomon permission to build an elaborate Temple to a new monotheistic God, YHWH. We cannot know whether the choice of YHWH was a new name or whether there was already in existence a god named YHWH whom the newcomers appropriated and developed. The reason why we cannot know is because we have already suggested that the pre-first-millennium BCE, biblical account is unreliable. We have also pointed out that this group could have been the community of tomb builders from *Deir el-Medina*. It is equally true to say that priests from one or more of the nearby temples might have joined them in their mini-exodus. It is equally true to say that other similar groups of Egyptians, whether priests or some other communities might equally fit the circumstances just described. The important element of our thesis is that this group was small, perhaps one or two hundred people, were skilled artisans and were laden with gold.

The first Temple at Jerusalem is described as an elaborately decorated Temple, lined with gold. This inevitably meant that the group who arrived with the request to build it must have had great wealth. They would not, of course, have carried that quantity of gold with them rather, as we have suggested above they would have buried it at various locations for later recovery when needed. There were after all no banks or depositories in those days. They would most likely have had a record of the locations, suitable encoded, much on the lines of the copper scroll discovered at Qumran with the other Dead Sea Scrolls. Indeed, it is possible that the copper scroll from Qumran is the actual record of burial sites of gold and other valuables brought out of Egypt by the mini-exodus group of escaping tomb builders.

There is one feature of the biblical account that supports the idea that the Temple priesthood began around the time of King Solomon. This is the concentration on the word Zadok, which was the name of the high priest who anointed King Solomon. Zadok is almost synonymous with Cohen, the modern family name of the sons-of Aaron and so holds an important place in this inquiry, and Zadok the priest was contemporaneous with Kings David and Solomon.

So far, what we have suggested is speculation. What we need in order to "firm-up" this proposition is some scientific evidence to set the Jerusalem temple priesthood, the sons-of-Aaron, the Cohanim, apart from the general Jewish population. We need something to show that they have a different genetic makeup to the rest of the Jews. Remarkably, such evidence is available. An article in the July 1998, edition of the science magazine Nature, entitled Origins of Old Testament priests provides strong support for our proposition. The researchers for this paper examined the DNA on the male Y chromosome, which is unaltered in each transmission: [appendix A provides a brief explanation of the genetic process during reproduction]. Mark Thomas, Karl Skoreckiad, Haim Ben-Amid, Tudor Parfitt, Neil Bradman and David Goldstein, from Universities in the U.K. and Israel, co-wrote this paper that holds some remarkable conclusions.

> According to Jewish tradition, following the Exodus from Egypt, males of the tribe of Levi, of which Moses was a member, were assigned special religious responsibilities, and male descendants of Aaron, his brother, were selected to serve as Priests (Cohanim). To the extent that patrilineal inheritance has been followed since sometime around the Temple period [from roughly 3,000 to 2,000 years before present], Y chromosomes of present-day Cohanim and Levites should not only be distinguishable from those of other Jews, but – given the dispersion of the priesthood following the Temple's destruction – they should derive from a common ancestral type no more recently than the Temple period. Here we show that although Levite Y chromosomes are diverse, Cohen chromosomes are homogeneous. We trace the origin of Cohen chromosomes to about 3,000 years before present, early during the Temple period.
>
> *Mark Thomas et al*
> *Origins of Old Testament Priests*

The Origins of Old Testament priests researchers based their findings on the results of the genetic analysis of 306 male Jews from Israel, the U.K. and Canada. They found that, for a particular "modal haplotype" or cluster of juxtaposed genes for Ashkenazic and Sephardic Cohanim Jews, the frequency is 0.449 and 0.561 respectively. That is to say, around half of all male Cohanim exhibited the same cluster of adjacent genes, a remarkable percentage. Ashkenazic Jews derive from those of the Diaspora who travelled around the north coast of the Mediterranean Sea and settled in Germany and adjoining countries. Sephardic Jews travelled along the north coast of Africa, settling along the way. Many Sephardic Jews then crossed the Mediterranean Sea to colonise Spain. Despite this huge geographical distance between the two groups, there is little difference in the research results.

They show that some half of the men tested for both groups had the same cluster of genes. This compares with results for the rest of the Jewish male population of 0.132 and 0.098 or roughly one-in-ten.

The researchers also concluded that the Levites, their description for the general Jewish population, are not patrilineal descendants of a "paternally related tribal group". Conversely, the Cohen family group appear to have gone to considerable lengths to preserve a patrilineal bloodline that pre-dates the split of the Diaspora into Ashkenazic and Sephardic groupings and survives in both groups to this day. The use of the term "Levites" for the general Jewish population is confusing, the Bible makes it clear that the Levite tribe were the Temple priesthood family, the Cohanim:

> And the anger of the Lord was kindled against Moses, and he said, is not Aaron the Levite thy brother? I know that he can speak well. And also, behold, he cometh forth to meet thee: and when he seeth thee, he will be glad in his heart.
>
> *Exodus 4:14*

The researchers put the date of coalescence - or origin - of the particular cluster of genes that they tested for, at between around 2,650 and 3,180 years ago. This places the timescale somewhere between the Biblical Exodus from Egypt and the destruction of King Solomon's Temple by the Babylonians in 586 BCE .

If the *Deir el-Medina* community were the original Cohanim, the biblical descendants of Aaron, then it would explain the differences between a Cohanim "Y" chromosome and that of a non-Cohen Jew. The *Deir el-Medina* community had lived in Egypt for hundreds of years while the archaeological evidence suggests that the local residents of the southern Levant highlands were mostly indigenous Canaanites. It is not difficult to speculate how some Cohanim "Y" chromosome markers were transmitted into the non-Cohen population. Over a period of three thousand years, there will have been many relationships between Cohen males and non-Cohen females, both legitimate and illegitimate. The occasional marriage between a low ranked (not able to secure a job in the Temple complex) *Deir el-Medina* (Cohanim) male and a Levite female was possible as were adulterous liaisons. Either of these routes would result in the Cohanim Y chromosome markers transferring to the non-Cohen male population.

Our suggestion of a small group of Egyptians arriving in Jerusalem would also explain why Moses needed someone to speak for him, because he couldn't speak a word of Hebrew. The Bible version of using Aaron to speak for Moses does not of course fit this explanation because Aaron, as Moses elder brother, was also Egyptian, but we have earlier poured cold water on the likelihood of Aaron being available at all to Moses.

Finally, if we take the latest date for which we have records of the village, 1070 BCE, and allow a period of ten years while they prepared to leave we have 1060 BCE, as the approximate date when the residents of *Deir el-Medina* left their village behind for good. If we then add the forty years spent in the desert, we arrive at the date of 1020 BCE. This is sufficiently close to the reign of King David, bearing in mind the variation in dates suggested for his reign. We are certainly within a decade or so and undoubtedly David would have had time to use the wealth brought by the arriving Egyptians to secure his united kingdom over Judaea and Israel. This done, it follows that the timing allows for his son Solomon to preside over the building or completion of the Temple at Jerusalem to YHWH.

The Origins of Old Testament priests research tells us two things:

1. The Temple priesthood, or Cohanim, had a different genetic make-up from the rest of the Jews.
2. The Cohanim have preserved their bloodline carefully until the present day.

These research conclusions are completely in keeping with the archaeological findings discussed in chapter 4, that the highlands of the Southern Levant were populated by Canaanites. They also support the notion that the Cohanim were not Canaanites but rather immigrants from another region. Indeed, this research supports the Biblical story that the Exodus people came from Egypt.

Item 1 above is the focus of our research at this time, but item 2, is also a remarkable observation that we will return to later.

We now have scientific evidence to support the idea of a much smaller Exodus, the arrival in Jerusalem of a small group of outsiders. This group could have had sufficient gold – or access to that gold – to facilitate the building of a Temple to YHWH. But what about the period immediately preceding this event, how does the archaeological reality match the Biblical report?

The indications, both biblical and archaeological, are that the earlier period of a loose tribal confederation (biblical Judges) was to everyone's liking but societies seldom exist in isolation for long. As the turn of the first millennium BCE, approached, the visible threat from the neighbouring states of Philistia and Samaria forced a rethink. The time had come for a monarchy and, as usual throughout history, "come the hour cometh the man" – this time in the person of Saul who was a Benjaminite. We can be reasonably confident that the normal accumulation of wealth flowed to the centre of the new Hebrew nation just as with other monarchies. Saul's home in Gebeah, just north of Jerusalem, has recently been excavated and signs of wealth are evident. Gebeah has the earliest example of a significant building so far discovered. Saul's reign turned out to be quite short, and after only eight years he committed suicide rather than be captured by the Philistines in a battle at Mount Gilboa.

> Then said Saul unto his armour-bearer, Draw thy sword, and thrust me through therewith; lest these uncircumcised come and thrust me through, and abuse me. But his armour-bearer would not; for he was sore afraid. Therefore Saul took a sword, and fell upon it.
>
> *1 Samuel 31:4*

The next King was David (circa 1010 – 970), who had been at Saul's court but he fell foul of Saul and had to escape to Philistia. After Saul's death David composed the famous eulogy, which begins:

> Thy glory, O Israel, is slain upon thy high places! How are the mighty fallen!
>
> *2 Samuel 1:4*

According to the Bible, it was David - noted warrior and slayer of Goliath that he was - who first united the twelve tribes of Israel and then looked outwards to extend his borders. The first major city to fall to David and his mercenaries was the purportedly heavily fortified Jebusite city of Jerusalem, and this is where he built his palace. This was before he became King of Israel. The knowledge that David gathered to his side mercenaries provides a glimpse of the possibility that he had obtained funds from somewhere, clearly his earnings as a shepherd would not have allowed such extravagance.

> And every one that was in distress, and every one that was in debt, and every one that was discontented, gathered themselves unto him [David]; and he became a captain over them: and there were with him about four hundred men.
>
> *1 Samuel 22:2*

However, Jerusalem was in Judaea where David was supposed to be King before he became King of Israel and so the biblical account is becoming confusing. If Jerusalem was excluded from Judaea then this kingdom had only around half the 9,000 people that we have assumed so far (see phase 5 in chapter 4). 4,500 people allows for around 900 adult males available as warriors. We can see from the extract from 1 Samuel 22:2 above, that David had only 400 men and this means that half of the male population of Judaea joined him on the battlefield. This is not an impossible number, especially if the women covered for guarding the sheep and goats, and so our archaeological evidence is actually supporting the Biblical version.

What is wholly improbably, though, is that 400 men could defeat a nation with 9,000 men available to fight. This in an age when weaponry was restricted to swords and spears, in other words one fighting man was about equal to any other one fighting man. The side with the most men would usually win. According to the Bible, David had now extended the state of Israel to include Judaea to the south and he promptly proclaimed Jerusalem as the capital city, the "city of David". He brought the Ark of the Covenant and the tabernacle to Jerusalem and made a vow to build a Temple to house the Ark. The reigns of David and his son Solomon were thus in every respect the zenith of the Jewish state.

David ruled for forty years, which looks suspiciously like the expected lifespan of those times, but is was the manner of his succession that is most curious. From his eight wives David had at least nineteen sons. Ammon, the eldest son was murdered on the orders of another son Absalom who attempted and almost succeeded with a coup d"etat. David recovered his position and Absalom was killed. Another pretender, the prince Adonijah was successfully diverted. The court prophet, Nathan, then helped Bathsheba – one of David's wives – to persuade David to appoint their son, Solomon, as co-regent. David died shortly after this event and Solomon swiftly eliminated any other claimants to the crown, beginning with Adonijah. The particular priest, who was in charge of the Tabernacle at the time that Solomon was proclaimed King was Zadok:

> And Zadok the priest took an horn of oil out of the tabernacle, and anointed Solomon. And they blew the trumpet; and all the people said, God save King Solomon.
>
> *1 Kings 1:39*

From this time the Temple priests were known as "sons of Zadok" or Zadokites:

> But the priests the Levites, the sons of Zadok, that kept the charge of my sanctuary when the children of Israel went astray from me, they shall come near to me to minister unto me, and they shall stand before me to offer unto me the fat and the blood, saith the Lord God:
>
> *Ezekiel 44:15*

There is no doubt therefore, that the "sons of Zadok" are Aaron's Levite dynasty and the same as our <u>Origins of Old Testament</u>

Priests researchers' Cohanim. To avoid confusion we will continue to use the term "Cohanim" to cover the priesthood. The introduction – in historical terms – of the word Zadok to describe the Temple priesthood can be explained in much the same manner as the appendage "Christ" is applied to Jesus. Just as Christ means "messiah" so "zadok" means "righteous". The absence of vowels in ancient written Hebrew produces various phonetic variations on zadok. For example, we find the names of certain people, such as Melchizedek – the priest and King of Salem (the early name of Jerusalem) of Abraham's time – having zadok, zadik or zedek appended to their names.

The introduction of Melchizedek suggests that the Zadokite order predated Solomon's priest, Zadok. Indeed the verses clearly tell us that the order predated Aaron and stretched back at least to the time of Abraham, who met Melchizedek. This is entirely consistent with the suggestion that among the people who travelled to Jerusalem, perhaps from *Deir el-Medina*, was an ancient priesthood family from which the Jerusalem high priests were chosen and which included Moses. All of this corroborates the notion that the Zadokite family tradition, or Cohanim, didn't really get established until the Temple priest, Zadok, anointed Solomon as King. The idea certainly has a certain authentic feel to it, and supports our earlier claim that the dispersal, or so-called "exodus" of the villagers of *Deir el-Medina* took place around the time of David.

Earlier we conjectured that the *Deir el-Medina* people might have spent some years at a desert oasis. It would be a perfectly normal action to convince them that they were not being followed in consequence of any tomb robbing that they may have committed. Such a period in the desert would have certainly have made dynastic control and record keeping more difficult. It is after all much easier to slip under the side of a tent in the dark for the caresses of an unsatisfied wife, than to wander through the streets under the watchful eyes of the neighbours. Such behaviour could explain a specific date from when the Cohen family began to preserve their identity. It also provides a reason why the "dynasty" was more fluid before that time.

The Origins of Old Testament priests researchers put the date of coalescence of the particular cluster of genes that they tested for, at between around 2,650 and 3,180 years ago. This gives an average date of 2,915 years ago, and that would have been around 910 BCE, very close to the 970 BCE, when Zadok anointed Solomon. It would, though, be wrong to read much into these coincident dates, based as they are on genetics research. Genetic statistics can only provide a very rough estimate on dates. Equally, we cannot be sure of exactly how the Zadokite role of high priest was passed from father to son. It is our view that the guidance given in Deuteronomy, of favouring the first-born son, is the most likely method:

> If a man have two wives, one beloved, and another hated, and they have born him children, both the beloved and the hated; and if the firstborn son be hers that was hated:
>
> Then it shall be, when he maketh his sons to inherit that which he hath, that he may not make the son of the beloved firstborn before the son of the hated, which is indeed the firstborn:
>
> *Deuteronomy 21:15 – 16*

We do now know, from the research described above, that for something like 3,000 years the Cohanim have been very careful, and the adjective "careful" is well applied, to marry within a strict definition of the family group. During the Temple period, there was a good reason for this genealogical prudence. The role of high priest, the most senior Judaic religious individual, was probably determined by the rule of primogenitor or first-born son. It was a dynastic role that was nearly on an equal footing with the monarchy and indeed for long periods replaced the monarchy. To make the issue of preserving the genealogy arguably even more important, any other male issue, from successive high priests, were awarded the supporting jobs in the Temple. The Cohen family was thus guaranteed full employment in the second - sometimes first - most privileged positions in the community. This was no small prize and one that more than warranted some care and attention over whom they could marry. That the Cohanim should have taken the necessary care and attention while the Temple existed is easy to explain. That they have continued to preserve this arrangement, after the destruction of the Herodian Temple until the present time, is less easy to account for.

Once again we need to recap on where we are in this enquiry. We have identified part of Jewish history – the Exodus – that modern archaeological findings tell us could not have happened as recorded in the Bible. Then there is the construction of a Temple in Jerusalem by a community of around 4,000 souls living at the very margins of existence. There is also the Biblical evidence that Solomon at least was not completely sold on monotheism.

> For Solomon went after Ashtoreth the goddess of the Zidonians, and after Milcom the abomination of the Ammonites.
>
> And Solomon did evil in the sight of the Lord, and went not fully after the Lord, as did David his father.
>
> Then did Solomon build an high place for Chemosh, the abomination of Moab, in the hill that is before Jerusalem, and for Molech, the abomination of the children of Ammon.
>
> *1King 11:5-7*

It is one thing to say that something could not have happened based on modern research but it is another matter completely to question the Bible. Before dismissing the case for an Exodus we can at least attempt to find a more plausible explanation for the events that we know did occur. This is necessarily speculation and we must be careful to recognise that fact. What we are suggesting is certainly plausible and offers an explanation for events that are otherwise difficult to explain.

We are suggesting the possible arrival in Jerusalem of a group of people who offered to build a gold lined Temple and make Kings David and his son Solomon wealthy. This proposition not only explains the existence of the Temple in Jerusalem, it would also have provided either King with the collateral to buy the mercenaries to create a united monarchy. We must bear in mind that during the period of the biblical united-monarchy, the archaeological evidence is that although Israel was growing and was wealthier than Judaea, the whole hilltop region was still poor. Gold, given to either monarch, would have bought mercenaries, weapons and chariots as well as stone defences for the strategically important towns. Indeed, force may not have been necessary. The sight of David or Solomon approaching Israel laden with gold and offering to enrich a united region was an offer that Israel would have found hard to refuse. To repeat the obvious, this group of latecomers – from Egypt – is only supposition but it is attractive in that it provides credible answers for several previously far-fetched Biblical assertions.

Having proposed a possible solution to the many biblical imponderables, we must now explore alternative candidates for the group of latecomers. The most obvious, and one who has been suggested before, is Akhenaten. Certainly as the reigning pharaoh over Egypt he would have had access to enough gold to meet all the needs for Temple building and the "purchase" of a united monarchy over the highlands of the southern Levant. Jerusalem would also have offered Akhenaten a home to satisfy his wish to worship his sun-god, Aten, away from the hostility of the supplanted Egyptian priesthood of the earlier pantheon of gods.

Dr. Kate Spence maintains, on the BBC history website, that Akhenaten died in the seventeenth year of his reign, around 1336 BCE. However, to this day no sign has been found of Akhenaten's mummy and this allows for conjecture. The problem for Akhenaten as the putative Moses is one of dating. Akhenaten reigned from 1352 to 1336 BCE, and this is at least 300 years too soon to fit our theory. We have already well made the point that this earlier Exodus did not occur, whether it was Moses or Akhenaten. For Akhenaten to have taken some of his wealth to the hilltop region of the southern Levant and built a Temple in 1336 BCE is unsustainable. There is no evidence of this archaeologically, but then there is no archaeological evidence of Solomon's Temple either. The biggest problem with this earlier date is that it is too soon for the construction methods used. They were unavailable at that time. It is probable that the Aten priests, perhaps led by a relative of Akhenaten's, considered emigration when Akhenaten's son-in-law Tutankhamun returned Egypt to polytheism and closed the Temples to Aten. The same argument, on dating, applies also to these disillusioned priests as for Akhenaten

In point of fact, the idea that an exodus occurred, but not as described in the Bible, has been explored before. Several authors have speculated on the nationality and background of Moses, and perhaps the most eminent of these was the psychiatrist Sigmund Freud. Freud[29] noted that "Moses" is an abridgement of the complete names of several pharaohs – such as Ah*mose* (meaning Ah-a-child), Thut*mose* and Ramses (Ra-*mose*) and concluded that the biblical Moses was an Egyptian. Freud suggests that Moses' father undoubtedly prefixed "*mose*" with the name of a god, such as Ptah or Amon, but that this element was lost in common use. Freud also points out that the final "s" in "Moses" was added during the Greek translations because it does not appear in the Hebrew version, which is "*Mosheh*". Freud continued his analysis by observing that the "origins of Moses" legend, that of being cast adrift by his mother in a wicker basket and then found by pharaoh's daughter, is a reversal of a common theme. The more usual version, adopted for Sargon of Agade, Cyrus the Great and Romulus of Rome is of a high-born child falling on hard times and being brought up in lowly surroundings. Inevitably the natural talents of the subject of the legend shine through and he attains greatness. Freud argues the legend of Moses upbringing had, necessarily, to be of either Hebrew or Egyptian origin and it made no sense for the Egyptians to so lionise Moses – he is after all not mentioned in Egyptian records. The Hebrews on the contrary, had every reason to hold Moses up as a hero, but could not concede to his birthright without admitting that the man who brought them their religion was an Egyptian. Hence the reversal of the usual legend, to show low-born origins for Moses.

Freud compared the polytheism of the Egyptians to the monotheism of the Jews and conceded that this was a problem. The mismatch of religions could only be corrected for one short pharaonic period, the reign of Akhenaten. Freud noted that Akhenaten's religion was monotheistic as is Judaism. It is common to confuse the worship of Aten with the sun-gods Horus, Re and Amon-re. Atenism, however, was not the "worship of the sun as a material object but as a symbol of a divine being whose energy was manifested in his rays". Another likeness between Atenism and early Judaism is that there was no acknowledgement of an afterlife.

> We were astonished – and rightly so – that the Jewish religion did not speak of anything beyond the grave, for such a doctrine is reconcilable with the strictest monotheism. This astonishment disappears if we go back from the Jewish religion to the Aton (sic) religion and surmise that this feature was taken over from the latter, since for Ikhnaton (sic) it was necessary in fighting the popular religion, where the death-god Osiris played perhaps a greater part than any god of the upper regions.
>
> *Sigmund Freud*
> *Moses and Monotheism*

Freud also cited circumcision and the dislike of swine as uniquely Egyptian practices in the region in those days. The question of circumcision has been confirmed by examination of mummies as well as Temple inscriptions. He continued to support his case by pointing out that the Bible mentions Moses' speech impediment to explain why his brother Aaron should accompany him to Egypt to speak to pharaoh. If Moses was an Egyptian he would have had difficulty in communicating with the Hebrews on the highlands of the southern Levant. Freud then quotes from *Mose und seine Bedeutung für die israelitisch-jüdische Religionsgenschichte*, a 1922 book by Ernst Sellin. This discusses how Sellin found in the book of the Prophet Hosea distinct traces of a tradition to the effect that Moses met a violent end during a rebellion of his "stubborn and refractory people". It is perhaps fitting to mention now, that when Freud wrote his three essays on this subject, it was perceived wisdom that the Exodus was an historical event. It was during the biblical account of the Exodus that Freud suggested that Moses obtained the original name Jahve (sic). Basing his writing on E. Meyer's *Die Israeliten und ihre Nachbarstämme,* Freud asserts that Moses discovered Jahve – a volcano god - from the Midianite priest, Jethro. Freud also suggests that Jethro was not as suggested in the Bible at mount Sinai, but at an oasis called Meribat-Qadeš. The suggestion is, that it is the deep and loud sound that volcanoes make as they erupt that provide the etymology of the name that was subsequently transliterated into (Jahweh) YHWH.

Freud remarks how JHWH is a fusion of the fierce Arabian god Jahve and the Egyptian Aten, and how by introducing the patriarchs into the story, Judaism is provided with roots into their own history. He also suggests, more provocatively, that it is not so much God who has selected the Jews to be His chosen people, but rather Moses who did the choosing. In the third, and last of Freud's essays, he analyses his findings just discussed, in a psychological context. As such, his essay moves too closely to theology for consideration in this book.

One of the first popular authors to explore Moses' antecedents was Ahmed Osman[30], and he drew the conclusion that Akhenaten and Moses were one and the same man. Another author, Ralph Ellis[31], extended the theories by equating the Jewish patriarchs with northern Egyptian pharaohs from the time that this area was ruled by the Hyksos. Ellis finds likenesses in the names of pharaohs to the patriarchs Abraham and Joseph sufficiently close to identify them as the same people. Ellis unfortunately makes the mistake of accepting Josephus' interpretation of Hyksos as meaning "shepherd", which provides a link through Judaism to Christianity. The term "Hyksos" was first used by the Egyptian historian Manetho at around 300 BCE, and Josephus, who was keen to show the antiquity of the Jews made the wrong translation, which Ellis then unwittingly used. Scholars are now agreed that Hyksos actually means "foreign" to show that the Hyksos pharaohs were not native Egyptians. They were a group of mixed Semitic-Asiatic invaders who successfully colonised northern Egypt in the 18th century BCE, and seized power around 1630 BCE. The Hyksos ruled northern Egypt until 1521 BCE, when the southern Egyptian pharaoh, Ahmose, finally expelled them. They had ruled over lower-Egypt for some 109 years.

What Ellis did do was to build on Osman's list of similarities between Judaism and Atenism to produce an extensive list:

a. The god of Akhenaten was called Aton (sic). The god of the Israelites was called Adonai. As the "t" and the "d" are interchangeable in Egyptian, the Israelite god could be called Atonai.
b. In the Talmud, the wife of Moses is called Adonith, which can be translated into Egyptian as Aton-it. Joseph's wife had a similar name, that of Asenath, a Phoenician god.
c. Akhenaton (sic) promoted a single god without an image, as did the Israelites.
d. The Ark of the Covenant bears more than a striking resemblance to the Ark of Tutankhamen. Tutankhamen was the last of the Amarna pharaohs.
e. The Israelites were commanded to make an altar that was not hewn with any tool, nor had steps leading up to it. The great altar of Karnak was made with the upper surface being of unhewn crystal and neither it nor the altars in the other Temples had steps before them.
f. The wearing of earrings was common in Egypt, and in the royal family it designated a prince who was not of the bloodline and could not become a pharaoh. Many of the Israelites used to wear earrings but were commanded not to when they reached Jerusalem.
g. The Egyptian priesthood had dietary prohibitions and ritual ablutions that were similar to those of Judaism.
h. The Egyptian priesthood had shaven heads. Although Celtic priests also sported shaven heads, other Christian priests altered this to a tonsure, which is similar to a Jewish yarmulke, or skullcap. Rabbis often sport a shaven forehead.
i. Orthodox Jews often wear long, curled side-locks of hair. In Egypt exactly this fashion denoted a young man – the uninitiated.
j. The symbol of the cross (in Christianity) is an Egyptian symbol. The Egyptian cross, the Ankh, was promoted by

Akhenaton into a major part of his theology where it symbolised life or the resurrection.

k. Christian churches are orientated towards east, as was the mobile Israelite Temple, the tabernacle. Similarly, all the Temples at Amarna face towards the rising sun.
l. Circumcision had been an early Egyptian custom and the ceremony is depicted in many Egyptian texts.
m. The carrying of religious shrines around the town or city was a common festival event in Egypt ... this same rite is still practised in many Catholic countries.
n. From Tuthmoses through Yuya to the Ramesside pharaohs of the nineteenth dynasty, the pharaohs typically display the long aquiline nasal phenotype, a feature typical of the Jewish race.

Ralph Ellis
Last of the Pharaohs

Ellis[31] supports his "Hyksos were shepherd-kings" thesis by drawing a time comparison with the astrological signs that various stars outline in the sky. He states that from 4,500 BCE, the star sign rising at the spring equinox was Taurus the Bull, and uses this - probably correctly - to explain the importance of the Apis Bulls in ancient Egypt. Ellis noted that in 1850 BCE, Taurus gave way to Aries the Ram and so opened the door religiously to the Shepherd kings. The twelve astrological star signs do indeed move through a 26,000-year cycle caused by the earth's wobble, known as precession, which takes this time to complete one 360° wobble. Ralph Ellis may be correct in his calculation of 1850 BCE, as the date when Taurus gave way to Aries. However, these calculations are supposition without the knowledge of where the ancients considered the boundaries of each constellation to be. All we have to go on are the stars that make up the constellation and a name. Therefore even a slight variation in where the limits are drawn means a variation of hundreds of years between the assumed change and the actual change from Taurus to Aries.

One final question mark that hangs over Ellis' work is that he asserts the pharaoh Akhenaten was isolated at Akhetaten (modern-day El-Amarna) and largely ignored by the rest of Egypt. This assertion is to some extent contradicted by the Amarna tablets that cover extensive correspondence between the royal palace and the rulers of adjacent lands such as Canaan. The obsequiousness of the various rulers to their suzerain pharaoh is not indicative of a pharaoh under threat in his homeland.

Another popular author, Robert Feather[32], who has decoded the copper scroll found at Qumran to identify the hiding places for substantial quantities of gold, also spends some time considering the origins of the Jews. Feather suggests that both "Aten" and "Jahweh" are two syllable words and that "Aten" transliterates to "Jati" which is not dissimilar to Jahweh. He also offers an alternative theory to "habiru" as the origin of the word "Hebrew", pointing out that the Egyptian word "khepru", which is also phonetically similar to "Hebrew", relates to the sun as the "soul of the high god". As well as these linguistic possibilities, Feather adds that the cherubim who guard the Ark of the Covenant are simply [winged] sphinxes. His thesis in this area is that after the death of Akhenaten and the move back to polytheism by Tutankhamen, the Aten priests went into exile at Elephantine Island and On (Heliopolis). Some one hundred and fifty years later, Moses, a prince became interested in Atenism and bought the freedom of the Aten priests and their descendants – who were assumed to be slaves – and took them to Canaan.

Having taken a short "Cook's tour" through some of the more popular theories of the alternative Exodus or origins for the Jews, the question remains. It is clear that none of these alternatives fit all the available data – both Biblical and independent – better than our *Deir el-Medina* community. Our proposed community meet all the genetic, biblical and archaeological requirements that would allow the Bible to be accepted as more or less correct from the time of King Solomon. We do indeed have an exodus of a - now small - group of people from Egypt under the leadership of someone who may well have been named Moses. We are also suggesting, along with others, that the date of the Exodus be moved forward some 400 years or so, to the time of kings David and Solomon. We have also offered an alternative life for Moses, not as the foster child of a pharaoh's daughter but rather an overseer or priest or scribe. Although these suggestions will doubtless offend those whose beliefs include biblical inerrancy, until this point there is little that should antagonise a curious Christian or Jew. It is the next presumption that should ease any foreboding in these groups.

According to the Bible, at an early stage of the Exodus, God made Himself known to Moses. He gave Moses the commandments and instructions on how to build a container that would become His point of contact with the human race. It is almost impossible to overstate the importance that this event had on the development of the western world. How we behave and how we think are in no small part a result of the commandments which God gave to Moses. It is hard to imagine a responsibility greater than that of safeguarding the Ark of the Covenant and its contents, the commandments we have just mentioned. The Ark was God's seat on earth and the place where He visited whenever He had a message for humanity, and so unsurprisingly Moses appointed his brother Aaron to this important task. To be more precise that decision was given to Moses by God:

> And take thou unto thee Aaron thy brother, and his sons with him, from among the children of Israel, that he may minister unto me in the priest's office, even Aaron, Nadab and Abihu, Eleazar and Ithamar, Aaron's sons.
>
> *Exodus 28:1*

> And I will sanctify the tabernacle of the congregation, and the altar: I will sanctify also both Aaron and his sons, to minister to me in the priest's office.
>
> *Exodus 29:44*

In identifying the *Deir el-Medina* community, or rather the remnants left when the village was finally abandoned, as possible candidates for the Exodus, we are not excluding other contemporary and similar groups. It is also part of this proposition that the group leader, and we shall continue to call him Moses, may have had an encounter with God exactly as the Bible states. Our variance from the biblical account is that we have moved the dates forward by around 400 years, reduced the numbers dramatically and offered an alternative group to the Israelite slaves put forward in the Bible. In other words, we have provided a model that fits the archaeological evidence, together with a group of real people who also fit the model.

Modern appraisement of the first high priest, Aaron, seems, unsurprisingly, to reflect the standing of whoever is giving the opinion. The Talmud and Midrash being Jewish guidance writings representing the combined wisdom of rabbis over the years, treat Aaron as a leading personality rather than any form of symbol. The rabbis appear as alternative religious leaders around the time of the Babylonian captivity and so this is understandable. The Temple priests had been taken into captivity leaving a vacuum of religious leadership in both Babylon and Israel. These alternative views on Aaron probably reflect the intellectual struggle that continued for generations after the return of the Jews - including the descendants of the Temple priesthood - from their Babylonian captivity. The battle for the religious hearts and minds of the Jewish people began when the returning priesthood naturally wished to exert their birthright as religious leaders of the Jews and the rabbis were doubtless reluctant to give up the role.

As we have just seen in the quotes from Exodus, God directed that the role of chief priest was to look after the Tabernacle and its important contents. With this command, He marked the defining moment when the Cohanim dynasty was founded. Aaron and his later male descendants would be solely responsible for guarding the tabernacle and its sacred contents including the Ark of the Covenant. This must have been the "theological trigger" that caused the Cohanim to embark on a stratagem of genetic isolation, identified from the Origins of Old Testament priests which we earlier discussed.

There is, though, our alternative explanation, based on the *Deir el-Medina* community, that Moses and his brother Aaron were foreigners in Judaea. In this case the question of the upper limit date identified by the researchers for when coalescence had taken place is unimportant. In this instance the upper limit date would in effect be sometime during the period when they had lived as a community before leaving the village. For the *Deir el-Medina* community this would certainly be within the times when the village is known to have existed.

Turning back to the biblical account of the Exodus, with the Ark of the Covenant safely in their care, Moses' charges are reported to have wandered the desert for forty years:

> And the children of Israel did eat manna forty years, until they came to a land inhabited; they did eat manna, until they came unto the borders of the land of Canaan.
>
> *Exodus 16:35*

This biblical period is, however, questioned by Biblical scholars partly because of the inhospitable nature of the Sinai wilderness and partly because the number forty is often used symbolically. There is another powerful reason for questioning this time of so-called "wandering" in the desert, as if lost. Whether the Exodus took place around the earliest estimation of the mid-fifteenth century BCE, or the later estimation of the mid-thirteenth century BCE, Palestine was under the control of a strong Egypt. Furthermore, it stood beside the main highway from Egypt to Asia and Babylonia. It is simply inconceivable that Moses, with his upbringing in the royal household, would have been unaware of the exact location of Palestine and also how to get there. It is also unthinkable that he and his people could have passed the many guard-posts placed along the exit routes. However, for our alternative group of no more than 100 *Deir el-Medina* villagers, escape from an Egypt that was racked in wars against Libya and with internal law and order falling apart, would have presented few problems. Equally, a sojourn of 40 years or longer would have presented no problems at all. They had all the skills to survive, provided food and water were available, and this ignores the biblical explanation of the manna and Moses striking the rock to bring forth water. The Sinai and bordering western end of Arabia have many oases, any one of which would have comfortably sustained a small group of fleeing tomb builders. After a delay of some forty years, the surviving older members of the *Deir el-Medina* villagers would have been very old. This observation would have especially applied for the life expectancy of those times, but this fact would also have given the group gravitas.

So, what happened when the huge biblical group of Exodus Jews, or the alternative small group of *Deir el-Medina* villagers reached Canaan? There is general agreement among biblical scholars, as discussed in chapter 5 that the next "big occasion", the conquest of Canaan did not happen. Under the leadership of Joshua, the River Jordan was not "split asunder" and the city of Jericho's walls did not fall down. The consensus is that immigration into Canaan was steady and over a prolonged period. The region was thus stable and not averse to outside settlers, and this would have made it an attractive destination for Moses and his followers. Perhaps the use of "forty years" for the exodus actually describes the period during which the Hebrews infiltrated Canaan: what Küng[18] describes as the "immigration model". The weakness of this so-called "immigration model" is that it does not address the reasons why the Levites did not get any land. Our new *Deir el-Medina* model more than satisfies this issue. The proposed newcomers were tomb builders with no interest in "tilling the land". They had never had to farm in all their years as tomb builders to the pharaohs and with their newly acquired gold they clearly had no intention of starting. Their life in Egypt had taught them well that running a temple was the business to be in with food in plenty provided by the animal sacrifices to the gods donated by the general population.

According to the Bible, after the deaths of Moses and Joshua there was a period during which the Hebrews were governed by one of Moses' innovations called Judges. This period lasted between 400 and 200 years dependant on the alternative Exodus dates mentioned above. The activities and deliberations of these Judges are given in the Bible books of the same name. Clearly, modern research is supporting the biblical version of events in the early years of Israel's history. During this period, the hilltop land in the southern Levant supported scattered families with no central leadership.

Perhaps we can discern from an examination of early "biblical" history of Israel and Judaea, how the biblical version arose. We have discussed the early period of the history of Canaan in the earlier chapters, but at the risk of some overlap, we will briefly revisit this period, but from the perspective of the priesthood. The early Canaanites were an agricultural society and so their religion had, as one might expect, a strong fertility bias. It is possible to discern evidence of syncretism – or the merging of religions – between the Canaanite gods and YHWH. The Canaanite male gods were Baalim meaning Lords, and the females Baalot, or Ashtoret. In the city of Shechem, close to where the present-day city of Nabulus stands, the local god was Baal-berith meaning Lord of the Covenant, or El-berith meaning God of the Covenant. We see here a parallelism between Canaanite and Jewry both entering into covenants with their god or God. Shechem was excavated during the 1960s, and the Temple of Baal-berith was partially reconstructed. There was a sacred pillar in the form of a phallic symbol positioned in front of the Temple entrance. Baal was the god of fertility who, as part of a fertility rite, sired a bull calf from a heifer. The Bible reports that when Moses first came down from mount Sinai with the stone tablets his followers were worshipping the golden calf. The sight of this so enraged him that he smashed the stone tablets on the ground and had to revisit God for replacements. There is another slender example of syncretism observable in the parallel between the attempt by Abraham to sacrifice his son, Isaac, to God and later sacrificial offerings of oxen to Yahweh at the Jerusalem Temple. The bull calf was, after all, the son of Baal.

Finally, we can briefly examine the founding tribes of Israel. That there were around twelve tribes is not questioned. As we identified above, Professor Dever has pointed to most of the locations of the traditional twelve tribes from archaeological artefacts. This is hardly unexpected because tribal groupings have formed the building blocks of larger communities around the world since *homo erectus* first stood on two legs. Against this background the legend, if that is what it is, of the twelve tribes of Israel originated. The twelve tribes are usually attributed to Jacob's sons - twelve altogether named Asher, Benjamin, Dan, Gad, Issachar, Joseph, Judah, Levi, Naphtali, Reuben, Simeon and Zebulum. The observant reader will notice that these are not the same as the twelve tribes recorded in the Bible. Joseph and Levi are missing and Manasseh and Ephraim have been added. The House of Levi was omitted by God's command because they were to be given another – more important – duty. They were directed to look after God's seat on earth, the Ark, and could not therefore head a tribe. It is to Reuben, Jacob's first-born son, that the changes are attributed. It seems that he upset his father by "sleeping" with Jacob's favourite concubine. To get even without creating public "waves", Jacob adopted two of the sons of Joseph, Manasseh and Ephraim, as replacements for Levi and Joseph himself.

Let us now consider a newly arriving group, who propose to build a glorious new Temple to a new God that will replace all other Gods. Surely such a group would spend time travelling the land and making a note of exactly who controlled what. They would want to know where the strength and the money lay. That the scribes should distil their findings down to twelve tribes was probably homage to the new religion's genesis in their native country, Egypt. The twelve zodiacal signs were especially important to the Egyptians. The zodiac signs do of course originate in Babylonia and this may explain why it was chosen as Abraham's birthplace.

In this chapter, we have taken the archaeological evidence that demonstrates beyond doubt that some of the biblical events down to around 1,000 BCE could not have happened. The biblical period of the Judges appears in line with the archaeological findings but the accounts of individual lives, from Abraham through to Joseph and his offspring appear, like the Exodus, to be based on myths. We have therefore suggested another model, one that moves the so-called "Exodus" forward to around 1,000 BCE and defines the people of this exodus as a small band of Egyptians. This small band of craftspeople, using wealth brought with them from Egypt, formed the nucleus of the Temple priesthood. This group could have been made up of existing Egyptian priests, laden with their temple's treasure, or some other similar small group. Alternatively and arguably more likely they may have been the occupants of the village of *Deir el-Medina*, the home of the tomb builders to the Egyptian pharaohs.

CHAPTER 7

THE ESSENES

We began this book by identifying the extraordinary amount of Judaic symbolism within Freemasonry, concluding that the Jews were involved in its formation. In Part 2, we are examining the history of the Jews to try and identify when they became involved with Freemasonry. We have looked at the geographical influences that helped to shape Israel and Judaea and we have discussed the political environment both internally and of their near and powerful neighbours. We also uncovered the fact that the Cohen family, who made up the Jerusalem Temple priesthood, have a different genetic structure to other Jews and they have preserved their bloodline to the present day.

Before we go any further, we need to clarify what we mean by "bloodline" and it is a sequence of direct ancestors as with a pedigree. An alternative word "dynasty" is appropriate only when a hereditary legacy passes to successive heirs, a legacy that is normally an overlord role such as king or duke. With dynasties, there are usually strict rules of inheritance, such as *primogeniture,* where the first-born son inherits the title. The word "bloodline, however, implies something much less. For example, a bloodline back to the Biblical King David would, if provable, be something far more common and thus of little if any, financial value. David's son and successor, Solomon, exemplifies this comment. According to the Bible, he was the result of the union between King David and Bathsheba. She was one of David's many wives and had earlier been the wife of the Hittite, Uriah, one of David's generals. Solomon married no fewer than seven hundred wives and acquired three hundred concubines. Clearly, within a few years, Solomon's progeny would have represented a sizeable proportion of the inhabitants of Jerusalem and be related, through Solomon, to David. This outcome was recorded in the Bible:

> As the host of heaven cannot be numbered, neither the sand of the sea measured: so will I multiply the seed of David my servant, and the Levites that minister unto me.
>
> *Jeremiah 33:22*

Modern science has now equipped us to examine our ancestry to a remarkable extent by examining mitochondrial DNA. This passes through the maternal line almost unaltered in each transmission. Using this technology, Professor Bryan Sykes[33] has traced the origins of the human race back to seven female archetypes, whom he names "the seven daughters of Eve". Professor Sykes' research clearly shows the devaluation in any bloodline after, say, 2,000 years because of the sheer numbers of people who will share any characteristics that it might bequeath.

Returning to the priesthood family, the Cohanim, it would be helpful if we could identify a simple formula that would enable us now to say the Jews preserved a stable Temple environment unless overwhelmed by some powerful external force. The sack of Jerusalem in 597 BCE by Nebuchadrezzar and the deportation of the royal family and priesthood clearly had a dramatic effect. This significant incident was followed by the return of a royal heir, Zerubbabel, with the next hereditary high priest Joshua, the son of the last high priest, Josedech, who had been taken to Babylon in exile. This return from exile allowed the Temple regime to restart effortlessly apart from the rebuilding work. Even the new rabbinic ideology appears to have been comfortably absorbed into mainstream Judaism.

Equally, it might be said that the liberal regime of Antiochus III allowed the inevitable rivalries and tensions that within any societal group often grow to the point where they explode into physical violence. This observation may be explained by the way that all external shocks have some effect that, over time alter societies in small ways, and that it is the cumulative effect that decides how they will end. We see this effect, known as "chaos theory", in the minute differences that sometimes result in a heavy storm turning into a hurricane.

The capture of Israel by Alexander the Great brought huge cultural changes that many resented. The dispute between

Alexander's heirs - the dynastic houses of Ptolemy and Seleucid – over who owned Israel festered for around a hundred years and was not resolved until around 200 BCE. The winning side, the Seleucids, were notable for their tolerance of local religions and the priesthoods that attended on them. This degree of freedom turned out to be all the Jewish leaders needed to turn in on themselves. What developed was a range of competing groupings, with the Hellenized priesthood at the complaisant end and the Hasideans, the "pious ones", at the other extreme. Eventually the Seleucid king Antiochus IV Epiphanes, became impatient with Israel and the resulting civil war pushed him into draconian remedies, including banning Judaism. This in turn brought about the successful Hasmonean revolt that resulted in "home rule" for the Jews which lasted for just over one-hundred years.

The manner in which the subsequent Maccabean dynasty seized and combined both regal and priestly power was discussed in chapter 5. It was the events shortly after the revolt that we might now see as having been a defining moment for the Cohanim. Perhaps unsurprisingly, the revolt had initially received strong support from the pious Hasideans. Their support had been ensured when, in 171 BCE, the incumbent high priest, Onias III, had been murdered and his brother, Jason, who was not a first-born son, took over the position. We can now see that this was probably the moment when the Cohanim, or Zadokite dynasty, the first-born sons of Aaron, lost their monopoly over the position of high priest. In reality we have no way of knowing exactly what criterion separated a Zadok – and thus high priest – from the other family members who performed the remaining temple duties. Sometimes, it is particular moments in history that provide the clues and the behaviour of the eldest son, Onias IV, provides some support for the suggestion that the role of high priest was transferred according to the rule of *primogeniture.*

When Jason was ousted and at first Menelaus, and then Alcimus were appointed high priests, the outrage was too much for the apparently rightful Zadokite heir Onias IV. Onias decamped to Egypt and erected a temple in Leontopolis in direct transgression of the Judaic law contained in Deuteronomy that prescribes a single temple in Jerusalem. Two "wrongs" do not make a "right" and there can be little doubt that this action by the apparent high priest elect must have caused considerable anguish for the pious Jews remaining in Jerusalem.

After the success of the revolt, the appointment of a Maccabean high priest, Alcimus, seems only to have antagonised the Hasideans and they then defected from the ruling elite. They must have regretted this precipitate action because Alcimus arranged for his Syrian allies to slaughter some sixty Hasideans in a single day. The usurpation of the Zadokites was completed when Jonathon Maccabeus, a priest but not a Zadok, accepted the position of high priest. When Jonathon was executed in 143 BCE, another Maccabee, Simon, took over and was appointed by the national assembly as "hereditary leader" and high priest. The Hasmoneans were then the new hereditary high priests. Although they clearly were members of the priestly bloodline, they do not appear to have been members of the Zadokite dynasty. We use the term "dynasty" to describe the Zadokites because the hereditary role of "high priest" was involved. The Hasmoneans did, though, have the support of one of the three politico-religious groups, the Sadducees. The second group, the Pharisees, supported the rabbinic wing of Judaism. The breakaway Hasideans, for their part, were drawn together by a charismatic individual, "the Righteous Teacher", to form the third group or sect, the Essenes. Josephus, the first century CE historiographer, had this to say of the three politico-religious groups:

> At this time there were three sects among the Jews, who had different opinions concerning human actions; the one was called the sect of the Pharisees, another the sect of the Sadducees, and the other the sect of the Essens [sic]. Now for the Pharisees, they say that some actions, but not all, are the work of fate, and some of them are in our own power, and that they are liable to fate, but are not caused by fate. But the sect of the Essens affirm, that fate governs all things, and that nothing befalls men but what is according to its determination. And for the Sadducees, they take away fate, and say there is no such thing, and that the events of human affairs are not at its disposal; but they suppose that all our actions are in our

own power, so that we are ourselves the causes of what is good, and receive what is evil from our own folly.

Flavius Josephus
Antiquitates Judaicae (The Antiquities of the Jews) – Book xiii

Gabriele Boccaccini[34], comments that "… the Damascus document has led scholars to the idea that the founders of the Qumran community were a group of Zadokite priests who separated themselves from the rest of Judaism when it became clear that they would never again regain their power in Jerusalem." It is abundantly clear from the Dead Sea Scrolls that the religious leaders of the Essenes, the priests, were considered by them to be Zadokites. They are referred to as such often and in different scrolls:

> The sons of Aaron alone shall command in matters of justice and property, and every rule concerning the men of the Community shall be determined according to their word.
>
> *The Community Rule*

> … under the sons of zadok the priests, [and] [under the direction] [of all the] heads of family of the congregation.
>
> When God engenders [the priest] Messiah, he shall come with them [at] the head of the whole congregation of Israel with all [his brethren, the sons] of Aaron the priests
>
> *The Damascus Rule*

One of the scrolls found at Qumran is the "Halakhic" (meaning legal discussion) Letter known as 4QMMT, from "*Miqsat Ma'ase ha-Torah*" meaning "some precepts of the law". This scroll lends support to our suggestion that the hereditary Temple priesthood sought refuge in Qumran. The full letter comprises six manuscripts, five of leather and one on papyrus, dated from between 75 BCE and 50 CE. In the legal discussion, the author states his beliefs and lists the twenty-four practices he feels that the priests of Jerusalem are compromising. These deal with priests accepting gifts as well as breaches of the laws of purity. The letter ends with two warnings to the effect that the last days have arrived. This letter is considered to have been what may well have been the last attempt at reconciliation between the Qumran sect and their Sadducean colleagues in Jerusalem and with the Hasmonaean leader. The attempt clearly failed because they never did return to Jerusalem.

In considering the legitimacy of the leader of the Qumran sect; if the rightful Zadokite heir, Onias IV, had emigrated to Egypt, then either he returned as the Righteous Teacher or his son or grandson did. This must have been so because the Zadokite dynasty had been carefully preserved over centuries and because of the known objections to non-Zadokite high priests in the Jerusalem Temple. Here was a group of pious Jews who had absented themselves from the goings-on in Jerusalem for the very reason that they felt that the Temple high priest was not entitled to hold the job. It seems unlikely, therefore, that a non-Zadokite could somehow assume the role of priest within the Essenes.

In looking back at historical events and superimposing motives to make sense of it, we must be careful not to try to fit modern ideas into ancient behaviour. Having made that caveat, the reality is that in behavioural terms man has not changed so much over the past 3,000 years. The seven deadly sins of greed, envy, pride, lust, gluttony, anger and sloth were just as applicable then as they are today. Against this background, it is not so difficult to imagine the individual and group feelings and emotions that would have brought about the actions that appear to have taken place. The Zadokites had been thrown out of the family business in the Temple and this would have hurt their pride and distressed many pious Jews who would have interpreted the actions as an affront to God's word. The ostensible head of the family, Onias IV, had taken off to Egypt and so the remainder – after perhaps witnessing the slaughter that befell the Hasidean objectors to the Maccabean high priest, Alcimus, – moved away to the comparative safety of Qumran. There they appear to have recreated a Zadokite dynasty in waiting.

Although doubters exist, we can be reasonably sure that Qumran was, indeed, the base for a settlement of Essenes because Pliny the Elder – the Roman historian – discusses their location as "south of Jericho on the north-western shore of the Dead Sea". Qumran is only eight miles south of Jericho and close to the Dead Sea. Vermes[35] provides a number of features and ideology common to Christianity and to the Essene movement recorded in the Dead Sea Scrolls:

1. They both used similar language – "sons of light" – to describe the faithful.
2. They both considered themselves to be the true Israel with 12 leaders representing the 12 tribes.
3. They both anticipated the imminent arrival of the Kingdom of God.
4. They both considered that their history truly reflected the words of the Old Testament prophets.
5. The Pope supported by his bishops for the Christians matches the hierarchical structure of a single leader (variously the master or guardian) and his overseers in the case of the Essenes.
6. The Essene prayer of Nabonidus, who was cured by a Jewish exorcist who forgave his sins, parallels the healing of the paralytic in Capernaum by Jesus, who used the same formula of forgiving the man's sins.
7. In a similar vein, the arrival of the final hour is reported in the Scrolls as the time when the blind will be cured, the wounded healed and the dead raised. This is mirrored in the gospel of Matthew with "the blind shall receive their sight and the lame walk, lepers are cleansed, etc".

Geza Vermes
The Complete Dead Sea Scrolls

It is the first item above that is perhaps the most important because the Essenes were not just a slightly different sect from Judaism but something rather more profound. The term "sons of light" for them represented a move away from the lunar calendar around which Judaism was structured, to a solar-based calendar. For any religion that keeps one day special and forbids any non-essential activity on that day, the calendar is of vital importance. The calendars of the Jews and the Essenes were quite different. The Jewish calendar comprised 12 months of 354 days in all, which was clearly out of synchronicity with the equinoxes and solstices. The Jews overcame this problem by inserting extra days – intercalation – to bring matters into balance. The Essenes adopted a solar year of 364 days giving 52 weeks of 7 days each.

> In tune with the great light of heaven
>
> *Scroll 1QH xii, 5*

It is immediately obvious that this new astronomical discovery took the Essenes perilously close to the worship of the sun. Sun-worship has, rather unsurprisingly, had a near universal appeal throughout history, although the second Roman *"sol"* god – *"sol invictus"* which was imported from Syria by the emperor Elagabalus around 220 CE – is perhaps the best known. There are still echoes of *sol invictus* within the Christian Church today as shown by the day of worship, Sunday, and the way many churches face east towards the rising sun.

Let us review our findings. Someone known to us only as "the Righteous Teacher" or "Teacher of Righteousness" founded the Essenes. Conventional scholarship based on archaeological and palaeographic evidence dates this event to the middle of the second century BCE, around 150 – 140 BCE. Qumran itself was destroyed by the Roman army, along with Jerusalem in 68 CE, after which all trace of the Essenes evaporates. The date for the "Righteous Teacher" creates problems for the various writers who have attempted to pin a name on him. Barbara Thiering[36], for example, suggests that he was John the Baptist and that Jesus Christ was the "wicked priest". Robert Eissenmann[37] prefers Jesus' brother James as the Righteous Teacher and the high priest Ananus as the wicked priest. Teicher[38], who started the speculation, cast Jesus as the Righteous Teacher and St. Paul as the wicked priest. Clearly, if the generally accepted founding date is more or less correct, then there is a time gap of the order of 180 years between the Righteous Teacher founding the Essenes and 30 CE when Jesus Christ was active in Palestine. Vermes[35] dismisses all of these suggestions out of hand:

> In other words, we neither know who the founder of the Essenes was, nor how, nor where, nor when he died.
>
> *Geza Vermes*
> *The Complete Dead Sea Scrolls*

The Dead Sea Scrolls and the consequent archaeological investigations that have taken place in Qumran enable us to understand better how the Essenes withdrew into a desert monastic retreat. There they were far away from the authorities in the Jerusalem. The cataclysmic events of the preceding hundred years or so for the Jewish nation had convinced the Essenes that their eschatological beliefs were coming to a conclusion. Judgement day was nigh. They poured over the Scriptures for further confirmation of their beliefs. They searched for signs that would help them to identify the messianic figures or signs that they believed were due. They desperately sought a Davidic or royal Messiah and an Aaronic or priestly Messiah.

An expectation of an Aaronic Messiah immediately provides an explanation as to why the Cohanim have been carefully preserving their bloodline because they hold the bloodline of the Aaronic dynasty in their genes. Here then is strong motivation to keep the Cohanim bloodline pure, to maintain the possibility for an Aaronic Messiah to emerge from within their ranks. Aaronic, Zadokite and Cohanim are synonymous terms for one family and for that reason an Aaronic Messiah can only come from within the Cohanim. According to their beliefs, the day will come - and who knows how soon - when two Cohens will become the proud parents of the next Aaronic Messiah and gain their place in history for eternity. Such a potential prize is worth preserving.

Josephus again provides a feel for the way of life among the Essenes:

> The doctrine of the Essens[sic] is this: That all things are best ascribed to God. They teach the immortality of souls, and esteem that the rewards of righteousness are to be earnestly striven for; and when they send what they have dedicated to God into the temple, they do not offer sacrifices because they have more pure lustrations of their own; on which account

> they are excluded from the common court of the temple, but offer their sacrifices themselves; yet is their course of life better than that of other men; and they entirely addict themselves to husbandry. It also deserves our admiration, how much they exceed all other men that addict themselves to virtue, and this in righteousness; and indeed to such a degree, that as it hath never appeared among any other men, neither Greeks nor barbarians, no, not for a little time, so hath it endured a long while among them. This is demonstrated by that institution of theirs, which will not suffer any thing to hinder them from having all things in common; so that a rich man enjoys no more of his own wealth than he who hath nothing at all. There are about four thousand men that live in this way, and neither marry wives, nor are desirous to keep servants; as thinking the latter tempts men to be unjust, and the former gives the handle to domestic quarrels; but as they live by themselves, they minister one to another.
>
> *Flavius Josephus*
> *Antiquitates Judaicae (The Antiquities of the Jews) – Book xviii*

With the added benefit of the Dead Sea Scrolls, we can now identify the Essenes as a group of people concerned more with the life hereafter than their earthly existence. For the record, although conventional Judaism allows a belief in the afterlife, this concept is not a law. The Essene emphasis on immortality of the soul, places them much closer to the Christian ideal than the Judaic one. The apparent nearness of Essene ideology to Christian doctrine invites a closer look at a reflection between the Christian foundation of Jesus Christ's crucifixion to absolve the sins of mankind and the Jewish "day of Atonement" or "*Yom Kippur*". This festival, which occurs on the tenth day of the seventh month, was instituted by Moses and is preceded by fasting. What sets the Day of Atonement apart is the elaborate ceremonial performed by the high priest.

Early in the morning the high priest, in his robes of office, offered the daily morning sacrifice and performed the ordinary morning ritual of dressing the lamps and burning incense. On this festival day, there followed the sacrifice of a bullock (contributed by the high priest), seven lambs, two rams and a goat. The high priest put on special linen vestments and with his hands on the bullock's head, made a confession of his own sins and of those of his household. Then two goats (contributed by the people) were brought in and one chosen by lot to be the "sin offering" to God. The other goat was to be the "scapegoat". One purpose of this festival was to purify the most holy place, the inner sanctum where the Ark of the Covenant rested, against any accidental or deliberate defilement that may have occurred during the preceding year. After sacrificing the animals and sprinkling their blood to purify the Tabernacle or Temple, the scapegoat was brought forward. The high priest laid his hand on the goat's head and confessed "all the iniquities of the Israelites, all their transgressions and all their sins", which were thus placed on the goat's head. Laden with the people's sins, the animal was sent away into the wilderness. The high priest then clothed himself in his usual vestments and sacrificed another goat as a sin-offering. Then two rams (one contributed by himself) would be sacrificed as burnt offerings. Finally the daily evening sacrifice was offered, the lamps were lit and incense burned. Immediately we can see that the notion of offering up to God a sacrifice to dispel the sins of the people was a model for the later sacrifice of Jesus Christ for the sins of all mankind. With this knowledge it is perhaps easier to understand why early Christianity was attractive to so many Jews.

Entry into the Essenes was only after an initiation followed by a long period of probation. Absolute loyalty and obedience to the head of the order, the master, was essential and any deviation led to punishment or expulsion from the order. The most important ritual was participation in a sacred meal to which only the full members who were free of error were admitted. Their decision to leave the Jerusalem temple and move to Qumran meant that they also left behind God's seat on earth. Consequently, communication with God was then only possible with the help of angels. In mentioning "God's seat on earth", in this context, we must make the point that the Ark of the Covenant, which was the "formal" seat for God on earth, ceased to be mentioned in the Bible after King Josias (641 - 611 BCE) ordered it to be returned to the temple. Whether the Ark was lost when Nebuchadrezzar sacked Jerusalem, or whether it was hidden and survives until today as

Byrne[1] suggests, makes no difference to the point being made here. In the absence of the Ark, it is clear that the Temple at Jerusalem remained the site of God's seat on earth. So, for the Essenes, a celibate lifestyle was necessary to ensure that some members remained in a sufficient state of purity to allow dialogue with the angels to take place. If we consider the suggestion above - that the Essenes were also the guardians of the Zadokian bloodline - has merit, then the knowledge that some Essenes were married makes sense. Marriages, or rather consummated marriages, were essential to preserve the dynasty and bloodline.

The Essene practice of a common meal was not unique but also practiced by the Pharisees. They, like the Pharisees, believed in resurrection and were therefore – subject to pious behaviour - guaranteed a place in the life hereafter. Mention of common meals invites a comparison with today's Freemasons. Clearly the everyday life of an Essene, in the monastic retreat of Qumran, can bear little resemblance to the life of a present-day Freemason. If, though, one compares aspects of their life with another monastic order – the Knights Templar – some similarities are immediately apparent. Templar Gold[1] identifies the Knights Templar as the forerunners of the Freemasons. Although it is far from clear, the existence of Essenes separate from the community at Qumran seems very likely. Josephus puts the number of Essenes at 4,000 and yet the numbers of bodies uncovered in the cemetery at Qumran indicate the numbers in residence there were unlikely to have exceeded 200. Josephus also hints at city based communities:

> They none of them differ from others of the Essens in their way of living, but do the most resemble those Dacae who are called *Polistae* [dwellers in cities].
>
> *Flavius Josephus*
> *Antiquitates Judaicae (The Antiquities of the Jews) – Book xviii*

One thing is clear and it is that the "community rule" Scroll describes a lifestyle for an ascetic monastic community while the "Damascus document" provides for an ordinary lay existence. If, then, we accept that some, perhaps a majority of Essenes, lived away from Qumran then their lifestyle would have been more "normal" and there seems to be a consensus that marriage was an option for them. We have shown that the Essenes appear to be the likely repository of the displaced Cohanim or Zadokites. We are similarly clear that the Temple priesthood also seems the most likely group to have formed Freemasonry because of a shared interest in the Ark of the Covenant. On this basis, it is worth examining the procedure for becoming an Essene and comparing it for that of becoming a Freemason.

	Essene	**Mason**
1	A potential postulant appeared before the leader of the Essenes, the Guardian or Master, and the congregation.	An applicant for Freemasonry first appears before a committee of senior members.
2	The Guardian inquired about the postulant's beliefs to ascertain whether he was suitable.	This is mirrored for an applicant for Freemasonry.
3	Satisfactory postulants entered into the "covenant" after taking vows of obedience.	A Freemason takes vows and becomes an Entered Apprentice Freemason.
4	The postulant was given instruction on the rules of the order.	An Entered Apprentice Freemason learns a few lines of responses to questions that are put at his next ceremony.
5	The postulant appeared again before the congregation for continued support or rejection.	A Freemason undergoes a second ceremony where he answers questions about his initiation. Further vows are taken and he becomes a Fellowcraft Freemason.
6	The postulant appeared for a third time when he was questioned on his understanding of the rule or laws of the order.	A Freemason undergoes a third ceremony where he answers questions about the Fellowcraft ceremony. More vows are taken and he becomes a Master Mason.

7	After two years the postulant handed over his worldly wealth, to be held in trust.	This is not a requirement of Freemasonry but it was of the Knights Templar.
8	After three years the postulant would be examined on his knowledge of the order and if successful would be admitted to full membership. At that point his possessions would become the property of the sect.	There is no comparable test after three years in Freemasonry but a Mason cannot become the master of his lodge until he has been a warden for a full year. It is most unlikely that the rank of warden could be achieved in less than three years.
9	The postulant would now begin a course of training, which would have lead to his becoming a member of the congregation. There were two "degrees" of membership within the Essenes, the lower one was the covenant and the senior one was the congregation.	This was mirrored within Freemasonry until the mid eighteenth century when the third degree, that of a Master Mason, was added to the original degrees of Entered Apprentice and Fellowcraft.

The idea that modern Freemasonry may be related to the Essenes is not new, and is discussed in some length in Albert Mackey - History of Freemasonry[5]; first published in 1909. Mackay suggests that, for him, the word "Essene" most likely derives from the Hebrew "*Chasid*" – meaning "holy" or "pious". This would also identify the Chasidim, or Hasideans as the founding sect of the Essenes. Mackay also quotes Alexander Laurie[39]:

> …and of whom Lawrie says, quoting from Scaliger, that they were "an order of the Knights of the Temple of Jerusalem, who bound themselves to adorn the porches of that magnificent structure, and to preserve it from injury and decay."
>
> *Albert Mackay*
> *The History of Freemasonry*

Largely on account of his lack of scholarship, questions were raised over Alexander Lawrie's authorship of his book. This lack of formal learning precluded him from understanding the many Greek and Latin authorities he quoted in the book. Dr. David Irving, the Librarian to the faculty of Advocates in Edinburgh, stated some 50 or so years later that he had personally declined the brief. He asserted that his acquaintance, David Brewster, compiled it for a "suitable remuneration".

Mackay provides a detailed account of life as an Essene drawing on more contemporaneous descriptions of them from Philo and Plato:

> They had a common treasury, in which was deposited whatever anyone of them possessed, and from this the wants of the whole community were supplied by stewards appointed by the brotherhood, so that they had everything in common. Hence there was no distinction among them between rich and poor, or masters and servants. The only gradation of rank, which they recognised, was derived from the Degrees or orders into which the members were divided, and which depended on holiness alone. They lived peaceably with all men, reprobated slavery and war, and would not manufacture any warlike instruments.
>
> *Albert Mackey*
> *Encyclopaedia of Freemasonry*

This last mention of a lack of "warlike" inclinations was made before the discovery of the War Scroll at Qumran, in which are described the preparations that were in hand for the "final conflict". Mackay continued:

> They were governed by a president, who was elected by the whole community; and members who had violated their rules were, after due trial, excommunicated or expelled. As they held no communication outside their own fraternity, they had to raise their own supplies, and some were engaged in tilling, some in tending flocks, others in making clothing, and others in preparing food. They got up before sunrise, and, after

> singing a hymn of praise for the return of light, which they did with their faces turned to the East, each one repaired to his appropriate task. At the fifth hour, or eleven in the forenoon, the morning labour terminated. The Brethren then again assembled, and after a lustration in cold water, they put on white garments and proceeded to the refectory, where they partook of the common meal, which was always of the most frugal character. A mysterious silence was observed during this meal, which, to some extent, had the character of a sacrament. The feast being ended, and the priest having returned thanks, the Brethren withdrew and put off their white garments, resumed their working-clothes and their several employments until evening, when they again assembled as before, to partake of a common meal.
>
> *Albert Mackey*
> *Encyclopaedia of Freemasonry*

There is here nothing unexpected from a group of monastic ascetics, and yet others detect a much deeper philosophy. The Reverend J. N. Cleland, M.A., D.D., in his paper, "The Kabbalah and Freemasonry" identifies the Essenes as early proponents of The Kabbalah. The Kabbalah is the esoteric doctrine passed on by the Jewish oral tradition to explain how "man may come to know God". Reverend Cleland notes that the Essenes shared many values with Freemasonry including shared garments. Some Masonic districts still provide a box of aprons for any brother to put on when entering a lodge room. Cleland lists four shared - between Essenes and Freemasons - attributes that he considers worthy of special note:

1. The great stress, which they laid upon Fellowship.
2. Their distinction from the general populace by their higher sanctity.
3. Their devotion to the study of the knowledge of God, and the beginnings of all things.
4. Their love of allegorical interpretation.

Reverend J. N. Cleland
The Kabbalah and Freemasonry

Cleland brought out another aspect of the Kabbalah, that it was earlier communicated only verbally "from mouth to ear". This definition describes the method by which at least one Masonic "secret-word" is passed to a new initiate. The Reverend Cleland continues to put the origins of the Kabbalah at least as early as 515 BCE at which time written evidence of it began. Cleland makes the point that the Kabbalah must have predated this period by some considerable time, as such complex philosophies do not suddenly appear. Reverend Cleland explains the underlying importance of number to an understanding of the Kabbalah, and identifies how the twenty-two characters of the Hebrew alphabet subdivide into three, seven and twelve letters. These are numbers, which together with five - the difference between twelve and seven - reverberate throughout the Masonic ritual performed during their ceremonies. The number five is also important to Jews, being, among other things, the number of books in the Torah as well as the hour of the day when they took their lunch-break.

Cleland's links, between the Kabbalah and Freemasonry, are undeniable and legion, but a couple more examples will make the point. The three so-called "Mother" letters, which define the three divisions of the Hebrew alphabet - mutes, sibilants and aspirates – are ALEPH, MEM and SHIN. The number of each character is 5, 3 and 4. To a Freemason, these are immediately recognisable as the sides – 3, 4 and 5 – of a right-angle triangle or square also representing the threefold deity. Temura is the branch of the Kabbalah that deals with ciphers. It overlays letters on a noughts-and-crosses square, substituting the sides of each box for the character as used by Masonic Mark Master Masons for the same purpose.

Albert Mackay had also noticed the connection between the Essenes, the Kabbalah and Freemasonry:

> The distinctive ordinances of the brotherhood [Essenes] and the mysteries connected with the Tetragrammaton [YHWH or Jehovah] and the angelic worlds, were the prominent topics of Sabbatical instruction. In particular, did they pay attention to the mysteries connected with the Tetragrammaton, or the *Shemhamphorah,* the Expository Name, and the other names

> of God which play so important a part in the mystical theosophy of the Jewish Cabalists [*sic*], a great deal of which has descended to the Freemasonry of our own age.
>
> *Albert Mackey*
> *Encyclopaedia of Freemasonry*

Mackay continued analysing the Essenes and making a comparison with Freemasonry by identifying Josephus' description of their attention to the charitable support of the needy, and to their inclination for showing mercy. Mackay also highlights Josephus' description of the ceremony by which a noviciate became an Essene brother, and, as described earlier, draws a comparison with the initiation into Freemasonry. Mackay continues:

> He then received a copy of the regulations of the brotherhood, and was presented with a spade, and apron, and a white robe. The spade was employed to bury excrement, the apron was used at the daily lustrations, and the white robe was worn as a symbol of purity.
>
> There was a third rank or Degree called the Disciple or Companion, in which there was a still closer union. Upon admission to this highest grade, the candidate was bound by a solemn oath to love God, to be just to all men, to practice charity, maintain truth, and to conceal the secrets of the society and the mysteries connected with the Tetragrammaton and the other names of God.
>
> When a candidate was proposed for admission, the strictest scrutiny was made into his character. If his life had hitherto been exemplary, and if he appeared capable of curbing his passions, and regulating his conduct, according to the virtuous, through austere maxims of their Order, he was presented, at the expiration of his novitiate, with a white garment, as an emblem of the regularity of his conduct, and the purity of his heart. A solemn oath was then administered to him, that he would never divulge the mysteries of the

> Order; that he would make no innovations on the doctrines of the society; and that he would continue in that honourable course of piety and virtue which he had begun to pursue.
>
> *Albert Mackey*
> *Encyclopaedia of Freemasonry*

It would at this stage be wrong to conclude, on the basis of shared doctrine and tenets, that Freemasonry originated with the Essenes; this would be far too great a leap of logic at this stage.

> Such a course of reasoning would place the Pythagoreans in the same category: a theory that has been rejected by the best modern critics.
>
> *Dr. W. Wynn Westcott*
> *Transactions (1915); Quator Coronati*

Whatever the relationship, there is an undeniable resemblance between the Essene sect and modern-day Freemasonry. We will examine later whether this likeness is coincidental or something stronger. Our attention is drawn once again, albeit tentatively, to the Freemasons, and also to the Knights Templar. It is, therefore, also worth noting something else that supports the co-author's thesis in Templar Gold - that the Templars created a "new Jerusalem" in the south of France:

> Similarly, the 'new Jerusalem' described in various manuscripts (cf. 1Q32; 2Q24; 4Q554; 5q15; 11Q18) does not match by definition the Holy City descending from above of 1. Enoch (xc, 28-9) or Revelation xxi, but could be an earthly city rebuilt according to the plans of angelic architects.
>
> *Geza Vermes*
> *The Complete Dead Sea Scrolls*

There is consensus that Vespasian's Roman soldiers destroyed or drove away the Essenes at Qumran. Vermes[35] makes the important point that subsequently no one from the Essene community ever returned to Qumran to salvage their important and presumably valuable manuscripts. This observation suggests that any survivors from the Roman defeat of the Jewish insurrection were probably deported as slaves.

We have just examined the known history of the Essenes and identified similarities between Masonic and Essene ritual that might point to a link between the two organisations. We have also revealed the Essenes as the spiritual and probable real home of the Cohanim following their expulsion from the Temple at Jerusalem. This is certainly unveiling a plausible linkage between a group or sect of Jews and Freemasonry with the Ark of the Covenant as a possible cause of that link. Our discovery, in chapter 2, that the footsteps made by an initiate spell out ZDK in "square-Hebrew", which transliterates to "Zadok", provides further compelling evidence of a link between these two groups. In our investigations into the Essenes, however, we have found not a single scrap of evidence to suggest that they were involved in the creation of Freemasonry. We will now pursue this line of enquiry a little further to see if any evidence of their being a link turns up.

To suggest at all that the Cohanim and the Freemasons are somehow linked seems an outrageous suggestion to make. Freemasonry although now non-denominational, was at one time purportedly a Christian order. And yet despite this, as proved in Part 1, Freemasonry contains an undue amount of Judaic symbolism. The use of a multiplicity of substitute names, such as "The Great Architect of the Universe" for God is simply the most obvious method of allowing Masonic Jews to conform to their religious rules. A tentative link between the Freemasons and the ancient Jerusalem temple priesthood is also evident from the Masonic regalia. The apron worn by a Freemason bears similarity to the ephod worn by ancient Jewish temple priests and a Freemason's collar, although less so, resembles the temple priest's breastplate.

FIGURE 12
TEMPLE PRIEST WEARING EPHOD AND BREASTPLATE

FIGURE 13
FREEMASON WEARING PROVINCIAL REGALIA

When we examine the apron of senior English Freemasons – that of a Provincial Grand Master - the resemblance to the robes of the high priest becomes more apparent.

FIGURE 14 - PROVINCIAL GRAND MASTER'S APRON

The Masonic Book of Constitutions describes the ornamentation on a Provincial Grand Master's apron as pomegranates alternating with lotuses. The pomegranates link directly with the Temple high priesthood as the following description of the high priest's robe or ephod portrays:

> And beneath upon the hem of it thou shalt make pomegranates of blue, and of purple, and of scarlet, round about the hem thereof; and bells of gold between them round about:
>
> A golden bell and a pomegranate, a golden bell and a pomegranate, upon the hem of the robe round about.
>
> *Exodus 28:33 and 34*

The ornate embroidery around the border of the apron of a Provincial Grand Master did not appear until the third quarter of the nineteenth century. Earlier aprons had a simple plain dark blue border. Having linked the pomegranates to the high priesthood, the lotus flowers are veiled a little more carefully in allegory. The lotus flower was used at ancient Egyptian funerals as a symbol of rebirth. Indeed, Tutankhamen's gold coffin had blue lotus petals scattered over it. Bearing in mind that we earlier put forward the tomb builders of *Deir el-Medina* as possible candidates forming the Exodus, they would have been well aware of the significance of the blue lotus plant. The lotus flower was an Egyptian symbol of the sun because at night the flower closes and sinks underwater and at dawn rises and reopens. The use of the lotus as a symbol of rebirth – important to tomb builders – also drew on the way the flower closed to await its opening with the morning sun. The Egyptians anticipated their souls coming back to life just like a lotus plant reopening. The ancient Egyptian Book of the Dead has a spell to allow the deceased to transform into one of these flowers:

> [The Chapter of] Making the Transformation into the Water Lily.
>
> The Osiris Ani, whose word is truth, saith:- I am the holy water lily that cometh forth from the light which belongeth to

> the nostrils of Ra, and which belongeth to the head of Hathor. I have made my way, and I seek after him, that is to say, Horus. I am the pure blue water lily that cometh forth from the field [of Ra].
>
> *Book of the Dead*

Although we have referred to this flower as a lotus, it is actually a *Nymphaea caerulea* or what we now call a blue water lily. The lotus has another facet which binds it into our investigation. In Mesopotamia, the lotus was the flower of Lilith, the goddess whom Jews claim was Adam's first wife. In addition to the pomegranates and lotuses some Provincial Grand Master's aprons have thistles embroidered in gold to clearly implicate Jerusalem. It is also worthy of mention that the circular leaves of the lotus flower could also be clever imagery to represent sleigh-bells and so meet the Biblical description of the high priest's robe given above.

Godfrey Higgin[3] prefers an etymological approach and sees Jesus as a flower, "Nazareth, the town of Nazir or Nazwfaioj, the flower, was situated in Carmel, the vineyard or garden of God". From whence, suggests Higgins came the adoration, by the Rossicrucians, of the Rose and Cross, which Rose was Ras, and this Ras, or knowledge or wisdom, was stolen from the garden. The God was also called Rose or Ras, because numerology gives a number 360 attributable to the characters ROZ signifying an everlasting circle. Higgins suggests that the "rose of the water", or "water-rose", as it is called to this day, is none other than the Rose of Sharon, the symbol of Jesus Christ.

Before leaving the intriguing water lily, there is another facet of this plant that deserves a mention. Emeritus Professor of Botany at the University of California, Los Angeles, William Emboden[40], asserts that the ancient Egyptians were aware of synergistic elements of the plant when combined with mandrake, and often soaked them in wine before drinking the brew.

> Although the usual interpretation of the water lily and the mandrake has been that of a part of ritual mourning ... it is argued that the dynastic Egyptians had developed a form of

> shamanistic trance induced by these two plants and used it in medicine as well as healing rituals. Analysis of the ritual and sacred iconography of dynastic Egypt, as seen on stelae, in magical papyri, and on vessels, indicates that these people possessed a profound knowledge of plant lore and altered states of consciousness. The abundant data indicate that the shamanistic priest, who was highly placed in the stratified society, guided the souls of the living and dead, provided for the transmutation of souls into other bodies and the personification of plants as possessed by human spirits, as well as performing other shamanistic activities.
>
> *The Sacred Journey in Dynastic Egypt*
> *Dr William Emboden*

The connection between the Essenes and the Cohanim is clearly important and so, at the risk of overstating the case, we will reiterate a few points. We identified in the previous chapter how, around 170 BCE, during the Maccabean revolt, the incumbent high priest, Onias III, was murdered and the dynasty of priests who tended the temple displaced. Throughout the temple period, 960 BCE to 70 CE, there were purportedly 78 high priests of whom at least 55 were hereditary Cohanim. We have also shown that around 170 BCE a group, or sect, of pious Jews gathered together and adopted the collective name of Essenes. The Essenes called themselves the "sons of Zadok", and the term "Zadok" – meaning "righteous" - appears to have been the honorific given to the high priest. The high priest was the most senior priest and the only one allowed to enter the inner sanctum of the Temple where the Ark of the Covenant rested. The Essenes were the probable repository of the dynasty of ex-temple priests for whom we have used the title "Cohanim."

We have touched on a possible connection between the Essenes and Freemasonry, but there is another curious coincidence that links the Essenes to Freemasonry. The linkage is slight but worthy of mention. In 1876, Alfred Edersheim wrote Sketches of Jewish Social Life, and in chapter 15 – "Relation of the Pharisees to the Sadducees and Essenes, and to the Gospel of Christ", he wrote:

> As a sect the Essenes never attained a larger number than four thousand; and as they lived apart from the rest, neither mingling in their society nor in their worship and as a general rule from marriage they soon became extinct. Indeed, Rabbinical writings allude to quite a number of what may probably be described as sectaries, all of them more or less distinctly belonging to the mystical and ascetic branch of Pharisaism. We here name, first, the "Vathikin," or "strong ones," who performed their prayers with the first dawn; secondly, the "Toble Shachrith," or "morning baptists," who immersed before morning prayer, so as to utter the Divine Name only in a state of purity; thirdly, the "Kehala Kadisha," or "holy congregation," who spent a third of the day in prayer, a third in study, and a third in labour; fourthly, **the "Banaim," or "builders,"** who, besides aiming after highest purity, occupied themselves with mystical studies about God and the world; fifthly, the "Zenuim," or "secret pious," who besides kept their views and writings secret; sixthly, the "Nekije hadaath," "men of a pure mind," who were really separatists from their brethren; seventhly, the "Chashaim," or "mysterious ones"; and lastly, the "Assiim," "helpers" or "healers," who professed to possess the right pronunciation of the sacred Name of Jehovah, with all that this implied.
>
> *Alfred Edersheim*
> *Sketches of Jewish Social Life,*

The final four words above, "all that this implied" deserve an explanation. The name of God referred to is the Tetragrammaton, YHWH, the pronunciation of which, contrary to common belief, is not forbidden in the Torah. Indeed, the earliest written account of the Jewish oral tradition, the *Mishnah*, confirms there was no ban on pronouncing YHWH in ancient times. The two major centres of Judaic learning eventually wrote down a commentary on this "oral tradition" as a permanent record, the *Talmud*. The first, known as the *Talmud Yerushalmi*, was produced by the Palestinian School in the fifth century CE. The second, known as the *Talmud Babli*, was produced by the Babylonian School in the sixth century CE. It was in these written laws, the *Talmuds*, where the directive not to pronounce the "Name" and to use substitutes such as "Adonai" was first introduced. YHWH had been regularly used in the Jerusalem Temple, but, when it was destroyed, pronouncing the Name outside the Temple was proscribed. Consequently the correct enunciation of the Name fell into disuse and although scholars passed down knowledge for generations, eventually the correct delivery was lost. Consequently, it was argued, anyone claiming to know the correct pronunciation must have access to God to have acquired such knowledge.

It is possible to identify the main strand of most of the above "sectaries" with some aspect of Essenism. For example the *Vathikin* performing their prayers with the first dawn and the *Toble Shachrith* immersing themselves before morning prayer. Similarly the *Kehala Kadisha*, *Banaim*, *Zenuim, Nekije hadaath* and *Assiim* all have particular identifying features that sit within our understanding of the Essene framework. It is however four of these last five sectaries that also share a likeness with Freemasonry. For instance, *Kehala Kadisha* spent a third of the day in prayer, a third in study, and a third in labour. Similarly, Freemasons are exhorted to spend "part [of their day] in labour and refreshment, part in prayer to Almighty God and part in helping a friend or brother in need." The *Banaim*, or builders, clearly share a synonymous name with Freemasons as well as aiming after the highest purity and occupying themselves with mystical studies about God. The *Zenuim* kept their views and writings secret, an issue over which Freemasonry is regularly criticised. It is though, the reference to the *Banaim* or "builders" that catches the eye when reading this passage, and the reason why we will now expand.

We now need to try and identify where the Essenes went after Titus Flavius Vespasianus razed Jerusalem in 70 AD, for after that date there is no record of them. There is consensus that Vespasian's Roman soldiers destroyed or drove away the Essenes at Qumran. Vermes[35] makes the important point that subsequently no one from the Essene community ever returned to Qumran to salvage their important and presumably valuable manuscripts. This observation suggests that any survivors from the Roman defeat of the Jewish insurrection were probably deported as slaves. We will concentrate on that point in history when the Essenes disappeared,

70 CE. The defeat of the Jews by the Romans resulted in some 70,000 Jews from Jerusalem and Judaea relocating to Rome as slaves. Of these 70,000 Jewish slaves, some 30,000 were employed building the new Coliseum. The emperor Caesar Vespasianus Augustus or Vespasian had ordered the construction of the Coliseum. Before he became emperor Vespasian's original name was Titus Flavius Vespasianus and he had returned to Rome to claim the now vacant title, on hearing of the death of the previous emperor, Nero. Coincidentally, it was his son, also called Titus, who had led the Roman army in their victory over those same Jews at Jerusalem.

Josephus reports the existence of four thousand Essenes, a number clearly acceptable to Alfred Edersheim as seen above. We can, as a guide, take the worst death rate recorded during the American Civil War of eighteen percent as a baseline. This figure allows us conservatively to state that not more than a quarter of the four thousand Essenes lost their lives during the destruction of the Jewish kingdom by Titus. We can also cautiously assume that at least half of the surviving Essenes were taken into captivity as slaves. We can now use these assumptions and the above figures of 70,000 Jewish captives and 30,000 workers on the Coliseum, to conclude that three-sevenths of the slaves ended up as Coliseum workers. From the original figure of 4,000 Essenes we can calculate that at least 1,200 were gathered together on building what was intended to be the eighth wonder of the world. This is a substantial core group for any organisation to muster in one place for the ten years during which the Coliseum was built. We must also consider it to have been extremely likely that among those Essenes working on the Coliseum would have been some hereditary priests. The hereditary priests, or Cohanim, were the most senior members of the Essenes, and arguably the very reason for the existence of the Essenes. Because of their importance to the group, it is unlikely that many, if any, hereditary priests would have been allowed to die in battle. More probable is that they would have been protected behind the front-line, in much the same way that later generals, dukes and even monarchs remained behind the frontlines.

Towards the end of the first century, therefore, we can see that on the building site of the Coliseum was most likely a nucleus of Cohanim, with their own "praetorian guard" of pious Jews. This group, this repository of the ancient temple priesthood, were now builders.

The next question has to be is there any way that any Essene slaves and especially any Cohanim among them might have found a channel in Rome that would allow them to keep intact their comradeship and knowledge? The answer to this question is a resounding "yes", and in the form of the Roman *collegia* or colleges and particularly the *collegium artificium* or college of artificers - artificers being skilled craftsmen - mainly those in the armed forces. The ancient Romans were skilful at spotting indigenous talent and exploiting it to the full. It did not matter whether this meant identifying potential gladiators or, as was often the case with Jews, identifying potential administrators. The Essenes were a learned group of Jews from a well-educated nation, by the standards of the day. It is unlikely the Romans would not have quickly identified such a group and put their reading and writing skills to good use. It is but a short step for at least some Essenes to become entrenched within the appropriate college – in this case a building college.

> *Amanuensis*, or *ad manum servus*, a slave, or freedman, whose office it was to write letters and other things under his master's direction. The *amanuensis* must not be confounded with another sort of slaves, also called *ad manum servi,* who were always kept ready to be employed in any business.
>
> *William Smith*
> *A Dictionary of Greek and Roman Antiquities.*

> Calcula'tor signifies a keeper of accounts in general, but was also used in the signification of a teacher of arithmetic; whence Martial classes him with the *notarius* or writing-master.

> The name was derived from *calculi,* which were commonly used in teaching arithmetic, and also in reckoning in general.
>
> *William Smith*
> *A Dictionary of Greek and Roman Antiquities.*

> *Libra'rii,* the name of slaves, who were employed by their masters in writing or copying in any way. They must be distinguished from the *Scribae publici*, who were freedmen, and also from the booksellers, to both of whom this name is occasionally applied.
>
> *William Smith*
> *A Dictionary of Greek and Roman Antiquities.*

The suggestion of Jewish slaves becoming members of a *collegium artificium* is of course speculative, because there are no surviving records of any such arrangements.

The chroniclers of the day were usually only interested in the rich and famous: *plus ça change plus c'est la même chose.* It is unlikely that any hard evidence to support this speculation will ever surface but that fact alone should not preclude us from exploring possibilities. Curiously, the idea that Freemasonry may find its roots in the Roman collegiate system is also not new and indeed finds notable favour with some Masonic researchers. The only difference between their research and the speculation outlined above is that we are trying to find a trail from the Temple priesthood, through the Essenes, into the Roman *collegia.*

It was our old Masonic friend Albert Mackey who summarised the available research on the proposition:

> It was the German writers on the history of the Institution, such as Krause, Heldmann, and some others of less repute, who first discovered, or at least first announced to the world, the connection that existed between the Roman Colleges of Architects and the Society of Freemasons. The theory of Krausse on this subject is to be found principally in his well-known book entitled *Die drei altesten Kunterskunden, The Three Oldest Craft Documents.* He there advances the doctrine that Freemasonry as it now exists is indebted for all its

> characteristics, religious and social, political and professional, its interior organisation, its modes of thought and action, and its very design and object, to the *Collegia Artificium* of the Romans, passing with but little characteristic changes through the *Corporationen von Baulunstlern,* or *Architectural Gilds,* of the Middle Ages up to the English organisation in the year 1717; so that he claims an almost absolute identity between the Roman Colleges of Numa, seven hundred years before Christ, and the Lodges of the nineteenth century. We need not, according to his view, go any farther back in history, nor look to any other influences for the origin and the character of Freemasonry.
>
> *Albert Mackey*
> *Encyclopaedia of Freemasonry.*

Mackey continues to analyse the various aspects of the Roman *collegia* system that appear to provide antecedents for Freemasonry. He begins with the "rule of three", *tres faciunt collegium* that needed a minimum of three members before a college could be recognised. Freemasonry has, over time, strengthened this rule to five with three rulers:

> Three rule a lodge, five hold a lodge and seven or more make it perfect.
>
> *Masonic ritual of the second degree tracing board*

The second similarity that Mackey quotes is the makeup of the senior officers of the college. The principal was called *Magister* and this translates into "master" exactly as in a Masonic lodge or indeed in earlier times, the ruler of the Knights Templar. Immediately beneath the *Magister* sat two *Decuriones*, just as there are two wardens in a Masonic lodge. Also, there were in each college a *Scriba* or secretary, a *Thesaurensis* or Treasurer and a *Tabularius* or Archivist. The former two offices find reflected images in any modern lodge but all three are offices that would have been ideally suited to literate and numerate Jewish slaves. They would also, just as in a modern Masonic lodge, have provided a fast track to the levers of power. The secretary, the treasurer and the archivist between them would have controlled the agenda, the money and the record of what was said and done. From a historical point of view this was complete power over what we now know of the period. Finally, Mackey points out how the *Sacerdos,* or Priest, was analogous to the modern Chaplain of a Masonic Lodge.

According to Mackey, the likeness between the Roman collegiate system and Freemasonry does not end there. For just as entry into Freemasonry is via the three stages of Entered Apprentice, Fellowcraft and finally Master Mason, so the entry into the Roman *collegium* was through the various stages of apprentices, journeymen and finally the *Seniores.* Mackey continues to elaborate on the collegiate structure of secret meetings to initiate neophytes into the college and of mystical and esoteric instructions to their apprentices and journeymen. He continues with the assertion that there were periodical collections from members for the support of the college and a common fund for the support of poor members and the relief of destitute strangers. This looks like strong support for the theory that the Roman colleges hold the key to the beginnings of Freemasonry. Well it does until we check the evidence.

The picture that Mackey is painting appears overwhelmingly conclusive, but, just as all that glitters is not gold: so, all that is written in Masonic encyclopaedias is not necessarily factual. Mackey relies heavily on the works of the Greek chronicler on Roman life, Plutarch, for contemporaneous evidence in support of his assertions. In reality Plutarch only mentions colleges once in the sixty-nine essays that have been translated into the English language:

> Tiberius, immediately on his attaining manhood, had such a reputation that he was admitted into the **college of the augurs,** and that in consideration more of his early virtue than of his noble birth. This appeared by what Appius Claudius did, who, though he had been consul and censor, and was now the head of the Roman senate, and had the highest sense of his own place and merit, at a public feast of the augurs, addressed

> himself openly to Tiberius, and with great expressions of kindness, offered him his daughter in marriage.
>
> *Plutarch*
> *Tiberius Gracchus*

In Roman antiquity, an "augur" was a diviner; a religious official who watched the behaviour of birds and other natural signs and interpreted them for guidance on the approval of the gods. The college of Augurs consisted of fifteen members. Each of them carried as his insignia a long, crooked staff with which he would mark a square space on the ground to detect auspicious omens. Plutarch's failure to mention colleges does not, though, mean that they did not exist. In reality most Roman skilled men grouped together into a variety of *collegia*. Alliances were and still are the most natural thing to do to gain strength from numbers and to disseminate relevant data within a confined group and thus hold power over the data.

> *Librator aquae*, a person whose knowledge was indispensable in the construction of aqueducts, sewers, and other structures for the purpose of conveying a fluid from one place to another. He examined by a hydrostatic balance [*libra aquaria*] the relative heights of the places from and to which the water was to be conducted. Some persons at Rome made this occupation their business, and were engaged under the *curatores aquarum*, though architects were also expected to be able to act as *libratores*.
>
> *John Murray*
> *A Dictionary of Greek and Roman Antiquities*

Our experience with Mackey's references to Roman Colleges extends to any collection of Jews, Cohanim or secular. There is simply no surviving evidence to suggest that they were permitted to organise themselves into recognisable groups, let alone early Freemasons. That the Freemasonic Constitution borrows from Essene ritual, and the Roman Collegia is almost beyond doubt, but this could have been done as late as 1717. There is another religious facet from Roman times that finds expression in

Freemasonic ritual and that concerns the various Roman gods. There is a Masonic connection to Jupiter that deserves to be noted. In an old – 1830 - book of Masonic ritual[12] is a curious piece of the initiation ceremony.

> Senior Warden: The right hand has ever been considered the seat of fidelity, and our ancient brethren worshipped a deity under the name of FIDES; which has sometimes been represented by two right hands joined together.
>
> 1831 *Avery Allyn*
> *A Ritual of Freemasonry*

An American Freemason, who had been severely shaken by the Morgan scandal of 1826, published this particular book of ritual. The Morgan affair concerned the disappearance of another Mason, who was never found, and who had threatened to publish some Masonic secrets. This book of ritual is one of the oldest existing written rituals in its complete form. The above reference to Fides is in uppercase, as if to emphasise it, and so unlikely to be a mistake. Fides was closely associated with Jupiter and was the goddess of good faith and honesty. Her duty was to oversee the moral integrity of the Roman people. Towards the end of the Roman era, Fides took over from Jupiter the role as guardian of state treaties and documents, which were deposited in her temple. In Fides, can be observed the concept of faith as an expression of mutual trust. In the case of Fides, or "faith", as a Roman religion, it encapsulated the trust between god and man. Whereas the Roman worshipper sought to gain the co-operation, benevolence, and peace of the gods (*pax deorum*), the modern-day Freemason seeks to achieve these constructs with his fellow man.

The Roman soldiers' second god of choice, *Mithras*, also holds out the promise of answers to many questions. *Mithras* or *Mithra* was the Persian god of light. Yet another reference to light after Jupiter, the bringer-of-light, mentioned earlier. This emphasis on "light" is of particular importance when considering Freemasonry where the whole experience for a new Mason is to be taken "from darkness to light". Mention of "light" would also have chimed with the Essenes as we saw earlier. *Mithraism* spread to the west after Alexander the Great conquered Persia. By the third century of the present era - thanks in no small part to the Roman soldiers - *Mithraism* was the single main alternative to the fast growing religion of Christianity. It became the norm for Roman emperors to be initiated into the mysteries of *Mithraism*. Commodus, Julian and Diocletian were all initiates. Just as Jupiter's favourite sacrifice was a white ox, so *Mithras* also had connections with an ox that would have made the cult an attractive "permitted" substitute for Jewish slaves. Mythology has it that *Mithras* killed the cosmic bull and this act created the earth and all the life on it, together with the cosmos. This myth provides an alternative to God's act of creation as recorded in the Bible. *Mithras* was thus the creator of life and so to replicate *Mithras*' achievement it became popular to sacrifice a bull as a ritual of fertility, and this finds echoes today in Spain. Inevitably, *Mithras*' role as god-of-light led to him being associated with *Helios*, the Greek sun-god and *Sol Invictus*, the Roman sun-god.

It was the Roman emperor Aurelian who first used the invincible sun-god, *Sol Invictus*, as a means of unifying the empire and thus his own position at its head. He announced that he was a protégé of the sun-god but this did not save him from being murdered by some army officers who believed that he threatened their lives. Aurelian is also remembered as the emperor who brought many of the Roman corporations and colleges under state - or to be more precise military - control. The notion of the Roman emperor as the representative on earth of *Sol Invictus* continued until the reign of Constantine the Great.

Arguably, it was the theological skills of the Christian bishop of Byzantium, Eusebius, who convinced Constantine there was only one God and that Christianity offered a means of unifying the Roman Empire under that one God. The practice of paying tribute to only one of the pantheon of Roman gods had by then become so routine that the short step to monotheism was not unduly difficult. Apparently Eusebius was able to keep Constantine's affection for *Sol Invictus* and somehow seamlessly substitute the Christian God by using the former as the physical expression of the latter. By getting the support of the Roman emperor, Eusebius ensured that Christianity would from then on become the dominant religion of the western world. Eusebius pronounced that Constantine was God's representative on earth and coupled his praising with references to "shine forth the image of his absolute power", and "the rays of which penetrate the world". In this way Eusebius juxtaposed the agreeable - for Constantine - perception of God as a shining light just like the sun or indeed *Sol Invictus*. Eusebius raised Christianity to the status of "Official State Religion" of the Roman Empire. However, the reality was that Christianity sat alongside the cult of *Sol Invictus* as is evident from the name we use for the day of Christian worship, Sunday. For his part, Constantine rode both religious horses until his death. He acted as *pontifex maximus* or high priest of the cult of *Sol Invictus* and de facto head of the Christian Church. His first choice of religions is arguably demonstrated by the way he delayed his baptism until he was on his deathbed.

When Constantine moved the capital city of the Roman Empire from Rome to Byzantium - which he later renamed Constantinople – it did nothing to slow the empire's decline. At its peak, around the end of the first century of the present era, Rome boasted an estimated one million residents. Many, if not most of this extraordinarily high number of people, lived in badly-made multi-storey houses with no water or sanitation, no heating and an almost constant risk of fire. It was then unsurprising that at the end of the second century Rome was hit by plague and the numbers of Roman citizens began what would become a permanent decline. Constantine's lasting monument to Rome came from his support of the city's Christians, which laid the foundations for the Papal Rome that survives to the present time.

A weakened Rome was clearly visible to those living outside its borders, people who had been under threat of Roman occupation for hundreds of years. By 408 CE Alaric had led his Visigoth army to the walls of Rome, completing the capture of the city in 410. It is said that during the fortnight long sack of Rome, the Vandals did less damage than the previous residents who for many years had stripped existing monuments for materials to build new homes. By the time 100 years had passed from the Visigoths' capture of Rome, the population had fallen by three-quarters to a quarter of a million. The Visigoths themselves had by then moved on to what are now France and Spain.

This look at the Roman Empire has been undertaken in the hope that evidence would be uncovered to show how the Essene sect of Jews established themselves in Rome. We sought a viable unit for the later – hoped for – recovery of their rightful role as Temple priesthood. The reality is that no such evidence exists. Another eminent Masonic historian, William Preston (1742 – 1818)[41], had this to say about Freemasonry in England during Roman times:

> On the arrival of the Romans in Britain, arts and sciences began to flourish. According to the progress of civilisation, Masonry rose into esteem; hence we find that Cæsar, and several of the Roman generals who succeeded him in the government of this island, ranked themselves as patrons and protectors of the [Masonic] Craft. At this period, the Fraternity were employed in erecting walls, forts, bridges, cities, temples, palaces, courts of justice, and other stately works; but history is silent respecting their mode of government, and affords no information with regard to the usages and customs prevalent among them. Their lodges or conventions were regularly held; but being open only to the initiated fellows, the legal restraints they were under prevented the public communication of their private transactions. The wars which afterwards broke out between the conquerors and conquered considerably obstructed the progress of Masonry in Britain; so that it continued in a very low state till the time of the emperor Carausius, by whom it was revived under his own immediate auspices.
>
> *William Preston*
> *Book 4, Illustrations of Masonry, 1812*

Now this may simply be a piece of literary licence created by Preston to cover a period of history when he, just like the authors, could find nothing relevant to architects. It may equally be restating a small piece of oral tradition that was passed on to him to help his researches, we will never know. Certainly Preston implicated the Knights Templar in the running of Freemasonry, and this supports Byrne[1].

> During the reign of Henry II. the Grand Master of the Knights Templars superintended the Masons, and employed them in building their Temple in Fleet-street, C.E. 1155. Masonry continued under the patronage of this order till the year 1199, when John succeeded his brother Richard on the throne of England.
>
> *William Preston*
> *Book 4, Illustrations of Masonry, 1812*

Preston is also almost unique, apart from Byrne[1], in bringing the Hospitallers – the other major order from the time of the Knights Templar – into the picture as leading lights in Freemasonry. The following excerpt suggests that the Hospitallers – referred to by Preston by one of their later names, the order of St. John at Rhodes – were indeed active in supervising Freemasonry:

> During the short reigns of Edward V and Richard III, Masonry was on the decline; but on the accession of Henry VII. C.E. 1485, it rose again into esteem, under the patronage of the Master and Fellows of the order of St. John at Rhodes [now Malta], who assembled their grand lodge in 1500, and chose Henry their protector. Under the auspices of this prince, the Fraternity once more revived their assemblies, and Masonry resumed its pristine splendour.
>
> *William Preston*
> *Book 4, Illustrations of Masonry, 1812*

Because we cannot find proof that a group of devout Jews did not outlast the Roman Empire as a functioning unit, is not to say that they did not survive. There is, though, no need to create speculation where none is necessary. All the indications are that Freemasonry did not – contrary to the views of several eminent Masonic historians – begin in Roman times. What is apparent is that the Masonic ritual draws on Essene ritual as building blocks for its own ceremonial. This may be an oblique way of signifying Cohanim involvement in early Masonry but that has to be speculation. The involvement of *Mithraic* style ceremonial likewise points to Roman times as a source of interesting ceremonial. Full membership of Mithraism involved passing through seven grades, each one representing one of the then known planets. Each ceremony involved ablutions or baptism, purification and chastisements, the application of fetters and subsequent liberation. During the ceremony certain ceremonial passwords were transferred as well as the symbolic passing through one of seven gates and ascending another step of a seven-rung ladder. These seven ceremonies were metaphors for the ascent of the novitiate past the planets, or lesser deities, into the realm of the stars. Ancient frescoes in Italy show blindfolded initiates, both kneeling and prostrated. It seems likely that a simulated death and resurrection was also included in the ceremony. After the rites, it was usual for the members to partake in a common meal with the new initiates. In chapter 1 we mentioned the Masonic order of *Rose Croix*. When joining this order, the candidate does allegorically circumnavigate the seven planets and "ascend" a ladder with seven rungs.

Our investigations into this period bear out those of an earlier Masonic researcher, Robert Freke Gould[10]. Gould, was a founder member and the second master of the UK's premier research lodge, Quatuor Coronati; he published his three-book historical opus between 1883 and 1887 and had this to say about the Essenes:

> What ultimately became of the Essenes is pure matter of conjecture, and in the attempted solution of this problem the speculation which connects them to other and later systems have their source. They are traced down to about C.E. 400, after which they fade away into obscurity. Epiphanius, Bishop of Constantia and metropolitan of Cyprus, who was born in Palestine early in the fourth century and died C.E. 402, alludes several times to them in his celebrated work, "Against the Heretics".
>
> *Robert Freke Gould*
> *History of Freemasonry, Its Antiquities, Constitutions, Customs*

We can conclude, with some confidence, that although there is no evidence that the Essenes or the Roman Colleges were direct ancestors of Freemasonry, it seems likely that some of their forms of ritual and organisation were borrowed by Freemasonry's founders.

CHAPTER 8

NARBONNE

In the previous chapter, we examined the Essenes and concluded that although much Masonic ceremonial was borrowed from them, there was no sign of Freemasonry originating either with them or in Rome. We will continue our investigation looking at what may have happened after the fall of Rome.

We now turn our attentions towards possible routes out of Rome for the Jews keeping a special watch on the activities of the Cohanim. At the beginning of the fifth century of the present era, the Roman Empire had collapsed into the hands of the Visigoths who were followers of Arian Christianity. The Arian Christian heresy was introduced by a priest from Alexandria called Arius. It argues that Christ could not be divine because God is unique, therefore the Son cannot be God without recognising Him as another God and so denying monotheism. The military skills of the Visigoths quickly enabled them to spread their authority south from Germany into Italy, then east into Greece, and west into Spain. After one hundred years, the Visigoths were forced into a slow retreat that left them with what is now Spain. It was a regrouping of the Ostrogoths who brought about this retreat; they, like the Visigoths were a breakaway group from the Germanic Goths. There was also another power rising in the region, a new force from northern Gaul, the Franks. The Ostrogoths took over the Visigoth assets in Italy and eastern Germany, reinstating Roman Christianity, while the Franks advanced to capture the Visigoth assets in the west. Clovis, who was the second leader of the Frankish Merovingian dynasty, is credited with consolidating their rule over Gaul, or most of what is now France. By the start of the sixth century, Clovis had defeated, Syagrius, the last Roman ruler in Gaul and extended the kingdom as far south as Aquitaine. He also moved east into a strip of around one-third of western Alemanni or what is now Germany.

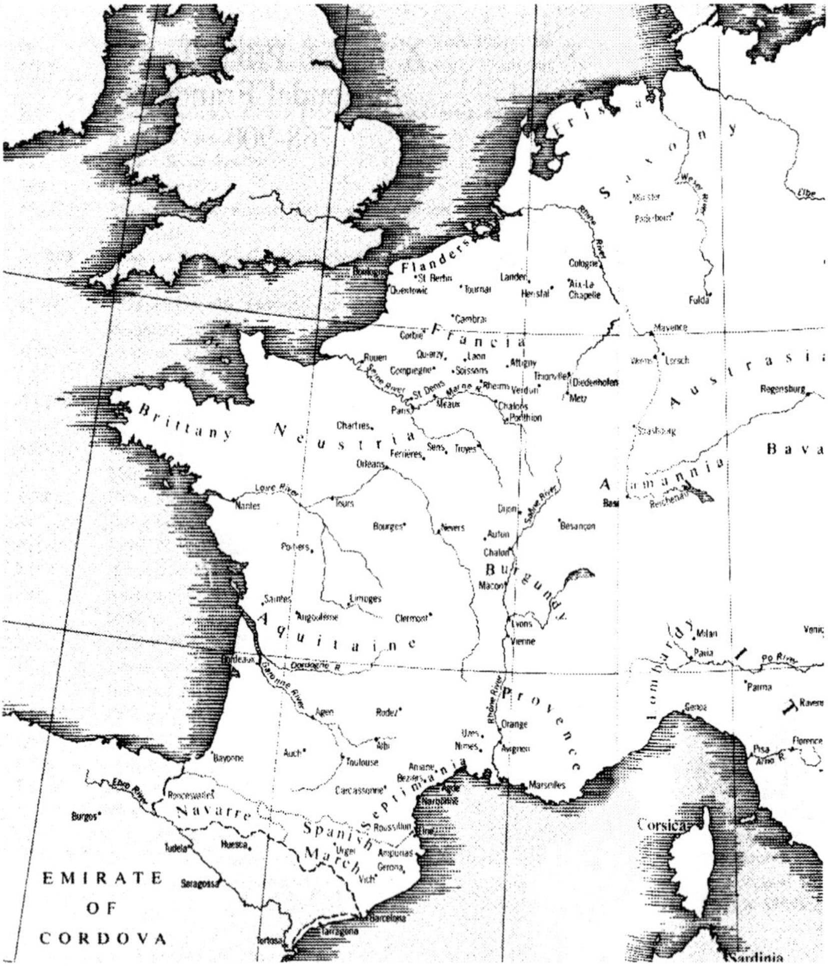

FIGURE 15 - MEDIEVAL FRANCE

Clovis' progress south to the Mediterranean Sea was halted at Septimania, which equated roughly to the present Languedoc and Roussilon region. It was the remnants of the retreating Visigoths, supported by the Ostrogoth Roman Emperor, Theodoric, who challenged his progress. Following a major battle in 496, Clovis, and his army, converted as a whole to Roman Christianity, in recognition of the God he believed had secured his victory. With the city of Paris as his capital, Clovis formed an alliance with the

Holy Roman Emperor that allowed him to use the imperial insignia. His four sons succeeded Clovis on his death, and this led to conflict between them. Some 47 years later, the expanded Frankish empire, by then including Burgundy, was united under the sole remaining son, Chlotar. On his death the kingdom was again divided among four sons and internecine strife continued. It was not until 613 that the kingdom was once again reunited under one king, Chlotar II. This unification continued under his son, Dagobert I. By the time that Dagobert died and his two sons once again divided the country, most of the power in the land had devolved to the "mayors of the palace". There followed just over one hundred years when these chief administrative officers manipulated their kings as puppets and the scene was set for a new royal household.

It was Pepin II's illegitimate son, Charles Martel, who was mayor-of-the-palace when the Merovingian king, Theodoric IV, died and left the throne vacant. The way was then clear for a mayor-of-the-palace to move up to the throne. Martel decided against taking this step himself, and on his death the effective rule over the realm was, yet again, divided between his sons Pepin III (also known as Pepin the Short) and Carloman. Carloman abdicated to enter a monastery leaving his brother Pepin as sole ruler. Although Charles Martel had prevented a successor Merovingian king from being crowned, his death enabled the royal heir, Childeric III, to be enthroned two years later. But, when Pepin the Short had consolidated his position he deposed Childeric and had himself elected king by the barons, with the support of the Pope. In 687, Pepin was crowned king of Gaul, so beginning the Carollingian dynasty. On the death of Pepin the land was again divided, but the death of one son, another Carloman, left the remaining son, Charles, as king. Charles is better known as Charlemagne and he extended the Frankish kingdom over what is now all France, the western side of Germany and into Italy. In 800, on Christmas Day, Charlemagne became Roman Emperor. Although Pope Leo II was present, Charlemagne placed the crown on his own head to emphasise his own superiority to the papacy.

As Europe settled into an arrangement of countries that we would almost recognise today, it was as early as 6 CE that Jews began to populate southern France. They are thought to have accompanied King Archelaus of Cappadocia – a small province in Anatolia – when he was exiled to Vienne[42]. Later additions are believed to have joined Herod's son Antipas when he too was banished, this time to Lyons, in 39 CE. The numbers of Jews settling there increased as they entered the region with the Roman army as soldiers or accompanying the army as traders. Under Visigoth rule, Jews had the status of Romans although Alaric II did substantially reduce the number of Roman laws. These Roman Laws, the so-called Theodosian Code, were named after the Roman Emperor, Theodosius II and applied then in Gaul. When Clovis drove Alaric out of Gaul, life for the resident Jews became harsher. Clovis had converted the Frankish nation to Christianity in 496 and the full force of anti-Jewish sentiment was liberated, spreading to southern France. The first new regulation banned Jews from marrying Christians or assaulting them.

It was fear of the high status afforded to Jews that triggered the anti-Jewish sentiments, supporting our earlier premise that the original Jewish slaves had been able to improve their station in life. The 5th Council of Merovingian Bishops, meeting in Paris, demanded that Jews in positions of authority over Christians should be baptised. Pope Gregory I was active in pressing for laws banning Jews from owning Christian slaves, although he was referring to permanent ownership rather than as a trader, for the Jews were then actively involved in the slave trade. Gregory was equally careful to exclude the Christian tenant farmers of Jewish landowners. Under the Merovingians, the position of Jews continued to worsen until 633 when King Dagobert offered baptism or exile to those remaining.

The anti-Semitism enacted under the Merovingians explains little about our search for a group of devout Jews who may hold some important secret. It does, though, weaken the argument put forward by others[43] that the Merovingians hold the key to a bloodline back to David. The unavoidable reality is that it is unthinkable that a royal family claiming descent from the first anointed king of Israel would cast out the very group of people who carried that bloodline. What is much more likely is that the Merovingians accepted the early Christian sentiment that the Jews had killed their Saviour and Son-of-God, and should be punished. That the Merovingian kings could have supported this early Christian view of Jewish culpability and at the same time proudly proclaimed descent from the most distinguished Jewish ancestor is implausible.

Perhaps the location of Septimania in the far south of France made control over it logistically more difficult, and so Jewry appears to have faired better there. Meanwhile, in Spain, the Visigoth rulers had also converted from Arianism to Catholicism and persecution of the Jews began there too. Indeed, many Spanish Jews fled north to Septimania where ownership of land by Jews was still permitted. The end of the 6th century and early 7th marked a favourable period for the Jews, particularly those in southern France and Spain. When the seventh century after the destruction of the Temple at Jerusalem dawned for the Jews, it brought an expectation that the inclusion of the mystical number seven would bring the long-awaited Messiah.

Coincidentally, the seventh century also saw the rise of Islam and its overwhelming success in rolling back the boundaries of the Christian empire. During the period 672 to 680, the weakness of the Christians in the face of the advancing Muslims prompted a revolt in Septimania and its bordering regions against the Spanish Visigoths. This revolt was at first successful but eventually put down. The effects of the revolt were to attract Jews from the surrounding areas to move to Septimania and to encourage many resident Christians to convert to Judaism. The eventual defeat of the uprising saw the Jews expelled from the region. The success by the Visigoths in restoring order was short-lived, and by 725 all Visigoth Spain and Septimania had fallen under Islamic control as the Arabs advanced out of Africa into Europe.

This was a promising time for those Jews who fell under the rule of the Muslims. It was the practice of the Muslim conquerors to place any Jewish residents in charge of the towns and cities they captured, Cordova, Toledo and Granada are examples. A few Muslims would remain behind with the Jews while the main army continued to move forward. Whether from the conversion of local Christians to the Jewish faith or because of increased immigration, some towns in Spain became all-Jewish or had a Jewish majority of the population[42]. It is not known whether Narbonne was similarly ceded to the Jews although it is a reasonable assumption. Without doubt, under the Muslims the Jews enjoyed a privileged role in Narbonne and managed the extensive Frankish trade that passed through the city heading south through Spain towards North Africa.

It was during this period, while the Muslims were busy bringing Spain and Septimania under their rule, that in Gaul the Merovingian rulers were weakened in consequence of their internecine quarrelling. The death of Dagobert I saw Gaul again divided, and the mayors-of-the-palace effectively running the country. Finally, in 750, Pepin the Short deposed the last Merovingian king, Childeric III, seized the throne and established the Carollingian dynasty.

The coronation of Pepin, in 751, saw the seeds of a Jewish renaissance in France metaphorically planted. At that time Pope Stephan III was under threat from the Lombards, whose expansive activities in Italy brought them closer to the papal lands, and Stephan needed support from a strong ruler in the west to counter these threats. Perhaps, though, there was a further reason for his extravagant support of Pepin. Jerusalem had proved impossible to recover from its Muslim captors; indeed, by 691 AD, Caliph 'Abd al-Malik ibn Marwan, had built the Dome of the Rock as a shrine for Muslim pilgrims on Jerusalem's Temple Mount itself. This may explain why Stephan elevated Pepin to the rank of God's appointed king, by anointing him in the same manner that king David had been anointed centuries earlier in Jerusalem. To emphasis the point, Pope Stephen said that Pepin's right to royal sway was a gift from God. Only three years later, Pope Stephan added to Pepin's honours by appointing him Patrician and Protector of the Church. Pepin's response was to keep a permanent royal delegation at the papal court. It is plain that this Papally endowed biblical succession arguably entitled Pepin to claim governance over Jerusalem itself. That Pepin did not take this step may be explained by his good rapport with the sovereign over Jerusalem, the Caliph of Baghdad. Maybe Pope Stephan had given more than a little thought to the coronation of Pepin.

It was Pepin's father and mayor of the palace, Charles Martel, who had in 738 halted the advance of the Arabs at Lyons and thrown them back to Narbonne. Although Charles laid siege to Narbonne he was unable to breach the walls and retired leaving the city outside Gaul. This was the position Pepin inherited when he assumed the throne of Gaul and was determined to redress. His first move in 752 was to form an alliance with Count Ansemond, and this brought him the surrounding towns from Nîmes to Béziers. With this support Pepin laid siege to Narbonne, a siege that would last seven years. There are conflicting records of who eventually assisted Pepin to break the defence of the siege[42]; one version attributes the success to the local Goths and the other to the Jews.

Whether it was Jew or Goth who helped Pepin to break the siege of Narbonne, the next few years saw a marked improvement of the status of the Jews in Gaul. After the collapse of the Roman Empire, Jews had been treated as Roman citizens, with all the attendant rights, under Roman statutes. Around 500 CE the old Roman law began to be replaced with Teutonic law that turned the Jews into aliens with almost no rights. Zuckerman[42] discusses this at length and concludes that the reality was closer to the position would have been if the Roman law had continued. Indeed, he cites many examples of extant documents granting special rights and privileges to the Jews during the Carollingian period. It is undeniable that if Pepin wished to exercise any control over Jerusalem he would need the tacit approval of the Frankish Jews. Pepin provided the solution to this problem with a masterstroke that demonstrated his complete control of the country. Pepin decided to cede part of the city of Narbonne and its surrounding area to a prince of the Jews, a prince with lineage back to king David.

To effect these plans, Pepin sent a delegation to the Caliph of Babylon requesting him to send a prince, or Nasi, of the Royal House of David to rule over Narbonne. The Caliph obliged and sent Rabbi Makhir, and Pepin responded by settling a large estate on Makhir. Jacob[6] defines the title of Nasi as "primarily one of religious authority but the Nasi also played an occasional political role". The usual title for the Nasis in Palestine, was "Rabban" meaning "Our Master". Jacobs[6] also provides the names of the first five Nasis of the present era:

Rabban Gamaliel (first half of the first century)
Rabban Simeon
Rabban Gamaliel
Rabban Simeon
Rabbi Judah the Prince
Rabban Gamaliel (first half of the third century)

Benbassa[4] puts a slightly different slant on the land settlement. She confirms that Narbonne was divided in three equal shares, between the Count, the bishop and the Jews, "whose leader bore the title 'king of the Jews'". The difference in Benbessa's approach is that she points out the surrender of the city by the Jews necessarily involved them in a breach of trust.

> Thus the Jews were said to have traitorously delivered Narbonne to the future emperor – though it was, of course, his father who conquered the city in 759.
>
> *Esther Bebessa*
> *The Jews of France*

Settling such large lands on a Jewish prince was not overlooked by Pope Stephan, who issued an epistle condemning the use of Christian workers in the vineyards of Jewish landowners. The letter bemoaned the fact that substantial freeholds belonged to the Jews at all. As well as the large Jewish land holdings in the Narbonne region, there is strong suggestion that large tracts of land were made over to the local Jewish leaders shortly after the fall of the city. This supports the claim that it was indeed the Jews who brought about the collapse of Narbonne from within. Zuckerman[42] gives further clarification on the question of whether it was Goth or Jew who helped Pepin's victory over Narbonne. He provides compelling evidence to show the local Goths gained little after the fall of Narbonne, quoting Theodulph, Bishop of Orléans (a fellow Goth), who visited the city at that time:

> As late as 797 – 98 there were only "remnants of the Goth folk" in Narbonne.
>
> *A Jewish Princedom in Feudal France*
> *Arthur Zuckerman*

Pepin's son Charlemagne acceded to the Frankish throne in 768 and, on the death of his brother, Carloman, three years later, gained complete control of Gaul. It was Charlemagne who - acting for his father - had personally presided over the capture of Narbonne and a thirteenth century account tells of him receiving 70,000 silver marks on behalf of the proposed Jewish prince. "He is of the stock of David and from Baghdad". Whether this is a true record is not important, for in early 768 CE the Jewish prince, Natronai, arrived and settled into his principate. There is little doubt that Pepin settled a huge portion of Narbonne on the Nasi. Accounts differ, but it is unlikely that it was less than one-third of the total land area of Narbonne. There is also some confusion over whether the Nasi was known as Natronai or Makhir, but his having one Hebrew name and a different Greek one explains this. To avoid confusion, we will use Natronai.

It is clear that Pepin – with the support of his two sons, Carloman and Charles – had brought a foreign prince into his kingdom and allotted him vast tracts of prime freehold land. Now this may simply have been a gesture to repay the help given to him by the Jews during his siege of Narbonne, the necessary price that brought him victory. But it is also clear the arrangement held many advantages. It cemented relations between the Frankish king and his counterpart in Baghdad. The caliph would have been pleased to have a friendly ambassador in the Frankish state as well as a tenuous claim to joint suzerainty with the Frankish king over a stretch of southern Gaul. Equally, the Carollingian claim to hold the throne by the will of God became more secure with a descendant of king David at hand. With it also came the possibility of later direct rule over Jerusalem. Finally, Pepin had secured a friendly and strong buffer state between Gaul and Muslim Spain.

We will now reflect on this investigation so far. We attempted to track deported Jews – after the sack of Jerusalem in 70 CE - on the assumption that some of them might have had some connection with the founding of Freemasonry. This connection may be connected with knowledge of the whereabouts of the Ark of the Covenant and that links the Cohanim into our investigation. We found nothing significant in Rome but in nearby Narbonne we find a secure haven, or as secure as anywhere might have been for a Jew in the Christian west. Narbonne is only 800 kilometres by sea from Rome or 1,000 kilometres overland. It is more or less where the Ashkenazic and Sephardic diasporas met, and arguably most important of all, it is only 50 kilometres from Pech Cardou. Pech Cardou is the mountain where Byrne[1] suggested that the Ark of the Covenant was hidden for several hundred years. This was indeed a golden location and the local main seat of learning – the Academy of Narbonne – would have been loyal to the new Nasi. This arrangement, a Jewish principate in southern Gaul - or at the least a strong Jewish presence - would last well over two hundred years until the end of the Carollingian dynasty.

Mention of Pech Cardou necessitates a brief explanation of the co-author, Patrick Byrne's, previous book, Templar Gold. This book examined the mystery surrounding a tiny village called Rennes-le-Château in the *Roussillon* region of Southern France. The "Rennes-le-Château mystery" concerns a legend suggesting there is some treasure buried there. The myth of buried treasure developed when a local priest Abbot Saunière made a discovery in 1885 that led to his becoming wealthy. Saunière promised to make his secret available before his death, but events dictated otherwise. There is, however, one aspect of the Rennes-le-Château mystery that was set on one side as an irrelevance. This is the suggestion that a bloodline exists dating back to the Biblical King David and, or Jesus Christ and for this reason is called the *Rex Deus* bloodline. The fact is that no matter how inconsequential this suggestion may be, the regular publication of books devoted in part, or in whole, to the subject suggests that unseen hands are actively cultivating the affair. The phenomenal success of the novel The Da Vinci Code[7], which is centred around a bloodline from Jesus Christ and His wife (according to the novel) Mary Magdalene, demonstrates that this line of enquiry should be kept in mind. The observation that we have already uncovered a Cohanim bloodline, which may have been preserved as a vehicle for an Aaronic Messiah makes certain that we will return in more detail to this matter in Part 3.

Narbonne holds a curious echo in this investigation. Just over a millennium later, the priest from Rennes-le-Château who created the mystery touched on above – Abbé Bérenger Saunière – was promoted, in 1882, to be professor at the seminary of Narbonne. A mundane coincidence perhaps as he only stayed there for one month, until one becomes aware of a curious episode that occurred at his death, as recorded by Gérard de Sède[45]:

> … where his earthly remains were set up in state, draped in a covering adorned with red tassels. All the villagers filed past to render him their final homage. In remembrance each one plucked a tassel as a keep-sake to take away.
>
> *The Accursed Treasure of Rennes-le-Château*
> *Gérard De Sède*

Various writers down the years have commented on this odd behaviour but not one has mentioned that this practice is common at a Jewish funeral. The shroud, over a Jewish male corpse, is called a *kittel* and is used in other ceremonies, such as weddings, as a reminder of mortality. This too finds an echo in the Masonic third-degree ceremony of "raising" where in earlier days a smock (*kittel* is from the German for smock) was actually worn by the candidate. As well as the *kittel*, men are also covered with their *tallit*, the white prayer shawl that they wore when they were alive. It is the Jewish custom at funerals to cut the fringes from the *tallit* to make it unusable by anyone else. We can only speculate on the reasons why Abbé Saunière had red tassels, perhaps an allusion to the red heifer, the *parah adumah* that is sacrificed to purify someone who has come in contact with a corpse. The Talmud states that the red signified its rarity. Perhaps this was the old Abbé's final joke, because the section of the Torah dealing with the *parah adumah* is read on the Sabbath after Purim. The *parah adumah* recalls Jerusalem Temple times and warns anyone who has been contaminated to purify themselves in readiness to offer the Paschal lamb at Passover[6], the festival to celebrate the escape of the Jews from Egypt. What if Saunière was actually a proselyte and had secretly converted to Judaism? This could explain why the priest who came to give him absolution only two days before his death, Abbé Rivière, the Curé from the neighbouring village of Esperanza, left "deathly pale and thrown into confusion". De Sède[45] reports Rivière as deeply affected by his last meeting with Saunière to the point where "he became withdrawn, taciturn and silent, up to his death he was not seen to laugh". There is a recent incident that supports this possibility. While writing Templar Gold, Byrne was told by a colleague who had visited the area, that many front doors had thistles pinned to them. This prompted some research into thistles that proved unproductive. Recently, though, Finkelstein and Silberman[22] discuss a verse from the Bible:

> And Jehoash the king of Israel sent to Amaziah king of Judah, saying, The thistle that was in Lebanon sent to the cedar that was in Lebanon, saying, Give thy daughter to my son to wife: and there passed by a wild beast that was in Lebanon, and trode down the thistle.
>
> *2 Kings 14:9*

Finkelstein and Silberman assert that the "thistle" refers to Jerusalem. While this snippet adds a slender measure of support for the thesis of Templar Gold, it may also point to a level of Judaic sympathy in the region around Rennes-le-Château that has previously gone unreported.

Zuckerman[42] is convinced the new Makhir, Natronai, married Alda, the daughter of Charles Martel, shortly after his arrival in Gaul. This would add weight to Charlemagne's epithet at court of "David", if he numbered a Jewish prince – a direct descendant of the Biblical king David – in his family. As if to further confuse the later chroniclers, the Franks preferred to use names that were more familiar to them and it seems that for the Natronai they selected Theodoricus, which was popular in Merovingian Gaul. Charlemagne was sufficiently happy with the way events turned out in southern France to issue a *privilegium* making the Principate of Narbonne a permanent institution. There is also some evidence to show that, even before Charlemagne had been made Roman Emperor, he turned "blind eye" to the Natronai being referred to as king. As late as the fourteenth century there are documents[42] that refer to a "king of the Jews" in Narbonne; and in 1216 a resident – Bernard de Cortone – left property and cash to "the son of the Jews' king".

Zuckerman[42] quotes G. Saige, Juifs de Narbonne, as reproducing a seal emblazoned on a heraldic shield with a lion rampant, a six-pointed star (the Magen David) and the name Kalonymos b. Todros Isaiah Cohen, on one side. Kalonymos is the Italian and Greek equivalent of Makhir and Todros has been identified as Theodoricus. Furthermore, only kings and barons were using heraldic symbols on their seals in the thirteenth century. What is, of course, of particular interest to this investigation is the surname "Cohen", which firmly settles the family group we seek in the region, and in a position of considerable power around the time of the Crusades. Zuckerman's assertion that the Natronai was Count Theodoricus is not universally accepted.

As if to further complicate matters, thousands of genealogical tables – particularly those of Mormons - claim lineage back to Jesus Christ based entirely on Zuckerman's claim. Noted authorities, such as Professors Constance Bouchard and Bernard Bachrach, from the Universities of Akron and California, dissent from this opinion.

> Thus it is disappointing that our author [Zuckerman] has discovered pyrites and cast a grotesque in fool's gold.
>
> *Bernard Bachrach*
> *American Historical Review December 1973*

Bachrach leans heavily for his criticism of Zuckerman on the latter's use of *chansons* (literally French "songs" dating back to the 12th century) and *responsa* (answers given by rabbinic scholars to questions about Jewish law, from the Hebrew *She'elot U-teshubot*). Professor Louis Rabinowitz[46] also mentions the Machir and so weakens the suggestion that these sources are not strong enough to support Zuckerman's thesis. Rabinowitz quotes Abraham ibn Daud from the *Sefer ha-Kabbalah* as well as well as Abraham Zacuto from the *Sefer Yuhasin*.

> The grant of one-third of the city of Narbonne was made, not to the Jewish community, but to a certain Rabbi Machir whom Charlemagne summoned from Babylon through the agency of Haroun al-Rashid.
>
> *Louis Rabinowitz*
> *Jewish Merchant Adventurers*

Bouchard[47] begins her treatise by discussing the difficulties of recreating family trees for ancient noble families:

> First of all, it must be stressed that the modern conception of the "family" did not exist in the central Middle Age... The medieval Latin term *familia* did not mean "family"; rather, it meant a household, including servants and attendants as well as actual relatives.
>
> *Constance Bouchard*
> *Those of My Blood*

While Professor Bouchard does not directly address the question of whether the Natronai and Theodoricus (Bouchard uses Theoderic) are the same person, she agrees with Zuckerman on Theoderic's mother as Alda (Zuckerman uses Aldana). Subsequent generations also display a high-level of agreement. Bouchard however, maintains that Theoderic is the first of the line of Dukes of Septimania and makes no mention of the Natronai, signalling that she too places no merit on Zuckerman's thesis.

Based on the available evidence, it is clearly unwise to accept Zuckerman's thesis as "beyond doubt". Equally it would be wrong to dismiss it out of hand; perhaps "not-proven" is a suitable compromise. To base one's family pedigree on such uncertain evidence does, though, look ill-advised. Whether Zuckerman's thesis is correct is largely immaterial to this chapter, the point of which is to identify a substantial Jewish community within striking distance of Rome. Zuckerman's opinions do find some support in later generations of Theodoric's family and so we will continue with his account.

In 791 the Natronai, known by his Frankish name as Count Theodoric [which we will use hereafter], participating in battle on behalf of Charlemagne against the Avars. The Avars were people from the east of Turkey who were then marauding through Europe. On this occasion they fled without offering any resistance, but it is notable that Theodoric commanded no less than one-third of the total army. In 793, in battle against the Saxons, Theodoric was killed and succeeded by his son William. William, was – according to Zuckerman - the son of a Carollingian Princess, and, if this is correct, the suggested Carollingian dream of uniting the Carollingian and Davidic bloodlines had been achieved. When William inherited the princedom, it had expanded to include the buffer state of the March of Spain. The March was a roughly rectangular territory bounded more or less by the eastern half of the present border between France and Spain and stretching as far south as Barcelona. William had earlier been given the title of Duke of Toulouse together with lands that accompanied it and added these to his father's princedom. William's land - Septimania and the Spanish march - now stretched from the Mediterranean shore to Toulouse in the north and from the Rhone river in the east to include the March of Spain in the south-west.

William's immediate inheritance was a baptism by fire. With Charlemagne – supported by Theodoric (until his death) – away in the east, the new Emir, Hisham I, brought his army across from Spain and plundered the March of Spain and western Septimania. William rushed back from the eastern front but Hisham's forces overwhelmed his army and he was lucky to escape with his life. Fortunately for William, Hisham was content to return to Spain laden with gold and slaves. Charlemagne, good general that he was, decided that his main threat was from the east and remained there. This action caused William to throw a tantrum and withdraw homage from the king of Aquitaine. Charlemagne's son Louis, who was the suzerain for William's title of Duke of Toulouse, settled matters by sending part of his army to assist William to hold the border. Zuckerman[42] refers to a contemporary ballad that suggests that Louis married William's sister – although the use of the word "married" – may have been artistic licence. Louis actually married Ermengarde, who was the daughter of Count Ingram, and Ingram's county was Hasbania in Saxony. Louis and Ermengarde together had four children, although Louis was known to have fathered two children before his marriage. If there is any truth in the ballad, then it is fitting to remember that Jewishness is transmitted down the female line.

The problems that William faced over the defence of his border with Spain must have caused more than a little soul-searching. It would have been easy for William to appeal to the Caliph of Baghdad to whom, if Zuckerman is correct, he was a subject (just like his father, Natronai, before him). This, though, would doubtless have offended Charlemagne who saw himself as William's suzerain. There was, however, another issue, which demanded that William kept a good relationship with Charlemagne. It was a problem that went to the heart of the theological differences between Jew and Christian. If William remained friendly with Charlemagne he would be allowed to keep the title of "king of the Jews" (in Europe). This enabled Jews to argue the Messiah had not yet come, in clear contradiction of the position held by Christians that Jesus Christ was the Messiah. For this exegesis, the Jews were relying on Exodus 49:10

> The sceptre shall not depart from Judah, nor the ruler's staff from between his feet, until Shiloh cometh.

Shiloh is another term for the Messiah and the convoluted argument was, that all the time a Jewish prince of the line of David exercised monarchical power then the Messiah cannot have arrived. According to this argument, if the messiah had arrived then the prince would have handed over his rule to him. It is always difficult to prove a negative and this Judaic versus Christian debate reverberated down the years.

The position of the Jewish people and their prince, in Gaul, was strengthened when the Patriarch of Jerusalem sent the keys to the Holy Sepulchre and of Calvary to Charlemagne. He also sent the Banner (*vexillum*) of Jerusalem thus placing the city under the authority of the West. A later report has Charlemagne giving the *vexillum* to William as a gift for services rendered. Ten years after assuming his father's title, William led an army into Spain and after a siege that lasted many months – some say over one year - Barcelona fell to the Franks. The emperor Charlemagne had provided support and king Louis of Aquitaine was in overall command, and because of his contribution to this successful military campaign, northern Spain was added to William's princedom. William died around 823 and the last twenty years of his life are shrouded in mystery, due in no small part to the activities of two monasteries. Doubtless William gave some properties to the monastery at Gellone, which is between Narbonne and Montpellier. This monastery, in time, came under the control of a neighbouring monastery, Aniane. It seems that over the years these two centres of ecclesiastical devotion competed with each other to the point of producing forgeries to claim credit for tempting William from Judaism into Christianity. The conversion of such a major Jewish dignitary would have been a significant catch for any Christian centre in any era. Zuckerman[42] casts doubts on the whole story of William's conversion and his later entry into the monastery at Gellone as a monk for the last years of his life. He prefers to see William's contribution of property as for an academy for religious and military study, *Bet-El* (House of God), is Zuckerman's preferred name for the institution. Whether William ended his life subservient to the rule of St. Benedict is difficult to contradict because the records that remain are minimal apart from the copies of ecclesiastical records compiled the monks of the two competing monasteries.

We must recognise that powerful forces are being tried to the limit by the very existence of William as the son of Nasi Natronai and thus a prince of the line of David. If Zuckerman is right then William is the first-born son to have both Carollingian and Davidic bloodlines coursing through his veins. Because of this, subsequent kings of France will – if this view is correct – have a Davidic bloodline. As we have mentioned before, Jewishness is carried down the female line and so the descendants of William would not be Jewish on his account, they would simply carry the bloodline. The existence, within the royal families of the Holy Roman Empire, of a Davidic Judaic bloodline would plainly pose a threat to the contemporary Church of Rome. The Church might therefore be forgiven for wanting William to convert to Christianity before his death. Whatever the truth of this interesting vignette from French history, the fact is that in 1066 William,

Count of Toulouse, was canonised and did become St. William of Gellone.

By 820, William's son Bernard had regained the March of Spain, which had earlier been detached from the princedom, possibly from his brother. Only seven or so years later Bernard achieved notable fame by successfully defending Barcelona unaided against a combined Goth and Saracen attack. In 829, Bernard, Count of Barcelona, was installed as chamberlain at the imperial court of Emperor Louis, who had succeeded his father Charlemagne. As chamberlain, Bernard was effectively number two in the realm after the emperor. When Bernard died, Septimania, by then safely back within the princedom, was referred to as a "kingdom", and Bernard as its king.

As so often happens, Louis' court was beset with intrigue as "friends" of Louis' various sons competed for the eventual shares of the empire. When the new chamberlain, Bernard, arrived, he cleared the palace of Louis' wife's enemies and replaced them with friendly faces. This act created enemies for Bernard and would in time contribute to his fall. Bearing in mind that Emperor Louis was known as "the Pious"; Bernard's cause was not helped when a deacon at court, Bodo, converted to Judaism. First Bodo broke off from a pilgrimage to Rome and then he went to southern France and sold his entourage into slavery. He was duly circumcised, let his hair grow and married a Jewess. Shortly after this momentous event, he took the name Eleazar and fled to Cordova.

In 840, Emperor Louis died and the distribution of his empire could not be agreed between his two competing sons, Charles the Bald and Lothar. The result was a battle between the two heirs with Bernard holding his army at a safe distance and not intervening on either side. Charles was the victor and shortly afterwards Bernard retired to the March of Spain. The royal family was not quite finished with Bernard. Pepin II, the king of Aquitaine refused to submit to Charles the Bald. In consequence, Charles gave Aquitaine, and with it Bernard's county of Toulouse, to another nobleman, Effroi. When Charles moved against Toulouse, Bernard made the fateful decision to lead its defence. He was captured early in the siege and executed for treason.

Bernard's fall from royal grace was the signal for the churchmen of southern France to sue for return of their various lost rights to tolls and other revenues. The loss of his previously loyal henchman caused Charles to rethink his defences along the Mediterranean coast and the border with Spain. The action Charles proposed was to weaken the incumbent prince of Septimania and to build up the Spanish settlers in the area. The incumbent prince was Bernard's eighteen-year-old son William and he immediately took up arms with Pepin II against king Charles. The first major battle between the two armies was at Angoumois where Charles' army was destroyed. It seems likely that following this victory, Pepin once more appointed William to the family title of Duke of Toulouse.

Meanwhile, the Church was dusting off its earlier draft legislation for the consideration of the king. In the space of only two years there were five church councils with resolutions seeking that:

1. No assignment of abbeys to laymen.
2. Jews be denied the right to have slaves.
3. Circumcised slaves to be freed.
4. Jews could not serve as attorneys or as soldiers.
5. Jews be denied public office.
6. Jews could no longer build synagogues.
7. Jews who converted freemen without consent be put to death.
8. On Christian festivals Jews were to stay out of public places.
9. Jewish children were to be taken from their parents and brought up as Christians.
10. In short, to suppress Judaism.

The list provides a flavour of the anti-Semitic feelings that permeated the Christian church in those days. To the consternation of the bishops, in 846 king Charles rejected sixty-four of the eighty-four articles including all the anti-Jewish canons.

With the bishops of France pressing Charles for anti-Jewish legislation, the ex-deacon of the Frankish court, Bodo now named Eleazar, had become increasingly fanatical about Judaism in his new country of Spain. He was eventually able to persuade the Muslim authorities to insist that all Christians convert to Islam or Judaism on pain of death. This demonstrates clearly that the antagonism between Christian and Jew was strong in both directions. During the whole of the period when Charles was under pressure on all fronts, William of Toulouse upheld his opposition to the king. William's hostility was completely undermined when in 845, Pepin II, rolled over and swore fealty to Charles the Bald. By 850, Charles' problems were improving and he was able to turn his attention to Willliam, who had returned to the March of Spain. With the help of Count Aléron of Troyes, William was trapped and engaged in battle. William's army fared worse and he fled to Barcelona where the local Goths accepted a bribe and handed him over to the king. William died, as had his father at the hands of the official executioner.

The loss, to the Natronai family, of William left one remaining male heir, Bernard, but he was only nine years old. Accordingly, another member of the Mahkir family, Solomon, took on the role of Nasi. Aléron of Troyes had added Barcelona to Troyes when William had been executed, but clearly Barcelona and Troyes are too far apart to govern effectively. Indeed, only two years later the Moors, with help from the resident Jews, captured Barcelona and slaughtered all of the remaining Christians. It took Solomon several years to settle and recover the titles and counties lost by Bernard and his son William. By 858, Solomon had established himself at the court of Charles and when the incumbent rebelled, Solomon was appointed to his titles of Count of Roussillon and Marquess of Barcelona. Solomon was assassinated by a young man from a local leading family, named Wilfred le Velu in 869.

The death of Solomon leaves the identity of the next Nasi open to debate. Zuckerman[42] settles on Bernard Plantevelue, Count of Auvergne, who, by 870 had moved to Narbonne. There were no fewer that three important Bernards at that time and so to avoid unnecessary speculation we will draw this location for our investigation to a close.

The last Carollingian king of France, Charles the Fat was deposed in November of 887 and died only two months later. Charles was succeeded in France by Eudes who was not a

Carollingian, but was the son of Robert the Strong, count of Anjou and Blois, from whom the following Capetian kings of France were descended. Eudes had successfully defended Paris from the Vikings in 886 and as a result was elected king. Eventually Hugh Capet was crowned in 987, marking the formal beginning of the Capetian dynasty of French kings.

During the early years of this period of turmoil, Zuckerman's[42] identified Nasi, William, tried to remain loyal to the titular rulers. However, his support for the Carollingian cause alienated King Eudes who divested him of his titles and estates and passed them to count Hugh of Bourges. The new claimant to the titles faced the earlier incumbent in battle and agreed to settle the dispute in hand-to-hand combat. The result was that William killed Hugh despite a plea for his life on the grounds of piety. After this William was reconciled with Eudes and his titles and estates were returned to him. It was in 910 that William, variously count, marquess, duke and prince, performed an act that provides a coincidental link to the Freemasons. William founded an institution at Bourges, which would eventually become the Benedictine Abbey of Cluny. Some 200 years later, the abbot of Cluny, one Peter the Venerable, had become a close friend of a Cistercian monk, Bernard, who later became the Saint Bernard who wrote the Templar rule.

We mentioned a little earlier how Aléron of Troyes had added Barcelona to his land around Troyes. This is, therefore, an appropriate moment to move our researches to another French centre for Judaism, Champagne. By the year 1,000 CE Jews were established in Troyes and Reims[5] with forty-three settlements totalling around 4,500 people. There, as elsewhere they protected their commerce by taking an oath, the *herem hayishuv*, which prevented newcomers from starting in competition with established businesses. Jewish communities would elect their "master" or mayor together with councilmen who would be recognised by the Christian authorities. These Jewish communities settled readily into a hierarchical structure targeted on the upper classes. Jews were well aware of the status enjoyed by the wealthy, and their merchant and money-lending activities ensured that many were eligible for such standing. It was the introduction of "non-retention laws" in 1198, which prohibited a Jew from leaving his lord's land without permission, which marked a turning point for them. The limitation that these laws imposed on the Jews sapped their entrepreneurship, and gradually the community became impoverished.

Champagne holds one of the keys to this enquiry, although that key will likely never be found. It was Champagne that produced Pope Urban II, who called the first Crusade. Urban was educated at Reims Cathedral school. It was in Troyes, capital city of Champagne that Rabbi Shlomo Yitzhaki, better known as Rashi from the initial letters of his name, was born. Rashi went on to become one of the foremost Rabbis known to Judaism and his *responsas* carry weight today. Rashi started his own school in 1070, teaching children and adults about the Torah and Jewish law. Rashi and his pupils started a movement that became known as the Tosafists. The name derives from *Tosafot* meaning additions to the Babylonian Talmud. The Tosafit examined the Talmud minutely and wrote extensive updates and amendments. It was also from Champagne that the first knights set off to form the Knights Templar in Jerusalem, shortly after the first Crusade. And it was in Champagne where Saint Bernard ran the Cistercian Monastery at Clairvaux. It was in Troyes that Saint Bernard compiled the Templar Rule by which the Knights Templar would live and die. Finally, it was the Knights Templar who Byrne[1] suggests found the Ark of the Covenant on Temple Mount and eventually took it back to France.

One thing is clear about Champagne and that is that Jews and gentiles lived for long periods in peaceful cooperation. There is even a legend that Jews joined the Christians gathered in Reims Cathedral to pray for rain during an exceptionally long drought. As the years passed, the strength of the Christian Church grew and with it a desire to snuff out the Judaism along with other schisms, and in 1030 the first burning of heretics took place in Champagne. It was during a period of intense pressure on Jews to convert to Christianity that Rashi issued an important *responsa*. He said that Jews who converted out of fear or weakness and who anticipated later return to Judaism were excused. He added that their legal status as Jews remained unchanged, using the words "An Israelite, even though he has sinned, [remains] an Israelite". When in 1096 the first Crusade began to wind its way across Europe towards the Levant, attacks on Jews by the religiously fired up crusaders were common. Usually the Jews were given the choice of conversion to Christianity or death. Rashi's rulings were therefore of extreme importance to European Jewry during this period. To the consternation of the crusaders, many Jews preferred suicide to conversion, on occasions killing their families along with themselves. The logic behind such actions was that Christians were unworthy to kill Jews and if anyone was going to kill a Jew then it would be a Jew. Although such slaughter did not take place in Champagne it affected both Christian and Jewish communities there.

After the first Crusade, Champagne began to flourish as the textile trade developed in the region. In Troyes, a second synagogue was built to accommodate the swelling ranks of Jews drawn to the area by its increasing wealth. Here, as in the south, Jews lived under the old Theodosian Code, that permitted them to make their own laws and to regulate and enforce them. Their Council of Elders dealt directly with the local Count as representatives of all the local Jewry. One important development, made possible by the increasing wealth, was the growth of Jewish schools and centres of learning. A comment from the times said that, "Jews were so zealous for learning that both rich and poor sent all their sons to school and even taught their daughters". A law passed by the Jewish synod of 1160 ruled that no Jew could take another to a gentile court unless both agreed. This expression of disdain for anything gentile, even the judiciary finds a curious impersonation in Freemasonry. The last of the "Ancient Charges" contains these words:

> And if any of them [other Freemasons] do you injury you must apply to your own or his lodge; and from thence you may appeal to the grand lodge at the quarterly communication, as has been the ancient laudable conduct of our forefathers in every nation; never taking a legal course but when the case cannot be otherwise decided, and patiently listening to the

> honest and friendly advice of master and fellows, when they would prevent your going to law with stranger …".

The similarity of this Masonic charge to the Jewish law is undeniable. It is, though, the words "as has been the ancient laudable conduct of our forefathers in every nation", which cements the argument. Who, apart from diaspora Jews can make such a claim? Who else has "forefathers" in every nation?

It was 1145, when King Louis VII issued an order banishing all Jews who had converted to Christianity and later reverted, that the spotlight turned again towards Jewry. Thirty-seven years later his son, Philip, expelled the Jews from Royal lands confiscating their lands in the process. This was a period when the nobility was under pressure to fund crusades and the wealth of the Jews, who provided them with loans, ensured the survival of Jewry in Champagne and elsewhere. The nobility also took a "cut" of the Jews' interest earnings on other loans in return for enforcing payment by defaulters. The "non-retention" treaties mentioned above, ensured the revenue of individual lords and counts, but began the decline of the wealth of the Jews that would seal their fate. As the wealth of the Champenois Jews declined, labouring for local gentiles became necessary, a style of living that Jewry found hard to accept. Emily Taitz[48] puts it succinctly:

> By assuming that all Jews were "like knights", Jews ignored the earlier terminology of the humble and the great (*ketanim* and *gedolim*) which had divided their own community.
>
> *Emily Taitz*
> *The Jews of Medieval France*

Apart from the obvious superiority that assumed "knighthood" brought with it, it also allowed Jews to travel anywhere unhindered, a benefit that will be seen to be important to this investigation. It is clear that the wealth of the Champenois Jewry had reinforced their views of superiority over the gentiles, a view doubtless derived from their status as God's chosen people. Such behaviour can, though, only have antagonised the indigenous gentile population. This attitude of superiority extended to theological matters and would have been enhanced by Christian scholars regularly consulting Jewish scholars on the Hebrew language in their search for the original meanings of early Bibles. Jewish feelings of superiority are exemplified by the ruling of another great Rabbi from Champagne, Rabbi Jacob Tam. He decreed that if a gentile overpaid a Jew, the overpayment need not be repaid. It is easy to see how knowledge of such a ruling by Christians would not have aided good relations. One aspect of Jewish business, money-lending, would not have endeared them to the local population. The normal rate of interest until 1206 was sixty-five percent, an excessive rate by modern standards. Even after 1206, the interest rate reduced to 43 percent, which is still very high by modern standards, especially when most loans were for short periods of around six weeks to cover the duration of a fair.

During the 1230s the Church of Rome initiated the Inquisition as a tool to root out heretics. Rome had been even-handed with the Jews for centuries but although the Inquisition was primarily aimed at Christian heresies, those enforcing it viewed Jewry as a legitimate target. They were particularly interested in Jews who had converted and later relapsed. By the 1250s Jews were obliged to wear the *rouelle* or round patch on the front and back of their clothing. Jews who converted to Christianity demonstrated their new loyalty by denouncing to the Inquisition the meaning of certain passages in the Hebrew Talmud. This resulted in twelve thousand copies of the Talmud being burned in Paris in 1242. Anti-Semitism continued and in 1288 thirteen Jews were burned alive in Troyes for the alleged murder of a Christian. Some measure of the importance of the Jews to the nobility is shown by the way the king ordered the Dominican Friars who had conducted the trial not to pursue or capture Jews without his permission.

As the thirteenth century drew to a close Champagne itself began to decline. Italian merchants began buying their textiles directly from the manufacturers in Flanders, bypassing the Champagne fairs that had brought wealth to the region. The growth of competition from Christian merchants had caused most Jewish traders to move into money-lending. Now, though, the reduction in trade brought major defaults by Christian merchants, and accumulating debts that were impossible to repay. This crisis brought laws providing moratoria on debts and suspension of interest charges. Champenois Jewry was itself now in serious economic difficulty. In consequence, several Rabbis emigrated to The Holy Land. The decline of the merchant class also allowed the Jewish scholar's to fill the void. Champagne became a rabbinic oligarchy. The local Tosafists were able to proclaim:

> The Talmudic texts, the commentaries, the novellae, the [*halakhic*] compositions, they are the teachers of men".

The use of the term "teachers of men" by a group of religious scholars provides a reminder of the term used for the leader of the Essenes, "righteous teacher".

The response by the Jews to the increasingly oppressive gentile regime was very human but unhelpful. Rabbi Issac of Dampierre urged Jews secretly to deny oaths made to gentiles. Passive hostility towards gentiles was another method of showing their dislike of the regime. Taitz[48] quotes a protest letter sent by Meir ben Simon of Narbonne to King Louis IX. There were also attempts to bring the Pope into the matter on the side of the Jews. This latter course of action did bear fruit and various Popes urged prudence on the bishops and counts but to no avail. After the introduction of the non-retention laws in 1198, the increasingly powerful secular authorities continued to undermine the position of Jewry. Increasing taxation, and replacing Jewish laws with laws of the realm reduced the communities control over its own members. As Champagne became closer to royal France the anti-Semitic royal decrees began to bite more heavily on Champenois Jewry. Even the Jewish claim to high social status was ending. As the large homes of Jews were confiscated to settle large tax debts, they were forced to move into houses more in line with those of their gentile neighbours. Evidenced by the question of whether a Jew should work as a labourer for a gentile. Rabbi Elijah of Paris argued that to support his wife a Jew should be prepared to take any work. Rabbi Tam disagreed and stated that while the job of "teacher to children" was acceptable a Jew was never required to hire himself out as a labourer. Rabbi Tam quoted the Talmud to support his argument, "we are servants of God not servants of His servants".

With the death of Philip III in 1285, Champagne was absorbed into the royal lands. The new king, Philip IV had plans for the Jews of an entirely different order. One by one the smaller Jewish communities were expelled and their possessions sequestrated by the king. The Jews of Gascony were first in 1288. In 1289 The Jews of Anjou followed. In 1290 the Jews of England were expelled Most of these exiles found their way to the large Jewish centres of France: Paris, Troyes and Reims. Having all of the Jews in a few locations was too great a temptation for Philip IV. In 1295 he ordered the arrest of all of the Jews and offered their release for a huge ransom. When the money failed to appear he raided their homes and seized any money and other valuables. Finally in 1306 Philip had all the Jews arrested again and this time confiscated their lands as well as their valuables. The Jews were then formally expelled from France. From Champagne alone it is estimated that some 20,000 Jews left with little more than the clothes they stood up in.

We have attempted in this chapter to show that the region in the south of France known now as the Languedoc and Roussillon was a Jewish stronghold during the Carollingian period of French history. In bringing this argument forward we have relied in large part on Arthur Zuckerman's[42] painstaking account of the history of the region during the Carollingian era. In so doing, it has proved impossible not to examine in detail Zuckerman's claim that a marriage took place between a Jewish prince of the House of David and a Carollingian princess. Today, thousands of families rely on Zuckerman's thesis to claim to be directly descended from the Biblical King David. Our researches have identified two authoritative scholars who disagree with Zuckerman's conclusions, and so complete confidence in them is not possible.

What cannot be denied is that the Jews of Narbonne and the surrounding region did enjoy an especially high status during the Carollingian era and we have supported this by examining another region in France, Champagne. Whether the Dukes of

Septimania carried Davidic blood in their veins is not the subject of this investigation. We are interested in the Cohanim, and so we have tracked a Jewish Aaronic bloodline not a Davidic one. In so doing, it is of interest to show there was, indeed, a special relationship between the Carollingian rulers and the Jews. The authenticity of this relationship, together with the special esteem that Narbonne held in those times is supported by another little-known fact. This is, that during the time of the Carollingians the Jews dominated international trade between the East and the West. This Jewish trade domination began around the beginning of the Carollingian rule over France and ended with its demise.

We would probably be unaware of this international commerce, carried out by Jewish merchants known as "Radanites", were it not for an Arab postmaster, Aboul Kassim Obaid Allah ibn Khordadbeh. Ibn Khordadbeh was the Director of Posts and Police for what is now Iran, and in his Kitab al Masalik w'al Mamalik (literally the "Book of the Roads and the Kingdoms") he mentions the Radanite trade. The postal service was created by Abd al-Malik, the fifth Umayyad Caliph, some 170 years earlier, around 700 CE, and radiated out from his base in Damascus. The postal service soon became much more that a facility for the delivery of mail and included a vast espionage system. Each provincial capital had its own post office and the mail was carried between these offices by mule and camel. The Umayyad dynasty initially ruled over what are now Syria and the Levant, but ambitious expansion plans would eventually bring them down. Their eventual demise had its origin at the time when they expanded north into Anatolia (modern Turkey) only to have the Byzantine Emperor Leo III defeat their army in 717 CE. The Umayyads turned west and drove along the Mediterranean coast of Africa before turning north to conquer what is now Spain. Their advance was halted at Poitiers, in France, in 732 CE.

The next few years saw the Umayyads suffer external attack and internal strife and in 750 CE, the last Umayyad Caliph, Marwan II, was defeated at the battle of the Great Zab River. The family members were hunted down and killed, apart from Abd ar-Rahman, who escaped to Spain to found the Muslim dynasty of the

Umayyads of Cordoba. Abu al-'Abbas as-Saffah, a Hashimite, was declared the first Abbasid Caliph.

The new Abbasid caliphate halted the advance to the West, north Africa and southern Europe, and turned to the East to establish a new capital at Baghdad. This move weakened their geographical links with the neighbouring Islamic states and heralded a rise in internationalism. They developed an emphasis on being a community of believers in Islam rather than existing as an Arab nation. It was the Abbasids who first acknowledged the embryonic Islamic law and established their rule based on it. For most of their first hundred years of rule, the Abbasids promoted commerce, industry, arts, and science, and so raised their prestige and power. It was during this period the Jewish merchants, the Radanites, also became established. The reason for the name "Radanite" is lost to us and Rabinowitz[46] suggests the town of Ray, on the eastern border of the province of Jibal (north-eastern Iraq), as the possible location of the first Jewish merchant traders. We can only speculate that perhaps the second syllable, "dan", refers to the original Jewish tribe to which those traders belonged.

When we look at the period of the Merovingians in France, from perhaps 700 CE until about 750 CE, international trade between east and west was managed by Jewish traders and the Syrians (under the Umayyad caliphs) from Anatolia. The date of 750 CE is auspicious because not only does the Umayyad dynasty collapse then but the Merovingian dynasty was also replaced by the Carollingians. This date, 750 CE, also saw the Radanites exert a monopoly over all trade between France to the west and India and China in the east, and all countries between. The Radanites would continue to control this trade until the end of the Carollingian era in 987 CE when they began to fade from history. There is a coincidence of timing between the Radanites, the Carolinian kings and the Babylonian caliphs that clearly suggests the Jewish traders provided a link between the two major powers. This would explain the favourable treatment granted to Jews in France during this period.

So, what do we know of these enigmatic Radanites? We must begin by recognising that at the beginning of the eighth century CE most Jews were living within the rapidly expanding empire of Islam. It was in 711 CE that Mohammed ibn Kasim captured the first piece of the Indian continent, the Province of Sind (now mostly in Pakistan). This region, which included the mouth of the river Indus, would be the Indian landfall for Radanite ships travelling both down the Red Sea and round the Arabian Peninsular or down the Persian Gulf and the Arabian Sea. We have discussed earlier how there was generally a climate of mutual trust between the Jews and the Arabs, although, as in Christendom, the occasional instance of persecution did take place. This trust went so far as to permit Jews to garrison towns in Spain that the Arabs had captured, so allowing the Arabs to move on to their next target. As Islam expanded, so did the trading empire of the Radanites. In India and later in China, settlements of Jews would settle themselves and provide local bases. They would quickly pick up the necessary local language skills and local produce to support developing international trade. Recent genetic research has indicated that the Cohanim were present among those Radanite merchants.

> Extensive DNA testing has found the Bene Israelis, clustered in and around the western city of Bombay, are direct descendants of a hereditary Israelite priesthood that can be traced back 3,000 years to Moses' brother, Aaron.
>
> *Terry Friel*
> *Reuters (March 1, 2003)*

By the ninth century, there were Jewish settlements along all the trade routes; throughout Spain and the north African coast, Egypt, Syria, Palestine and Babylon, as well as in Christian Europe. There are fewer records of the settlements east of Babylon, but we can be sure of Jewish settlements at Merv, Balkh, Ghazna, Heart, Nishapur and Bokhara in what is now Afghanistan. There also exists a record of Jewish settlements in Tibet, Uzbekistan, India and China. The various Jewish colonies just mentioned varied from being a small community in a bigger town to towns that were almost entirely Jewish. Indeed one region in Europe, Khazaria, which equates to the modern Crimea was a Jewish state from 740 when the king, Bulan, converted to Judaism. Khazaria maintained an important position in international trade until they were crushed by what is now Ukraine in 965.

To show the vast trade empire the Radanites controlled, we will touch briefly on the four routes between the east and the west. Apparently a disservice has been done to this group of Jewish merchants by not recording their incredible feats of seafaring and navigation for posterity.

Route 1 - Was the sea route beginning on the Mediterranean coast of France, usually Narbonne, Nice or Marseilles. The Radanite ships, and there must have been hundreds of them, would hug the coast round the Italian, Greek and Turkish coasts, sometimes stopping at various ports to offload and take-on cargo. The ships would then cross to Farama, the major Egyptian port, and Biblical city of Sin, which silted up years ago and the coastline moved north to what is now Port Said. At Farama the Radanite ships would be offloaded and the cargo taken overland, on camel and mule, to Kolzum (modern Suez) where it was reloaded on to more Radanite ships for transit to India. It is worth mentioning here that before the branch of the river Nile on which Farama was built silted up, there was a man-made canal that ran from this branch of the Nile to the Red Sea. The difference in sea levels must have needed the cargo to be offloaded at various points and trans-shipped to other vessels because there were no locks in those days, but it was still a remarkable achievement. From Kolzum, the ships would sail down the Red Sea and around the coast to the river Indus. This particular voyage was particularly difficult and solved by an Egyptian captain who discovered that during the monsoon period the prevailing winds ensured that a ship could sail out of sight of land and safely arrive in India. Any cargo that was not offloaded for India would continue around the coast to the final destination, Canton.

Route 2 – Was the same as route 1 until the ships reached Greece where, instead of crossing directly to Farama they would continue to hug the coast as far as Antioch. There the cargo would be offloaded and taken overland to Damascus and thence to al-Jabia on the river Euphrates where they would be transported by riverboat to Al-Fāw on the Persian Gulf. The Radanite ships would then sail down the Persian Gulf to the river Indus estuary where they joined route 1 to China.

Route 3 – Was almost entirely overland starting in France and travelling down through Spain and across to North Africa. There the route went along the coast to Egypt where it then followed either the King's-Highway or the Way-of-the-Sea (discussed in chapter 4) to Damascus and then Baghdad. From Baghdad the route went directly east in the Szechwan region of China and surroundings.

Route 4 - Was similar to route 3 but went directly east from mid-France to Venice, then to Khazaria before turning south through Azerbaijan. At Gilan, the cargo would be loaded on to boats in the Caspian Sea and taken across to the eastern side at Mazanderan. Gilan was the home of the secretive sect of Ismailis who eventually became known as the Assassins. From Mazanderan, the route headed due east to arrive in the Szechwan region of China.

So, having described who the Radanites were and the routes they operated, it only remains to mention what cargo they carried. When they travelled from the west towards the east, they usually transported eunuchs and other slaves of both sexes. Apart from this human cargo, they took silk, hair oils, embalming fluid, soap, lubricants, marten and other furs swords and castor oil; this last item being used in cosmetics. For the return trip they brought musk (for perfume), aloes (which is a purgative and treatment for burns), camphor (an ingredient of incense), cinnamon and other spices.

Mention has already been made earlier of the problems the slave trade created between Christian and Jew although the issue was simply one of Jews owning Christian slaves. Apart from the international - west to east - trade in slaves, which the Radanites controlled, the Jews were in fact major players in the slave trade within Europe. This was a particularly profitable business and provided several Jewish families with the necessary wealth to enable them in later years to dominate the international banking business. It is difficult for us today to imagine the wealth that would have been controlled by the Radanites. We were all made aware at a young age of the exploits of such seafaring trailblazers as Ferdinand Magellan, Henry the Navigator and Christopher Columbus. Yet here were men - whose exploits have gone almost unmentioned - opening silk roads and spice routes some seven hundred years earlier that were every bit as transoceanic and inaccessible.

This chapter has described a special relationship between the French Carollingian kings and the Jewish nobility, some aspects of which, even today, we know very little. We can, though, plainly see the Languedoc region of the south of France was a place where the Jews prospered over a long period. It also becomes clear that if Byrne[1] is correct, and the guardians did choose to conceal the Ark of the Covenant in this area it was a fortunate or inspired decision on their part. There, in the territory that includes the mountain, Pech Cardou, which mimics the temple of Jerusalem, was a regime of sympathetic tolerance towards Jews unknown until modern times. If there was such a thing as a "grand design", then it was there in the Languedoc region of France during the three hundred or so years each side of the first millennium. During that time, conditions existed for taking any such plan forward. During the first half of this period was a dynasty of kings who, for reasons that had to do with the "divine right to rule", may have wished to add Davidic Jewish genes to their bloodline. This period allowed the local Jews to gain a large measure of control over the region. During the second half the large areas of the region, particularly around Pech Cardou were under the control of the Knights Templar and their castles stand to this day. Whether these circumstances triggered ambition of greater things or simply that it had always been an unstated aim, we shall never know. What is obvious, though, is that a dream became a little closer, a dream to meet the demands of the Old Testament prophets that the Messiah would bring about the worship of YHWH by all men:

> And it shall come to pass in the last days, that the mountain of the LORD's house shall be established in the top of the

> mountains, and shall be exalted above the hills; and all nations shall flow unto it.
>
> *Isaiah 2:2*

We demonstrated above how the Jewish Davidic bloodline might have been introduced into the upper reaches of the French nobility by Charles Martel, from where it would have spread throughout the royal families of Europe. It was, though, if Templar Gold's is to be given credence, the court of Champagne where the spark that was to ignite the first Crusade was struck. This chapter has not provided any definitive answers to our investigation but it has thrown up some remarkable coincidences.

One region, Champagne, where all of the early players were assembled, Pope Urban II, Saint Bernard, the first Knights Templar and illustrious Hebrew scholars such as Rashi. These people had between them the knowledge of where the Ark of the Covenant was hidden and the military strength to recover The Holy Land from Islam. Another region, the Languedoc and Rousillon holds Pech Cardou and provides an inkling of how the Jews, who knew the region intimately, may have supported the Knights Templar and Jews to secure the Ark from prying eyes. Neither Champagne nor Narbonne provides any answers to the question of who created Freemasonry but some intriguing facts have been thrown up, not least being the strong feelings of superiority over gentiles held by Jews during the middle-ages. There is little doubt that Freemasonry did not originate during the period discussed above, but there is an almost intangible sense that the circumstances necessary to the birth of Freemasonry were somehow being shaped.

CHAPTER 9

THE MARRANOS

In our endeavours to identify the group of people – almost certainly Jews – who founded Freemasonry, we have been analysing the history of the Jewish people to explore the proposition that a group of Jews formed themselves into a secret society and remained "underground" for perhaps hundreds of years. In fact, we should not become too focused on the words "group" and "society", the reality might have been little more than an idea carried across time. If this latter paradigm is closer to what happened then the "idea" may have coalesced at various points in history to create real groups, possibly at different times. If we can identify such a group, then we may be getting closer to the founders of Freemasonry. Our examination of the history of the Jews to date - until the fourteenth century - has yielded no sign of any secret Jewish organisations, let alone one that might have developed into Freemasonry. As our investigations move into the fifteenth century, we do at last find what we seek, a group of Jews who have kept their religion secret for some five hundred years. They are the Sephardic Marranos, or Christian-Jews or Crypto-Jews of Spain.

The relationship between Jew and gentile became more complicated when Christianity moved clearly away from Judaism by admitting gentiles into the faith. St. Paul addressed this issue head-on in his letter to the Galatians:

> But when I saw that they walked not uprightly according to the truth of the gospel, I said unto Peter before them all, If thou, being a Jew, livest after the manner of Gentiles, and not as do the Jews, why compellest thou the Gentiles to live as do the Jews?
>
> *Galatians 2:14*

The early Christians, as we have said earlier, were all Jews but as the religion opened its doors more widely to gentiles, the tensions began to build. To understand how this might have happened, it is necessary to recognise that the alternative religions to Judaism were all pagan. There was only one monotheistic religion in Israel and it was Judaism. So, when many gentiles (pagans) became Christians – as compared to Jewish Christians – many also became "Judaizers". That is to say they found the whole panoply of Jewish customs and festivals fascinating to the point where they insisted that gentiles should adhere to teachings of the Torah. This insistence included circumcision and adherence to the Jewish food laws. We mention this fact to reiterate that early Christianity was really a branch of Judaism rather than the present day separate religion. It was only when Christian and Jewish theologians picked over the available written words, and came to their different interpretations, that the gulf between the two religions widened to the point where each considered the other to be a heresy. Against this background, it is unsurprising that when threatened with converting to Christianity, or, being expelled from the country where they lived, many Jews opted for conversion. This is especially understandable with the interventions discussed in the previous chapter of Rabbis Rashi and Issac of Dampierre. Rashi had ruled that it was excusable to convert to Christianity under threat of expulsion and Issac had ruled that oaths made to Christians could be denied.

We have observed in the earlier chapters how, for Israel and Judaea's temple period, Judaism came under pressure from the competing religions of invading forces. Nothing, however, quite prepared the Jews for the impact that Christianity would have on them and their religion. From the early part of the 4th century CE, when the emperor Constantine made Christianity the religion of Rome and thus of the "western world", Judaism would be progressively forced into a subservient position. As we noticed in chapter 8, even with the support of the Carollingian kings, Jews were still less secure legally than Christians. Fortunately for the Jews, the Pope and most bishops never viewed them in the same light as they viewed the various Christian sects that were designated "heretical". Such a definition usually brought the threat of death or attack by "crusaders" or both. The Jews were, though, seen as enough of a threat for them to be confined to separated enclaves where they could not take part in the full privileges of Christendom. To live a full life in the West needed a belief in Jesus Christ and the teachings of His Church.

In the 7th century CE, emerging Islam confronted Judaism with yet another religion that worshipped the same God as Judaism and Christianity, but proclaimed essential differences from both. These three religions are collectively known as the Abrahamic religions, from the name of the earliest prophet whom they share. The monotheism, which should have bound them, had already foundered on the "rocks" of iconism and trinitarianism for Christianity and Judaism. These matters, though, were not an issue between Judaism and Islam. There can be little doubt the emergence of theologians and philosophers from within Islam, who challenged Judaism head on and at the highest intellectual level, produced an atmosphere of mutual respect. While most nations conquered by the Muslims were obliged to convert to Islam, Judaism was generally - there were exceptions - treated as an acceptable alternative religion. The rise, of Islam and the increasing land area that it covered resulted in Jews occupying in roughly equal proportions lands where either Islam or Christianity was the state religion.

While Jewry, in Islamic countries, was usually treated fairly benignly, the Christian countries became increasingly less tolerant of the religious beliefs of Jews, and tended to isolate them into sealed areas of their towns. Edward I, of England, was the first monarch to extend this ghettoisation of the Jews into a countrywide expulsion. Edward came to the throne burdened with considerable debts created by his father, Henry III's, extravagance and internal feuding. One of Henry's financially imprudent acts was the sending his son, Edward, and a group of knights to Jerusalem in support of the seventh Crusade. In addition, Henry made many large charitable donations, including one for the rebuilding of Westminster Abbey. It was, though the marriage of Henry's sister to Simon de Montfort that led him into a disastrous military campaign in France. The resulting disagreements between Henry and De Montfort over culpability for the fiasco led to civil war. The effects of this civil war were still not settled when

Edward I assumed the throne and de Montfort's supporters fought to recover the lands which Henry had confiscated.

The sale of these confiscated lands back to their original owners plus the profitable imposition of export duties on wool helped Edward to restore the royal finances. The regular revenue from this and other such duties also enabled Edward to borrow substantially from Italian bankers using the duties as collateral. These Italian bankers were willing and able to finance Edward's activities and so caused the indigenous Jews to be viewed by him as no longer necessary.

The British Jews had mostly arrived from Normandy with William the Conqueror during the eleventh century, and continued their long tradition as bankers to the ruling and business classes. Christians were forbidden to charge interest on loans making banking a banned occupation for them. The Jews had provided King Henry with his financial needs, but when Edward ascended the throne of England the Jews were considerably impoverished because of Henry's increasingly heavy tax impositions on them. The influx of new Italian finance meant that Edward had no further need of the Jews or any obligation to protect them from his other subjects who generally disliked them. Borrowing money is usually easy, while the repayment seldom is. It is effortless to blame the lender for the stress of finding the money to repay a debt, and, as has happened since anti-Semitic feelings grew in the community, and Jews were made scapegoats for the country's financial problems. In 1287, Edward I imprisoned and ransomed 3,000 Jews and although the ransom was paid, he followed this action up in 1290 with an order expelling all Jews from England. The obvious opportunities for a quick "financial killing" were not lost on the European monarchy. Only 16 years later, in 1306, the French king, Philip IV not only expelled the Jews from France but also expropriated their property as he did so.

After the expulsion of Jews from England, economic resentment coupled with Christian religious prejudice resulted in the continued growth of anti-Jewish sentiment and the exclusions continued. Germany followed suit in 1350, Spain in 1392, Portugal in 1496, Provence – which had not been included in the earlier French expulsion – in 1512, and even the Papal States in 1569. It was, though, in Spain where perhaps the Jews felt the greatest pain. Because under an earlier fanatical Muslim leader, Almohades, many Jews had fled to escape persecutions, the Jews only represented around two per cent of the population, but Spain still had the largest community of Jews worldwide. The anti-Jewish sentiment discussed above was building and Spain was not immune. These sentiments were fanned by anti-Jewish canons coming from the Fourth Lateran Council and the Council of Arles in 1235. In 1380, Spain succumbed to the fanatical preaching of Archdeacon Ferrant Martinez, and in 1391, townspeople began attacking local Jews. Many Jews were killed in these riots and in August, the survivors were given the ultimatum of conversion to Christianity or exile. Many left, some moving to the Muslim Ottoman Empire, while others transferred to north-eastern Europe: many, particularly the middle classes, decided to remain and adopt the Christian faith.

These converts, and there were at least one hundred thousand of them, perhaps three times that number, were known locally as *conversos* or "converts", and the term was also applied to their descendants. For many, when all vestige of Judaism had long been forgotten, they and their descendants kept the title *conversos* and were marked out from other Christians. This seemingly curious observation is readily explained because the *conversos* continued to occupy the same professions of cobblers, tailors, merchants, tax agents and moneylenders.

With much of Europe now barred to them, it is understandable that so many Jews chose to convert to Roman Catholicism rather than move. Many Jews had, in earlier and better times, been the backbone of the Spanish middle classes, they were well educated and provided large numbers of doctors and other professional men to the community. Therefore, the second-generation *conversos* were able to marry other Christians. Their wealth and intelligence brought them influence and with it important positions within the Spanish establishment. The "not-so-wealthy" *conversos* practised medicine and law and taught at the universities, and even encouraged their children to follow ecclesiastical careers. By 1478, when the Spanish Inquisition was created, *conversos* held five of the most senior posts in Aragon.

They also held some of the highest posts in provincial courts and in the Spanish church. Inevitably the "old Christian" aristocracy began to circulate conspiracy theories to the effect that the *conversos* were deliberately infiltrating the Catholic Church with a view to changing it.

Subsequent history tells us that most of these *conversos* unsurprisingly had not internalised Christianity and that they did not act as faithful Catholics but rather continued to follow their Jewish customs in secret. The term used to describe these unwilling Catholics was "*Marrano*", the etymology of which is uncertain. One suggestion is that its root was "*marrón*" the Spanish word for maroon or chestnut, which was the colour of a bishop's robes; the explanation being that converted Jews came under the direct supervision of the local bishop. Another suggestion takes the literal Spanish meaning of "*marrano*", which is "pig". Attaching the term "pig" to a group of people who – according to their original beliefs could not eat pork – is clearly unsubtle. It is said that during the Spanish Inquisition it was not unusual for *Marrano* families to have a pot of pork simmering on the stove at all times. This was a display, not so much of Catholic belief but rather of a non-Jewish one. The habit of keeping a cauldron of pork simmering resulted in the converted Jews of Majorca being called "*Chuetas*", meaning "pork lard". Because of the possibility of insult, we shall from now on generally use the term "crypto-Jews".

It is important to distinguish between crypto-Jews, who continued to follow Judaism in secret, and those who were less attached to their religion of birth. The latter were happy to exchange the oppressed life as a Jew for the freedom which Christianity brought. The Internet Jewish Encyclopaedia has this to say on the subject:

> They simulated the Christian faith when it was to their advantage, and mocked at Jews and Judaism. A number of Spanish poets belong to this category, such as Pero Ferrus, Juan de Valladolid, Rodrigo Cota, and Juan de España of Toledo, called also "El Viejo" (the old one), who was considered a sound Talmudist, and who, like the monk Diego

> de Valencia, himself a baptized Jew, introduced in his pasquinades [anti-Papal poems] Hebrew and Talmudic words to mock the Jews.
>
> *JewishEncyclopedia.com*

The crypto-Jews, although able to uphold a façade of Christianity could not easily hide their devotion to Judaism. By way of example, in the city of Seville an inquisitor is said to have taken the regent to the top of a tower one Saturday. There he asked him to observe those houses which had no smoke rising from their chimneys. "Those", he remarked "are the houses of *Marranos* because in spite of the severe cold they set no fire on the Sabbath". The dietary requirement on Jews to eat only *kosher*, or "fit", food also raised important problems particularly when animals were slaughtered for eating. The Judaic law requires a special method of slaughtering animals, called *shehitah*, which involves cutting the animal's neck and draining the blood. Clearly this practice could not be performed openly and so men had to be employed to carry out the task in secret. Even that most fundamental requirement for male Jews, circumcision, had to be carried out in secret.

The crypto-Jews were, to some extent, helped in their decisions to adopt – although under threat – an alternative religion by the teachings of Rashi, as we mentioned earlier. Another Jewish philosopher, Moses ben Maimon, or as he is usually known, Maimonides (1135 – 1204) supported Rashi's ruling. Maimonides was himself required to become a *converso* although in his case to Islam. He was thirteen years old when the fanatical Muslim leader, Almohades, captured his hometown of Cordova. Maimonides' family chose a nomadic life rather than open conversion to Islam, but it soon became necessary for them to adopt an Islamic façade. Indeed Maimonides was at one point charged with having relapsed from Islam, and was only saved from death by the intercession of a friendly Moslem theologian. Maimonides wrote extensively on the subject of personal ethics, he established rules deduced from the Torah as well as the *responsas* of earlier Rabbis. He decreed that a man's duties to himself included the need to keep in good health by regular living, by seeking medical advice in sickness, by cleanliness and by earning a livelihood. He also wrote an essay on forced conversions, although his authorship has been questioned. It is generally held that in this case Maimonides preached "*pro domo sua*", he and his family having themselves been forced to embrace Islam. "*Pro domo sua*" directs *conversos* to revert as soon as was convenient to the beliefs of their ancestors; or, more accurately, to the values of their paternal households.

Inevitably, the wealth and favoured status of the crypto-Jews, just like the Jews before them induced envy in the other Spaniards, and this was seized on by the clergy to foment discord. Eventually rioting broke out, the first one was in Toledo in 1449. The crypto-Jews did not take the attacks on them submissively and in 1467 mounted a counter-attack to try to gain control of the city. It was in vain and the ringleaders were hanged. Six years later, the events of Toledo were imitated in Cordova when the accidental splashing of water – by a young crypto-Jewish girl - on an image of the Virgin Mary that was being paraded, exploded into a riot. Despite the arrival of a troop of soldiers who tried to quell the violence the commotion raged for three days during which hundreds died. To avoid any repetition, crypto-Jews were banned from Cordova and from holding public office. Just as in 1391, suppressing the crypto-Jews spread to other cities. Probably the worst riot was at Segovia in 1474 where corpses of crypto-Jews were piled high in the streets. Reports of the revolt say that not a single crypto-Jew survived.

There are still crypto-Jews in north-western Spain and northern Portugal to this day and they are the descendants of those who fled from Spain to Portugal. The practice of adopting, albeit as a façade, an alternative religion to Judaism was not restricted to conversions to Christianity, as we saw above with Maimonides, and even today there are outwardly Muslim crypto-Jews in Iran, and in Turkey. The largest surviving crypto-Jewish communities are to be found in southern USA and South American countries such as Colombia and Mexico where Spain at one time ruled. These communities still practice secrecy and perform such Jewish practices as lighting candles on Friday nights[49].

In Spain, things were about to take yet another turn for the worse for the Sephardic crypto-Jews. This terrifying event was the institution of the Spanish Inquisition. Although there are no existing records to show that the children of *conversos* who had become clerics of the Catholic Church had any hidden motives, envy had been whipped up into rioting. The monarchy was beset on several fronts by civil wars, anti-Jewish riots, the usual dissent by nobles and a general breakdown of law and order. From 1482, what would turn out to be a long and expensive war against the Muslim kingdom of Granada was added to their problems. Because of all of these concurrent threats the King decided to devolve one of the problems to others. It was the crypto-Jewish problem.

The Inquisition was bitterly opposed by the crypto-Jews especially those who held high office. Tit-for-tat killings occurred, including Christians in the cathedral of Jaen assassinating the Constable of Castile, Miguel Lucas de Iranzo. The revenge murder of the inquisitor Pedro Arbues followed twelve years later in the cathedral of Saragossa. Alongside the introduction of the Inquisition an order went out that Jews must live within their defined area and be separated from the crypto-Jews. This law had little real effect and the authentic Jews continued to communicate with their crypto-Jewish brethren. The Jews were anxious to return the crypto-Jews to their faith and so they coached the crypto-Jews in Judaic ceremonial and Mosaic Law. They provided unleavened bread for the festival of Passover and kosher meat at other times.

The first Inquisition, in France, was authorised by Pope Gregory IX in his Bull "Declinante jam mundi" of 26th May 1232. Its purpose was to root out, with the use of torture, an heretical sect called Catharism, which had taken hold in the Languedoc region of France. The Spanish Inquisition, however, was authorised by Pope Sixtus IV in 1478. The grounds for the Inquisition were that pseudo-converts from Judaism and Islam endangered the Catholic faith. The Inquisition was an ecclesiastic-legal process and the judges had to be at least forty years old. In addition they had to be of unimpeachable reputation, distinguished for virtue and wisdom, masters of theology, or doctors or licentiates of canon law, and they had to follow the usual ecclesiastical rules and regulations.

The precondition for “wisdom” in the judges appears to have been to no avail for after only two years the first two Dominican inquisitors, Miguel de Morillo and Juan de San Martin were reported to Pope Sixtus. Their infractions were, "unjustly imprisoning many people, subjecting them to cruel tortures, declaring them false believers, and sequestrating the property of the executed". The two senior inquisitors would have been deposed had not the king and queen, Ferdinand and Isabella, not interceded on their behalf. The direct outcome of this maladministration was a new appointment, that of Grand Inquisitor as the highest official in the inquisitorial court. This appointment went to Tomás de Torquemada who had previously been one of the assistant inquisitors. Torquemada had joined the Dominican monastery at Valladolid as a youth and rose to become Prior of the Monastery of Santa Cruz at Segovia. While there he became confessor to the Infanta Isabella and when she became Queen, Torquemada became one of her trusted councillors. The pre-expulsion crypto-Jews had successfully evaded Torquemada's tribunals by involving on their side the Jews, who had by then been allowed back into Spain. The riches of these returning Jews had given them much influence; also, the Inquisition had no jurisdiction over genuine Jews. Frustrated at these impediments to his office, Torquemada brought the examples of religious direction and help given by Jews to the crypto-Jews, mentioned above, and appealed to the King to force all Jews to become Christians or leave Spain. The Jews offered to pay the state 30,000 ducats, a sum of money in excess of £10 million at today's values in return for retaining their religion. It is said that when King Ferdinand was about to accept the offer Torquemada walked forward holding a crucifix above his head. As he did he said, "Judas Iscariot sold Christ for 30 pieces of silver; your Highness is about to sell him for 30,000 ducats. Here He is; take Him and sell Him." Then, leaving the crucifix on the table he left the room. It is generally accepted that this action, or one like it resulted in the Jews being once again expelled from Spain in 1492. The Spanish Inquisition remained in force until the Revolution of 1820, apart from a brief break from 1808 until 1814.

The Grand Inquisitor could delegate his powers to suitably qualified assistants leaving himself free to hear appeals from the Spanish Courts. The High Council consisting of the Grand Inquisitor and five Apostolic Inquisitors, who were appointed by the Grand Inquisitor and approved by the king, heard appeals. As well as appeals, the High Council ruled on important defendants. No priest, knight, or noble could be imprisoned, and no *auto-da-fé* (act of faith) held without the sanction of the High Council. The *sermo generalis* or more usually *auto-da-fé* was the solemn ceremonial when the final decision was pronounced to the defendant.

It is usual to attribute barbaric practices to the various inquisitions but the reality was that – for the time – they were remarkable well regulated and policed. The very idea now that one can place a red-hot piece of iron on or in a person and if God wills it he would feel no pain is incredible. In those days, however, it was firmly believed by all except those undergoing the "punishment". The procedures were well documented and had to be followed. After a charge had been laid the defendant had a period of grace – usually thirty to forty days – during which to prepare his defence. Imprisonment was only used when the Inquisitors unanimously agreed that the defendant was guilty or definite proof had been laid before the tribunal. Examination of the accused – a euphemism for torture - could take place only if two "disinterested" priests were present. Their duty was to restrain any arbitrary act and to ensure the protocol had been read out twice to the accused. A lawyer always handled the defence. Most importantly, the witnesses - often unknown to the accused - were sworn and severe punishment even death befell those giving false witness. It is easy to see how such an atmosphere of fear would have driven some *conversos* to emphasis their Christian credentials by denouncing other *conversos*, and so it was. The greater the fear - and hundreds of thousands went to their death courtesy of the Inquisition - the greater became the spirituality, real or feigned, of the *conversos* and crypto-Jews.

Those crypto-Jews who did manage to escape the inquisition, either in groups or as individuals did not have a huge choice of countries to resettle in. Many made it to Italy where the climate and language were similar to Spain. Twenty-one of them settled at Ferrara where the Duke, Ercole I, granted them the right to remain. Others chose Bologna, Pisa, Naples, Reggio, Venice, Florence Milan and Livorno, this last town they transformed into a popular seaport. Throughout Italy the crypto-Jews dropped their Christianity and openly avowed Judaism. In Rome Pope Paul III, received them for commercial reasons, and granted complete liberty to them. The peace was short-lived and in 1555, Pope Paul IV had all the crypto-Jews thrown into the prisons of a new Inquisition which he had just set up. Sixty reaffirmed the Catholic faith and were transported to Malta. Another twenty-four, refused to renounce Judaism and were burned at the stake.

Other Spanish and Portuguese crypto-Jews headed northwest and sought refuge in France. They settled in St. Jean de Luz, Tarbes, Bayonne, Bordeaux, Marseilles, and Montpellier living outwardly as Christians. They attended Catholic churches, had their children baptised, and displayed all of the normal behaviour of Christians; but in secret they circumcised their children, kept the Sabbath and feast-days and prayed together. The lives of the crypto-Jews in France was not without problems and many had to leave within a short time. Under Louis XIII, the crypto-Jews of Bayonne were ghettoised into the suburb of St. Esprit. However, in the south-west of France, well away from Paris, they were eventually able to declare their true faith. By 1640 several hundred crypto-Jews, were living openly as Jews and in 1660 the first synagogue was built in St. Esprit.

In Europe, it was Flanders which offered the most peaceful future to the fleeing Spanish crypto-Jews. Whether this was due to the mix of races that made up the region: Romance, Frankish, Germanic, Saxon and Dutch; or because Flanders was a great trading centre is not known. What is known is that the benign environment attracted huge numbers of crypto-Sephadic-Jews and Antwerp was a particular favourite. Another was Amsterdam, where so many crypto-Jews settled that it was called the "new Jerusalem". Whereas in Flanders the crypto-Jews were quickly able to revert to their religion of choice, other Sephadic crypto-Jews moved to Germany and in particular to Hamburg and Altona where they had to maintain their disguise of Christianity. One ruler, Christian IV, of Denmark went further and invited crypto-Jewish families to settle at Glückstadt and Emden.

Of the large number of crypto-Jews who remained on the Iberian Peninsula and survived the Inquisition it was the crypto-

Jews of Portugal who gained the first reprieve. In 1601 the King of Portugal, Philip III, passed a law allowing them the unrestricted sale of their properties and free departure for themselves, their families, and their possessions. This relaxation only lasted a few years after which the Inquisition resumed its work.

When the Sephardic crypto-Jews settled across Europe, from Amsterdam to Venice, they carried with them the education that they had picked up while living among the upper classes of Spain. They also had the Christian customs and ideology, to which they had been exposed for many years. It was this prior exposure to Christian conventions that, perhaps more than anything, began the *Haskala* or "Jewish Enlightenment", which brought the Jews into the mainstream of modern European culture. Conversely, the Ashkenazim Jews of central Europe - who had not benefited from the exposure of the Sephardim to the Spanish establishment - did not begin their *Haskala* until the eighteenth century. The Jewish Enlightenment followed much the same lines as the Christian one, the expression and application of reason. It might be argued that the Christian Enlightment saw the beginning of the end of religious domination of knowledge, for before that time the Church decided such matters as whether the sun revolved around the earth. The Enlightenment, therefore, heralded the beginning of the weakening of the Church.

The leading Jewish philosopher during that period was Moses Mendelssohn. He favoured a departure from the usual preoccupation with the Talmud and a redirection towards the universal religion of reason, of which - he suggested - Judaism was but a single manifestation. Mendelssohn's message was unequivocally that Jews should become Westerners, and actively pursue the Enlightenment. He co-operated with Naphtali Wessely in transliterating the Torah into German. Mendelssohn's aim was to explain to his fellow Jews that they could, indeed, join Western society without sacrificing Judaism. He successfully demonstrated that Judaic intellectual processes were simply those of universal reason.

These last two chapters have shown how dangerous was the practice of Judaism in Europe over several centuries. Even conversion to Christianity did not remove the danger of being denounced as a crypto-Jew and possible consignment to the fire. And yet we know that these communities survived and in time went on to blossom and expand. So how did they do it? How did they communicate with each other? We do not here mean the sort of discussions that would have taken place daily in each town and village, between crypto-Jew and crypto-Jew who were well known to each other, but rather crypto-Jew from one town with crypto-Jews from another. There was news of family members and there were business contracts to be exchanged. In addition, Judaism is a very prescriptive religion. There are rules and laws for most activities and as society develops so these Judaic laws and rules needed to be reinterpreted to take account of these societal changes. These changes were, and still are, debated by the spiritual leaders of Judaism, the rabbis. Jews everywhere, whether living openly as Jews or covertly as crypto-Jews would have wanted to know the latest rabbinical opinions to ensure that their observance of Judaism was proper and in accordance with the latest thinking. All of these newsworthy matters needed to be communicated to the crypto-Jewish communities, who had no way of obtaining this information other than covertly by way of a secret news-carrying organisation. The news-carrier simply must have had some form of secret recognition, for being uncovered meant a roasting at the stake. What better form of communication was there than the use of square-Hebrew, a language with which only Jews were familiar and one which not even the educated Christian clergy had any knowledge of? In chapter 2, we saw an example of how such covert recognition might take place:

> Another sign is placing their right heel to the inside of their left in the form of a square so walk a few steps backward and forward and at every third step make a little stand placing the feet square as afores. This done, any if masons perceive it they will presently come to you if you come where any masons tools lie in the form of a square. It is a sign to discover him.
>
> *The Sloane Manuscript*

Square

This unobtrusive display - leading hopefully to recognition by a fellow Mason - makes no sense whatsoever if all that is required is to identify a fellow tradesman. It does, however carry extraordinary weight if the person being identified was a crypto-Jew for whom exposure would probably lead to death on one of the many the inquisition bonfires. We can speculate how such an arrangement first developed. The first stage of the identification process was by means of a special stance, a slightly different way of standing. This was done by placing the right heel into the hollow of the left foot forming a crude representation of three Hebrew characters Z, D or K. This stance is a little unusual but not overtly so, not enough to draw attention to anyone other than a Jew, versed in the language of the Torah, Hebrew. Indeed, this particular posture is almost normal when leaning against the bar of an inn or alehouse. Certainly a travelling man visiting a distant inn and standing with his feet turned out in the form of a square would not attract attention. That is unless the observer was a crypto-Jew, a Jew hiding among the gentiles and fearful of having his true religion uncovered. Such a crypto-Jew would feel obliged to approach the man with the unusually placed feet and ask the question:

"Are you on the square."

If the answer was affirmative, one can readily picture a careful verbal dance ending in a request for a password. A password which was only given one syllable at a time and which required the other man to provide the next syllable before the third syllable was given. Few if any gentiles would have known the name of the cave where Abraham is buried, but most Jews certainly would. The exchange might have gone like this:

First man, "Mac,"
Second man, "pel,"
First man, "ah."
Second man, "Machpelah."

And away they would scurry to catch up on the news and latest directives from the distant rabbis. But what if the request, "are you on the square?" brought forth the response:

"What do you mean?"

It is not difficult to contrive an innocuous response, such as:

> "I'm sorry, sir, you looked like a travelling mason, my cousin is a mason and he always talks about being on the square. I think it's the thing they use to measure corners."

Speculation this may be, because we will probably never know exactly how they communicated during those dark days when they had to conceal their true religion under pain of death. But it is informed speculation because contact each other they most certainly did and with great success, as today's thriving Jewish communities will attest.

By the seventeenth century alternative philosophies such as Illuminatism, Pantheism and Deism were evolving out of the general Enlightenment. The whole enlightenment movement found favour, as we have just mentioned, with Jewry itself and they too joined the search for the ultimate truth about themselves. These intellectual concepts provided a framework which would soon be displayed in a new organisation, Freemasonry. We have identified the means and opportunity by which the explicitly Judaic Freemasonry evolved. What we lack is supporting evidence of what happened between the periods of expulsion of the Jews including the Inquisition, and the emergence into the light of Freemasonry in 1717. Let us turn our attentions to country where Freemasonry first emerged into the light, England.

It was not until after 1066 that Jews first began to settle in England in numbers. The Jews of Normandy followed William the Conqueror into England expecting the favourable treatment that they had experienced in France. During the 12th century, their position had improved to the point where Jewish visitors regularly visited from Europe. In London, as a demonstration of their improving position, they built "the great Synagogue" close to the Tower. When Henry I, died the welfare of the Jews continued to improve; the new king was Stephen and he declared his fondness for them. The improving climate for Jews brought new communities in Norwich, Cambridge and Oxford. By the time

Stephen's heir Henry II, had ascended the throne of England, more Jewish communities could be found in Lincoln, Northampton, Norfolk, Suffolk, Gloucestershire, Hampshire and Wiltshire. It was near the end of the twelfth century that events took a turn for the worse for the Jews of England, as Christian anti-Semitism began to take hold. In 1192, the local population killed Isaac of Saint Edmund's at Thetford during an uprising against the Jews. Other massacres followed. After one such massacre in 1264, many Jews returned to Normandy, and by the thirteenth century it was illegal for Jews to live outside the larger towns without a special licence, which could only be purchased from the King.

These controls only applied to the permanent homes of Jews in larger towns; travel was still permitted. Indeed, Jews could travel all over the country as their charter allowed. Some Jews would travel to a town where they owned property, stay a few days during which they would carry out their business of money-lending, and then return to their permanent residence. "Coinage clipping", that is to say, the filing off of a small part of the gold or silver of coins of the realm marked the beginning of the end for the Jews of England. These clippings could be melted down and sold as bullion or turned into jewellery. Rightly or wrongly, this particular offence was placed at the door of the Jews and in November 1278 a house-to-house search took place and the heads of all Jewish families arrested. Several hundred were sent to the Tower, executed and their property confiscated by the King. It is known that some Jews survived by converting to Christianity, just as the crypto-Jews of Spain were to do some two hundred years later. This was not an unwise decision because only three Christians were hanged for clipping the coinage and melting it down into bullion. The sale and export of bullion by Jews was prohibited and the coin of the realm became trustworthy once more.

In 1290 the final expulsion of the Jews took place, but even then it is known that not all of the Jews left England. Mundill[50] reports the observation made by John of Oxnead:

> The Lord King condemned all Jews of whatever sex or age living throughout England into perpetual exile without any

> hope of return. In truth, out of all that large number of Jews, whose total number from young to old was reckoned to be 17,511; no one who would not be converted to the Christian faith either by promise or allurement remained beyond the fixed and decided date of departure.
>
> *Robin Mundill*
> *England's Jewish Solution*

Robin Mundill also recorded John Stowe's comment that "the number of Jews now expelled was 15,060 persons whose houses being sold the King made a mighty masse of money". It is plain that the difference between 17,511 and 15,060 represents the number of Jews, 2,451, remaining in England either as conversos or as crypto-Jews. Other historians put the number as probably between 2,000 and 4,000. Hyamson[51] says there were indeed crypto-Jews, as well as some Jews living openly in England - particularly in East Anglia - during the period between the expulsion and the resettlement. In his paper, Some Sephardic Jews in Freemasonry, delivered at his installation as Master of the Montefiore Lodge of Installed Masters, Leon Zeldis, had this to say in the matter:

> In England, where the Jews had been expelled by King Edward I in the year 1290, some "secret" Jews entered the country surreptitiously, under the appearance of being Spanish or Portuguese Catholics … Enjoying the more liberal environment prevailing in England and Holland, some Jews gradually revealed themselves as such. In 1655, the Sephardic Rabbi Menasseh ben Israel (also known as Manoel Días Soeiro, 1604-1657) from Amsterdam, submitted a petition to Oliver Cromwell to allow the official residence of Jews in England. No record has been found of the result of this démarche, but a small congregation of Sephardim was officially recognized by King Charles II in 1664, after the Restoration of the Stuart monarchy.
>
> *www.geocities.com/fmisrael*

www.geocities.com/fmisrael

It is easy to understate the importance of the Jews to England during their stay before the expulsion. This is evidenced by the existence of a separate Jewish exchequer in Westminster with its own royal seal. The exchequer kept their own records in both Latin and Hebrew, it had its own Justices, clerks and sergeants. One profession where Jews were welcomed after the expulsion, even in the royal household, was that of physician or surgeon. Other Jews, learned in philosophy and other specialist areas of knowledge are also mentioned from the fourteenth century onwards in public life.

Armed with this knowledge, we can readily appreciate how the speculation we introduced above, about a need for a travelling news-carrying service for the crypto-Jews, became a reality. Even 2,000 crypto-Jews spread around the southern parts of England would have needed someone to carry the news between the scattered groups. They would have craved news of the other groups and news from abroad, in short Hebrew news, news telling how Jews were faring elsewhere, as well as the latest dictates from senior rabbis. They needed some means of communicating news about their forbidden Jewish relations elsewhere in the kingdom and abroad. This would have needed men who could travel and who possessed the means by which they could be recognised and accepted as safe to exchange news with.

The Internet History Sourcebooks Project is a world-wide-web academic project designed to provide easy access to primary sources and other teaching materials in a non-commercial environment. Fordham University hosts one such site and at www.fordham.edu/halsall/jewish/jewishsbook.htm can be found a great number of primary source documents translated into English. The site editor, Dr. Paul Halsall - Senior Teaching Fellow at Fordham University - has this to say of the medieval Jews:

> There is a lot of evidence that scattered Jewish communities kept in contact with each other.
>
> *Internet Jewish History Sourcebook*

An example of the way in which the diaspora kept in contact can be found in a letter from Rabbi Hasdai, son of Isaac ibn Shaprut, to the king of the Khazars:

www.fordham.edu/halsall/jewish/jewishbook.htm.

> I always ask the ambassadors of these monarchs who bring gifts about our brethren the Israelites, the remnant of the captivity, whether they have heard anything concerning the deliverance of those who have languished in bondage and have found no rest.
>
> *Internet Jewish History Sourcebook*

What better cover could there have been than travelling masons? Some, if not all of these travelling or free masons would have been skilled working masons. They could have used each stopover as an opportunity to build a wall or two and so make some money before setting off for the next group of crypto-Jews awaiting his news. Such earnings would have supplemented the fees paid for their news carrying services.

As the guild of masons became settled, they would have wanted - just like the other guilds – to have ceremonials that centred on bringing new apprentices into the trade and recognising newly qualified craftsmen. It was then that the crypto-Jewish masons would unavoidably have been drawn into ceremonial matters if their cover was to be maintained. Having been brought up as Jews, their abilities to read would have catapulted them to leading roles in presenting the ceremonials and so they would have gained tacit control over the ritual. They would undoubtedly have discussed these matters with Jewish intellectuals some of whom, like surgeons, were permitted openly to practice as Jews. The Jewish intellectuals would not have overlooked an opportunity unobtrusively to mould at least one guild to their own image. The crypto-Jewish "news" organisation served them well for there are no recorded examples of their cover being "blown" for some 350 years before Oliver Cromwell allowed the Jewish resettlement. Coincidentally, just as the Jews were allowed back into England, the power and influence of the guild of masons was waning. At the end of the seventeenth century the guild sold its London building to the Freemasons. Was this event fortuitous or manipulated? Is the reality simply that, with the disappearance of the need for Jews to live clandestinely, there was simply no further need for the mason-Jews acting as news-carriers to prop up a guild of masons: we mentioned earlier how many Jews despised manual work. They now had a "heaven-sent" opportunity to turn the guild into something of their own.

Once the Jews returned legally to England, there was no further need for a crypto-Jewish-masonic-news-carrying service. If our earlier speculation is right, then what happened next is history. We can premise that the Jewish intellectuals decided to develop their cryptic news-carrying organisation into something altogether greater. They would turn it into a middle-class dining club, and use it as a vehicle to hasten their penetration of the upper classes of English society. Later, it appears that they decided to expose the gentile gentry of England to some Hebrew culture, thinly veiled behind a philosophical curtain. But could they possibly have known how well it would travel?

Perhaps the moment is right for another small indulgence in speculation. Earlier we conjectured that the crypto-Jews, that we know were living in England during the period when they were banned, would have needed a "news-carrying" service. These news-carriers would have needed secret passwords and signs to identify his potential news-targets. Towards the end of the seventeenth century we have evidence of meetings of Freemasons who were clearly not operative masons. We can say this because of the introduction into the ritual of the "mason-words" and the secret signs and tokens. It is surely inconceivable that an operative mason would not have found the idea of secret words extremely curious as well as meetings with gentlemen who had no knowledge whatever of operative masonry. That a few working masons later joined in these meetings is undeniable, but they cannot have considered them as anything other than a social event, certainly nothing to do with their trade apart from sharing a name.

John Robinson[52] speculated that Freemasonry originated in a secret organisation to provide cover for ex-knights Templar who were fleeing from persecution after the order was proscribed by papal decree in 1312. Robinson's authoritative work is compelling but loses some credibility from the period after the first wave of ex-Templars had died. Let us say from the end of the fourteenth century. What possible reason would there be to preserve an organisation of which membership meant excommunication? The underlying idea is sound but the client group is wrong. Surely far more believable is a group of crypto-Jews working under cover in a climate of extreme hostility towards their religion of birth. This is not of course to rule out the possibility that some first generation ex-Templars were provided with cover within the then new crypto-Jewish-masonic news carrying service.

Indeed, the reference made in chapter 2, in *The Sloane Manuscript,* to methods of identifying Freemasons abroad, points to this "news-carrying" service being international. We have made a speculative case that the original Masonic ritual probably had its origins in an organisation designed to provide security and cover for covert news-carriers acting for the various groups of crypto-Jews scattered throughout England. Sometime after 1290, when the Jews were expelled from England, they created a secret group of masons whose job it was to travel around the country between the various clusters of crypto-Jews. The role of this "news-carrying service" was to deliver to the crypto-Jews, who were living ostensibly as Christians, news, rabbinical decrees, commercial agreements and contracts etc., and to take the same on to the next group. They must have developed a complex code of words and signs, built around square Hebrew and Judaic history, by which they could identify the crypto-Jews they wanted to meet in a way that ensured that their cover would not be blown. The model was so successful that when other countries, such as Spain and France expelled their Jews, an international network of crypto-Jewish-masons developed. This network carried news not only within any given country, but also abroad to other countries where Jews were forbidden to live openly. The inclusion of Spain is supported by the fact that in 1730, the only Masonic lodge recorded outside the United Kingdom was in Spain. Indeed, the monastery of San Lorenzo El Escorial, 50 Km north-west of Madrid, which was built between 1563 and 1584, was built to represent King Solomon's temple and contains a wealth of Masonic symbolism. We cannot exclude the possibility that the crypto-Jewish-news-gathering service started in Spain and later spread to England.

In Leon Zeldis' paper, Some Sephardic Jews in Freemasonry, Zeldis reports on a letter from Companion [the term for a brother in Royal Arch] Samuel W. Freedman of Wilmington,

Delaware, printed in the USA Winter, 1967 issue of *The Royal Arch Mason*, entitled Did Jews Introduce Masonry in America? This letter mentions an historical pamphlet put out by the Touro Synagogue, which is the oldest synagogue on the American continent. The pamphlet includes the following statement:

> The first documentary evidence of the presence of Jews in Newport dates from 1658. In that year the document reads: **"Wee mett att ye House of Mordecai Campannall and after Synagog Wee gave Abm Moses the degrees of Maçonrie."** This not only points to the early settlement of Jews in Rhode Island, but it is the basis for the theory, which has been questioned by some, that the craft of Masonry was first introduced into America through the early Jewish settlers in Rhode Island, who seemed to have worked the degrees after religious services which were held in private houses.'

Samuel Freedman reported that these Jews were either Spanish or Portuguese, who first went to Brazil and Curaçao in South America before moving to Newport.

This revelation certainly supports the suggestion that Freemasonry began with the Jews. If the Newport Jews of 1658 had travelled there from South America then there was simply no way that they could possibly have learned about Freemasonry in England first. As mentioned above, Menasseh ben Israel did not submit his petition to Oliver Cromwell to allow Jews to return to England until 1655. The only conclusion possible is that they became aware of Freemasonry from within worldwide Jewry.

In 1656 Oliver Cromwell allowed the Jews once more to live in England and so the need for the secret group was ended. With Jewish people once more settling in England legitimately, they decided that their organisation of crypto-masons offered a unique opportunity to advance social relations with the middle and upper-class gentlemen of England. The crypto-Jewish-masons began to develop a sophisticated philosophy built around their old operative masonic (with a small "m") ceremonies and at the same time invited English gentlemen to join them for what was – in reality - a fashionable drinking and dining club. The idea of

Paper

keeping the old signs and passwords, which had been used previously to identify another crypto-Jew was inspirational. Before developing this issue, now is an appropriate moment to remind the reader of an observation we made in chapter 1:

> In this exposure the Master Masons' [Master's] word is said to be "Macbenach". The pronunciation of this word after years of slight changes resulting from oral transfers has varied it in many areas of modern Freemasonry to "Machbenah"... Can it once again be simply coincidence that the name of the cave where Abraham is buried is "Machpelah"? The syllabic and phonetic similarities are remarkable for a word that has for hundreds of years been verbally transferred from man to man.

We have suggested, in this chapter, how the re-admittance of the Jews by Oliver Cromwell provided the opportunity for some of those Jews to re-orientate an organisation that they had used to carry news, into a social club for the English middle-class gentlemen. What we lack, thus far, is any contemporaneous evidence to support such speculation; but it exists thanks to professor Margaret Jacobs[50].

> Yet a century later we find continental freemasons, writing in French in the 1770s and 1780s, telling themselves that Cromwell was the founder of modern freemasonry.
>
> *Margaret Jacobs*
> *Living the Enlightenment*

There is no suggestion in extant records that Oliver Cromwell was a Freemason or was involved in founding the institution. So why would such a rumour arise in France? Professor Jacobs makes other similar references to Cromwell's involvement in early Freemasonry:

> We have Masonic histories by French freemasons stating, almost in passing, that freemasonry was associated with Oliver Cromwell. These devout freemasons accepted Cromwell as their founder, and they wanted to believe that

> although they were descended from the events that transformed seventeenth-century England [the civil war], they were not responsible for them.
>
> Even the official history of French freemasonry located the beginning of speculative freemasonry in mid-seventeenth-century England, mentioning, in passing, Christopher Wren's involvement in the lodges. The official history discretely left out the Cromwell story.
>
> *Margaret Jacobs*
> *Living the Enlightenment*

Surely, it is now clear that Cromwell did not - himself - found Freemasonry, it was his action in permitting Jews once more to live unfettered in England that brought this about. The idea that a small group of crypto-Jewish news carrying operative masons could expand and provide an attractive organisation for English gentlemen to join is not so outlandish. The reality would have been that far more Jews would have been aware of the crypto-Jewish masons and their passwords and signs than just the masons themselves. In each community of crypto-Jews there must have been men who would make contact with the newly arrived crypto-Jewish mason. We use the term "men" deliberately because it would have been dangerous to the reputation of any woman to take up in conversation with a strange man arriving in a village. In any event Judaism was then still male dominated and so the "all-male" aspects would not have been at all unusual. It would have been essential for local crypto-Jews to be familiar with any signs, symbols and passwords because it was essential to convince a visiting crypto-Jew of their authenticity. Any failure to convince the visiting crypto-Jewish mason of their credentials would have resulted in the visitor leaving without passing on the latest news. Equally, in the eighteenth century there were no telephones and so there was no possibility of phoning ahead to set up a meeting. The visiting crypto-Jewish mason might arrive at any time and there had to be men in the crypto-Jewish community capable of going through the recognition process. It is easy to see how, in these circumstances, each local community of crypto-Jewish men might gather regularly to practice the recognition signs, symbols and words. It is also easy to imagine how extreme penalties for writing those secrets on anything that might lead to their discovery by a Christian would have evolved. Similar punishments would have awaited anyone who passed them on to someone who should not have known them - for the penalty that awaited the discovered crypto-Jew was death.

Nietszche said, "there are no facts, only interpretations," and here we have put forward a completely plausible explanation that takes all the known information and sits it comfortably within a theory. It is, furthermore, a theory which is at ease with every facet of the available evidence. What is proposed is that the forerunner to Freemasonry, comprised operative-news-carrying-masons - and crypto-Jewish-non-masons who were the recipients of the news carrying service. The inspirational idea to admit gentiles was therefore an easy step, and one that would have been unlikely to arouse any suspicions among the new-made Freemasons. Perhaps those early Jews should have looked back into history and remembered the way that Christianity borrowed their ideas and subsequently outnumbered them.

This supposition poses the question that "surely the new gentile members would have been surprised to find so many Jews as members"? However, we must remember that the Jews who were already members were crypto-Jews living as Christians. The experience of Spanish crypto-Jews is that it took many years before they felt secure enough to revert openly to Judaism, indeed there are crypto-Jews living in South America to this day. Subsequent events are written into history and the new "club", called Freemasonry, took hold and soon it became *de riguer* for an English gentlemen to become a member. The international existence of the earlier "news-carrying" service gave nascent Freemasonry an international flavour adding to its prestige. In 1717, several English Freemasons were persuaded to take the organisation into the public arena and so The Premier Grand Lodge, or Moderns as it became known, was formed.

It only remains to try to identify whether any particular group of Jews, or one particular tribe, played a leading role. Here, it is difficult not to point to the tribe or family with whom we began this investigation, the Cohanim. The likeness of the Masonic aprons to the dress of the old temple priests is but one clue, made all the stronger when we examined the ceremonial dress of a Provincial Grand Master in chapter 7. The existence of a Masonic order of Temple Priests is of minor support but it demonstrates the general direction that Freemasonry takes. Likewise, as we discussed in chapter 2, the way that a Masonic initiate takes steps that spell out "Zadok", the name of the high-priest who officiated at King Solomon's Temple, and interchangeable with the name "Cohanim", which have used to describe the temple priesthood, also adds support for their involvement.

It is, however, the involvement of Freemasonry with the Ark of the Covenant that brings the Cohanim openly into the debate. All direct references to the Ark have long been removed from modern Masonic ritual; however, traces remain. We mentioned in chapter 1 the "tracing boards" that have imagery of each ceremony painted on them; and how these are discussed in lengthy lectures given during the ceremonies. The second-degree tracing board depicts the inside of King Solomon's Temple, highlighting a staircase leading to a "middle-chamber". The purpose of the lecture is to explain how the password originated and at its conclusion it describes how a Fellowcraft Freemason - going to collect his wages - would arrive at the door of the middle-chamber and, on giving the correct passwords, be admitted. So far, so good: except, that during the time when the masons were building the temple this upper floor was one of the last parts to be built. What makes this narrative even more implausible is that once the mason has entered the middle-chamber of the temple, his attention was drawn to "certain Hebrew characters, here depicted by the letter G denoting God ...". The reference to "certain Hebrew characters" clearly refers to YHWH or, יהוה; and the only artefact inside King Solomon's Temple that justified association with God was the Ark of the Covenant. The Bible informs us that the Ark was only placed in the temple when it was complete.

> And the priests brought in the ark of the covenant of the LORD unto his place, into the oracle of the house, to the most holy place, even under the wings of the cherubim.
>
> *1 Kings 8:6*

This additional piece of information, in the second-degree lecture, clearly tells us that when the Ark of the Covenant was in place in the middle-chamber of the temple or Holy of Holies, the building work was complete and therefore all the masons had left the site. By inference, the only people "working" within the temple complex when the Ark was there were the priests, the Cohanim. It must follow from this observation that the Freemasons referred to in the second-degree lecture were temple priests.

Guarding the Ark has been the Cohen family business since Moses appointed his brother Aaron to the role more than three thousand years ago. It is almost inconceivable that the Knights Hospitaller would be involved in guarding the Ark without some members of the Cohen family in close proximity, whether openly or covertly as crypto-Jews. There are a couple of amusing clues within the ritual that display support for the idea that the Cohanim were directly involved with the creation of the Masonic ritual.

The direction to the Tyler or outer guard "to keep out all intruders and cowans to Freemasonry" is one. The meaning of the word "cowan" has been discussed by Masons over the centuries, indeed, a Scottish meaning has even crept into the dictionary, as "one who works as a mason without serving an apprenticeship". Cowan is, in fact, an alternative transliteration of Cohen, along with Cowen, Kohn, Cohn and Cohan. The significance of this can be better understood when the third degree ceremony is examined. In this ceremony a candidate is required to step over the mock grave of the dead temple architect Hiram Abif. A curious ceremony that most Mason's complete without question other than the occasional "I wonder what that was about?" Indeed, in some lodges all of the members parade around and step over the "grave" during the third degree ceremony. In reality it is the temple priesthood, the Cohanim who are forbidden to step over a grave. It is for this reason that emergency graves in Israel – the dead need to be buried quickly because of the heat that decomposes their bodies rapidly – are usually marked with a sprig of acacia, just as the third degree ceremony, the Hiramic legend displays. Taken together, the act of stepping over a grave – a "selection" test albeit a mock one – and banning Cohens (cowans) completes the illusion.

The illusion is that Freemasons do not want any of the rightful guardians of the Ark of the Covenant - the temple priesthood, the Cohanim - to come into the lodge and realise that the Freemasons had the Ark all along. All of course a clever charade in all probability introduced by the Cohanim, out of a sense of humour. Perhaps it was that same mischievous sense of humour that decided the early Jewish Masonic ritual compilers to build the ritual around a metaphor for conversion to Judaism. Whatever the answer, the ceremony was designed as a metaphor for a *mikvah* and not a real grave. Therefore stepping over it was not a problem for them. This explanation is of course pure speculation and evidence to support it is unlikely ever be found. However, it was during the period when the Holy Royal Arch was being introduced into Freemasonry that the third degree, the Hiramic legend, was also launched. This concurrence of dates would, if the above conjecture is even partly correct put the Cohanim in the right place and at the right time to influence the Masonic ritual. We can only speculate that perhaps the crypto-Jewish news carrying service, which we have suggested predated Freemasonry and from which Freemasonry evolved, was staffed entirely by Cohanim. As the family charged with protecting the Ark of the Covenant, as well as tending to any future temple at Jerusalem, they had – and still have – a vested interest in keeping Judaism alive and well. Such an interest would have included bringing crypto-Jews back into the fold at the earliest opportunity. As John Maynard Keynes put it:

> The difficulty lies, not in the new ideas, but in escaping the old ones, which ramify, for those brought up as most of us have been, into every corner of our minds.

We have identified that some Jews were involved in the early creation of Masonic ritual and ceremonial. The level of Judaic influence, down to the metaphorical conversion ceremony, is so overwhelming as to suggest that these Jews acted either alone or dictated the eventual outcome if gentiles were also involved with Freemasonry at that early stage. What we do not know is exactly when this event occurred. We can date, fairly accurately, the manuscripts that advise us of the content of the early Masonic rituals and we know when the Jews could live legally in England and the need for a covert news-carrying service evaporated. This places the emergence of Freemasonry firmly in the second half of the seventeenth century.

We have now provided overwhelming evidence of the involvement of Jews in the creation of Freemasonry and we have provided a coherent and plausible explanation of when, where, why and how they carried out this audacious act.

PART 3

A MESSIANIC BLOODLINE

CHAPTER 10

REX DEUS

In Parts 1 and 2 of this book, our investigations concluded that crypto-Jews created an organisation to carry news and contracts between distant groups of crypto-Jews. This "news-carrying" service must have had code words and signs that enabled them to be recognised by fellow crypto-Jews in the towns and villages they visited. Finally, when this news-carrying service was no longer required, they allowed it to be joined by non-Jews as a means of penetrating the gentile middle-classes. They named this new organisation the Freemasons.

In the course of studying the activities of the Jews, especially those displaced from the Southern Levant, we uncovered in chapter 6 a bloodline back to Moses' brother Aaron, carefully preserved by the Jerusalem Temple priesthood family, the Cohanim. The existence of this bloodline was secondary to our investigation into the origins of Freemasonry; in chapter 6 we were more concerned to identify proof of a different genetic makcup for the Cohanim from the general run of Jews. It is, however, impossible to mention a Biblical bloodline without examining the infamous *Rex Deus*, more recently known as the *Da Vinci* bloodline. This has generated so much debate, that deciding whether it is in any way connected with the Messianic bloodline being preserved by the Cohanim almost demands to be examined. Is the Cohanim "bloodline" the same one that weaves its way through the Rennes-le-Château mystery? The idea has attractions; for the duty of the Cohanim or family of Temple priests was to guard the Ark of the Covenant, which Byrne[1] speculated reposed for hundreds of years near Rennes-le-Château and is now in the hands of the Freemasons. If we can show that the so-called *Rex Deus* bloodline and the Messianic Cohanim bloodline, which we have made use of, are one and the same then it supports the suggestion that the Freemasons are guardians of the Ark. Where else would the Cohanim be than close to the Ark that they were charged by God to guard?

It was a French author, Gérard de Sède with his book L'Or de Rennes, who probably first raised the possibility that Jesus did indeed sire children and so begin a *Rex Deus* dynasty of God Kings. However, a trio of writers, Michael Baigent, Henry Leigh and Henry Lincoln initially introduced the English-speaking world to the idea with their book published in 1982, The Holy Blood and the Holy Grail[54]. This book was also the first in the English language to open the Rennes-le-Château mystery to a wide readership. Baigent, Leigh and Lincoln's thoughts turned towards *Rex Deus* lines – although they never used the term – when they received a curious message from a retired Anglican priest who stated that:

> The secret of Rennes-le-Château consisted of incontrovertible proof the crucifixion was a fraud and that Jesus was alive as late as 45 CE.
>
> *The Holy Blood and the Holy Grail*

The Anglican priest is unknown, so this interesting snippet has undefined provenance. The book stated that the retired priest had received the information from yet another Anglican priest, Canon Alfred Leslie Lilley, who died in 1940. Lilley published widely and had many contacts with the church of St. Sulpice in Paris.

What we must now do is to analyse whether a bloodline from Jesus Christ is a realistic possibility, and in so doing determine whether the Cohanim – Messianic – bloodline could possibly include Jesus Christ. If we can do this then it will indicate that our Cohanim bloodline is one and the same as the so-called *Rex Deus* bloodline, for it seems inconceivable that there are two such lineages.

The two pieces of information, Christ not dying on the cross and the link to St. Sulpice, led Baigent, Leigh and Lincoln in two directions. At first they explored the St. Sulpice link back to the Merovingians, the first Frankish monarchs. Saint Sulpice or Sulpicius, as we know him, died in 647; and apart from his distinction in aiding the poor from an early age, it was his robust defence of his people against the tyranny of the Merovingian mayors-of-the-palace which brought him to fame.

We briefly discussed the Merovingians in chapter 8 and concluded that the possibility of their being descended from either Jesus Christ or King David was most unlikely. As we now examine the bloodline theory in more detail, we will look more closely at their credentials. The Merovingian dynasty of Frankish kings gained the title from their 5th-century leader Merovech. A curious group of monarchs, they claimed divine right of rule. They also, reportedly, had long blonde hair, which was the source of their strength and therefore never cut. As with so much religious symbolism, this notion finds an echo from an early period, this time with Samson. Samson's mother was told by God, "and no rasor shall come on his head: for the child shall be a Nazarite unto God from the womb". The Merovingian kings regarded the day-to-day administration of their kingdoms to be beneath them and delegated the administrative power to the "mayor-of-the-palace". The inevitable result was the mayors took over to form the next dynasty – the Carollingians.

There is an apparent misconception that the Merovingians were Jewish as a means of explaining their claimed divine right to reign, and this suggestion extends to the existence of a bloodline back to Jesus Christ. An earlier legend provides a clue how the term "divine right" originated, or perhaps "high-jacked" is a better word. The legend states that a sea monster sired Merovech, and this explained his having syndactyly, or webbed fingers. Syndactyly is one of the signs of a "great-man" in Buddhism - indeed Buddha himself supposedly had it. This might explain how the story came to be borrowed. In reality we know almost nothing of Merovech and there is also nothing in known Merovingian history to support the suggestion that they descended from Jesus Christ. Furthermore, their long blonde hair – and yellow was used to describe it – almost certainly rules out an original near-eastern ancestry. Although it is not **now** unusual for Jews to have blonde hair, especially Ashkenazies, this is a product of Diaspora Jews intermarrying with the indigenous people where they settled. It was – and indeed still is – popular to portray Jesus Christ as a blue-eyed blonde; the reality is the dominant appearance of Semites is dark in both complexion and hair colour.

Because indigenous Semites usually have black hair, which has a dominant gene, the suggestion of Semitic roots for the Merovingians is remote. For Meovingian blonde hair genes to have been dominant over the house-of-Judah Semitic dark-hair genes would have needed many generations to develop. This implies that house-of-Judah Semites migrated to Germany long before the Merovingian dynasty emerged. There is no evidence to support this proposition: indeed, all the evidence points to the opposite and to the migration from Germany being in a southerly direction. The clear inference is the likelihood of a Jewish bloodline for the Merovingians is improbable, let alone any suggestion that the Merovingian bloodline was Jesus Christ's.

With any myth, there has to be a fragment of truth around which to weave the fable, and so it is with this recently created myth about a Merovingian *Rex Deus* dynasty. The theoretical possibility of a group of Jews leaving Judaea as early as 720 BCE, travelling to and settling in Northern Europe, evidently exists. It could have been when the Assyrian ruler, Tiglath-pileser, overran Israel and deported the ruling and administrative classes back to Nineveh and Asur, in what is today Kurdistan. The deportees never returned and ten of the twelve founding tribes are known as "the ten lost tribes of Israel". Although the possibility of dispersion, to Northern Europe is possible, the defeated Israeli people were actually deported to Kurdistan. Either way, this is long before the birth of Jesus Christ and so descent from Him can be ruled out in this theoretical circumstance. The next and perhaps most significant Diaspora was the "Babylonian Exile" of 586, BCE, with many Jews declining to return to Judaea. Once again the centre for the Diaspora was the region of Mesopotamia.

Recent research, by Dr. Doron Behar[55], under the supervision of professor Karl Skorecki, strongly supports these assertions. Behar, Karl Skorecki and Dror Rosengarten of the Technion and Rambam Medical Centre, Haifa; together with Michael Hammer, Matthew Caplan and Daniel Garrigan of the University of Arizona; Richard Villems, of the Tartu University; Batsheva Bonne-Tamir and David Gurwitz of the Sackler School of Medicine; Martin Richards, of the University of Huddersfield; Sergio Della Pergola, of the Hebrew University, Jerusalem; and

Lluis Quintana-Murci, of the Institut Pasteur, Paris, identified a "bottleneck" of only four Ashkenazi women during the early part of the first millennium from whom nearly half of all living Ashkenazim females are descended.

> The term Ashkenazi refers to Jewish people of recent European ancestry, with an historical separation from other major Jewish populations in North Africa and the Middle eat. The contemporary Ashenazi gene pool is thought to have originated from a founding deme (closely related group) that migrated from the Near-East within the last two millennia.
>
> *Dr. Doron Behar et al*
> *MtDNA Evidence for a Genetic Bottleneck in the Early History of the Ashkenazi Jewish Population*

Behar's research also supports an assertion made in chapter 4, that Jews and Canaanites shared a common ancestry.

> In contrast, the 224-234-311 haplotype is rare among European and Near-Eastern non-Jewish populations. A single direct match was found in a sample of Palestinian Arabs.
>
> *Dr. Doron Behar et al*
> *MtDNA Evidence for a Genetic Bottleneck in the Early History of the Ashkenazi Jewish Population*

By the first century BCE, the Egyptian city of Alexandria contained the largest Jewish Diaspora, demonstrating the tendency of Jews to disperse, but usually only to civilised areas. Other, more far-flung centres of the Jewish Diaspora appeared, some much later, in Persia, Spain, France, Germany, Poland, Russia, Ukraine and, more recently, the United States of America, Canada and South America. Evidence of the movement of Jews into Europe followed firstly the expanding Greek empire and secondly the Roman Empire. Evidence of Jewish settlement in central and northern Europe only began with the campaigns of Julius Caesar around 55, BCE, and this is not hard to understand. The Germanic tribes advancing south as far as the Danube River and west of the Rhine into Gaul forced Caesar to take the war to them. Before the civilising effects of the Roman occupation on Gaul fierce Celtic tribes populated these regions and, therefore, they offered little reward to an educated Jew to move there. Indeed Gibbon[56] provides a good description of life in Germany during Roman times:

> The religious system of the Germans (if the wild opinions of savages can deserve that name) was dictated by their wants, their fears, and their ignorance. They adored the great visible objects and agents of nature, the Sun and the Moon, the Fire and the Earth; together with those imaginary deities, who were supposed to preside over the most important occupations of human life. They were persuaded that, by some ridiculous arts of divination, they could discover the will of the superior beings, and that human sacrifices were the most precious and acceptable offering to their altars. Some applause has been hastily bestowed on the sublime notion, entertained by that people, of the Deity, whom they neither confined within the walls of a temple, nor represented by any human figure. But, when we recollect that the Germans were unskilled in architecture, and totally unacquainted with the art of sculpture, we shall readily assign the true reason of a scruple which arose not so much from a superiority of reason as from a want of ingenuity. The only temples in Germany were dark and ancient groves, consecrated by the reverence of succeeding generations. Their secret gloom, the imagined residence of an invisible power, by presenting no distinct object of fear or worship, impressed the mind with a still deeper sense of religious horror; and the priests, rude and illiterate as they were, had been taught by experience the use of every artifice that could preserve and fortify impressions so well suited to their own interest.
>
> *Edward Gibbon*
> *The Decline and Fall of the Roman Empire*

This debate has taken us into the various Jewish dispersions, and it is necessary to identify an important difference between expanding Jewish communities and those of the Christians. Largely, it was the movement of people, the Jews themselves, who achieved the spread of Judaism, whereas the spread of Christianity involved converting the local population of a region to the new religion. This is an important factor when considering the effect that a group of immigrant Jews might have on their new location. It takes many years for population numbers to increase to a size where they represent the significant proportion of the inhabitants from which rulers might emerge. The dispersed Jews in Germany, even if there were any before the emerging Merovingian dynasty, would have been a tiny minority and most unlikely to provide the nation's head. Judaism is not generally an evangelising religion and therefore the wholesale religious conversion of the locals could not speed-up this development.

Further consideration of the possibility of a "divine" bloodline for the Merovingians proves similarly unproductive. We can reasonably dismiss the legend, which claims that a fabulous sea monster fathered Merovech, although in it may lie the origins of claims of divinity. Further ammunition to discard these claims to divine status lies in the notorious polygamy of the Merovingians. To preserve a dynasty, some minimal concern for patrilineal, or for that matter matrilineal, inheritance is necessary to maintain any semblance of credibility. If we suggest the Merovingian bloodline was so powerful that even a concubine could not dilute its effects, it must follow that the number of generations since then will have deposited some of their powerful genes in each of us. If the Merovingian genes were that powerful and divine, statistically, if we accept the *Rex Deus* notion, most of us are gods because of the way genes spread out rapidly among later generations. Indeed, Dr. Bryan Sykes, professor of genetics at Oxford University, whom we quoted in chapter 1, believes that genes from Genghis Khan can be identified in 16 million living males. Dr. Sykes' remarkable proposition follows from Genghis Khan's appetite for raping his conquests. The suggestion, though, that we each have god-like Merovingian genes is discredited by the reality that we lack the fundamental divine ability to walk on water without artificial aids.

Having poured a measure of scorn on the idea that the Merovingian dynasty were somehow related to the Biblical King

David or even Jesus Christ, the rumour itself deserves some explanation. The origin of the story may lie with the earliest Merovingian King who expanded the dynasty's lands beyond a small area of present day Belgium, to cover much of France. This dynasty's King was Clovis I, and when Clovis assumed the Frankish throne in 481, he was in fact a pagan. There is an explanation which sets Clovis apart and appears to place the Merovingian dynasty in a pre-eminent position among those interested in divine bloodlines. It is the observation that Clovis converted to Christianity late in life and effectively made Catholicism the religion of France.

The story of Clovis' conversion has his Catholic wife, Clotilde, as the major influence on this decision. Clotilde was the granddaughter of the Catholic Burgundian King Gonderic, by Chilperic one of his four sons. At Gonderic's death his four sons battled for the succession. Chilperic was Catholic, and another son, Gondebaud, was Arian. During the battles for the crown, Chilperic and his family were all killed except for of his two daughters, Chrona and Clotilde. The story of how Clovis wooed Clotilde, by sending a courtier disguised as a beggar to entice her away from her guardian, is pure Disney. However, they did indeed marry and eventually Saint Remi baptised Clovis in Reims cathedral.

It was during this ceremony that the next episode in this extraordinary story occurred. To mark the important entry of King Clovis into Christianity, Saint Remi was about to anoint the King with oil. This was a clear allusion to the anointing of King David, and intended to mark Clovis' approval by God. However, when the phial of anointing oil was opened it proved to be empty. Saint Remi raised his hands to heaven and a white dove flew to him with a phial of oil in its beak. Now this event was an embellishment, an example of judicious bird training or an act of God, depending on one's personal preferences. However this event is viewed, it does link Clovis irrevocably with the early Hebrew kings David and Solomon and forever settled the act of anointing with oil for future Christian kings and queens. It is to Georgius Florentius, writer and bishop of Tours, that Clovis owes his posthumous religious elevation. Saint Gregory of Tours, as we know Georgius, wrote the Ten Books of Histories in which he repeats much of the above and refers to Clovis as a "new Constantine". In Ten Books of Histories, Gregory equates the Franks with the ancient Hebrews, and Clovis to King David. Here then is the most likely source of the Merovingian legend of Davidic ancestry - the grateful writings of a Christian bishop, praising the life of Clovis as an expression of gratitude for converting France to Catholicism.

Having explored the possibility of a divine bloodline from the Merovingians, Baigent, Leigh and Lincoln turned their attentions to another possibility - the likelihood that Jesus Christ survived the crucifixion. They implied that, having already married Mary Magdeleine, Jesus fathered a son who went on to found a sacred – or *Rex Deus* - dynasty. They produce an argument to suggest the "Holy Grail" is a phonetic development from *Sang Raal* – Royal Blood - the bloodline of Jesus. It would be easy to dismiss these fanciful ideas out of hand, but for the constant reminders that some – occasionally powerful - figures wish to sustain them. For example, Baigent, Leigh and Lincoln quote an event from the 16th century life of Henri I de Lorraine, Duke of Guise. It seems that rapturous crowds greeted Henri, when he entered the town of Joinville in Champagne, with cries of "Hosannah to the Son-of-David". This cry clearly suggests that the Duke of Guise was content to have his name linked with the Biblical king.

The controversial Laurence Gardner[57] continued this Jesus bloodline theme by suggesting that Jesus, as the chief representative of the "chosen people" - that is, of the dynasty of David - was not a member of the priesthood. The reason he gave was that such rights belonged to the order of Aaron and the tribe of Levi. Gardner then argues that it was the ascension of Christ that formalised His priesthood:

> Wherefore, holy brethren, partakers of the heavenly calling, consider the Apostle and High Priest of our profession, Christ Jesus.
>
> *Hebrews 3:1*

> So also Christ glorified not himself to be made an high priest; but he that said unto him, Thou art my Son, today have I begotten thee.
>
> As he saith also in another place, Thou art a priest forever after the order of Melchisedec.
>
> *Hebrews 5:5 and 6*

The weakness is this polemic is there is nothing in the Biblical text to support the idea that His priesthood was not recognised during His life. Laurence Gardner[57] also produced genealogical lists, the correctness of which have been extensively questioned, showing that Prince Michael of Albany, otherwise known as Michel Lafosse, is the rightful heir to the crown of David. Gardner has, though, revised this opinion of late. In an interview with Tracy Twyman[58], the earlier recipient of Gardner's genealogical research, Prince Michael, stated that:

> One thing you could say in your article is that Mary, Queen of Scots, for example, was very aware of her Merovingian and Davidic descent, because she actually had a book that had her family tree back to King David via Jesus and so forth. And that came from the Lorraine family, de Guise-Lorraine. And again, if you go back to The Forgotten Monarchy of Scotland then you see the descent of Marie de Guise-Lorraine from the Crusader Kingdom of Jerusalem, i.e. Baldwin II.

We can observe that Prince Michael, like Baigent, Leigh and Lincoln, also uses the Lorraine family to provide a genealogical link back to Jesus Christ. By bringing Mary Queen of Scots into the debate the "unseen hands" we referred to in chapter 8 may have supporters of the Stuart pretenders to the English Crown behind them.

No one has suggested that David was a god, and so a "*Rex*" or Davidic bloodline would only have regal implications, and in the absence of a defined dynasty, even that would be slight. The real interest appears to be generated by the addition of the word "*Deus*". The first (recent) use of the term "*Rex Deus*" probably belongs to Knight and Lomas[59] who continued and expanded the "Jesus Christ did marry and had children" polemic. More recently, Tim Wallace-Murphy, Marilyn Hopkins and Graham Simmans[43] published their unambiguous book Rex Deus which continues the argument that Christ married.

The idea of a *Rex Deus* – a God King – two bloodlines in one-person - one regal, one directly from God, is not new. Indeed, the idea is as old as the institution of monarchy itself. We have just used the term "recent" in parentheses because the words *Rex Deus* do appear in the Vulgate (circa 400 CE) version of the Bible. Here, though, the meaning is more "Oh king, God most High hath made you …" rather than King and God.

> O rex Deus altissimus regnum et magnificentiam gloriam et honorem dedit Nabuchodonosor patri tuo.
>
> *Daniel 5:18*

Because the suggested *Rex Deus* bloodline – that we are discussing here - emanates from Jesus Christ, it is from within the framework of Christianity that we address this concept in the rest of this chapter: no other Abrahamic religion recognizes Jesus Christ as God on earth. It will become apparent that from within Christianity, the idea of *Rex Deus* is more difficult to accept. The Christian God – and similarly of course the Jewish and Muslim God alike – is all around and everywhere but only in spirit. Records of God "physically" visiting humans on earth occurred only in ancient Judaic, pre-Christian meetings with only a few special people such as Abraham and Moses. God also visited the Ark of the Covenant in the tabernacle and the Temple at Jerusalem. In Templar Gold, Patrick Byrne identified the Freemasons as the current guardians of the Ark. However, the observation the Ark still exists doesn't alter the fact that it appears to have been "out of action" as God's seat on earth for some 2500 years. Despite this observation, there is no suggestion anywhere that God ever harboured any wish to procreate with any of His earthly subjects. According to Christian doctrine, even the birth of His son by a human – Mary – did not involve any physical contact. Indeed, descriptions of God's physical being suggest that contact between God and humans may have been more than a little problematic:

> In my distress I called upon the Lord, and cried unto my God: he heard my voice out of his temple, and my cry came before him, even into his ears.
>
> Then the earth shook and trembled; the foundations also of the hills moved and were shaken, because he was wroth.
>
> There went up a smoke out of his nostrils, and fire out of his mouth devoured: coals were kindled by it.
>
> *Psalm 18:6-9*
>
> A fiery stream issued and came forth from before him: thousand thousands ministered unto him, and ten thousand times ten thousand stood before him: the judgement was set, and the books were opened.
>
> *Daniel 7:9-10*

Further evidence is available of the power of God's presence from Moses' encounters with Him:

> And it came to pass, when Moses came down from mount Sinai with the two tables of testimony in Moses' hand, when he came down from the mount, that Moses wist not that the skin of his face shone while he talked with him.
>
> And when Aaron and all the children of Israel saw Moses, behold, the skin of his face shone; and they were afraid to come nigh him.
>
> *Exodus 34:29-30*

Before leaving this line of argument, we must acknowledge an occasion when God may have had physical contact with a man, in this instance, Jacob.

> And Jacob was left alone; and there wrestled a man with him until the breaking of the day.
>
> *Genesis 32:24*

It is widely believed that the "man" referred to in this extract is in fact God, because Jacob later says, "for I have seen God face to face, and my life is preserved." Once again, though, this is a matter of Biblical interpretation. The fact remains, that to this day there is not a single scrap of evidence to suggest that El Shaddai, YHWH, the God of the Jews, the God of the Christians - or any other name for God - ever had sexual relations with any human. It is relatively easy, then, to dismiss the possibility of YHWH impregnating any human females because His "physical" appearance - as just described above - rules it out on practical grounds. Furthermore, there has never been any suggestion that He ever did any such thing.

One of YHWH's early acts was to transfer "sonship" from the rulers – pharaohs in Moses' region of the world – to the people. All Jews became "sons-of-God" - an interesting idea that provides room for debate on the later proclamation that Jesus Christ was "The Son-of-God". During the period when the Ark of the Covenant was available in the tabernacle and later in the Temple at Jerusalem, it was not unusual for God to visit His "seat-on-earth" to deliver instructions to the high priest. After the time from when the Ark was no longer mentioned – around 650 BCE – it became more usual for an angel to deliver God's directives to His "chosen" individuals.

Christians, though, do believe there was one epoch when the bloodline of God did exist on earth and that was during the lifetime of Jesus Christ. The Christian doctrine states that Jesus was the "Son-of-God" and an equal partner in the trinity of Father, Son and Holy Ghost, which makes up the single entity of the Christian God. Jesus was, according to Christian belief, both God and man simultaneously. Therefore, we must admit to at least the "theoretical possibility" according to Christian doctrine – that, during the lifetime of Jesus Christ – the bloodline of God did pass into the human race. However, if Jesus had sired children, and if they survived and sired or bore children through several generations, by now most of us will have some genetic code that had originated with God. This is a possibility that we will carefully examine.

We showed in chapter 7, how Professor Bryan Sykes' research[33] upheld the statement just made, "by now most of us will have some genetic code that had originated with God." Further support is available from recent studies by the University of Michigan. There, a group of researchers from Penn State, Yale, Rome and Witwatersrand Universities explain the way genetic code spreads throughout the population and remain as "markers". The researchers were looking at genetic information on mitochondrial DNA, which does not alter during the reproductive process (see appendix A).

> Using these markers to trace lineages, we find that modern humans appear to have emerged from Africa between 100,000 and 150,000 years ago and the population that left Africa was rather small.
>
> *Bryan Sykes*
> *The Seven Daughters of Eve*

We can gain a clearer understanding of these findings by examining the reproductive behaviour of Jews themselves. Jews have, since Bible days, been strongly encouraged to marry by the age of eighteen; therefore, we can conservatively argue that a generation lasts 25 years. If each female member of every generation produces an average of 2 children, then, after 1500 years there will have been 60 generations. The number of related offspring from a single couple – assuming 2 children for every female offspring - after 60 generations is therefore 2^{60}. This number is 10 followed by 17 zeros, and is larger, by far, than there are human beings on earth today, a figure which is around 10 billion. The effects of disease, famine and wars, in regularly reducing the population, can explain the massive difference between the two figures. As an example, the bubonic plague or "black death" of the middle ages killed around one-third of the population. Clearly any genetic variation – once it fixes in the

2
Children

mitochondrial DNA - will, over a long enough period, permeate vast tracts of the human race.

If we consider the alternative, that this is more than a bloodline, and may even be a dynasty, then we must examine how such a dynasty might have been preserved. *Primogeniture* is of course a difficult avenue to venture down because it similarly questions the Davidic bloodline. The King who followed David was of course Solomon and he was fifth in line and at least one of David's more senior sons, Adonijah, was still alive when Solomon became King of Israel. The picture becomes even more blurred with the knowledge that Solomon had around seven-hundred wives. According to Biblical accounts, Solomon's eldest – or at least "favourite" – son Rehoboam succeeded him and reigned for seventeen years. Rehoboam preceded his "favourite" son, Abijah, and Asa, his son, in turn, followed him. Asa's son, Jehoshaphat, then became king, and his son, Jehoram, succeeded him. Jehoram, however, was not a good King and it was his youngest son, Ahaziah, whom the people chose to replace him. After only six generations from David, we have at least two Biblically recorded breaches in the rule of *primogeniture*. We hardly need any more evidence to show that, for the early Jews, *primogeniture* was not an essential factor in deciding the royal succession. This "dynasty" then, is, as we have demonstrated above, little more than a bloodline.

All of this interest in the idea that Jesus left a legacy of a miraculous inheritance of people related to God can only have two possible explanations. Either the whole business is reification:

> The regarding or treating of an abstraction as if it had a concrete or material existence.

In other words someone came up with an idea and wrote about it in a book and others have come along subsequently and repeated the matter as if it were real. Or, alternatively, Jesus Christ married, had children and they founded a dynasty. It is the implications of this latter notion that we will continue to explore.

The difficulty that anyone seeking to question the argument - that Jesus founded a dynasty - has to face is that there is simply no contemporary evidence to confirm or deny the suggestion. The Bible provides the main source of information about Jesus' life but the earliest books of the New Testament draw from the various letters to churches written by the apostle Paul as he travelled throughout the Levant. We now know these were written between 20 and 30 years after Jesus' death. The first gospel, that of Mark, probably did not appear until 40 years after the death of Jesus. These are long periods through which we must rely entirely on an oral tradition of transmitting information. The absence of the written-word as evidence creates an "easy target" for those choosing to present almost any theory; but this absence of the written-word does not preclude the development of counter-arguments.

We have recognised that a theoretical opportunity existed, within Christianity, for *Rex Deus* dynastic foundations to evolve. That opportunity arrived when Jesus Christ entered the scene as an adult. It is certainly not the purpose of this book to question Christian or any other belief. The reality is that apart from the New Testament and brief mentions by Josephus in Testimonium Flavianum, Tacitus, Pliny the Younger and possibly Suetonius, there is precious little contemporary documentation about the life of Jesus. Therefore, we must examine carefully whatever there is to decide its credibility.

Confusion surrounding the early life of Christ increases when Matthew has Him travelling to Egypt at an early age and remaining there until Herod was dead. Mark, Luke and John make no mention of a trip to Egypt. This example is an indication of the paucity of solid data on the early life of Jesus Christ, and the quality does not improve for His later life.

Returning to the *Rex Deus* theory, clearly it has two constituent parts, *Rex* and *Deus*. Having accepted that, according to Christian doctrine that Jesus was God – an issue to which we will come back shortly – then we have in Christ the second half or *Deus*. It remains to settle whether Jesus Christ also held the first half, *Rex*. The term *Rex Deus* requires that, in Christ, the *Rex* or Davidic bloodline merged with the *Deus* half, which came from God, Jesus' father. To prove the authenticity of Jesus' Davidic, or *Rex*, consanguinity, the Biblical books of Luke and Matthew both provide detailed genealogies. Matthew's genealogical tree extends back to Abraham and Luke's goes back to Adam. Unfortunately the genealogies do not agree one with the other.

LUKE	MATTHEW
Adam	**There are no entries until Abraham**
Seth	
Enos	
Cainan	
Maleleel	
Jared	
Enoch	
Mathusala	
Lamech	
Noe	
Sem	
Arphaxad	
Cainan	
Sala	
Heber	
Phalec	
Ragau	
Saruch	
Nachor	
Thara	
Abraham	**Abraham**
Isaac	Isaac
Jacob	Jacob
Juda	Judas
Phares	Phares
Esrom	Esrom
Aram	Aram
Aminadab	Aminadab
Nasson	Naasson
Salmon	Salmon
Booz	Booz
Obed	Obed
Jesse	Jesse
David	**David**
Natham	Solomon
Mattatha	Roboam
Menan	Abia

Melea	Asa
Eliakim	Josaphat
Jonan	Joram
Joseph	Ozias
Juda	Joatham
Simeon	Achaz
Levi	Ezekias
Matthat	Manasses
Jorim	Amon
Eliezier	Josias
Jose	Jechonias
Er	Salathiel
Elmodam	
Cosam	
Addi	
Melchi	
Neri	
Salathiel	
Zorobabel	**Zorobabel**
Rhesa	Abind
Joanna	
Juda	Eliakim
Joseph	
Semei	Azor
Mattathias	
Maath	Sadoc
Nagge	
Esli	Achim
Naum	
Amos	Eliud
Mattathias	
Joseph	Eliazer
Jamia	
Melchi	Mattan
Levi	
Matthat	Jacob
Heli	
Joseph	Joseph
Jesus	**Jesus**
Luke 3: 23 – 38	**Matthew 1: 1 - 16**

The use of the Bible as a source of "integrity" to make the following point is unavoidable as no other source exists to support the idea that Jesus was of the Davidic bloodline. However, a cursory examination immediately highlights some serious inconsistencies. Starting with the numbers of generations. Matthew boasts what must be a measure of metaphorical licence. From Abraham to David, he has 14 generations, from David to the Babylonian exile is also 14 generations and from the Babylonian exile to the birth of Jesus is a further 14 generations. What little we know of Abraham points to his having lived around 1900 BCE. Even accepting that he was 100 years old when Isaac was born, this is still pointing to at least 700 years for 14 generations, a generation span of 50 years and not very probable. From David to the Babylonian exile was around 600 years and a little less to the birth of Jesus. Even these reduced numbers point to generation spans of 35 years, still unrealistically high. The genealogical tree provided by Luke has a much more realistic timescale - some 42 generations from David until Jesus, an average of around 24 years for each generation.

Comparing the two lists for the period from Adam to Abraham, Matthew gives no genealogy upholding Abraham as the "father" of the Jews. The fact that Luke provides a genealogical history from Adam casts serious doubt on its efficacy. From Abraham to David there is an exact correlation – apart from a couple of minor spelling differences. It is easy to suppose that both lists came from a common source. From David on, however, the only correlation is where well-known figures from Jewish history appear in the family tree - Zorobabel, Joseph and of course Jesus. Now we might argue that the ancestral records simply record alternative routes down the same genealogical history. This argument, though, does not withstand analysis. If we start with Jesus and, for the sake of discussion, accept Joseph as his father, then we move one generation back to Heli for Luke's records and Jacob for Matthew's. Now the one detail that we can be sure of is that Joseph did not have two fathers, so one or both of the records is wrong. The same argument applies for Zorobabel's father Salathiel. Both genealogies cannot be correct and both, we have argued above, are so flawed as to be of questionable value.

There is a suggestion that one of the genealogies belongs to Mary and the other to Joseph. We can reasonably discount this argument as an attempt to ameliorate an obviously inaccurate record. Both genealogies identify Joseph as Jesus' father and thus clearly display Joseph's family tree. If we stretch credibility to the utmost we might accept that one genealogy belongs to Mary, whose father we must then accept was also called Joseph. Excluding Jesus' father and the names before Abraham, only some three-percent of the names are "Joseph", which when added to the criticisms already made of both lists, makes acceptance a matter of faith rather than statistical probability. The final rebuttal to this particular explanation comes from the Biblical texts. Matthew leaves no doubt that the genealogy of Jesus is for the male line:

> The book of the generation of Jesus Christ, the son of David, the son of Abraham. Abraham begat Isaac; and Isaac begat Jacob; and Jacob begat Judas and his brethren; And Judas begat Phares and Zara of Thamar; and Phares begat Esrom; and Esrom begat Aram; And Aram begat Aminadab; and Aminadab begat Naasson; and Naasson begat Salmon;
>
> *Matthew 1:1-4*

Luke too removes any doubt that he refers to the male line:

> And Jesus himself began to be about thirty years of age, being (as was supposed) the son of Joseph, which was the son of Heli, Which was the son of Matthat, which was the son of Levi, which was the son of Melchi, which was the son of Janna, which was the son of Joseph, Which was the son of Mattathias, which was the son of Amos, which was the son of Naum, which was the son of Esli, which was the son of Nagge,
>
> *Luke 3:23-25*

It follows, on the balance of available evidence, that we can say with confidence that a Davidic bloodline for Jesus is slight. It is statistically only the same as that of random chance, or of anyone born, in that region, at that time being of the royal-blood of David. This supports the view of historians that the dynasty of David died out after the Babylonian captivity. In making that comment, we must emphasise that historians are referring to a "dynasty", a succession of first-born sons, or something close. A "bloodline" from David is another matter and as discussed earlier is by now spread across most of humanity.

In fact, the debate has been taken out of our hands because the Catholic Church of Rome, which for centuries was the principal controlling body of Christianity, has decreed that Jesus' mother Mary was a virgin. To avoid room for disagreement, Protestants and the Eastern Orthodox Christian Church also holds that Mary was a virgin. The doctrine that Mary conceived Jesus, with the help of only The Holy Spirit, has been a universal principle of the Church since the second century and included in the Apostle's creed.

> I believe in God the Father Almighty maker of heaven and earth, and in Jesus Christ, His only Son, our Lord, who was conceived by the Holy Spirit, born of the Virgin Mary…

The church Council of Nicaea varied this only slightly in 325 to:

> I believe in one God the Father Almighty maker of heaven and earth and of all things visible and invisible, and in one Lord Jesus Christ. For our salvation came down from heaven and was incarnate by the Holy Spirit of the Virgin Mary and was made man…

It is worth noting that Muslims also accept that Jesus was a virgin birth. For Christians, therefore, the long and painstakingly detailed genealogies are irrelevant. Joseph may or may not have been heir to the throne of David but according to Christian doctrine his blood never flowed in the body of Jesus Christ. The idea that Jesus was conceived by another "immaculate conception" – the first was Mary's birth - is not without some evidence for debate, even within the Bible:

> For it is evident that our Lord sprang out of Judah; of which tribe Moses spake nothing concerning priesthood.
>
> *Hebrews 7:14*

In considering Jesus' patrilineal forebears, this is perhaps an unnecessary confusion because Judah was the fourth son born to Jacob and his first wife, Leah. Therefore, if Jesus was of the tribe of Judah, then His father was Joseph rather than God.

Although the above quote, Hebrews 7:14, suggests that Jesus was not heir to any priestly inheritance, some writers attribute a Zadokite inheritance to His mother Mary. This priestly status – in their opinion - brought the priestly (Zadokite) and kingly (Davidic) bloodlines together. This argument can only stand if Jesus held a Davidic bloodline and we described above how we have difficulty in attributing such a pedigree to Him. With regard to Jesus' mother, Mary, being of Zadokite or Cohanim bloodline, there is a persuasive clue in the Bible. Indeed, apart from this clue, the Bible has surprisingly little to say about the Virgin Mary. The Bible clue is in the gospel according to Luke:

> There was in the days of Herod, the King of Judaea, a certain priest named Zacharias, of the course of Abia: and his wife was of the daughters of Aaron, and her name was Elisabeth.
>
> *Luke.1:5*

Luke explains how the priest, Zacharias, could not have children because his wife, Elisabeth, was barren, but God answered his prayers:

> But the angel said unto him, Fear not, Zacharias: for thy prayer is heard; and thy wife Elisabeth shall bear thee a son, and thou shalt call his name John.
>
> *Luke.1:13*

The son born later to Elisabeth and Zacharias would grow up to be John the Baptist and by his mother's lineage he was a Cohanim (see Luke 1:5 above), a descendent of Aaron. By the time of

Herod, the Temple priesthood extended beyond the Cohanim. However, it was generally only the position of high priest which was purchased. Because Zacharias was simply a Temple priest, we can safely assert that he was a Levite and a direct descendent of Aaron. Thus, on his mother's side, John the Baptist was eligible to join the Essenes, if - as we speculated in chapter 7 - that is where some of the male heirs of Aaron lived. Luke's words on this matter continue with an equally important observation:

> And in the sixth month the angel Gabriel was sent from God unto a city of Galilee, named Nazareth, To a virgin espoused to a man whose name was Joseph, of the house of David; and the virgin's name was Mary.
>
> *Luke.1:26-27*

The angel Gabriel brought the news of Mary's coming birth of the Messiah, Jesus, and another most important piece of information:

> And, behold, thy cousin Elisabeth, she hath also conceived a son in her old age: and this is the sixth month with her, who was called barren.
>
> For with God nothing shall be impossible.
>
> *Luke.1:36-37*

What Luke is saying plainly here, is that Jesus' mother, Mary was a cousin of Elisabeth, the mother of John the Baptist. Luke has already shown that Elisabeth was a Cohanim and this makes the likelihood of Mary also being Cohanim quite high. The Levite tribe were careful to marry within the Levite tribe, and this is confirmed by the Origins of Old Testament priests research reviewed in chapter 6. Indeed, a priest could not take up his duties unless his wife could also prove that she was a Levite through several generations. These two cousins necessarily shared the same family tree although removed from each other by a branch or two. We can therefore surmise that, if John was a Cohanim, then there it was probable that his cousin, Jesus, was also a Cohanim.

The belief, that the Virgin Mary was a Zadokite also comes from a second century "Gospel of James", a Gnostic work not included in the Bible. Although Gnosticism predates Christianity, Simon Magus is said to have set in motion the "Christian" Gnostic movement, some suggest around the end of the first century, as a splinter group within Christianity. It could be argued that the Gnostics helped – or perhaps "forced" would be a better word – the Christian church to resolve the complex issues surrounding Jesus as the Son-of-God. The Christians were having problems reconciling two matters:

1. The existence of a single God having His son born of human parents and at the same time being the Son-of-God.
2. James, mentioned in the gospels, as Jesus' brother.

There is another problem, because the version of the birth of Christ to the Virgin Mary in his Gospel mimics the Old Testament story of the birth of Samuel to a virgin. This reference requires caution, though, because although the Bible appears to imply that Samuel's mother, Hannah, was a virgin, it is actually saying that Hannah was barren and could not have children.

> But unto Hannah he gave a worthy portion; for he loved Hannah: but the Lord had shut up her womb.
>
> *1 Samuel 1:4 and 5*

But Hannah entreated the Lord to give her a male child and the plea was successful:

> Wherefore it came to pass, when the time was come about after Hannah had conceived, that she bare a son, and called his name Samuel, saying, Because I have asked him of the Lord.
>
> *1 Samuel 1:19 and 20*

In the Syriac version of the Gospel of James, Mary's mother was either Dina or Hanna and her father was Zadok Yonakhir. At twelve years old, Mary was taken to the temple and entrusted to an elderly priest also called Zadok. In the Greek version of the same

Gospel, Mary stayed at the temple from the age of three until she was twelve.

In chapter 2, we mentioned how the two original English Grand Lodges merged on 27th December, 1813. This day, as we noted, is St. John the Evangelist's day and the venerating of his day, and by association the saint himself, provides another clue as to whether Jesus Christ was a Cohanim. In the New Testament book of John, we find the following text, written about the discovery that Christ had risen again and departed his tomb.

> The first day of the week cometh Mary Magdalene early, when it was yet dark, unto the sepulchre, and seeth the stone taken away from the sepulchre.
>
> Then she runneth, and cometh to Simon Peter, and to the other disciple, whom Jesus loved [St. John the Evangelist], and saith unto them, They have taken away the Lord out of the sepulchre, and we know not where they have laid him.
>
> Peter therefore went forth, and that other disciple, and came to the sepulchre.
>
> So they ran both together: and the other disciple did outrun Peter, and came first to the sepulchre.
>
> And he stooping down, and looking in, saw the linen clothes lying; yet went he not in.
>
> *St. John 20:2-5*

The important observation is that St. John the Evangelist did not enter the tomb. This indicates that he was a member of the Temple priesthood, of the Cohen family, and so forbidden to approach a dead body.

> Then cometh Simon Peter following him, and went into the sepulchre, and seeth the linen clothes lie,

> And the napkin, that was about his head, not lying with the linen clothes, but wrapped together in a place by itself. Then went in also that other disciple, which came first to the sepulchre, and he saw, and believed.
>
> *St. John 20:6-8*

Only when St. John is satisfied that there is no body in the tomb does he enter, to satisfy himself that Christ is risen from the dead. This short piece of Biblical text has confirmed the connection between the Freemasons and the Cohanim as well as supporting the suggestion that Jesus was also a Cohanim. The clue here is in verse 3 above in the words "whom Jesus loved", indicating that St. John the Evangelist was also of the same family as Jesus Christ.

It is frankly impossible to be dogmatic about what texts are historically accurate and what were later compilations added for public consumption. As explained above, reference to modern analysis is also no guarantee of accuracy. These decisions are more a matter of faith than scientific analysis. In any event, as the Biblical genealogies of Luke and Matthew testify, dynastic inheritance was patrilineal not matrilineal at that period of Jewish history. On the basis, therefore, of the available evidence, we may reasonably discount the likelihood of a "*Rex*" or kingly dynasty emanating from Jesus Christ. It does appear much more likely that, rather than a royal bloodline, Jesus actually enjoyed a priestly one.

If this comment is correct, then we must seriously consider the possibility that Jesus Christ shared the Cohanim – Messianic – bloodline.

CHAPTER 11

THE JESUS GENE

Before we examine a possible link between the Cohanim and Christ, we need to establish whether Jesus Christ could, indeed, have founded a *Deus* bloodline, directly from God. We must first explore the notion – fundamental to the Christian faith – that Christ is "of-one-substance-with-God". The introduction of the Church of Rome into a debate on matters of Christian doctrine has profound implications. The issue of Jesus' divinity, perhaps more than any other issue, divides Christianity from Judaism. For Jews, the expected messiah was to be a new King who would lead them to freedom from under the yoke of Roman oppression. Jesus' teachings, of "turning the other cheek" and of the "meek inheriting the earth" did not meet that expectation. The survival and growth of Christianity evidence the fact that the ideas, which Jesus represents, are by any standard extraordinary. But curiously, from the Bible writings, it was Saul who took Christ's comment "I and my Father are one", [from St. John, chapter 10, verse 9] and promoted the concept of Jesus being, literally, the Son-of-God. Saul was a rabbi who headed a commission sent from Jerusalem to Damascus to persecute Christians. The story of how he fell from his horse and lost his sight is well known, as is his hearing Jesus' voice calling on him to stop the harassment. Saul then went to Damascus where a Christian named Ananias cured his blindness. At this point Saul joined the Christians, changed his name to Paul (a result of the change from Hebrew to Greek records), and went to the local synagogue to preach that Jesus was the Son-of-God.

Paul made three missionary journeys covering some 7,000 miles through what is now Turkey and Greece. He then travelled to Rome via Rhodes, Crete and Malta, a journey that would be replicated many years later by the Knights of the Hospital of St. John, more commonly known as the Hospitallers.

The assertion that Jesus was the Son-of-God, as a reality rather than metaphor, drove a wedge between Judaism and Christianity: this wedge proved irreconcilable. Judaism relies on the Old Testament books of the Bible and they clearly state "there is only one God"; indeed, the Ten commandments state that, "I am the Lord thy God. Thou shalt not have strange gods before Me", (Catholic version). Or, "Thou shalt have no other gods before Me", (Protestant version). To have a Son-of-God "appears" to require two Gods – a "family of Gods" may be a better interpretation. This issue - so fundamental to Christianity - reverberated throughout the faith. Indeed, an Alexandrian lay official, called Arius, tried to move the faith back to its Judaic roots by proposing that Jesus was created and therefore not divine. He argued that – according to the Old Testament – God is unique and immutable and therefore cannot be shared with a Son. The counter argument is - if one tries to sustain a messianic role for Jesus - that Jesus must be a demigod and that simply moves Christianity back to polytheism. A partial resolution of the heresy occurred in the year 325, when the church leaders called a council meeting at Nicaea. Here the council ruled the Son is of "one-substance" with the Father. A creed emerged (see earlier), which was to be repeated by Christians everywhere as part of the service of worship. This creed settled beyond question that God the Father, God the Son and God the Holy Ghost are one and the same, a trinity equalling one.

It is perhaps not surprising the issue would not lie down. The followers of Arius, known as Arians, were banished but refused to give up the fight. Two more church councils, one at Antioch in 341 and another in what is now Sofia in 342, blurred the issue slightly by dropping the "one-substance" clause. The next 18 years saw the followers of the Nicene decision persecuted by rulers who preferred the Arian interpretation but the "dispute" would not go away and the outcome was uncertain. In 381 the Nicene group re-established themselves and the council of Constantinople re-imposed the Nicene Creed as the official doctrine of the Christian church. Another council held at Chalcedon in 451 reinforced the Nicene Creed and finally settled the issue within the Catholic Church.

The important point made here is that the whole question of Jesus being God is one of Christian faith. It was the Christian church that first decided that Jesus was "of one-substance" with

God, and they made the acceptance of this "ordained reality" an irrefutable condition of faith for all Christians. An immutable part of the dogma is the issue of "virgin birth" mentioned in the previous chapter. The Bible describes Mary as a virgin:

> Behold, a virgin shall be with child, and shall bring forth a son, and they shall call his name Emmanuel, which being interpreted is, God with us.
>
> *Matthew 1:23*

This fulfilled Isaiah's prophecy:

> Therefore the Lord himself shall give you a sign; Behold, a virgin shall conceive, and bear a son, and shall call his name Immanuel.
>
> *Isaiah 7:14*

However, the earliest copy of Isaiah's prophecy was written in Hebrew and actually stated that a "young woman" would give birth to the Messiah. It was when the Hebrew was translated into Greek that the word "virgin" replace "young woman." Some scholars suggest that the Greek Septuagint mistranslated the Hebrew word for young woman, "almah", into the Greek word "parthenos", meaning virgin. If this interpretation is correct, then St. Matthew's gospel looks uncomfortably like an attempt to describe the fulfillment of a prophecy that was actually not made. Other scholars, however, suggest that the Septuagint was translated from an alternative – long lost - Hebrew text. This alternative version is based on comparisons between existing Masoretic texts, Septuagint texts, Dead Sea Scrolls, and some Samaritan texts.

Clearly for Jesus to be the Son-of-God, a human could not have sired Him, but for Him to be God-on-earth and human, He had to originate from the womb of a human woman, Mary. This does of course create all sorts of contradictions for the church to have addressed over many years. The formalisation of the "virgin birth" took place at the council of Chalcedon in 451. There had existed a general acceptance by early Christians that Mary remained a virgin all her life. But, as the New Testament books of the Bible came together, the references to Jesus' brothers and sisters cast some doubt on this suggestion.

> Is not this the carpenter's son? is not his mother called Mary? and his brethren, James, and Joses, and Simon, and Judas?
>
> And his sisters, are they not all with us? Whence then hath this man all these things?
>
> *Matthew 13:55-56*

The Roman Catholic Church decrees that Jesus' mother Mary remained a virgin all her life and overcomes the biblical references to brothers and sisters of Jesus by attributing them to Joseph's earlier marriage, making them stepbrothers and stepsisters. An alternative exegesis was that the Greek biblical text translated as "cousins". These doubts persisted from as early as the 6th century but Pope Pius IX did not address them formally until 1854. He declared in his *Bull Ineffabilis*, under the protection of papal infallibility, that Mary's mother was a virgin at the time of Mary's birth and so Mary had an "immaculate conception", relieving her of the possibility of "original-sin" during her lifetime. "Conception" as here defined refers to the moment when the soul is created and infused into the body, and not the physical act of egg fertilisation that occurs during sexual intercourse.

> We declare pronounce and define that the doctrine which asserts that the Blessed Virgin Mary, from the first moment of her conception, by a singular grace and privilege of almighty God, and in view of the merits of Jesus Christ, saviour of the human race, was preserved free from every stain of original sin is a doctrine revealed by God and for this reason must be firmly and constantly believed by all the faithful.
>
> *Pope Pius IX*
> *Bull Ineffabilis*

The above definition - that conception refers to the moment when the soul is infused - does of course permit the theological possibility of two fathers. In the case of Jesus, this would allow Joseph to have been the physical father responsible for fertilising the egg, while God was responsible for infusing the soul of Jesus. To debate this idea would, however, take us even further down a theological path. To illustrate the potential for debate, St. Augustine and St. Thomas Aquinas determined that the foetus acquired a soul after 40 days for males and after 90 days for females. As just mentioned, it is not our aim to enter into the theological aspects of this debate and, having already gone further than we wished, we will move on.

On the basis, therefore, of the teachings of the Christian church a "*Deus*" bloodline from Jesus' appears impossible. It is the Church that has determined that Jesus is the Son-of-God and "of-one-substance" with God. As a condition of this decision or perhaps because of it, the Church has also ruled that Jesus did not have any brothers:

> For God so loved the world, that he gave his only begotten Son, that whosoever believeth in him should not perish, but have everlasting life.
>
> He that believeth on him is not condemned: but he that believeth not is condemned already, because he hath not believed in the name of the only begotten Son of God.
>
> *John 3:16 and 18*

The rulings just quoted only apply to the Catholic Church of Rome. Other Christian groups, such as the Orthodox, the Copts and the Protestant denominations accept that Jesus had siblings.

There is one aspect of the divine birth of Jesus, which we must mention. It is that – just like the earlier mention of Samson, and the early life of Moses, discussed in chapter 4 – we find that it follows uncomfortably closely an earlier legend. In this instance it is the biblical book of Matthew that follows the legend most closely. Toynbee[60] quotes from Meyer[61] on this coincidence:

> The correspondence between Matthew and the legend of the birth of Plato is as exact as it could possibly be.
>
> *Arnold Toynbee*
> *A Study of History*

Toynbee discusses how, when Joseph first discovers that Mary is pregnant, and aware that the child could not be his, proposes to put her away. However, an angel visits Joseph and reveals the future that awaits the unborn child, and so Joseph marries Mary but does not "sleep with her" until the birth of baby Jesus.

> The exact instructions that are given to Plato's father. This divine paternity of a saviour born of a woman is a form of epiphany which brings the saviour-god into a perfect intimacy with human kind.
>
> *Arnold Toynbee*
> *A Study of History*

Having brought the Church of Rome into the debate, we see that one conclusion jumps out at us. This observation is, that if a divine bloodline existed from Jesus, then the one place where it surely would have settled is the papacy. It seems to go without saying that if direct descendents of Jesus exist then they should lead Jesus' church, or hold a special place within it. Such a group did claim to exist, the "desposyni", a Greek term meaning "beloved of God". Evidence of their existence is limited to Eusebius quoting a second century historian, Hegessipus, who recounted how the emperor Domitian Caesar – the youngest son of Vespasian – discounted a group of them as harmless peasants. There is also a persistent legend which asserts that a delegation of desposyni to Rome failed to gain recognition by Pope Sylvester in 318. There is, however, no evidence that the desposyni were directly descended from Jesus but rather that they were related to His brothers and sisters, and this rules out a "*Deus*" bloodline from this group.

The earliest popes nominated their successors, but this soon changed to the present arrangement whereby successive popes have been elected with no pretence to preserving a bloodline or dynasty. The fact the papacy makes no claim to such an inheritance is probably all the proof needed to confirm that no such bloodline exists. Indeed, we can show decisively that the church's earliest historian Eusebius[62] ignored a similar possibility even when he had a tempting opportunity. In 336, when Constantine the Great reached his thirtieth year as Emperor, it fell to Eusebius to deliver his *Oratio de Laudibus Constantini*. This was a massive address in praise of Constantine delivered to the Emperor in the imperial court. Constantine had, just before overthrowing the previous Emperor, Maxentius, adopted the early Christian "Chi-Rho" sign. This uses two overlain letters from the Greek alphabet, Chi (X) with Rho (P) through the centre ☧ short for **XRISTOS**, which is Greek for Christ. This was the device given to him in a vision in the sky with the message "by this sign you will conquer". His success at the Battle of Milvian Bridge led Constantine to relax the persecution of Christians and enabled their religion to flourish.

Eusebius, therefore, had many reasons - within his oration - to elevate Constantine, alongside Jesus, to the deity: something that would not have troubled the Emperor who maintained a relaxed attitude to the God of the Christians alongside the other Roman gods[62]. But the fact is that Eusebius never praised Constantine above "godlike qualities" placing him above other men but below God. Eusebius points to Constantine as the new Messiah - studiously avoiding all reference to Jesus Christ, an action, which Kee[62] takes to signal Constantine's ambivalence to Christianity.

The final issue that intrudes into this debate is the difficult question of whether Jesus had any children - through whom a dynasty, or even a bloodline could develop. The problem arises from the lack of evidence in the Bible to say definitively whether Jesus was even married let alone whether He had any children. The fact that John the Baptist was clearly celibate raises the heat of the debate without throwing any light on it. Certainly Jesus condoned John's celibacy and recognised it as an acceptable option and this went strongly against the teaching of Judaism. The Old Testament and particularly the Pentateuch - the first five books which form the Torah - positively overflow with exhortations to procreate.

> And God blessed them, and God said unto them, be fruitful, and multiply, and replenish the earth, and subdue it: and have dominion over the fish of the sea, and over the fowl of the air, and over every living thing that moveth upon the earth.
>
> *Genesis 1:28*

> That in blessing I will bless thee, and in multiplying I will multiply thy seed as the stars of the heaven, and as the sand which is upon the sea shore; and thy seed shall possess the gate of his enemies;
>
> *Genesis 22:17*

> And when Rachel saw that she bare Jacob no children, Rachel envied her sister; and said unto Jacob, Give me children, or else I die.
>
> *Genesis 30:1*

The use of the term "celibacy" could open the debate to etymological interpretation, but in reality the difference between celibacy and chastity is paper-thin. "Celibacy" can mean either to remain unmarried or to abstain from sexual relations. "Chastity" can mean either the latter or to abstain from sexual relations outside marriage. We are here discussing Christianity, so it seems appropriate to consult a theologian, Leonard Weber[63], in discussing the issue in relation to the priesthood:

> Celibacy is here understood as the unmarried state chosen in the light of the Christian faith, and in particular as one of the duties of the state in life of the clergy of the Latin Church, by which they are forbidden to marry and obliged to live in total continence.
>
> *Leonard Weber*
> *Encyclopaedia of Theology*

One source of documentary evidence that might support the idea that Jesus was married is the *Nag Hammadi* Library. This is a collection of some fifty ancient manuscripts bound up into thirteen volumes. They were discovered in 1945 in Egypt in the small-town of *Nag Hammadi* and date to the first centuries of the Christian era. There is one particular manuscript that those who argue that Jesus was married identify to support their case. This is the Gospel of Philip:

> There were three who always walked with the Lord: Mary, his mother, and her sister, and Magdalene, the one who was called his companion. His sister and his mother and his companion were each a Mary.
>
> *Gospel of Philip*
> *Nag Hammadi Scrolls*

Those who support the "Jesus was married" school point out that in the original Greek the word "companion" meant "consort" or "sexual partner". Also in the Gospel of Philip is the tantalising comment:

> Christ loved her [Magdalene] more than all the disciples and used to kiss her often on the mouth.
>
> *Gospel of Philip*
> *Nag Hammadi Scrolls*

In fact the first word "Christ" has not been deciphered and translated. The full available text is:

> As for the Wisdom who is called "the barren," she is the mother of the angels. And the companion of the [...] Mary Magdalene. [...] loved her more than all the disciples, and used to kiss her often on her mouth. The rest of the disciples [...]. They said to him "Why do you love her more than all of us?" The Saviour answered and said to them, "Why do I not love you like her? When a blind man and one who sees are both together in darkness, they are no different from one another.

When the light comes, then he who sees will see the light, and he who is blind will remain in darkness."

Gospel of Philip
Nag Hammadi Scrolls

Mary Magdalene, around whom the saga that Jesus was married developed, is little mentioned in the Bible. She was one of the three women present at the crucifixion; however, her main claim to fame is that she was the first to discover that Jesus' body had gone from the sepulcher. It was also Mary who saw two angels sitting where Jesus had lain and who then saw Him standing nearby. Mary Magdalene's role, as possible "wife of Jesus", has grown from the general religious doctrine of Gnosticism, which derives from the Greek word "*gnosis*" meaning knowledge. When Christianity arrived the Gnostics appear to have found their natural home. We can only speculate as to why this happened although the judicious selection of historical records by the established Church can only have fed the flames on which mistrust burns. Gnostics soon claimed to be the true Christians and this threat was attacked by the founding fathers of Christianity with a determination to uproot it completely. The lack of contemporaneous records from the period of Christ may, or may not, be explained by the actions of one early Christian leader, Athenasius, Archbishop of Alexandria. In 315 AD, he identified the 27 Books, which comprise the New Testament. Elaine Pagels[64] asserts that Athenasius ordered his monks to destroy all other documents relating to the life of Christ, but this assertion appears to be mistaken. The discovery of the *Nag Hammadi* scrolls does, however, suggest that they were buried in a manner designed to preserve them and the absence of similar documents further suggests that other copies were destroyed. This, though, is speculation and there may be an uncontentious explanation for the recovery to date of only one copy of gospels omitted from the official version of the New Testament. That the early Church did go to considerable lengths to destroy the Gnostic heresy is evidenced by the actions of Iranaeus, Bishop of Lyons. His five volumes - from the second century - entitled The Destruction and Overthrow of Falsely So-called Knowledge: include the comment

"You may urge all those with whom you are connected to avoid such an abyss of madness and of blasphemy against Christ."

The veracity of the Gnostic doctrine was unintentionally enhanced when, in 591 AD, Pope Gregory the Great falsely denounced Mary Magdalene as "the one whom Luke calls the sinful woman". It was not until 1969 that the Catholic Church corrected this error and identified Mary of Bethany (the sinful woman) as separate from Mary Magdalene. The status of Mary was also improved with the discovery of the *Nag Hammadi* scrolls, because among them is a gospel of Mary Magdalene. It is clear that Mary did play an important role in the very early Christian church and was probably a disciple. The actions of Pope Gregory might now be seen as simply the actions of a church ruler intent on keeping the leading roles in the Church as a male preserve. No matter how these matters are interpreted, there persists an ongoing belief that Mary Magdalene was married to Jesus Christ and had children by him. The reality is that there is no proof for this belief whatsoever. It is clear the case for a married Jesus is far from made although to be fair it is equally impossible to rule it out. There is evidence that Jesus became a rabbi at the age of thirty and that was normal; indeed, no one can become a rabbi earlier than thirty, and marriage is a continuing precondition for a rabbi. This particular proposition is, to a large extent, disarmed by the Bible texts, which clearly show that Jesus did not live by the prevailing cultural expectations. He was, in almost every sense of the word, a rebel; and it was his rebellious behaviour that brought about His death on the cross. One conjecture that meets most of the needs of both sides of the debate is that Jesus had an earlier wife who died and left Him a widower. Without more archaeological or palaeographic information, we will never know.

In recent years, the idea that Mary Magdalene was married to Christ, and that a bloodline from Him existed, found expression through two "legend-based" strands. Baigent, Leigh and Lincoln introduced the first strand in their book, which we mentioned in the previous chapter, The Holy Blood and the Holy Grail[54]. There, they postulated an idea that would generate huge interest: it was that a bloodline from Jesus Christ existed and that a secret sect had carefully nurtured this bloodline until today. To support this romance, the above authors quoted two historical sources. The first was the use of the term "*sang real*", meaning royal blood, by a fifteenth century cleric, John Harding; but this has been shown to be a unique transposition error of *san greal* meaning the Holy Grail. Importantly, this transposition error was not replicated by him or anyone else until the above authors lighted upon it. Baigent, Leigh and Lincoln supported their claim drawing on the 1275 writings of Jacobus de Voragine - Archbishop of Genoa - the *Aurea Legenda,* or Golden Legend. This huge work, comprising some nine-hundred extant manuscripts, describes the life and times of Jesus and many early saints. It was later printed by Caxton and others and remained a popular book until the Reformation when its abundance of miraculous stories and lack of historical credibility made it unacceptable. With the dawn of the enlightenment, the Golden Legend slipped into obscurity. By way of example, Jacobus de Voragine's story of Mary Magdalene repeats the mistake of Pope Gregory the Great in confusing her with Mary of Bethany:

> Therefore she lost her right name, and was called customably a sinner. And when our Lord Jesu Christ preached there and in other places, she was inspired with the Holy Ghost, and went into the house of Simon leprous, whereas our Lord dined. Then she durst not, because she was a sinner, appear tofore the just and good people, but remained behind at the feet of our Lord, and washed his feet with the tears of her eyes and dryed them with the hair of her head, and anointed them with precious ointments.
>
> *Jacobus de Voragine*
> *The Golden Legend*

De Voragine's version of the journey of Mary Magdalene to France is equally discredited:

> When the disciples were departed, S. Maximin, Mary Magdalene, and Lazarus her brother, Martha her sister, Marcelle, chamberer of Martha, and S. Cedony which was born blind, and after enlumined of our Lord; all these together,

> and many other christian men were taken of the miscreants and put in a ship in the sea, without any tackle or rudder, for to be drowned. But by the purveyance of Almighty God they came all to Marseilles, where, as none would receive them to be lodged, they dwelled and abode under a porch tofore a temple of the people of that country.
>
> *Jacobus de Voragine*
> *The Golden Legend*

It is generally assumed that the story in the Golden Legend resulted from the erroneous borrowing of a similar tale, which is celebrated in the French seaside town of *Les Saintes-Marie-de- la-Mer* to this day. These villagers hold a festival on 25th May each year to celebrate the arrival, not of Mary Magdalene, but rather Mary Jacobi, Mary Salome and Sarah, their servant girl. The two Marys' are credited with taking Christianity to the Roman province of Gaul.

It was Lynn Picknett and Clive Prince who introduced the second "legend-based" strand supporting Mary Magdalene as the wife of Jesus, in their book, The Templar Revelation[65]. Their well-researched findings draw on the mural, painted by Leonardo da Vinci, on the wall of the Santa Maria della Grazie church in Milan. The feminine countenance of the person sitting to the right of Christ, coupled with the clearly discernable "M" shape made out by their two bodies, caused Picknett and Prince to conclude that Leonardo was suggesting that Mary Magdalene – from the "M" shape and the feminine face on St. John – was one of the disciples. From this plausible hypothesis the above earlier propositions flow. The counter-arguments are that Leonardo da Vinci was a known homosexual and occasionally painted men with feminine features. The obvious "M" feature may equally be taken with any of the "L" features made up from various columns and the side of the table, to provide the initials of the Duke of Milan, who sponsored the painting: the Duke, Lodovico Sforza, was also known as **L**odovico il **M**oro (the moor). It may also have been that Leonardo was obliquely acknowledging Jesus Christ's ascension with the introduction of an "M" to signify the heavenly chariot, Mercavah, which we touched on in chapter one:

> From all these considerations I am induced to believe that the word Mercavah is formed of M, (meaning chief or arch).
>
> *Godfrey Higgins*
> *Anacalypsis*

Whether Leonardo da Vinci really had any insight into Jesus' marital status has to be seriously doubted. The *Nag Hammadi* scrolls were not found until 1945 and so any earlier knowledge was necessarily founded on gossip. The Gnostic chronicle was strengthened by the Rennes-le Château whodunit, which includes reference to a secret sect called the "Priory-of-Sion". A Priory document emerged naming Leonardo as one of the *Nautoniers* or Grand Masters. The author of this document, Gerard de Sède, has since named it a forgery: and without that connection, there is nothing to suggest that Leonardo might have had any special knowledge about Christ. The question must be posed as to why a Renaissance painter would be privy to secret knowledge about Jesus Christ some 1,500 years after Christ had died; knowledge that emerged again some 500 years later by the hand of a self-confessed fraudster?

So where has this analysis led us? We can safely say from the available evidence that a *Rex* or kingly bloodline emanating from David and continuing through Jesus Christ is statistically implausible. The second half of the ostensible dynastic title is contestable with certainty. A *Deus* bloodline option is simply not available. That Jesus has the status of God - equal to and of "one-substance" with God - is a matter entirely within the ownership of the Christian Church. It might be easier to argue that it holds the copyright on this concept. Equally, the Christian church has made it abundantly clear that, according to their rules, Jesus was single and had no children - indeed he was celibate in the "abstaining from sex entirely" sense. Put another way, it is theologically acceptable to accept Jesus Christ as of one substance with God and so to be God. Within that Christian framework, it is unacceptable to suggest that He had children.

This statement does leave some room for speculation. That a married Jesus could have had children and a priestly inheritance cannot be ruled out. There is simply not enough evidence to form a definitive conclusion. However, to argue that - in defiance of Christian doctrine - Jesus had children, from inside or outside marriage, is to remove oneself from mainstream Christendom and into the realms of heresy. It is arguably inconsistent to try to use Christian ideology and dogma when it suits and to ignore it when it doesn't. The obvious conclusion must be that if Jesus did have children, He was **not** the Son-of-God and therefore not of one-substance with God. From this we can infer with safety there cannot be a "*Deus*" bloodline. We have already made the point in the previous chapter that a "*Rex*" bloodline is statistically implausible.

The question of whether Jesus did have children must, however, remain open. For anyone to consider that they have Jesus Christ as an ancestor requires them to deny the conventional Christian doctrine. In so doing they also deny to themselves that having Christ as an ancestor is of any significance. Once Christ is removed from His position within Christianity of the "Son of God", He becomes but another man mentioned in the Bible. It must also follow that to claim Christ as an ancestor demands admitting hundreds of thousands perhaps millions of similar "family members" who also number Jesus Christ among their ancestors. We explained earlier how after 1,500 years the offspring from one couple could multiply to 10^{17}. It must, therefore follow, that after 2,000 years the number would be substantially higher. We must recognise the inclination of the Jews to marry within their religious group. However, enough Jews have - over the years - married outside of Jewry for the genetic strain of any of Jesus' children to have spread throughout the population of the civilised world.

It is now clear that this debate ends as a classic "catch-22" problem. You can have Jesus Christ as the Son-of-God or you can have Him in your family tree, but you cannot have both.

Having forcefully argued that a *Rex Deus* bloodline cannot exist from Jesus Christ we are left with the theoretical possibility that

Christ did have children. In this eventuality, or possibility, what exactly would Christ have passed down to any children? What happens when a man and a woman create a new life? What are the implications of a "bloodline"? To appreciate what Jesus may, or may not have physically bequeathed to humanity, we need to understand a little about the fundamentals of genetics. Genetics are at the heart of this part of our investigation and for this reason, there is an explanation of the genetic processes behind human reproduction at appendix A.

The knowledge of genetics has brought with it a serious scientific hurdle for those who argue that Jesus is of one-substance-with-God. This statement asserts that a human male was not involved in fertilising the egg cell that Mary carried which developed into Christ. For those readers who believe that Jesus Christ is the Son-of-God and of one-substance-with-God, the following discussion is irrelevant. Christians believe that God can do whatever He wishes, and the rules of science are but a prop for man's fallibility. For the more sceptical reader, there is a scientific weakness in the Christian case for a virgin birth. It centres on the sex chromosomes X and Y. The fact is that an X chromosome can only come from the mother and a Y chromosome can only come from the father. If, therefore, Jesus was the result of a "virgin birth", where did His Y chromosome come from? To be a man, and it is not suggested that Jesus was anything but male, He had to have a Y chromosome, which could **not** originate from his mother. The scientific assertion is that a human male must introduce a Y chromosome at conception, before a boy is possible.

This observation does at least suggest the "Jesus was **not** of one-substance-with-God" argument is scientifically possible and opens the door to the possibility that he married and had children. If, for the sake of discussion, we admit that Jesus Christ could have sired children, where exactly does that leave us? It is fair to say that if Jesus Christ did sire a child or children, then Christianity as ordained by the Church of Rome stands on a false premise. In that event, He could not now be of "one-substance-with-God". The harsh reality, however, is that - apart from the Bible - there is no reliable evidence to say whether Jesus was married, single or widowed. There is also no reliable evidence to say whether Jesus had children. The issue then is one of faith. One can believe that Jesus is of "one-substance-with-God" or one does not believe that proposition or one neither knows nor cares. It is not the purpose of this book to question religious beliefs. To state, though, that an alternative reality was possible, is another matter. Setting aside dogma, surely we must concede that it is possible for Jesus to have had children. It is also now clear that even if Jesus had sired a child and the dynasty was traceable until the present-day, the amount of Jesus' genetic material in the present-day heir would be minuscule. It is even possible that Jesus' genetic material in a modern heir could be zero. It would only have taken a near descendent or two to have all female children for His personal Y chromosome to be lost forever.

As we discussed in chapter 6, the Origins of Old Testament priests research opened a whole new perspective on this debate. Mark Thomas and his research colleagues discovered that Cohanim Jews, the descendents of the Jerusalem Temple priesthood had preserved their genetic inheritance to a remarkable degree over three millennia. Research into the Y chromosome has shown that in the earliest period of human evolution, all but one of the Y chromosomes became lost because couples had no children or only daughters. Consequently all Y chromosomes today share a common ancestry with a single male – a genetic Adam - who probably lived some 140,000 years ago.

Were it not for the occasional damage that occurs during replication, all males would have an identical sequence of DNA letters on their Y chromosomes. There are, however, occasional mistakes or misspellings, which then duplicate into following generations. These small variations allow us to identify particular lineages - or bloodlines - all stemming from the original family tree started by the genetic Adam we have just mentioned.

More recently, Dr. Michael Hammer of the University of Arizona continued this particular line of research. He was assisted by A. J. Redd, E. T. Wood, M. R. Bonner, H. Jarjanazi, T. Karafet, S. Santachiara-Benerecetti, A. Oppenheim, M. A. Jobling, T. Jenkins, H. Ostrer, and B. Bonné-Tamir, from the United States, Italy, Israel, England and South Africa. These researchers examined the DNA from a large sample of nearly 1,350 males of whom:

> <u>Jews:</u>
> 336 from the USA, Europe Africa and the Near East
> 34 from southern Africa who claim Jewish paternal ancestry
>
> <u>Non-Jews:</u>
> 206 from the Middle East
> 337 European
> 137 North African
> 199 sub-Saharan
> 98 Turks

What Dr. Hammer and his colleagues found was that:

> Both Jewish and Middle Eastern non-Jewish populations share a common pool of Y chromosome biallelic haplotypes.
>
> *Proceedings of the National Academy of Sciences*
> *9th May 2000*

What this means is that an identifiable cluster of juxtaposed genes is present on the Y chromosomes of both Jewish and non-Jewish Middle Eastern males. This research also supports the propositions made in Part 2 of this book that the Exodus as described in the Bible did not take place. These findings have profound implications for the Jews because it implies that Middle Eastern males all share the same male ancestor, or bloodline. This later research also supported the earlier work mentioned above - <u>Origins of Old Testament priests</u> – carried out by Drs. Thomas, Skoreckiad, Ben-Amid, Parfitt, Bradman and Goldstein. The "Origins" conclusion was that, except for the Cohanim, the Jewish diaspora population displays evidence of intermarriage with their host populations. In contrast, the Cohanim have, to a remarkable extent, kept their biological identity.

The main conclusion is the lineages observable in present-day Arab and Jewish populations are distinct from those of European populations and both groups differ widely from sub-Saharan Africans. Dr. Hammer's findings were that the Ashkenazi

Jews are descended from Roman Jews. Despite the long period that Ashkenazi Jews had lived in Europe, their Y chromosome signature has remained distinct from that of non-Jewish Europeans.

So, what might we deduce from these rather surprising results? One thing is for certain: the Diaspora Jews do occasionally marry with non-Jews. The priestly family - Cohens - take their bloodline much more seriously and rarely marry with Gentiles. They go even further and tend not to marry non-Cohen Jews. This points out a behavioural pattern that didn't alter across two separate groups of migrant Jews (Ashkenazic and Sephardic). Two groups separated by thousands of miles for at least two thousand years when no telephones and only a limited postal service existed. By any standard this is a remarkable achievement, one that would need extraordinarily strong motivation to sustain it for so long.

We now have a group of people, Cohanim Jews, for whom science has demonstrated that they have preserved their family purity over at least 3,000 years. This is the family from whom, during most of the Jerusalem temple period, the priesthood derived. Is this the "bloodline" which weaves its way throughout the Rennes-le-Château mystery? The idea has attractions, for the duty of the Cohanim or temple priests was to guard the Ark of the Covenant, which Byrne[1] speculated reposed for hundreds of years near Rennes-le-Château and is now in the hands of the Freemasons. This convenient piece of evidence does lack any link to Jesus Christ; nonetheless He figures strongly in the "bloodline strand" of the Rennes-le-Château mystery. Finally, we can now examine whether a connection between the Cohanim and Jesus Christ exists.

There are many references in the New Testament of the Bible to Jesus' membership in the priesthood, but we must be careful what we read into this.

> And Melchizedek King of Salem brought forth bread and wine: and he was the priest of the most high God. And he blessed him, and said, Blessed be Abram of the most high God, possessor of heaven and earth:
>
> *Genesis 14:18-19*

> So also Christ glorified not himself to be made an high priest; but he that said unto him, Thou art my Son, to day have I begotten thee.
>
> As he saith also in another place, Thou art a priest for ever after the order of Melchisedec.
>
> *Hebrews 5:5-6*

The reason why we need to take care over reference to Jesus Christ as "a priest for ever after the order of Melchisedec," is that it can be argued that Melchisedec was not a Jew. We can suggest this because he predates the Exodus from Egypt (if it happened). This would make Melchisedec more a forerunner or archetypical priest. Thus, as a prototype priest, he was somehow superior to the subsequent Jewish Aaronic and Levitical priesthood. We must bear in mind that when Paul wrote that Jesus was "a priest after the order of Melchisedec", he was removing Christ from association with a discredited priesthood. Discredited perhaps, by its lack of Cohanim content. This was a period when the high priesthood was for sale by the Roman occupiers.

It is of course possible, but we cannot take it as fact, that Paul was simply mistaking Melchisedec with Zadok, the High priest of David and Solomon's time. Alternatively, a later scribe may have altered the script to lift Christ above the earthly bound Zadok family tree.

St. Peter continued with the suggestion that Jesus was a priest:

> But ye are a chosen generation, a royal priesthood, an holy nation, a peculiar people; that ye should shew forth the praises of him who hath called you out of darkness into his marvelous light:
>
> *1 Peter 2:9*

St. Mark also provides a hint of Jesus' priestly status; and St. Luke repeats this reference almost verbatim:

> How he went into the house of God in the days of Abiathar the high priest, and did eat the shewbread, which is not lawful to eat but for the priests, and gave also to them which were with him?
>
> *Mark 2:26*

The idea of Jesus Christ as a member of the priesthood, that is to say, the "legitimate priesthood", the male descendants of Aaron, makes sense when viewed against the record of His life. The evidence of his time in Jerusalem is one of an almost constant battle of wills with the existing priesthood. It was a psychological battle that would end with the priests handing Christ over to Pontius Pilate for sentencing to death by crucifixion.

> And when the chief priests and scribes saw the wonderful things that he did, and the children crying in the temple, and saying, Hosanna to the Son of David; they were sore displeased.
>
> And when the chief priests and Pharisees had heard his parables, they perceived that he spake of them.
>
> *Matthew 21:15,45*

> And the scribes and chief priests heard it, and sought how they might destroy him: for they feared him, because all the people was astonished at his doctrine.
>
> *Mark 11:18*

> And he taught daily in the temple. But the chief priests and the scribes and the chief of the people sought to destroy him,
>
> *Luke 19:47*

There is another facet of the life of Jesus which supports His priesthood lineage. The Essenes were a Jewish cult around the time of Jesus, and there is circumstantial evidence to suggest that they might have been the legitimate heirs of the Zadokite priesthood. Reference to the Essenes reminds us that some commentators believe John the Baptist's diet of locusts and honey, his interests in sacramentology and his water rites, which compare closely to Qumran ablutions, demonstrate that he was an Essene. The Bible supports this discussion:

> There was in the days of Herod, the King of Judaea, a certain priest named Zacharias, of the course of Abia: and his wife was of the daughters of Aaron, and her name was Elisabeth.
> But the angel said unto him, Fear not, Zacharias: for thy prayer is heard; and thy wife Elisabeth shall bear thee a son, and thou shalt call his name John.
>
> *Luke 1:5, 13*

If, therefore, St John the Baptist's father was a priest then St. John was himself probably a Levite. Although this was a time when the Roman rulers regularly sold the high priesthood, the lower ranks of the priesthood were still in the hands of the Levite family. The Bible continues to aid this debate by confirming that St John the Baptist and Jesus Christ were cousins, as we have just discussed above.

> And in the sixth month the angel Gabriel was sent from God unto a city of Galilee, named Nazareth.
>
> To a virgin espoused to a man whose name was Joseph, of the house of David; and the virgin's name was Mary.
>
> And, behold, thou shalt conceive in thy womb, and bring forth a son, and shalt call his name Jesus.
>
> He shall be great, and shall be called the Son of the Highest: and the Lord God shall give unto him the throne of his father David:
>
> And, behold, thy cousin Elisabeth, she hath also conceived a son in her old age: and this is the sixth month with her, who was called barren.
>
> *Luke 1:26, 27, 31, 32, 36*

We have seen from the Origins of Old Testament priests research how the Cohanim generally married within the family. These two cousins, therefore, shared the same family tree although removed from each other by a branch or two. We can therefore surmise that, if John had joined the Essenes, then there was at least the likelihood that his cousin, Jesus, may also have joined them. If this argument holds water, then it is probable that both St John and Jesus were both members of the hereditary priesthood family, the Cohanim.

We can identify further evidence in the Bible to support the notion that Jesus was an Essene, and it emerges from the date of the "Last Supper". In the Gospels of Matthew, Mark and Luke, the "Last Supper" was a "Passover" meal. Geza Vermes[66] makes the observation that if the Passover supper was taken around 6.00 pm on 15th Nisan [the first and springtime month of the Hebrew lunar calendar] then the trial of Jesus would - unrealistically - have occurred on a feast-day. In John's Gospel, the "Last Supper" was not a "Passover" meal and taken a day earlier: this, though, misses the "Passover" symbolism of the Paschal lamb, the unleavened bread and the subsequent Passover-Sabbath theme of renewal and final redemption in the Messianic age. It appears that the three synoptic Gospels are more likely, and the only way that the problem just identified - of the trial falling on a feast-day - could have been avoided, was if Jesus and his group worked on the Essene calendar, which we discussed in chapter 7. This would have resulted in Jesus being crucified on a Wednesday and His resurrection could not then have been on a Sabbath and so this explanation is not without controversy.

The possibility that Jesus Christ was a Zadokite priest has indeed been made before, usually drawing on the evidence of the *Nag Hammadi* scrolls discussed in chapter 1. Surprisingly this notion finds compelling support in the New Testament portion of the Bible:

> Wherefore, holy brethren, partakers of the heavenly calling, consider the Apostle and High Priest of our profession, Christ Jesus.
>
> *Hebrews 3:1*

> Seeing then that we have a great high priest, that is passed into the heavens, Jesus the Son of God, let us hold fast our profession.
>
> *Hebrews 4:14*

> And no man taketh this honour unto himself, but he that is called of God, as was Aaron.
>
> *Hebrews 5:4*

Here then is further unequivocal evidence, from the Bible, that Jesus was considered to be a "lawful" high priest, in other words a Zadok or Cohanim. The hypothesis put forward earlier, is that when the Zadokite priesthood was displaced from the temple, they set up as the Essenes. It follows that if Jesus Christ was also a Zadok, then He too could also have been an Essene.

If Jesus Christ had a human father, rather than God as His sire, then a remarkable conclusion flows from our analysis. It is that Jesus was probably a Cohanim, and His Y chromosome was, in almost every respect, identical with the Y chromosome of any modern male member of the Cohen family.

If this supposition is correct then we can now define the Y chromosome of Jesus Christ. It is the one identified by the Origins of Old Testament priests researchers as coursing through the veins of the Cohanim.

APPENDIX A

GENETICS

The science of genetics began in 1902, when Walter Sutton suggested that chromosomes held the key to inherited features. The next big step forward in knowledge followed quickly, in 1910, when Thomas Morgan, showed how groups of genes on each chromosome formed linked groups that were passed on intact to the next generation. It was, though, not until 1944 that Oswald Avery was able to demonstrate that a substance named deoxyribonucleic acid, or DNA, is what the genes are made from and where the genetic information is actually stored.

For centuries, the medical profession has had a fairly accurate knowledge of the functions of the various organs in the human body. What has only become evident in the last 50 years is that a human being is made up of around 1,000,000,000,000,000 identical cells. A few cells are different and these are the reproductive cells and mature red blood cells. What is quite staggering about this huge number of individual building blocks, that make up each and every one of us, is that every cell – apart from the reproductive cells – carries a complete set of instructions for building the particular person in which they reside. This huge level of redundancy is rather like having a complete set of manufacturing manuals embedded into every one of the million or so components that go to make up a jumbo jet airliner.

The full set of instructions is carried in each cell, on 46 chromosomes, 23 maternal chromosomes donated by the mother and 23 paternal chromosomes donated by the father. This full set of human chromosomes is called a "genome". When a male sperm and a female egg merge during mating the chromosomes are reorganised. It is this process of re-organising the instruction set that decides what we will look like and what innate qualities we will each possess. Of the two sets of 23 chromosomes, 2 chromosomes - one from each parent - are concerned entirely with the sexuality of the individual. In a normal female these two sexuality chromosomes will both be type "X", whereas a normal male will have a type "X" and a type "Y". It is important to understand that these sex-determining chromosomes, types "X" and "Y" do not go through a process that we are about to describe – called crossover.

So we can now see that the remaining two sets of 22 chromosomes carry between them the remaining building instructions. This is again rather difficult to visualise, so it may help to think of the two sets of 23 chromosomes rather like two sets of slightly different encyclopaedias, of 23 volumes each, with the first volume covering subjects from A to C; and the next from D to F etc. Most people will be aware of the "double helix" shape of a chromosome, which is most easily visualised by imagining a rope ladder hanging from a high ceiling and being twisted throughout its whole length down to the ground. Each of the rungs on the ladder is made up of two parts, called nucleotides, one attached to the left side "rope" and the other attached to the right side "rope".

Anyone who takes the time to sit back and ponder the wonder of mankind, and who hasn't, must conclude that we are remarkably complex animals. And yet the complete instruction set for building a human is based on only four different types of nucleotide. The nucleotides are nitrogen-containing molecules called bases and referred to as - A (adenine), T (thymine), C (cytosine) and G (guanine). When a rung is formed between the two ropes, to start to construct a chromosome, very strict rules apply. An "A" nucleotide can only join with a "T" and a "C" can only join with a "G". Thus the only possible combinations of nucleotides making up the "rungs" on the analogous rope ladder are AT, TA, CG and GC. The four different nucleotides are identical throughout nature; thus, an "A" or "G" nucleotide in a horse or fish or bird is identical to an "A" or "G" nucleotide in a human. The analogy of a rope ladder can be further refined if the rope is viewed as more like a bead necklace. The construction is in fact one phosphate molecule – think of it as one bead – then one sugar molecule followed by another phosphate molecule; this sequence repeats throughout the length of the chromosome. The nucleotides, A, T, C or G are attached to the sugar molecule in the "rope" strand and to the matching nucleotide from the other "rope" strand. The phosphate molecules act rather like spacers or washers to separate the pairs of nucleotides.

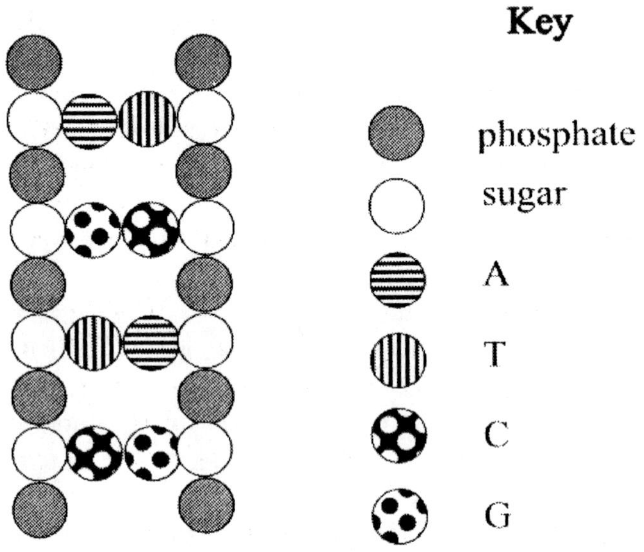

FIGURE 16 – ILLUSTRATION OF A STRAND OF CHROMOSOME (UNTWISTED)

It is not difficult to envisage a complete chromosome based on the illustration above until the numbers are considered. The two chromosomes concerned with sexuality each have some 50 million nucleotides and the other 44 chromosomes have up to 250 million nucleotides each. The entire human genome of 46 chromosomes comprises no less than 3 billion nucleotides.

We have already mentioned how the full set of 46 chromosomes contains all of the instructions necessary to construct the human being within whom they reside. However, if the massive redundancy of including a full set of manufacturing instructions within every one of trillions of cells is not wasteful enough, we now know that some 90 percent of the human genome – the complete set of chromosomes – appears to contain no known function other than to act as markers or spacers between individual genes. The building instructions are contained in a mere 10 percent of the genome; this does however represent some 300 million "active" nucleotides. The pairs of nucleotides, joining the two "rope" strands together to form a chromosome, are divided into groups called genes. Each gene carries specific instructions for a particular part of the host body. It may be the colour of the person's eyes or the shape of his fingernails or something more important to his future development. An average sized gene will thus contain some 3,000 pairs of nucleotides. The recently completed "human genome project" has identified the location and number of nucleotides of each one of the 80,000 or so genes in a human genome.

All normal human life begins with a single cell containing, *inter alia*, one genome. This cell divides into two identical cells, which then further divide into four until the number of cells is in the trillions and a human baby is born into the world. The method of division into two cells is divinely simple. The two "ropes" making up each chromosome split, taking the nucleotides in contact with the "rope" with them. Each – now single – rope "sucks" molecules out of the surrounding fluid; "A" nucleotides attract "T" nucleotides, "C" nucleotides attract "G" nucleotides and vice versa. As a base-pair of nucleotides is completed a sugar molecule joins at the free end followed by a phosphate molecule each side of the sugar molecule. Soon the whole empty side of each chromosome has been rebuilt and two identical chromosomes exist where previously there had been one. With the two complete sets of 46 chromosomes in place the cell divides into two identical cells.

The following is unfortunately complex and represents our best efforts to explain it simply. On the basis of what we have just said, one might be forgiven for asking why everyone is not identical to the same-sex parent. The answer to this hypothetical question occurs shortly after the fertilisation of the egg. When a human reaches maturity and is ready to reproduce a new process is triggered. This involves the creation of a completely different type of cell: in the case of a female she will produce eggs and the male will produce sperm, or more correctly in the case of the male, millions of them in a system that thrives on redundancy. It is only when an egg and a sperm fuse that a process, called meiosis commences. This decides what features and attributes the child will develop. Each of the "sex-cells" – that is to say, female eggs and male sperm – contain only 23 chromosomes, including one sex-deciding "X" (female) chromosome in each egg and "Y" (male) chromosome in each sperm. Only when fusion of the two "X" and "Y" chromosomes has taken place is a "complete" cell with 46 chromosomes formed. During meiosis the male and female donated chromosomes (but not types "X" or "Y") align themselves in pairs. Not pairs of ropes forming a metaphorical rope ladder but two pairs of rope ladders, one maternal chromosome, donated by the mother and one paternal chromosome (Figure 17 - Stage A). The two pairs of chromosomes now split, just as if they were going to form two new cells as in the process described earlier but with a significant difference (Stage B). Two of the single strands, or "ropes" touch together at about mid-length. The top half from one strand then joins with the bottom half of the other strand and they break away to form a new strand comprising the bottom half of the first strand and the top half of the second strand (Stage C). There are now two entirely new sequences of chromosome about to be created when the matching nucleotides are attracted onto the open strings, and the ladders are formed (Stage D). Chromosome types "X" or "Y" in the cell simply replicate themselves - without crossover - as explained above, by splitting into two single ropes which "suck" molecules out of the surrounding fluid to build two identical chromosomes. With the two complete sets of 46 chromosomes in place the cell divides into two identical cells.

At stage "D" the original 2 chromosomes, 1 maternal and 1 paternal have become 4 - 1 maternal and 1 paternal - exactly as at the start, plus 2 new chromosomes which are a combination of parts of the original maternal and paternal chromosomes. There are you will recall 22 pairs of chromosomes all going through this process of producing 2 additional "recombinant" chromosomes, plus the two "X" or "Y" chromosomes which have simply replicated themselves. This makes a full set of 2 x 46 chromosomes.

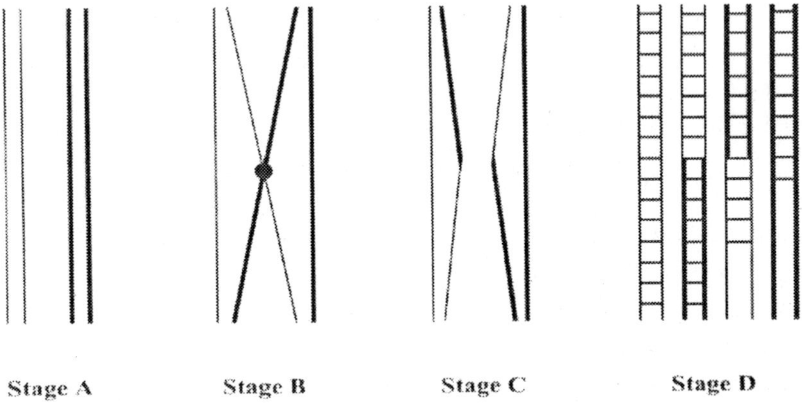

FIGURE 17 – MEIOSIS

An important point must be made here, and it is that the process of "crossover" during which new recombinant chromosomes are created, the illustration used above may not be the one that happens. Sometimes the chromosomes touch at 2 points and 2 crossovers take place to create a recombinant chromosome made up from 3 different sections:

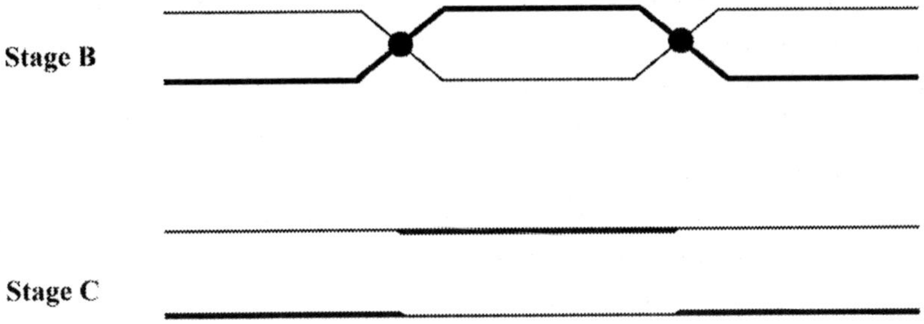

FIGURE 18 – ILLUSTRATION OF A TWO-POINT CROSSOVER DURING MEIOSIS STAGES B AND C

Returning to stage "D", the 4 sets of chromosomes now gather together at the two ends of the cells two sets at each end. Although 2 chromosomes from each set of 4 will go to one end of the cell, there is no pre-arranged order in which they will do this. Thus 1 maternal chromosome and 1 paternal chromosome may go to one end of the cell and the 2 recombinant chromosomes go to the other end of the cell. Alternatively 1 paternal chromosome and 1 recombinant chromosome will go to one end. This process is completely random, and when half of the chromosomes are at each end of the cell the cell divides into 2 non-identical cells. Each of these two new cells now goes through exactly the same process as just described except that 1 chromosome goes to one end of the cell and the other chromosome to the opposite end of the cell. Once again the selection of which chromosome goes to which end is entirely random. When this further cell division is complete there are 4 cells where originally there had been 1 and each cell contains just 23 chromosomes – one of which is an "X" or "Y" sex chromosome - instead of the usual 23 pairs. These cells are now either eggs or sperm and will take part in the reproductive process. The "basic building blocks" of mankind – eggs and sperm – are no longer replicas of their parental donors but rather they contain a shuffled set of DNA just as if they were playing cards.

The creation process begins when an egg, created as just described, fuses with a sperm that was created in an identical manner to produce a new cell with the correct number of 23 pairs of chromosomes. This cell will divide thousands of times to make a new human being. It is hopefully now clear that the process of "shuffling" the deck of genes to produce an offspring is inordinately thorough. It is possible to simulate, on a much smaller scale, this process. If you take a deck of 52 playing cards and deal out four hands of 13 cards which we shall call a, b, c and d. The cards in each hand should then be written down for future reference. Now place hand "a" on top of hand "c" and place hand "b" on top of hand "d". Now place "b and d" on top of "a and c" and re-deal four hands of 13 cards each. Write down the cards in each hand and compare them with the first deal. The only difference between this card simulation and life is that in the card simulation there are 52 cards and in life there are some 80,000 genes all being shuffled. The point is hopefully made that, when a father says, "that's my son" the actual genetic contribution he has made may be quite small. Heredity is an emotional experience as much as it is a physical transfer of attributes from parent to child.

In fact, the process is even more random because the 23 pairs of chromosomes are just that. Each set of 22 chromosomes, one shuffled set from the father and one similarly shuffled set from the mother, plus an "XX" or an "XY", carries the full set of instruction for making a new human being. Which particular gene is chosen to select, say the colour of the new child's eyes, is decided by which of the 2 genes is dominant or indeed if both are recessive. As we mentioned above, this is not an academic treatise on reproduction, simply an aid to the curious reader who should turn to academic books on the subject for a thorough explanation. The purpose of this chapter is to explain briefly how heredity operates and that point has hopefully been made.

An aspect of procreation that deserves a mention is selective breeding. If, as has been hypothesised by some, Jesus Christ did have a child or children, might His genetic makeup have been preserved within a family-tree. This can be achieved by selective breeding within the immediate family. Father mating with daughter and brother with sister. Such arrangements are common with the breeding of race-horses and pedigree-dogs as a means of setting the genes for traits or qualities, such as speed or endurance. We can realistically rule this out for Jesus because incest was and remains forbidden within both Judaism and Christianity. There is a common presumption that incest results in the birth of albino babes or worse but this is not strictly speaking correct. Incest will increase the chances of any trait, carried by the parents, being transferred to the child, whether it is a potential strength or a weakness such as an inheritable disease. This is because recessive faulty genes – those carrying inheritable diseases (and most of us carry some) – are more likely to exhibit themselves if breeding takes place within a restricted pool of individuals (deme).

Examples of the prevalence for some families to exhibit defects can readily be found among the aristocratic families of Europe where close interbreeding - often first cousins - is encouraged for lineage reasons. The recessed chin and protruding bottom lip of the Hapsburg family and the haemophilia of Queen Victoria's offspring - which ravaged the thrones of Europe - are a couple of better known examples.

The two examples just given, of genetic disorders, arise from the selection process that takes place when the cells divide to create a new human being. Each cell has, as mentioned above, two sets of genes - one set transmitted from the mother and one from the father. The selection of one possible gene over another has already been explained in chapter 10, by a procedure of defining genes as dominant or recessive. To quickly reiterate, for each attribute of the new body the cell has two possible genes to choose from. If both of those available genes are dominant - as with say brown for eye colour - then there is no choice but for the dominant gene to hold sway. If one gene is dominant and the other recessive, then again the dominant gene will prevail. Only if both genes are recessive will that gene decide the pattern of particular attribute. This possibility is only one in four as will be seen:

Possible genes	**Result**
Dominant + dominant	dominant
Dominant + recessive	dominant
Recessive + dominant	dominant
Recessive + recessive	recessive

Clearly, if a family member creates, by mutation, a faulty gene or mates with someone carrying a faulty gene then - depending on whether the gene is dominant or recessive - it is possible to statistically calculate the chances of an offspring exhibiting the characteristics of that gene. By mating too closely within the bloodline the chances of the mutant gene remaining are increased. Conversely, by mating from non-linked bloodlines, the possibility exists for the mutated gene to drop out of the bloodline altogether.

The reader will be forgiven for posing the question, "if we can now catalogue the human genome, surely we can now identify the gene that controls our soul"? It is a fair question but one that is still not capable of being answered with any reasonable level of scientific confidence. The point has already been made that we can only identify 10% of the total number of nucleotides in a human cell as having any recognisable purpose. This still leaves 90% of the total nucleotides that appear to have no discernible purpose. Perhaps, as has already been said by others, God is in the spaces, that is the 90% of nucleotides - between the genes - for which no apparent purpose has been identified.

APPENDIX B

HEBREW KINGS

UNITED MONARCHY

Saul	1,025 – 1,005
David	1,005 – 965
Solomon	968 – 928

JUDAEA			ISRAEL		
Rehoboam		928 - 911	Jeroboam I		928 - 907
Abijam		911 - 908	Nadab		907 - 906
Asa		908 - 867	Baasha		906 - 883
			Elah		883 - 882
			Zimri		882
			Tibni	(4 year dispute)	882 - 878
			Omri	(4 year dispute)	882 - 871
Jehoshaphat	(co-reg)	870 - 846	Ahab		873 - 852
Jehoram	(co-regent)	851 - 843	Ahaziah		852 - 851
Ahaziah		843 - 842	Joram		851 - 842
Athaliah		842 - 836	Jehu		842 - 814
Joash		836 - 798	Jehoahaz	(co- regent)	817 - 800
Amaziah		798 - 769	Jehoash		800 - 784
Azariah	(co-regent)	785 - 733	Jeroboam II	(co-regent)	788 - 747
Jotham	(co-regent)	759 - 743	Zechariah		747
			Shallum		747
Ahaz	(co-regent)	743 - 727	Menahem		747 - 737
			Pekahiah		737 - 735
			Pekah		735 - 732
Hezekiah		727 - 698	Hoshea		732 - 724
Manasseh		698 - 642			
Amon		641 - 640			
Josiah		639 - 609			
Jehoahaz		609			
Jehoiakim		608 - 598			
Jehoiachin		597			
Zedekiah		596 - 586			

APPENDIX C

THE COOKE MANUSCRIPT

Original

Thonkyd be god our glorious ffadir and founder and former of heuen and of erthe and of all thygis that in hym is that he wolde fochesaue of his glorius god hed for to make so mony thyngis of duers vertu for mankynd. ffor he mader all thyngis for to be abedient & soget to man ffor all thyngis that ben comes tible of holsome nature he ordeyned hit for manys sustynans. And all to be hath yif to man wittys and conyng of dyvers thyngys and craft tys by the whiche we may trauayle in this worlde to gete wit our lyuyg to make diuers thingys to goddis plesans and also for our ese and profyt. The whiche thingis if I scholde reherse hem hit wre to longe to telle and to wryte.

Wherfor I woll leue. but I schall schew you some that is to sey ho and in what wyse the sciens of Gemetry firste be ganne and who wer the founders therof and of othur craftis mo as hit is notid in the bybill and in othur stories.

How and in what maner that this worthy sciens of Gemetry began began I wole tell you as I sayde bifore. ye schall undirstondethat ther ben vii liberall sciens by the whiche vii all sciens and craftis in the world were fyrste founde. and in especiall for he is causer of all. that is to sey the sciens of Gemetry of all other that be. the whiche vii sciens ben called thus. as for the

Recent

Thanks be to God, our glorious father, founder and maker of heaven and earth and of all things that are in Him, that He would vouchsafe, of his glorious God-head, to make so many things of divers virtue for mankind. For He made all things to be obedient and subject to man, for all things that are come to the table of wholesome nature he ordained it for men's sustenance. And also he hath given to man wits and cunning of divers things, and crafts, by which we may travel in this world to make our living; to make divers things to God's pleasure and also for our ease and profit. The things, which, if I should repeat them, would be too long to tell, and to write.

Therefore I will leave them, but I shall show you some, that is to say how and in what way the science of Geometry first began, and who were the founders thereof, and of other crafts more, as it is noted in the Bible and in other stories.

How and in what manner that this worthy science of geometry began, I will tell you, as I said before. You shall understand that there are seven liberal sciences: by which seven all sciences and crafts in the world were first found. And in especial for He is the cause of all, that is to say the science of geometry and of all others; the seven sciences are called thus. As

first that is called fundament of sciens his name is grammer he techith a man rygthfully to speke and to write truly.
The seconde is rethorik. and he techith a man to speke formabely and fayre. The thrid is dioleticus. and that sciens techith a man to discerne the trowthe fro the fals and comenly it is tellid art or soph'stry. The fourth ys callid arsmetryk the whiche techeth a man the crafte of nowmbers for to rekyn and to make a count of all thyge
The ffte Gemetry the which techith a man all the mettand mesurs and onderaton of wyghtis of all mans craft. The. vi. is musik that techith a man the crafte of song in notys of voys and organ & trompe and harp and of all othur pteynyng to hem. The vii is astronomy that techith man the cours of the sonne and of the moune and of other sterrys & planetys of heuen.

Owr entent is princi pally to trete of fyrstfundacion of the worthe scyens of Gemetry and we were the founders therof as I seyde by fore there ben vii liberallscyens that is to say vii sciens or scyens that is to say vii sciens or craftys that ben fre in hem selfe the whiche vii. lyuen only by Gemetry. And Gemetry is as moche to sey as the mesure of the erth Et sic dicit a geo ge quin R ter a latine & metron quod e mensura. Una Gemetria. i, mensur terrc uel terrarum. that is to say in englische that Gemetria is I seyd of geo that is in gru. crthe, and metron that is to sey mesure. And thus is this nam of Gemetria compounyd as isseyd the mesur of the erthe.

for the first, which is called the fundamental of science, its name is grammar, it teaches a man to speak and to write truly.
The second is rhetoric, and it teaches a man to speak formally and fair. The third is dialectics, and that science teaches a man to discern the truth from the false, and commonly it is called art or sophistry. The fourth is called arithmetic, which teaches a man the craft of numbers, to reckon and to make account of all things.
The fifth is geometry, which teaches a man all the measures, and to reflect on the weight of all mans craft. The sixth is music, which teaches a man the craft of song, in notes of voice and organ, and trumpet, and harp, and of all others pertaining to them. The seventh is astronomy, which teaches man the course of the sun, and of the moon, and of the other stars and planets of heaven.
Our intent is principally to treat of the first foundation of the worthy science of geometry, and we were the founders thereof. As I said before there are seven liberal sciences; that is to say, seven sciences, or crafts, which are free in themselves. These seven live only by geometry. And geometry is as much to say as the measure of the earth, *"Et sic dicitur a geo ge quin R ter a latin et metron quod est mensura. Una Geometria in mensura terra vel terrarum,"* that is to say in English, that geometry is, I said, of "geo" or "gru", meaning earth, and "metron", meaning "measure". Thus is the name of Geometry

Mervile ye not that I seyd that all sciens lyue all only by the sciens of Gemetry. ffor there is none artifici all ne honcrafte that is wrogth by manys hond bot hit iswrougght by Gemetry. and a notabull cause. for if a man worche wit his hondis he worchyth wit some manner tole and ther is none instrument of materiall thingis in this worlde but hit come of the kynde of erthe and to erthe hit wole turne a yen. and ther is none instrument that is to say a tole to wirche wit but hit hathsome prooprorcion more or lasseAnd some proporcion is mesure the tole er the instrment is erthe.

And Gemetry is said the mesure of erthe Where fore I may sey that men lyuen all by Gemetry. ffor all men here in this worlde lyue by the labour of her hondys. Mony mo pbacions I wole telle yow why that Gemetry is the sciens that all reasonable men lyue by. but I leue hit at this tyme for the loge processe of wrytyng. And now I woll prpcede forther on me mater. ye schall understonde that amonge all the craftys of the worlde of mannes crafte masonry hath the moste notabilite and moste parte of this sciens Gemetry as hit is notid and seyd in storiall as in the bybyll and in the master of stories. And in policronico a cronycle prinyd and in the stories that is named Beda

De Imagine mundi & Isodorus ethomologiarum. Methodius epus & martirus. And other meny mo seyd that masonry is principall of Gemetry as me thenkyth hit may

compounded and is said to be the measure of the earth. Marvel not that I said that all sciences live only by the science of geometry. For there is none of them artificial; no handicraft that is wrought by mans hand but it is wrought by geometry, and a notable cause, for if a man work with his hands he works with some manner of tool, and there is no instrument, of material things in this world but that it comes of the kind of earth, and to the earth it will turn again, and there is no instrument, that is to say a tool to work with, but that it has some proportion, more or less. And proportion is measure, the tool, or the instrument, is earth.

And geometry is said to be the measure of the earth. Therefore, I may say that men live by geometry, for all men here in this world live by the labour of their hands. Many more probations [tests of individual conduct] I will tell you, why geometry is the science that all reasonable men live by, but I leave it, at this time, for the long process of writing. And now I will proceed further with my subject. You shall understand that among all the crafts in the world of man's craft, Masonry is the most notable; and most part of this science, geometry, as it is noted and said in history, is in the Bible, and in the mastery of history. And in the *Policronicon* - a printed chronicle - and in the histories that is named Bede. *De Imagine Mundi et Isodorus Ethomolegiarum. Methodius, Episcopus et Martiris.* And others, many more, said that masonry is the principal of geometry, as I think well be sayd for hit was the first that was foundon as hit is notid in the bybull in the first boke of Genesis in the iiii chapter. And also all the doctours aforsayde acordeth therto. And sume of hem seythe hit more openly and playnly rygt as his seithe in the by bull Genesis Adam is line linyalle sone descendyng doune the vii age of adam byfore noes flode ther was a man that was clepyd lameth the whiche hadde ii wyffes the on hyght ada & a nothersella by the fyrst wyffe thathyght ada he be gate ii sonys that one hyght Jobel and the other height juball.

The elder sone Jobell he was the fists man that ever found gemetry and masonry. and he made howsis & namyd in the bybull Pater habitantcium in tentoris atque pastorum That is to say fader of men dwellyng in tentis that is dwellyng howsis. And he was Cayin is master mason and governor of all his werkys whan he made the Cite of Enoch that was the firste Cite that was the first Cite that ever was made and that made Kayme Adam is sone. and yaf to his owne sone. Enoch and yaff the Cyte the name of his sone and kallyd hit Enoch. and now hit is callyd Effraym and ther was sciens of Gemetry and masonri fyrst occupied and contrenyd for a sciens and for a crafte and so we maysey that hit was cavse & fun dacion of all craftys and sciens. And also this man Jobell was called Pater Pastorum

The master of stories seith and beda de ymagyna mundi policronicon & other mo seyn that he was the first

it may well be said, for it was the first that was founded, as it is noted in the Bible, in the first book of Genesis in the fourth chapter. And also all the doctors before mentioned accorded with it, and some of them said it more openly, and plainly, right as it said in the Bible, Genesis. Adam's male line, descending down to the seventh age of Adam. Before Noah's flood, there was a man that was named Lamech who had two wives, the one named Adah, and another Zillah. By the first wife, named Adah, he had two sons called Jabal, and Jubal.

The elder son, Jabal was the first man that discovered geometry and Masonry, and he made houses, and is named in the Bible *Pater habitancium in tentoris atque pastorum.* That is to say, father of men dwelling in tents and dwelling in houses. And he was Cain's master mason, and governor of all his works. When he made the city of Enoch, it was the first city. It was the first city that ever was made, and Cain, Adam's son, gave to the city the name of his son, and called it Enoch. And now it is called Ephraim, and there was the science of Geometry, and masonry, first occupied, and contended to be a science and a craft, and so we may say that it was the cause and foundation of all crafts, and sciences, and also this man, Jaball, was called *pater pastorum.*

The master of stories said, and the Bede, in *De Imagine Mundi,* and the *Policronicon,* and others say that made deperceson of lond that every man myght knowe his owne grounde and laboure there on as for his owne. And also he departid flockes of schepe that every man myght know his owne schepe and so we may sey that he was the first founder of that sciens. And his brother Juball. or tuball was founder of mysyke & song as pictogoras seyth in policronycon and the same seythe ylodoure in his ethemologii in the vi boke there he seythe that he was the first foundere of mysyke and song and of organ & trompe and he founde that sciens by the soune of ponderacion of his brotheris hamers that was tubalcaym.

Sothely as the bybull seyth in the chapitre that is to sey the iiii of Genes' that is to sey the iiii of Genes' that he seyth lameth gate apon his other wiffe that height sella a sone & a dooucter the names of them were clepid tubalcaym that was the sone. & his doghter that was the sone. & his doghter hight neema & as the policronycon seyth that some men sey that sche was noes wyffe wether hit be so other no we afferme hit nott

Ye schulle understonde that this sone tubalcaym was founder of smythis craft and other craft of meteil that is to sey of eyron of braffe of golde & of silver as some docturs seyn & his syster neema was fynder of weverscraft. for by fore that time was no cloth weuyn but they did spynne yerne and knytte hit & made hem suche clothyng as they couthe but as the woman neema founde the craft of weuyng& therfore hit was kalled

that he was the first to disperse the land, so that every man might know his own ground, and labour thereon, was for himself. And also he dispersed flocks of sheep, that every man might know his own sheep, and so we may say that he was the first founder of that science. And his brother Jubal, or Tubal, was the founder of music and song, as Pythagoras said in the *Policronicon* and also Isodore in his *Ethemologies,* in the sixth book, there he said that he was the first founder of music, and song, and of organ and trumpet, and he found that science by the sound of the pounding of his brother's hammers, that was Tubal Cain.

Truly, as the Bible says in the fourth chapter of Genesis, that he said Lamech gave his other wife, named Zillah, a son and a daughter, the names of them were called Tubal Cain, that was the son, and his daughter was called Naamah, and as the *Policronicon* said, that some men say that she was Noah's wife: whether it be so, or no, we cannot say.

You shall understand that this son Tubal Cain was the founder of the blacksmiths' craft, and of other crafts of metal, that is to say, of iron, of brass, of gold, and of silver, as some doctors say. His sister, Naamah, was the founder of the weavers craft, for before that time was no cloth woven, but they did spin yarn and knit it, and made them such clothing as they could, but as the woman, Naamah, founded the craft of weaving, and wo menys craft. and thes iii brotheryn aforesayd had know lyche that god wold take ven gans for synne other by fyre or watir and they had greter care how they myst do to saue the sciens that they founde and they toke her conselle togedyr & by all her witts they seyde that were. ii maner of stonn of suche vertu that the one wolde never brenne & that stone is callyd marbyll. & that other stone that woll not synke in water. & that stone is named latrus.

And so they deuysyed to wryte all the sciens that they had ffounde in the sciens that they had ffounde in this ii stonys if that god wolde take vengns by fyre that themarbyll scholde not brenne And yf god sende vengansby water that the other scholde not droune. & so they prayed ther elder brother jobell that wold make ii. pillers of thes. ii stones that is to sey of marbyll and of latrus and that he wold write in the ii. pylers all the sciens & crafts that all they had founde. and so he did and therfor we may sey that he was most connyng in sciens for he fyrst bygan& performed the end by for noes flode.

Kyndly knowyng of that venganns that god wolde send whether hit scholde be bi fyre or by water the bretherne hadde hit not by a maner of a prophecy they wist that god wold send one therhere sciens in the. ii. Pilers of stone. And sume men sey that they writen in the. stonis all the. vii sciens. but as they in here mynde that a ven ganns scholde come. And to hit was that god sentd ven ganns so that ther

therefore it was called women's craft, and these three brethren, aforesaid, had knowledge that God would take vengeance for sin, either by fire, or water, and they had greater care how they might do to save the sciences that they had found, and they took their counsel together and, by all their wits, they said that there were two types of stones of such virtue that the one would never burn, and that stone is called marble, and that the other stone that will not sink in water and that stone is called pumice.

And so they devised to write all of the sciences that they had found in these two stones, so that if God takes vengeance, by fire, that the marble should not burn. And if God sent vengeance, by water, that the other should not drown, and so they prayed that their elder brother Jabal that he would make two pillars of these two stones, that is to say of marble and pumice, and that he would write in the two pillars all the sciences and crafts that they had found, and so he did and, therefore, we may say that he was most cunning in science, for he first began and worked before Noah's flood.

Kindly knowing of the vengeance, that God would send, whether it should be by fire, or by water, the brethren had not the skill of prophecy, they thought that God would send one and therefore they wrote their sciences in the two pillars of stone, and some men say that they wrote in the stones all the seven sciences, but as they had in their minds that vengeance would come. And so it was that God sent come suche a flode that alle the worl was drowned. and alle men wer dede ther in saue. viii. Personis And that was noe and his wyffe. and his iii. sonys & here wyffes. of whiche. iii sones all the world cam of. and here namys were namyd in this maner. Sem. Cam. & Japhet. And this flode was kalled noes flode ffor he & his children were sauyed ther in.

And after this flode many yeres as the cronycle telleth thes. ii pillers were founde& as the polycronicon seyth that a grete clerke that callede puto-gorasfonde that one and hermes the philisophre fonde that other. & thei tought forthe the sciens that thei fonde ther y wryten. Every cronycle and storiall and meny other clerkys and the bybull in princi pall wittenes of the makynge of the toure of babilon and hit is writen in the bibull Genesis Capter x wo that Cam noessone gate nembrothe and he war a myghty man apon the erthe and he war a stronge man like a Gyant and he was a grete Kyng. and the bygyn ynge of his kyngdom was trew kyngdom of babilon and arach. and archad. & talan & the lond if sennare. And this same CamNemroth began the towre of babilon and he taught and he taught to his werkemwn the crafte of masuri and he had wit hym mony masonys mo thanxl thousand. and he louyd & cheresched them well. and hit is wryten in policronicon and in the master of stories and in other stories mo. and this a part wytnes bybull in the samex. chapter he seyth that asure that was nye

vengeance so that there came such a flood that all the world was drowned, and all men were dead, save eight persons, And that was Noah, and his wife, and his three sons, and their wives. From these three sons came all of the world and their names were named in this manner, Shem, Ham, and Japhet. And this flood was called Noah's flood, for he, and his children, were saved therein.

And after this flood many years, as the chronicle told, these 2 pillars were found, and as the *Pilicronicon* saith, that a great clerk that was called Pythagoras found that one, and Hermes, the philosopher, found that other, and they taught forth the sciences that they found therein written. Every chronicle, and history, and many other clerks, and the Bible in principal, witnesses of the making of the tower of Babel, and it is written in the Bible, Genesis Chapter x, how that Ham, Noah's son begot Nimrod, and he waxed a mighty man upon the earth, and he waxed a strong man, like a giant, and he was a great king. And the beginning of his kingdom was that of the true kingdom of Babylon, and Arach, and Archad, and Calan, and the land of Sennare. And this same Nimrod began the tower of Babylon . . . and he taught to his workmen the craft of measures, and he had with him many masons, more than 40 thousand. And he loved and cherished them well. And it is written in the *Policronicon,* and in the master of stories, and in other stories more, and this in part is witnessed in the Bible, in the kynne to CamNembrothe yede owt of the londe of senare and he bylled the Cie Nunyve and plateas and other mo thus he seyth. De tra illa& de sennare egreffus est asure & edificauit Nunyven & plateas ciuiyate & cale & Jesu qoqz inter nunyven & hec est Ciuitas magna.

Reson wolde that we schold tell opunly how & in what maner that the charges of masoncraft was fyrst foun dyd & ho yaf first the name to hit of masonri and ye and writen in policronicon & in methodus episcopus and marter that asur that was a worthy lord of sennare sende to nembroththe kynge to sende hym masons and workemen of craft that might helpe hym to make his Cite that he was in wyll to make. And nembroth sende hym xxx C. of masons. And whan they scholde go & sende hem forth. he callyd hem by for hym and seyd to hem ye most go to my cosyn asure to helpe hym to bilde a cyte but loke that ye be well gouernyd and I schall yeue yov a charge profitable for you & me.

When ye come to that lord loke that ye be trewe to hym lyke as ye wolde be to me. and truly do your labour and craft and takyt resonabull your mede therfor as ye may deserue and also that ye loue to gedyr as ye were bretheryn and holde to gedyrtruly. & he that hath most conyng teche hit to hys felaw and louke ye gouerne you ayenst yowr lord and a monge yowr selfe.

same chapter 10, of Genesis, where he said that Asur, that was nigh of kin to Nimrod, and went out of the land of Senare and he built the city of Nineveh, and Plateas, and other more, this he said "*de tra illa et de Sennare egressus est Asur, et edificavit Nineven et Plateas civitatum et Cale et Jesu quoque, inter Nineven et hoec est Civitas magna.*"

Reason would that we should tell openly how, and in what manner, that the charges of mason-craft was first founded and who gave first the name of it of masonry. And you shall know well that it is told and written in the *Policronicon* and in Methodius Episcopus and Martyrus that assure, that was a worthy lord of Sennare, sent to Nimrod the king, to send him masons and workmen of craft that might help him to make his city that he was in will to make. And Nimrod sent him three hundred masons. And when they should go and he should send them forth he called them before him and said to them--"You must go to my cousin Asure, to help him to build a city; but look to it that you be well governed, and I shall give you a charge profitable for you and me.

When you come to that lord look that you are true to him like as you would be to me, and truly do your labour and craft, and take reasonable your mead therefore as you may deserve, and also that you love together as you were brethren, and hold together truly; and he that hath most cunning teach it to his fellow; and look you govern you against your lord and among that I may haue worchyppe and thonke for me sendyng and techyng you the crafte. and they resceyuyd the charge of hym that was here maister and here lorde. and wente forthe to asure. & hit is seyd of y lodour Ethemologiarum in the v. boke. Ethemologiarum Capitolo p'mo. Seyth that Enclyde was on of the first founders of Gemetry & his tyme ther was a water in that lond of Egypt that is callyd Nilo and hit flowid so ferre in to the londe that men myght not dwelle ther in Then this worthi clerke Enclide taught hem to make grete wallys and diches to holde owt the watyr.

And he by Gemet' mesured the londe and departyd hit in dyvers partys. & mad every man to close his awne parte wit walles and diches an theen hit be came a plentuos conuntre of all maner of freute and of yonge peple of men and women that ther was so myche pepull of yonge frute that they couth' not well lyue. And the lordys of the countre drew hem to gedyr and made a councell how they myght helpe her childeryn that had no lyflode compotente & abull for to fynde hem selfe and here childron for they had so many. and a mong hem all in councell was this worthy clerke Enclidnis and when he sawe that all they couthe not btynge a bout this mater. he seyd to hem woll ye take your sonys in gouernanns & I schall teche hen suche a sciens that they schall iyue ther by jentelmanly vnder condicion that ye wyll be swore to me toperfourme the gouernanns that I schall sette you too and hem

yourselves, that I may have worship and thanks for my sending, and teaching, you the craft." and they received the charge of him that was their master and their lord, and went forth to Asur, and it is said of Isodour, E*themologiarum,* in the 5th book *Ethemolegiarum,* who understood it first, said that Euclid was one of the first founders of geometry, for in his time that was a water in that land of Egypt that is called the Nile, and it flowed so far into the land that men might not dwell therein. Then this worthy clerk, Euclid, taught them to make walls and ditches to hold out the water.

And he, by Geometry measured the land and divided it between many parties. And made every man to choose his own part with walls and ditches and then it became a plentious country with all manner of fruit and young people and men and women that there was so many young people that they could not cope. And the lords of the Country drew them together and made a council that might help the children who had no lifelong constituent for or able to find himself and the children because there were so many of them. And among them was this worthy clerk called Euclid and when he saw that they could not understand about the matter he said to them "I will take your sons and governors and I will teach them such a science that they shall become gentlemanly". This condition will allow them to govern themselves and he swore to me that the governors would settle you too and both the king and the lords by

bothe and the kyng of the londe and all the lordys by one assent grauntyd ther too.
Reson wolde that euery man woulde graunte to that thyng that were profetable to himself. and they toke here so nys to enclide to gouerne hem at his owne wylle & he taught to hem the craft Masonry and yaf hit the name of Gemetry by cavse of the partyng of the grounde that he had taught to the peple in the time of the makyng of the wallys and diches a for sayd to clawse out the watyr. & Isodor seyth in his Ethemolegies that Enclide callith the craft Gemetrya And ther this worthye clerke yaf hit name and taught hitt the lordis sonys of the londe that he had in his teching And he yaf hem a charge that they scholde calle here eche other ffelowe & no nother wise by cavse that they were all of one crafte & of one gentyll berthe bore & lords' sonys. And also he that were most of connyng scholde be gouernour of the werke and scholde be callyd maister & other charges mo that ben wryten in the boke of chargys. And so they wrought with lordys of the lond & made cities and tounys castelis & templis and lordis placis. What tyme that the children of isrl dwellidin egypte they lernyd the craft of masonry.

And afturward they were dryuen ont of Egypte they come in to the lond of bihest and is now callyd ierlem and hit was ocupied & chargys y holde. And the makyng of salomonis tempull that Kyng Dauid be gan. kyng dauid louyd well masons and he yaf hem rygt

one assent will be granted this too.

Reason would that every manwould grant the that thing that were profitable to himself and they took so nicely to Euclid for him to govern them at his own will and he taught them the craft of Masonry and gave it the name of Geometry by cause of the dividing of the ground that he had taught to the people in the time of making the walls and ditches aforesaid to keep out the water. And Isodore said, in his *Ethemologies,* that Euclid calleth the craft geometry; and there was this worthy clerk gave it name, and taught it the lords' sons of the land that he had in his teaching. And he gave them a charge that they should call here each other fellow, and no otherwise, because that they were all of one craft, and of one gentle birth born, and lords' sons.
And also he that were most of cunning should be governor of the work, and should be called master, and other charges more that are written in the book of charges. And so they wrought with lords of the land, and made cities and towns, castles and temples, and lords' palaces. What time that the children of Israel dwelt in Egypt they learned the craft of masonry.
And afterward, when they were driven out of Egypt, they came into the land of behest, and is now called Jerusalem, and it was occupied and charges there held. And the making of Solomon's temple that king David began. King David loved well masons, and he

nye as they be nowe. And at the makyng of the temple in salomonis tyme as hit is seyd in the bibull in the iii boke of Regu in tercio Regum Capitolo quinto. That Salomon had iiii. score thowsand masons at his werke. And the kyng is sone of Tyry was his master masen.

And other crony clos hit is seyd & in olde bokys of masonry that Salomon confirmed the char gys that dauid has fadir had yeue to masons. And salo mon hym self taught hem here maners byt lityll differans fro the maners that now ben usyd. And fro thens this worthy sciens was brought in to fraunce And in to many other regions Sum tyme ther was a worthye kyng in ffrauns that was clepyd Carolus s'cundus that ys to sey Charlys the secunde. And this Charlys was elyte kyng of ffrauns by the grace of god & by lynage also. And summe men sey that he was elite by fortune the whiche is fals as by cronycle he was of the kynges blode Royal.

And this same kyng Charlys was a mason bi for that he was kyng. And after that he was kyng he louyd masons & cherschid them and yaf hem chargys and manerys at his deuise the whiche sum ben yet used in fraunce and he ordeynyd that they scholde haue a semly onys in the yere and come and speke to gedyr and for to be reuled by masters & felows of thynges a mysse. And soone after that comes eynt ad habell in to Englondand he conuertyd seynt Albonto cristendome. And seynt Albon lovyd well masons and he yaf hem

gave them right nigh as they be now. And at the making of the temple in Solomon's time as it is said in the Bible, in the 3rd book of *Regum in tercio Regum capitolo quinto*, that Solomon had four score thousand masons at his work. And the king's son, of Tyre, was his master Mason.

And in other chronicles it is said, and in old books of masonry, that Solomon confirmed the charges that David, his father, had given to masons. And Solomon himself taught them there manners with but little difference from the manners that now are used. And from thence this worthy science was brought into France and into many other regions Sometime there was a worthy king in France that was called Carolus secundus, that is to say, Charles the Second, and this Charles was elected king of France, by the grace of God and by lineage also. And some men say that he was elected by fortune, which is false, as by the chronicle he was of the king's blood royal.

And this same King, Charles, was a mason before that he was king, and after that he was king he loved Masons and cherished them, and gave them charges and manners at his device, of the which some are yet used in France; and he ordained that they should have an assembly once in the year, and come and speak together, and for to be ruled by masters and fellows of all things amiss. And soon after that came Saint Adhabell into England, and converted Saint Alban to Christianity. And Saint Alban loved well masons, and he gave them first

fyrst here charges & maners fyrst in Englond. And he or deyned conuenyent to pay for the trauayle. And after theat was a worthy kynge in Englond that was callyd Athelstone and his yongest sone lovyd well the sciens of Gemetry. and he wyst well that hand craft had the practyke of the sciens of Gemetry to well as masons wherefore he drewe hym to consell and lernyd practyke of that sciens to his speculatyf.
For of specculatyfe he was a master and he lovyd well masonry and masons. And he bicome a mason hym selfe. And he yaf hem chargesand names as hit is now othere countries. And heordyned that they schulde haue resonabull pay. And purchased a fre patent of the kyng that they schoulde make asembly whan thei sawe resonably tyme a cu to gedir tohere counselle of the whiche Charges manors & sembleas is write and taught in the boke of our charges wher for I leue hit at this tyme. Good men for this cause and this maner masonry toke firste begynnyng. hit befyll sumtyme that grete lordis had not sogrete possessions that they myghte not a vaunce here fre bigeton childeryn forthey had so many. Therefore they toke counsell howe theyand ordeyn hem onestly tolyue. And sende after wysemaisters of the worthy sci ens of Gemetry that they thorou here wysdome schold ordey/nehem sum honest lyuyngname whiche was callyd Englet that was most sotell& wise founder ordeyned and art and callyd hit masonry. and so with his art ho nestly he thogt the childeren

their charges and manners first in England. And he ordained convenient times to pay for the travail. And after that was a worthy king in England that was called Athelstan, and his youngest son loved well the science of geometry, and he was well that hand-craft had the practice of the science of geometry so well as masons, wherefore he drew him to council and learned the practice of that science to his speculative.
For of speculative he was a master, and he loved well masonry and masons. And he became a mason himself, and he gave them charges and names as it is now used in England, and in other countries. And he ordained that they should have reasonable pay and purchased a free patent of the king that they should make an assembly when they saw a reasonable time and come together to their councillors of which charges, manners, and assembly, as it is written and taught in the book of our charges, wherefore I leave it at this time. Good men for this cause and this manner Masonry took its first beginning. It befell sometimes that great lords had not so great possessions that they might not advance their free begotten children, for they had so many, therefore they took counsel how they might their children advance and ordain them honestly to live. And they sent after wise masters of the worthy science of geometry that they, through their wisdom, should ordain them some honest living. Then one of them, that had the name which was called Englet, that

of get lordis bi the pray er of the fathers and the frewill of here children. The wiche when thei taugt with hie Cure bi a serteyn tymethey were not all ilyke abull for to take of the forseyde art Wherefore the forsayde maister Englet ordeynet thei were passing of conyng schold be passing honoured. And ded to call the connynger maister for to enforme the lasse of con nyng masters of the wiche were callyd masters of nobilite of witte and connyng of that art.

Neverthelesse thei commaundid that thei that were lasse of witte schold not be callyd seruanter ner sogett but felau ffor nobilite of here gentyll nlode. In this maner was the forsayde art begunne in the lond of Egypte by the forsayde ordeyned a certayne reule a mongys hom on tyme of the yere or in iii yere as nede were to the kyng and gret lordys of the londe and all the comente fro proynce to proynce and fro countre to countre congregacions scholde be made by maisters of all maisters masons and felaus in the forsayd art. And so at suche congregacons they that be mad masters schold be examined of the articuls after writen. & be ransakyd whether thei be abull and kunnyng to the prfyte of the lordys hem to serue and to the honour of the forsaidart and more ouer they schulde receyue here charge that they schuld well and trewly dispende the goodys of here lordis and as well the lowist as the hiest

was most subtle and wise founder, ordained an art and called it Masonry, and so with his art, honestly, he taught the children of great lords, by the prayer of the fathers and the freewill of their children, the which when they were taught with high care, by a certain time, they were not all alike able for to take of the aforesaid art wherefore the aforesaid master, Englet, ordained that they who were passing of cunning should be passing honoured, and did call the cunning master to inform the less of cunning masters, of the which were called masters, of nobility of wit and cunning of that art.

Nevertheless they commanded that they that were less of wit should not be called servant, nor subject, but fellow, for nobility of their gentle blood. In this manner was the aforesaid art begun in the land of Egypt, by the aforesaid master Englet, they ordained a certain rule amongst them: one time of the year, or in 3 years as need were to the king and great lords of the land, and all the commonalty, from province to province, and from country to country, congregations should be made, by masters, of all masters, Masons, and fellows in the aforesaid art, and so, at such congregations, they that be made masters should be examined, of the articles after written, and be ransacked whether they be able and cunning to the profit of the lords having them to serve and to the honour of the aforesaid art. And, moreover, they should receive their charge that they should well and truly dispend the goods of their for they ben her lordys for the tyme of whom hei take here pay for here cervyce and for here trauayle.

lords, as well the lowest as the highest, for hey be their lords, for the time, of whom they take their pay for their service and for their travail.

The firste article ys this that euery maister of this art schulde be wysse and trewe to the lord that he seruyth dispendyng his godis trule as he wolde his awne were dispendyd. and not yefe more pay to no mason than he wot he may diserue after the derthe of korne & vytayl in the contry no fauour with stondyg for euery man to be rewardyd after his trauayle.

The secnd article is this that euery master of this art scholde be warned by fore to cum to his cogregat that thei com dewly but yf thei may asscusyd by sume maner cause. But neuerlesse if they be founde rebell at suche congregacions or fauty in eny maner harme of here lordys and reprene of this art thei schulde not be excusyd in no manere out take perell of dethe and thow they be in peryll of dethe they scall warne the maister that is pryncipall of the gederyng of his dessese.

The article is this that no master take noprentes for lasse terme than vii yer at the lest. bycause whi suche as ben with I lasse terme may not profitely come to his art. nor abull to serue truly his lorde to take as a mason schulde take.

The iiii article is this that no master for no profyte take no prentis for to be lernyd that is bore of bonde blode fore bicause of his lorde to whom he is bonde woll take hym as he well may fro his art & lede hym

The first Article is this, - That every master of this art should be wise and true to the lord that he served, dispending his goods truly as he would his own were dispensed, and not give more pay to any mason than what he may deserve, after the dearth of corn and victual in the country, no favour withstanding, for every man to be rewarded after his travail.

The second Article is this, - That every master of this art should be warned, before, to come to his congregation, that they come duly, but if they may be excused by some manner of cause. But, nevertheless, if they be found rebellious at such congregations, or faulty in any manner of harm of their lords, and reproof of this art, they should not be excused in any manner without taking peril of death, and though they be in peril of death, they shall warn the master that is principal of the gathering of his decease.

The third Article is this, -That no master take an apprentice for a less term than 7 years at the least, because such as be within a less term may not, profitably, come to his art nor able to serve, truly, his lord and to take as a mason should take.

The fourth Article is this, - That no master, for no profit, take an apprentice, for to be learned, that is born of bond blood, for, because of his lord, to whom he is bond, will take him as he well may, from his with hym out of his logge or out of his place that he worchyth in for his felaus perauenter wold help hym and debte for hym. And thereoff manslaughter mygt ryse hit is forbede. And also for a nother cause of his art hit toke begynnyng of grete lordis children frely begetyn as hit is iseyd bi for.

The v. article is thys that no master yef more to his prentis in tyme of his prentis hode for no prophite to be take than he note well he may disserue of the lorde that he seruith nor not so moche that the lorde of the place that he is taught inne may haue sum profyte bi his techyng.

The vi. article is this that no master for no couetyse ner profite take no prentis to teche that is unperfyte that is to sey havyng eny maym for the whiche he may not trewely worche as hym ought for to do.

The vii.article is this that np maister bey founde wittyngly or help or procure to be mayntener & susteyner any comyn nygt walker to robbe bi the whiche maner of nygt walking thei may not fulfyll ther days werke and traueyell thorow the condicion her felaus mygt be made wrowthe.

The viii article is this that yf hit befall that any mason that be perfyte and connyng come for to seche werke and fynde any vnperfit and vnkunnyng worchyng the master of the place schall receyue the perfite and do a wey the vnperfite to the profite of his lord

The ix. article is this that no maister schall supplanta nother for hit is

art and lead him, with him, out of his lodge, or out of his place, that he worked in, for his fellows, peradventure, would help him and debate for him, and thereof manslaughter might arise, it is forbidden. And also for another cause of his art, it took beginning of great lords' children, freely begotten, as it is said before.

The fifth Article is this, - That no master give more to his apprentice in time of his apprenticeship, for any profit to be taken, than he notes well he may deserve of the lord that he served, nor not so much that the lord, of the place that he is taught in, may have some profit of his teaching.

The sixth Article is this, - That no master for no covetousness, nor profit, take no apprentice to teach that is imperfect, that is to say, having any maim for the which he may not truly work as he ought for to do.

The seventh Article is this, - That no master be found wittingly, or help or procure, to be a maintainer and sustainer of any common night walker to rob, by the which manner of night-walking they may not fulfil their day's work and travail, and through the condition their fellows might be made wroth.

The eigth Article is this, - That if it befall that any mason that be perfect, and cunning, come for to seek work and find an imperfect and uncunning working, the master of the place shall receive the perfect, and do away the imperfect, to the profit of his lord.

The ninth Article is this, -That no master shall supplant another for it

seyd in the art of masonry that no man scholde make ende so well of werke bigonne bi a no ther to the profite of his lorde as he bigan hit for to end hit bi his maters or to whome he scheweth his maters.
This councell ys made bi dy uers lordis & maisters of dyvers provynces and diuers congregacions of masonry and hit is to wyte that who that covetyth for to come to the state of that forseyd art hit be hoveth hem fyrst principally to god and holy chyrche & all halowis and his master and his felowis as his awne brotheryn. The seconde poynthe most fulfylle his dayes werke truly that he takyth for his pay. The. iii. point he can **hele** the councell of his felows in logge and in chambere and in euery place ther as masons beth. The iiii. poynt that he be no disseyver of the forseyd art ne do no preiudice ne susteyne none articles ayenst the art ne a yenst none of the art but he schall susteyne hit in all honovre in as moche as he may. The. v. poynt whan he schall take his pay that he take hit mekely as the tyme ys ordeynyd bi the maister to be done and that he fulfylle the accepcions of trauayle and of his resty ordeyned and sette by the maister.

The. vi. poynt yf eny discorde schall be bitwe ne hym & his felows he schall a bey hym mekely & be stylle at the byddyng of his master or of the wardeyne of his master in his masters absens to the holy day folowyng and that he accorde then at the dispocion of his felaus and not upon the werkeday for lettyng of here werke and

is said, in the art of masonry, that no man should make end so well of work begun by another, to the profit of his lord, as he that began it, for to end it by his matters, or to whom he showed his matters. This council is made by divers lords and masters of divers provinces and divers congregations of masonry and it is, to wit, that who that coveted to come to the state of the aforesaid art it behoved them first, principally, to God and holy church, and allhallows, and his master and his fellows as his own brethren.
The second Point, - He must fulfil his day's work truly that he took for his pay. The third Point. - That he can hele the counsel of his fellows in lodge, and in chamber, and in every place there as Masons be.
The fourth Point, - That he be no deceiver of the aforesaid art, nor do no prejudice, nor sustain no articles, against the art, nor against none of the art, but he shall sustain it in all honour, inasmuch as he may. The fifth Point, - When he shall take his pay, that he take it meekly, as the time is ordained by the master to be done, and that he fulfil the acceptations of travail, and of rest, ordained and set by the master.
The sixth Point, - If any discord shall be between him and his fellows he shall obey him meekly, and be still at the bidding of his master, or of the warden of his master, in his master's absence, to the holy-day following, and that he accord then at the disposition of his fellows, and not upon the workday for letting of their work and profit

profyte of his lord The. vii. poynt that he covet not the wyfe ne the doughter of his masters nother of his felaws but yf hit be in matuge nor holde concubines for dyscord that mygt fall amonges them. The. Viii poynt yf hit befalle hym ffor to be wardeyne vndyr his master that he be trewe mene bitwene his master & his felaws and that he be besy in the absence of his master to the honor of his master and profit to the lorde that he serueth

The. ix. poynt yf he be wiser and sotellere than his felaweworchyng with hym in his logge or in eny other place and he perseyue hit that he schold lefe the stone that he worchyt apon for defawte of connyng and can teche hym and a mende the stone he schall enforme hym and helpe him that the more loue may encrese among hem and that the werke of the lorde be not

lost. Whan the master and the felawes be for warned ben y come to suche congregaconns if nede be the Schereffe of the countre or the mayer of the Cyte or alderman of the towne in wyche the congregacons ys holden schall be felaw and so ciat to the master of the congregacion in helpe of hym ayenst rebelles and vpberyng the rygt of the reme.

At the fyrst begynnyng new men that neuer were chargyd bifore beth charged in this manere that schold neuer be theuys nor theuys meynteners and that schuld tryuly fulfyll here dayes

werke and truayle for he repay that they schull take of here lord and trewe a count yeue to here felaus in thyngys that be to be a countyd of

of his lord. The seventh Point, - That he covet not the wife, not the daughter, of his masters, neither of his fellows, but if it be in marriage, nor hold concubines, for discord that might fall amongst them. The eighth Point, - If it befall him for to be warden under his master, that he be true mean between his master and his fellows, and that he is busy in the absence of his master to the honour of his master and profit of the lord that he served.

The ninth Point, - If he be wiser, and subtler than his fellow working with him in his lodge, or any other place, and he perceive it that he should leave the stone that he worked upon, for default of cunning, and can teach him and amend the stone, he shall inform him and help him, that the more love may increase among them, and that the work of the lord be not lost. When the master and the fellows be forewarned and are come to such congregations, if need be, the Sheriff of the Country, or the Mayor of the City, or Alderman of the Town, in which the congregations is held, shall be fellow, and associate, to the master of the congregation, in help of him, against rebels and for the upholding the right of the realm.

At the first beginning new men, that never were charged before, be charged in this manner, - That they should never be thieves, nor thieves' maintainers, and that they should truly fulfil their day's work, and travail, for their pay that they shall take of their lord, and a true account give to their fellows, in things that be to be accounted of hem and to here and hem loue as hem selfe and they schall be trew to the kynge of englond and to the reme and that they kepe with all ther mygt and all the articles a for sayd. After that hit schall be enqueryd if ony master or felaw that is y warnyd haue y broke ony article be forsayd the whiche if they haue done hit schall be de termyned ther. Therefore hit is to wyte if eny master or felawe that is warnyd bifore to come to suche congregaconns and berebell and woll not come or els haue trespassed a yenst any article befor sayd if hit may be prouyd he schall forswere his masonri and schal no more vse his craft.

The whiche if he presume for to do the Scherefe of the countre in the which he may be founde worchynge he schall prison him & take all his godys into the kynges hond tyll his grace be grantyd him & y schewed for this cause principally wher thes congregatonns ben y ordeyned that as well the lowist as as the hiest schuld be welland trewely y seruyd in his art biforesayd thorow owt all the kyngdom of Englond. Amen so mote hit be

them, and to hear, and them love as themselves. And they shall be true to the King of England, and to the realm, and that they keep, with all their might, and all the Articles aforesaid. After that it shall be enquired if any master, or fellow, that is warned, have broken any Article before said, the which, if they have done, it shall be determined there. Therefore, it is to wit, if any master, or fellow, that is warned before to come to such congregations and be rebellious, and will not come, or else have trespassed against any Article before said, if it may be proved, he shall forswear his Masonry and shall no more use his craft;

The which, if he presume for to do, the Sheriff of the County, in which he may be found working, he shall imprison him and take all his goods into the king's hand till his grace be granted him and showed. For this cause, principally, where these congregations ordained that as well the lowest, as the highest, should be well and truly served in his art, before said, throughout all the kingdom of England.

Amen: so mote it be.

REFERENCES

1. Patrick Byrne, *Templar Gold* (2001)
2. Harry Carr, *The Freemason at Work* (1976)
3. Manly Hall, *The Secret Teachings of All Ages* (1999)
3. Godfrey Higgins, *Anacalypsis* (1986)
4. David Stevenson, *The Origins of Freemasonry* (1988)
5. Albert Mackay, *A History of Freemasonry* (1909)
6. Louis Jacobs, *Oxford Concise Companion to the Jewish Religion* (1999)
7. Dan Brown, *The Da Vinci Code* (2004)
8. Dr. Bing Johnson, *An Address to The Grand Junction Scottish Rite Bodies* (2001)
9. John Hamill, *The Craft* (1986)
10. Robert Gould, *History of Freemasonry* (2003)
11. Douglas Knoop, *The Early Masonic Catechisms* (1943)
12. Avery Allyn, *A Ritual of Freemasonry* (1831)
13. A. Jackson, *English Masonic Exposure* (1986)
14. John Shaftesley, *Jews in English Regular Freemasonry* (1975)
15. John Clapham, *Bank of England* (1944)
16. Abraham Maslow, *Motivation and Personality* (1987)
17. Kevin MacDonald, *The Culture of Critique* (2002)
18. Hans Küng, *Judaism* (1992)
19. Kathleen Kenyon, *Archaeology in the Holy Land* (1985)
20. William Dever, *What Did the Biblical Writers Know and When Did They Know It* (2001)
21. Donald Redford, *Egypt, Canaan and Israel in Ancient Times* (1992)
22. Israel Finkelstein, *The Bible Unearthed* (2001)
23. M. Hasel, *Israel in the Merneptah Stela* (1994)
24. James Pritchard, *The Ancient Near East* (1958)
25. Walter Elwell, *Evangelical Dictionary of Biblical Theology* (1996)

26. Morris Bierbrier, *The Tomb-Builders of the Pharaohs* (1982)
27. James Jordan, *Biblical Chronology* (1992)
28. James Vanderkam, *An Introduction to Early Judaism* (2001)
29. Sigmund Freud, *Moses and Monotheism* (1967)
30. Ahmed Osman, *Moses and Akhenaten* (2002)
31. Ralph Ellis, *Jesus Last of the Pharaohs* (1998)
32. Robert Feather, *The Copper Scroll Decoded* (1999)
33. Bryan Sykes, *The Seven daughters of Eve* (2001)
34. Gabriele Boccaccini, *Beyond the Essene Hypothesis* (1998)
35. Geza Vermes, *The Complete Dead Sea Scrolls* (1998)
36. Barbara Thiering, *Jesus the Man* (1992)
37. Robert Eisenmann, *The Dea Sea Scrolls and the First Christians* (1996)
38. Jacob Teicher, *Hebrew printed fragments*
39. Alexander Lawrie, *The History of Freemasonry* (1804)
40. Dr. William Emboden, *The Sacred Journey in Dynastic Egypt*
41. Andrew Prescott, *Preston's Illustrations of Masonry* (2001)
42. Arthur Zuckerman, *A Jewish Princedom in Feudal France* (1972)
43. Tim Wallace-Murphy, *Rex Deus* (2000)
44. Esther Benbassa, *The Jews of France* (1999)
45. Gérard De Sède, *The Accursed Treasure of Rennes-le-Château* (2001)
46. Louis Rabinowitz, *Jewish Merchant Adventurers* (1948)
47. Constance Bouchard, *Those of My Blood* (2001)
48. Emily Taitz, *The Jews of Medieval France* (1994)
49. Martin Cohen, *The Canonization of a Myth* (2003)
50. Robin Mundill, *England's Jewish Solution* (1998)
51. Albert Hyamson, *A History of the Jews in England* (2001)
52. John Robinson, *Born in Blood* (1990)
53. Margaret Jacobs, *Living the Enlightenment* (1991)
54. Michael Baigent, *The Holy Blood and the Holy Grail* (1982)

55. Doron Behar, *MtDNA Evidence for a Genetic Bottleneck in the Early History of the Ashkenazi Jewish Population* (2004)
56. Edward Gibbon, *The Decline and Fall of the Roman Empire* (1996)
57. Laurence Gardner, *The Bloodline of the Holy Grail* (1996)
58. Dagobert's Revenge Magazine,
59. Christopher Knight, *The Hiram Key* (1996)
60. Arnold Toynbee, *A Study of History* (1979)
61. E. Meyer, *Ursprung und Anfange des Christentums* (1921)
62. Alistair Key, *Constantine Versus Christ* (1982)
63. Leonard Weber, *Encyclopaedia of Theology* (1975)
64. Elaine Pagels, *Beyond Belief* (2004)
65. Lynn Picknett, *The Templar Revelation* (1997)
66. Geza Vermes, *The Passion* (2002)

BIBLIOGRAPHY

Albright, W. F. - *The Archaeology Of Palestine* - Librairie du Liban, 1960

Allyn, Avery. - *A Ritual of Freemasonry Illustrated by Numerous Engravings* – Philadelphia: John Clarke, 1831

Andrews, Richard and Schellenberger, Paul - *The Tomb of God: The Body of Jesus and the Solution to a 2,000-Year-Old Mystery* – London: Little Brown & Company, 1996

Andrews, Richard - *Blood on the Mountain: A History of the Temple Mount from the Ark to the Present* – London: Phoenix, 1999

Anonymous - *A Ritual of Freemasonry* - William Reeves, c.1912

Aristidou, Dr. Ekaterini - *Kolossi Castle through the Centuries* – Nicosia: 1983

Aveling, J. C. H. - *The Jesuits* – London: Blond and Briggs, 1981

Baigent, Michael & Leigh, Henry - *The Temple and the Lodge* – London: Cape, 1989

Baigent, Michael & Leigh, Henry; and Lincoln, Henry - *The Holy Blood and the Holy Grail* – London; Jonathan Cape, 1982

Barringer, Tim - *The Pre-Raphaelites: Reading the Image* – London: Weidenfeld and Nicholson, 1988

Barker-Cryer, Rev. Neville - *The Shamir* - Masonic Research Paper

Bauval, Robert & Hancock, Graham - *Keeper of Genesis: A Quest for theHidden Legacy of Mankind* – London: Heinemann, 1996

Begg, E.& Begg, D. - *In Search of the Holy Grail and the Precious Blood* –London: Aquarian, 1995

Behar, Doron et al – *MtDNA Evidence for a Genetic Bottleneck in the Early History of the Ashkenazi Jewish Population* – European Journal of Human Genetics (12), 2004

Benbassa, Esther – *The Jews of France; The History from Antiquity to the Present* – New Jersey: Princeton University Press, 1999

Boardman, John; Griffin, Jasper; Murray, Oswyn (eds). – *The Oxford Illustrated History of the Roman World* – Oxford: Oxford University Press, 1986

Breffny, Brian de - *The Synagogue* - 1978.

Briggs, Allan H. – *Retrospect; A Primer of Freemasonry*

Brown, Dan – *The Da Vinci Code* – Corgi Adult, 2004

Bierbrier, Morris – *The Tomb-Builders of the Pharaohs* – Cairo: American University in Cairo, 1982

Boccaccini, Gabriele - *Beyond the Essene Hypothesis: The Parting of the Ways Between Qumran and Enochic Judaism* – Michigan: William Eerdmans Publishing, 1998

Bouchard, Constance B. – *Those of My Blood; Constructing Noble Families in Medieval Francia* – Philadelphia: University of Pennsylvania, 2001

Burman, Edward - *Supremely Abominable Crimes: The Trial of the Knights Templar* – London: Allison and Busby, 1994

Byrne, Patrick – *Templar Gold; Discovering the Ark of the Covenant* – Nevada USA: Symposium, 2001

Captain Wilson & Captain Warren - *Recovery of Jerusalem* - 1971

Carr, Harry – *The Freemason at Work* – UK: Harry Carr, 1976

Castells, Rev. F. De - *Arithmetic in Freemasonry* - 1925

Chadwick, Owen - *A History of Christianity* – London, Weidenfeld and Nicolson, 1995

Charpentier, Louis (translated by Sir Ronald Fraser) - *The Mysteries of Chartres Cathedral* - 1972

Clapham, John – *Bank of England* – Cambridge: Cambridge University Press, 1944

Cohen, Martin A. - *The Canonization of a Myth: Portugal's "Jewish Problem" and the Assembly of Tomar 1629 (Hebrew Union College Annual. Supplements, No. 5)* – Michigan: Wayne State University Press, 2003

Coogan, Michael (Ed) - *The Oxford History of the Biblical World* – Oxford, Oxford University Press, 1998

Cohane, John - *The Key* – 1971

Dagobert's Revenge Magazine, Dragon Key Press, Portland, USA

De Sède, Gérard (Bill Kersey translator) – *The Accursed Treasure of Rennes-le-Château* – Worcester: DEK Publishing, 2001

Dever, William – *What Did the Biblical Writers Know and When Did They Know It: What Archaeology Can Tell Us About the Reality of Ancient Israel* – Michigan: William Eerdman, 2001

Dilke, O.A.W. – *The Ancient Romans: How they Lived and Worked* – Newton Abbot, David and Charles, 1975

Douglas, J. D. (Ed.) - *The New International Dictionary of the Christian Church* – Exeter: Paternoster Press, 1974

Eliade, Mircea (Ed.) - *The Encyclopaedia of Religion* – London, Collier Macmillan, 1987

Ellis, Ralph – *Jesus Last of the Pharaohs* – Dorset: EDFU Books, 1998

Elwell, Walter - *Evangelical Dictionary of Biblical Theology* – Carlisle: Paternoster Press, 1996

Eisenmann, Robert. – *The Dea Sea Scrolls and the First Christians.* – Shaftesbury: Element, 1996

Emboden, Dr. William - *The Sacred Journey in Dynastic Egypt; Shamanistic Trance in the Context of the Narcotic Water Lily and the Mandrak* – The Journal of Psychoactive Drugs 21, San Francisco: Haight-Ashbury Publications.

ETHRN Federation - *A Brief History of the Knights Templa*r - Internet, 1998

Evans, Joan - *Life in Medieval France* – London: Phaidon, 1969

Every, George - *Christian Mythology* – Middlesex, Hamlyn Publishing, 1970

Farah, Caesar E. – *Islam: Beliefs and Practices* - 1970

Feather, Robert – *The Copper Scroll Decoded* – Hammersmith, Thorsons, 1999

Finke, H. - *Acta Aragonensia, Vol. 2* - 1923

Finkelstein, Israel and Silberman, Neil, Asher – *The Bible Unearthed: Archaeology's New Vision of Ancient Israel* – London: Simon & Schuster, 2001

Fosse, Michael - *The Founding of the Jesuits* - 1969

Fox-Davies, Arthur - *A Complete Guide to Heraldry* – London: Bracken Books, 1993

Frère, Jean-Claude - *Leonardo: Painter, Inventor, Visionary, Mathematician,Philosopher, Engineer* – Paris: Terrail, 1995

Freud, Sigmund (translator Jones, Katherine) – *Moses and Monotheism* – New York: Vintage Books, 1967

Gardner, Laurence - *The Bloodline of the Holy Grail: The Hidden Lineage of Jesus Revealed* - Shaftesbury: Element, 1996.

Gibbon, Edward. – *The Decline and Fall of the Roman Empire* – Penguin Books, 1996

Goldscheider, Ludwig - *Michelangelo: Paintings, Sculpture, Architecture* - London: Phaidon, 1975.

Goodman, Martin. – *The Roman World 44 BC to AD 180* – London, Routledge, 1997

Gould, Robert F. – *History of Freemasonry, Its Antiquities, Symbols, Constitutions, Customs* – Edinburgh: Kessinger Publishing, 2003

Greer, John - *An Introduction to Corpus Hermeticu*m - Internet, 1997.

Hall, P, Manly - *The Secret Teachings of All Ages: An Encylopedic Outline of Masonic, Hermetic, Qabbalistic, and Rosicrucian Symbolical Philosophy* – USA: Philosophical Research Society, 1999

Hamill, John. *The Craft: A History of English Freemasonry.* Wellingborough: Crucible, 1986.

Hancock, Graham - *The Sign and the Seal: A Quest for the Ark of the Covenant* - London: Heinemann, 1992.

Hancock, Graham - *Fingerprints of the Gods: A Quest for the Beginning and the End.* London: Heinemann, 1995.

Hasel, M.G. - *Israel in the Merneptah Stela* - Bulletin of the American Schools of Oriental Research, 1994

Higgins, Godfrey - *Anacalypsis: An Attempt to Draw Aside the Veil of the Saitic Isis: Or an Inquiry into the Origin of Languages, Nations and Religions* - Society of Metaphysicians, 1986

Hinnells, John (Ed.) - *Penguin Dictionary of Religions* - London: Allen Lane, 1984.

Howarth, Stephen - *The Knights Templar* - London: Collins 1982.

Hyamson, Albert Montefiore – *A History of the Jews in England* – University Press of the Pacific, 2001

Jacobs C. Margaret – *Living the Enlightenment: Freemasonry and Politics in Eighteenth-Century Europe* – Oxford: Oxford University Press, 1991

Jacobs, Louis – *Oxford Concise Companion to the Jewish religion* – Oxford: Oxford University Press, 1999

Jackson, A. C. F. – *English Masonic Exposure 1760 – 1769* – Shepperton: Lewis Masonic, 1986

James, Stanley - *The Treasure Maps of Rennes-le-Chateau* - London: Max-bow, 1984.

Johnson, Dr. Bing - *An Address by the Orator of the Monrtose Lodge of Perfection To The Grand Junction Scottish Rite Bodies* – 2001

Johnson, Paul. – *The Civilization of Ancient Egypt.* – London: Weidenfield and Nicholson, 1978

Jones, Bernard E. - *Freemasons' Book of the Royal Arc* -. London: Harrap, 1957.

Jones, Terry & Ereira, Alan – *Crusades* - London: BBC Books, 1994.

Jordan, James - *Biblical Chronology; Vol. 4, No. 2* - February, 1992

Kenyon, Kathleen - *Archaeology in the Holy Land* – Nashville: Thomas Nelson Inc, 1985

Key, Alistair - *Constantine Versus Christ; The Triumph of Ideology* – London: SCM Press, 1982

Knight, Christopher & Lomas, Robert. *The Hiram Key: Pharaohs, Freema-sons and the Discovery of the Secret Scrolls of Jesus.* London: Century, 1996.

Knoop, Douglas; Jones, G. P. and Hamer, Douglas – *The Early Masonic Catechisms* – Manchester: Manchester University Press, 1943

Küng, Hans. – *Judaism: The Religious Situation of our Time.* – London: SCM Press, 1992

Laidler, Dr. Keith - *The Head of God: The Lost Treasure of the Templars* - London: Weidenfeld, 1998.

Law, Colin - *Kabbalah FAQ* - Internet, 1996.

Lawrie, Alexander. – *The History of Freemasonry* – Edinburgh: Alexander Lawrie, 1804

Lewis, Bernard - *The Middle East: 2000 Years of History from the Rise of Christianity* - London: Weidenfeld, 1995.

Lincoln, Henry - *The Holy Place: The Mystery of Rennes-le-Château: Discov-ering the Eighth Wonder of the Ancient World* - London: Jonathon Cape, 1991.

Lincoln, Henry - *The Key to the Sacred Pattern: The Untold Story of Rennes-le-Château* - Moreton-in-the-Marsh: Windrush, 1997.

Longford, Frank Pakenham – *Saints* - London: Hutchinson, 1987.

Luke, Sir Harry - *Cyprus: A Portrait and an Appreciation* - London: Harrap, 1973.

Mackay, Albert Gallatin. - *A History of Freemasonry* – USA: The Masonic History Company, 1909

Maslow, Abraham, H. – *Motivation and Personality* – Harlow, Longman, 1987

MacDonald, Kevin - *The Culture of Critique: An Evolutionary Analysis of Jewish Involvement in Twentieth-Century Intellectual and Political Movements* - 1st Books Library, 2002

McKenzie, Steven; Römer, Thomas and Schmid, Hans (eds). – *Rethinking the Foundations: Historiography in the Ancient World and in the Bible.* – Berlin: Walter de Gruyter, 2000

McLeish, Kenneth - *Myth: Myths and Legends of the World Explored* - London: Bloomsbury, 1996.

Meyer, E. – *Ursprung und Anfange des Christentums* – Stuttgart and Berlin, 1921

Morgan, Gareth - *Images of Organisation* - London: Sage, 1986.

Mundill, Robin, R. – *England's Jewish Solution; Experiment and Expulsion 1262 – 1290* – Cambridge: Cambridge University Press, 1998

Osman, Ahmed - *Moses and Akhenaten; The Secret History of Egypt at the Time of the Exodus* – Sante Fe: Bear & Company, 2002

Pagels, Elaine – *Beyond Belief; The Secret Gospel of Thomas* – USA: Vintage Books, 2004

Picknett, Lynn & Prince, Clive - *The Templar Revelation: Secret Guardians of the True Identity of Christ* - London: Bantam, 1997.

Pike, General Albert - *Morals and Dogma* - 1977.

Prescott, Andrew (ed) - *Preston's Illustrations of Masonry* – Sheffield: Academy Electronic Publications Ltd, 2001

Price, Roger - *Concise History of France (Cambridge Concise Histories)* - Cambridge: Cambridge University Press, 1993.

Pritchard, James - *The Ancient Near East: an Anthology of Texts and Pictures* - Princetown: Princeton University Press, 1958

Rabinowitz, Louis – *Jewish Merchant Adventurers; A study of the Radanites* – London: Edward Goldston,1948

Read, Piers Paul - *The Templars: The Dramatic History of the Knights Templar, the Most Powerful Military Order of the Crusades* - London: Weidenfeld & Nicholson, 1999.

Redford, Donald – *Egypt, Canaan and Israel in Ancient Times* – Princetown: Princetown University Press, 1992

Reeves, Nicholas. – *The Complete Tutankhamun: The King, The Tomb, The Royal Treasure.* – London: Thames and Hudson, 1990

Rheeders, Kate - *Qabalah: A Beginners Guide* - London: Headway, 1996.

Rigby, Greg - *On Earth As It Is in Heaven* - Belmont: Rhaedus, 1996.

Riley-Smith, Jonathon (Ed). - *The Oxford Illustrated History of the Crusades* - Oxford: Oxford University Press, 1995.

Ritmeyer, Leen - *The Temple and the Rock* - York: Ritmeyer Archaeological Design, 1996.

Robinson, John. *Born in Blood: The Lost Secrets of Freemasonry.* London: Century, 1990.

Robinson, John - *Dungeon, Fire and Sword: The Knights Templar in the Crusades.* London: Michael O'Mara, 1994.

Runciman, Steven - *A History of the Crusades Vol. 1: The First Crusade and the Foundation of the Kingdom of Jerusalem* - Harmondsworth: Penguin, 1978.

Runciman, Steven - *A History of the Crusades Vol. 2: The Kingdom of Jerusalem and the Frankish East* - Harmondsworth: Penguin, 1978.

Runciman, Steven - *A History of the Crusades Vol. 3: The Kingdom of Acre and the Later Crusades* - Cambridge: Cambridge University Press, 1954.

Sadleir, Richard (translation) - *Titian (1487 – 1575)* - Arnoldo Mondadori (Arte), 1991.

Sède, Gérard de - *L'Or de Rennes* - 1967.

Shaftesley, John – *Jews in English Regular Freemasonry 1717 to 1860* – Paper delivered to the Jewish Historical Society of England on 4th June 1975.

Shanks, Hershel - *The Mystery and meaning of the Dead Sea Scrolls* – USA, Random House, 1998

Simon, Edith - *The Piebald Standard: A Biography of the Knights Templar* - London: Cassels, 1959.

Sinclair, Andrew - *The Sword and the Grail* - London: Century, 1988.

Sitchin, Zecharia - *The Stairway to Heaven* - Sante Fe: Bear & Co., 1993.

Smith, William. - *A Dictionary of Greek and Roman Antiquities* – London, John Murray, 1875

Sobel, Dava - *Longitude: The True Story of a Lone Genius Who Solved the Greatest Scientific Problem of the Time* - London: Fourth Estate, 1995.

Speake, Jennifer - *The Dent Dictionary of Symbols in Christian Art* - London: Dent, 1994.

Stevenson, David - *The Origins of Freemasonry: Scotland's Century 1590-1710* - Cambridge: Cambridge University Press, 1988

Sykes, Bryan. – *The Seven daughters of Eve: The Science that Reveals our Genetic Ancestry* – New York: W. W. Norton & Company, 2001

Taitz, Emily – *The Jews of Medieval France: the Community of Champagne* – Westport: Greenwood Press, 1994

Teicher, Jacob - *Hebrew printed fragments*

Thiering, Barbara - *Jesus the Man: New Interpretation from the Dead Sea Scrolls* – Doubleday, 1992

Toynbee, Arnold. – *A Study of History* – Oxford: Oxford University Press, 1979

Toynbee, Arnold - *Mankind and Mother Earth: A Narrative History of the World* - London: Oxford University Press, 1976.

Troyes, Chrétien de (Translated by Nigel Bryant) – *Perlesvaus* - Ipswich: Brewer, 1982.

Tuchman, Barbara - *A Distant Mirror: The Calamitous 14th Century* - London: Papermac, 1978.

Uden, Grant - *A Dictionary of Chivalry* - London: Longman, 1968.

Vanderkam, James – *An Introduction to Early Judaism* – Michigan: William Eerdman, 2001

Vermes, Geza. – *The Complete Dead Sea Scrolls.* – London: Penguin Books, 1998

Vermes, Geza – *The Passion* – London, Penguin Books, 2002

Wallace-Murphy, Tim; Hopkins, Marilyn; and Simmans, Graham - *Rex Deus; the True Mystery of Rennes Le Chateau and the Dynasty of Jesus* – London: Harper Collins, 2000

Walsh, Michael - *The Roots of Christianity* – Grafton Books, 1986

Weber, Leonard - *Encyclopaedia of Theology* – 1975

West, John - *Serpent in the Sky: The High Wisdom of Ancient Egypt* - London: Wildword, 1979.

Wilenski, R. H. - *Poussin (1594–1665* -. London: Faber, 1958.

Wilson, Ian - *The Blood and the Shroud: The Passionate Controversy Still Enflaming the World* - London: Weidenfeld, 1998.

Wood, David - *Genisis: The First Book of Revelations* - Tunbridge Wells: Baton, 1985.

Wood, David & Campbell, Ian - *Geneset: Target Earth* - Sunbury-on-Thames: Bellevue, 1994.

Woodward, John & Burnett, George - *A Treatise on Heraldry* - 1892.

Zuckerman, Arthur. - *A Jewish Princedom in Feudal France 768 – 900* – New York: Columbia University Press, 1972

INDEX

THE AUTHORS

Patrick Byrne is a retired civil engineer and training company director, married with 4 children and 5 grandchildren. At the age of 49 he took a part-time masters' degree at De Montfort University Leicester in Human Resource Management.

A Freemason for 38 years; in craft Patrick holds the past provincial rank of Junior Grand Warden in both Surrey and Leicestershire. In the Royal Arch he holds the past provincial rank of Grand Registrar in Surrey. In the Masonic Knights Templar he is a past Provincial Herald and is Marshal in his Leicestershire Preceptory.

Enrique Bozzo is 53 and lives in Montevideo, Uruguay. He is a chemical engineer and has studied in Uruguay, the USA and Japan.

Enrique has published several books including "The Seven Tools of Quality Control"; his main hobby is history, which he has avidly read since his early teens.
Enrique's speciality subject is World War 2. Other interests include sports, photography, geography, ships and the internet, which he believes to be the best invention since the Guttenberg press. Enrique particularly enjoys the Grail sagas and defines himself as a skeptical atheist.

Ray Hudson was born in London in 1942. A retired International Banker and Restauranteur, Ray has been a Masonic researcher and historian for two decades. Many of his papers are held in the Masonic Library at UGLE.

Lead writer for "thefreemason.com" for the first 18months of its development, he is active in over 20 Masonic Orders and holds many senior offices, including provincial assistant Grand Director of Ceremonies in Kent. Past provincial assistant Grand Sojourner in the Royal Arch and provincial Grand Counsellor in the Order of the Secret Monitor.

Printed in the United Kingdom
by Lightning Source UK Ltd.
1437UKS00002B/37-255

9 780955 268007